Natalie Marena Nobitz
History's Queer Stories

Queer Studies | Volume 19

Natalie Marena Nobitz, born in 1989, works in the office for equal opportunities at the University of Hagen, Germany, and teaches Literary Studies and Gender Studies at the University of Kiel, Germany.

NATALIE MARENA NOBITZ

History's Queer Stories

Retrieving and Navigating Homosexuality in British Fiction about the Second World War

[transcript]

Funded by the State graduate scholarship Schleswig-Holstein.

Bibliographic information published by the Deutsche Nationalbibliothek
The Deutsche Nationalbibliothek lists this publication in the Deutsche Nationalbibliografie; detailed bibliographic data are available in the Internet at http://dnb.d-nb.de

Cover layout: Maria Arndt, Bielefeld
Cover illustration: Natalie Marena Nobitz
Printed by Majuskel Medienproduktion GmbH, Wetzlar
Print-ISBN 978-3-8376-4543-9
PDF-ISBN 978-3-8394-4543-3
https://doi.org/10.14361/9783839445433

Contents

Acknowledgements

It was in 2013 when I first learned about Michel Foucault's *History of Sexuality*, about Judith Butler's theory on gender performativity and when I began to grasp the vast and controversial landscape of gender studies. Thenceforth I was hooked. I devoured not only theories, trying to catch up on a century of engaging thoughts, but also novels that had not been part of any standardised reading list I had thus far encountered. Sarah Waters' historical novels particularly caught my attention and I began to wonder how a history of silence and invisibility is retrieved and represented by a modern novelist whose own lived experiences are so vastly different from her characters and settings.

This book is the result of my journey to find answers to this and other questions regarding the development of a queer literary history as well as my attempt to broaden dominant knowledge of war, sexuality and gender roles. I could not have completed my work without the encouragement of Prof. Dr. Anna-Margaretha Horatschek who generously offered guidance and advice whenever needed. I also want to thank Laura Hair whose incredible patience and constructive criticism enabled me to continue working well beyond my limits. Whilst professional advice helps the shaping of one's work, emotional guidance keeps the spirit sound. I therefore want to thank my parents without whom I could not have written a single word: *Ihr habt immer an mich geglaubt. Danke.*

Jan, für dich – mit dir.

List of Abbreviations

LD	Walter Baxter, *Look Down in Mercy*, [1951], (Virginia: Valancourt Books, 2014)
MD	Adam Fitzroy, *Make Do and Mend* (UK: Manifold Press, 2012)
TC	Mary Renault, *The Charioteer*, [1953], (New York: Vintage Books, 2003)
TN	Quentin Crisp, *The Naked Civil Servant*, [1968], (London: Harper Perennial, 2007)
TNW	Sarah Waters, *The Night Watch* (London: Virago, 2006)
TW	Radclyffe Hall, *The Well of Loneliness*, [1928], (New York: Anchor Books, 1990)
WL	Han Suyin, *Winter Love*, [1962], (London: Virago Press, 1994)

A.R.P.	Air Raid Precautions
BBC	British Broadcasting Corporation
Conshie/ Conchie	Conscientious objector
DSO Medal	Distinguished Service Order Medal
GLF	Gay Liberation Front
LGBTQI	Lesbian, Gay, Bisexual, Trans*, Queer, Intersectional
OED	Oxford English Dictionary
RAF	Royal Air Force
Wren/ WRNS	Women's Royal Naval Service

Introduction: "Never in the History of Sex was so Much Offered to so Many by so Few"

Narrating War and Homosexuality

QUENTIN CRISP'S WAR

The women of London had gone butch. At all ages and on every social level, they had taken to uniforms – or near-uniforms. They wore jackets, trousers and sensible shoes. I could now buy easily the footwear that I had always favoured – black lace-up shoes with firm, medium heels. I became indistinguishable from a woman.
Once, as I stood at a bus stop, a policeman accused me of this. After looking me up and down for nearly a minute he asked me what I was doing.
Me: I'm waiting for a bus.
Policeman: You're dressed as a woman.
Me (amazed): I'm wearing trousers.
Policeman: Women wear trousers.
Me: Are you blaming me because everybody else is so eccentric?

Quentin Crisp, *The Naked Civil Servant* (152 -153) [1]

As arguably the best-known example of eccentricity of his time, Quentin Crisp recaps his experiences before, during and after the Second World War in the auto-biography *The Naked Civil Servant* (1968). He invites the reader to join him in being amazed, shocked, flabbergasted and in the end enlightened for having glimpsed into a world completely detached from anything considered 'normal'. Throughout his life, Crisp – born in Sutton, England, as Denis Charles Pratt (1908-1999) – lived as a "self-confessed", "self-evident" (5) and consequently outcast homosexual, who wore make-up, high heels and strove for effeminacy

1 Quentin Crisp, *The Naked Civil Servant*, [1968], (London: Harper Perennial, 2007).

long before signs of an organised gay liberation movement were detectable in Western Europe. His lifestyle was not only unsavoury to 'civil society', but also to other homosexuals, who did not identify with Crisp's open effeminacy. This led to him being excluded from the heteronormative community as well as from its homosexual subculture. The above excerpt exemplifies Crisp's sarcasm and sharp humour when disclosing his excluded position and his unwillingness to conform to social standards. Moreover, Crisp's auto-biography denotes an often disengaged attitude towards the Second World War and its regulation of subjects, as well as his refusal to apologise for being homosexual.

After his discharge from military service in April 1940 on the grounds of "suffer[ing] from sexual perversion" (118), a friend of Crisp's responded to the military terminology by musing: "Shouldn't it be 'glorying in'?" (118) And glory Crisp did: during the war he continued to live his extravagant lifestyle, which he was slightly less harassed for as the war dominated life. Crisp therefore welcomed the imposed darkness on London, and the number of foreign soldiers and sailors entering the city because of the war. He gleefully states that "[n]ever in the history of sex was so much offered to so many by so few" (160).

However, whilst enjoying more freedoms, Crisp was excluded from the overarching discourse of combat. Self-consciously, he observes that "[p]eople did not like that sort of thing [being different] and could now add patriotism to their other less easily named reasons for hating me" (153). Rather than shaming Crisp for his homosexuality, people now censured him for not fighting. This collective patriotism altered the significance of class, gender, sexuality and other differentiating factors, as it emphasised the importance of distinguishing between *us*, the fighting nation, and *them*, the enemy, but also the non-fighter or conscientious objector, at times of national crisis. As a non-fighter and a homosexual, Crisp was thus doubly marginalised and excluded from the grand narrative of his time. He unsurprisingly recalls the war in very different ways compared to those authors, who were integrated in the war effort. His auto-biography *The Naked Civil Servant* thus exemplifies the difficulty of categorising war stories as either supportive or critical of the historical events taking place. Instead of displaying a coherent attitude, Crisp, and homosexual wartime fiction more broadly, often cover a spectrum of responses to the war that may be inherently contradictory and inconsistent.

Although Victoria Stewart rightly observes that "[t]he bringing into focus of the unfamiliar, via the narration of an individual's experiences and memories, is [...] another means by which our understanding of the historical can be deepened"[2], Crisp's auto-biography is, to my knowledge, not being read as part of the expanding canon of Second World War writings. This lack of attention derives from Crisp's narration of a war story that is disengaged from hegemonic discourse because it represents the increasing availability of sex, and the male soldier as the embodiment of homosexual fantasies. Petra Rau critically alludes to further themes often missing from hegemonic dramatisations of the Second World War:

> looting, striking, or black marketeering have been written out of the popular home front narrative altogether as have conscientious objectors or pacifists, many of whom did agricultural or clerical work or served in the fire or ambulance service.[3]

What Rau's observation most strikingly implies is a rethinking of the heroic soldier narrative when she detects "conscientious objectors or pacifists", who voluntarily passed on what Crisp sarcastically identifies as "a glorious and convenient death" (119) on the battlefield. In this book I will engage with four novels from different periods that concentrate on these sub-narratives identified by Rau in an effort to begin to close a glaring gap in the canonised recollection of an allegedly homogeneous and heteronormative war: Walter Baxter's *Look Down in Mercy* (1951), Mary Renault's *The Charioteer* (1953), Sarah Waters' *The Night Watch* (2006) and Adam Fitzroy's *Make Do and Mend* (2012)[4]. In order to give an overview of these novels, I shall briefly summarise the most significant storylines and character developments.

Walter Baxter's *Look Down in Mercy* (1951) comes closest to what can be considered a 'traditional' war writing: the protagonist Anthony Kent, known as Tony, is a heterosexual, married officer, who is responsible for an English platoon in Burma. The battle scenes between the English army and the Japanese are brutal and capture the atrocities of war. However, Kent's growing self-doubts over his masculine performance invest the text with a compassion for an increasingly compromised protagonist. When Kent additionally becomes conscious of his attraction to his batman Anson, the novel devastates heteronormative pa-

2 Victoria Stewart, *The Second World War in Contemporary British Fiction: Secret Histories* (Edinburgh: Edinburgh University Press, 2011), p. 14.

3 Petra Rau (ed.), *Long Shadows: The Second World War in British Fiction and Film* (Evanston, Illinois: Northwestern University Press, 2016), p. 7.

4 Walter Baxter, *Look Down in Mercy*, [1951], (Virginia: Valancourt Books, 2014), Mary Renault, *The Charioteer*, [1953], (New York: Vintage Books, 2003), Sarah Waters, *The Night Watch* (London: Virago, 2006) and Adam Fitzroy, *Make Do and Mend* (UK: Manifold Press, 2012).

rameters of war fiction by illustrating the transformation of Kent's identity from being a married officer to a homosexual war victim. *Look Down in Mercy* consequently challenges traditional accounts of the war, in favour of negotiating homosexuality at times of extraordinary circumstances.

Mary Renault's *The Charioteer* (1953) portrays a group of conscientious objectors who condemn the war due to their Quaker beliefs.[5] They perform alternative service as male orderlies in a hospital where the protagonist Laurie Odell (sometimes called Spud) is recovering from a knee injury incurred at the battle of Dunkirk. Laurie immediately falls in love with the young orderly Andrew Raynes, but because Laurie does not want to sacrifice Andrew's innocence, their love remains an abstract fantasy. The protagonist instead re-encounters Ralph Lanyon, his schoolboy crush, who introduces him to the homosexual subculture. Despite latently associating with these "advanced psychopaths" (199) – as Laurie calls them, signalling his strong aversion to effeminate homosexuals – neither Ralph nor Laurie want to fully identify with its promiscuity and flamboyancy. Laurie has to consequentially find a way of living up to his self-imposed standards of morality and integrity, which leaves him with few opportunities and eventually drives him away from Andrew and into the arms of Ralph.

In Adam Fitzroy's *Make Do and Mend* (2012), the protagonist Harry Lyon has a similar choice to make: he can either plunge into the homosexual subculture that is depicted in even more voyeuristic and promiscuous terms than in *The Charioteer* or enlighten the innocent farm labourer Jim Brynawel about his love for him. When Harry returns home on convalescent leave to his family estate in Wales called Hendra, he encounters Jim for the first time. Harry is immediately attracted to Jim and confesses his homosexuality, which enables the two men to fashion a relationship in surprisingly open terms. I am approaching *Make Do and Mend* as a modern re-write of Renault's novel that opts for an idealistic ending to signal its liberationist consciousness.

Contrasting *Make Do and Mend*, Sarah Waters' *The Night Watch* (2006) tries to be less obviously invested in its modern mindset and captures the lives of five

5 The *Oxford English Dictionary* (*OED*) defines Quaker as: "A member of the Religious Society of Friends, a religious movement founded by the Christian preacher George Fox in 1648–50, and distinguished by its emphasis on the direct relationship of the individual with the divine, and its rejection of sacraments, ordained ministry, and set forms of worship. The Society is also noted for pacifist principles and an emphasis on simplicity of life, formerly particularly associated with plainness of dress and speech. The name has never been officially adopted by the Friends themselves, but is not now regarded as a derogatory term." "Quaker, n." *OED Online*. Oxford University Press, June 2017. Web. 31 August 2017.

protagonists in more bleak ways than Fitzroy's novel. Proceeding back in time, *The Night Watch* consists of three parts moving from 1947 to 1944 and concluding in 1941. The characters Vivian (Viv) Pearce, Duncan Pearce, Helen Geniver, Julia Standing and Kay Langrish are variously connected and form interlinking bonds with each other. Viv is having an illicit affair with Reggie Nigri, who is a married soldier with two children. Their relationship begins with a chance encounter in a toilet stall on a train and subsequently takes place in various shabby hotel rooms ending with a botched abortion that almost kills Viv. Her brother Duncan Pearce has been convicted of attempted suicide and experiences the war behind prison bars. His past and sexuality are unknown for most of the novel, which substantiate the air of secrecy surrounding him. After the war, Duncan lives with Mr Mundy (a former prison guard), because his shameful history leads to his self-imposed exclusion from his childhood home. Duncan's relationship with Mr Mundy is governed by dependence and sexual assault until he re-encounters his former cell-mate Robert Fraser and falls in love with him. Not returning Duncan's affection, Fraser is instead attracted to Duncan's sister Viv, who is no longer involved with Reggie because she cannot forgive him for abandoning her after the abortion of their unwanted child. Rather than Reggie, it is the ambulance driver Kay who rescues Viv and gives her a ring to simultaneously conceal that Viv is not married, and that the alleged miscarriage was in fact an illegal abortion. Kay is in a lesbian relationship with Helen Giniver and the ring symbolises their unconventional love in the most conventional form. Helen later starts an affair with Julia Standing, a novelist who once was in love with Kay. The tragic love triangle between Kay, Helen and Julia leaves all involved unhappy and alone in the end. Since Duncan's love for Fraser is equally left unrequited, it seems that *The Night Watch* depicts homosexuality as failing. Viv, in contrast, becomes involved in a heteronormative relationship with Fraser that can be lived out in the street and does not need concealment like her affair with Reggie. However, Duncan is happy for his sister and the failure of Kay, Helen and Julia's relationships derives from their dishonesty and betrayal, which suggests a critique of modern, superficial relationships. Consequently, Waters' retrospective narrative infiltrates contemporary issues into a Second World War setting, to the effect of questioning both its heteronormative literary representation and modern conceptions of homosexuality, relationships and lifestyles.

Whilst these four novels form the centre of my analysis in this study, I am giving Quentin Crisp's *The Naked Civil Servant* leading position in this opening chapter in order to demonstrate that there is a variety of writings of and about the Second World War remarkably unaccounted for. It also shows that the selected novels can only stand as examples for an unknown number of other neglected works that are not discussed here. Crisp's experiences during the war begin to bring into conversation the seemingly oppositional parameters of homosexuality and warfare. In order to elaborate on this controversial relationship, this study will focus on how the four novels represent homosexuality at times of war and to what extent the fictionalisation of same-sex desire challenges wartime order grounded in gender segregation. What effect has the scale of destruction on the characters' performance of gender when various scripts of peacetime heteronormativity lose their determining footing? At what point is the narrative of national patriotism, deriving its traction from a communal feeling of fighting in a People's War, challenged, and how does this collapse facilitate a re-negotiation of men's role during the war? In order to situate the novels into a broader framework with regard to their time of publication I will additionally analyse the place of pre-Stonewall literature within a growing canon of gay and lesbian fiction by asking if novels of the 1950s indeed rehearse a narrative of stigmatisation deriving from the homophobic discourse in which they were written. Can historical fiction refurbish a homosexual past in less woebegone language, or is it condemned to inscribe a modern consciousness into past times making it a derivative haunted by the present?

I will pursue a two-fold approach in answering these questions by simultaneously examining the structure of gender norms that organise social life at times of national crisis, and investigating how the novels challenge the dominant order when homosexual desire is inscribed into the discourse of war. My thesis proposes that the novels under discussion open scope for re-negotiating parameters that govern traditional wartime fiction such as nationalism and propaganda, in order to contest the relentless inscription of heteronormative masculinity onto the figurehead of warfare – namely the soldier. This reading against the grain of entrenched stereotypes is complemented by an analysis of the home as controversially protecting conservative scripts of conduct and sheltering the public from encountering deviance. In a close reading of the gendered politics of space, I shall disclose that gender norms remain deeply embedded within the foundation of society. Only through the symbolic as well as physical devastation of the home due to the war, can non-conforming characters begin to conceptualise an autonomous identity.

In 1970, Robin Morgan coined the term 'herstory' in her inspiring resistance book *Sisterhood is Powerful*[6] to denote the long-standing restriction and subordination of women within society. Later, the term was used by Second Wave Feminism to demonstrate firstly the consistent focus on men's lives when writ-

6 Robin Morgan, Sisterhood is Powerful: An Anthology of Writings from the Women's Liberation Movement (New York: Random House, 1970).

ing *his*tory, and secondly to point out biases in academic research more broadly. The *Oxford English Dictionary* (*OED*) has included the word and defines it as a "history emphasizing the role of women or told from a woman's point of view; also, a piece of historical writing by or about women"[7]. I propose that beyond *her*story there lingers an as yet largely unrecognised *queer*story that awaits retrieval and negotiation. Investigating history's queer stories simultaneously enables a re-reading of the canon of war literature and challenges the perception of gay writings before 1969 as homophobic[8], bleak and damaging for post-Stonewall gay and lesbian politics. The title of this study not only alludes to affectionate touches between historical fictions re-writing a homosexual past and novels written and published before Stonewall, it also points towards the multiplicity of stories that have not yet been told. In order to place *History's Queer Stories* into a wider context, I will now undertake an overview of the existing critical terrain surrounding war literature, examining in particular the retrospective and retroactive function of this genre within gay and lesbian studies. This introduction will take its lead from two distinct positions by calling to attention first the dominance of the male authored heteronormative war narrative, and second the historical and literary amnesia of the gay community deriving from the Stonewall riots in 1969 and the formation of a modern gay consciousness in its aftermath.

---

7 "Herstory, n." *OED Online*. Oxford University Press, September 2016. Web. 6 October 2016.

8 The term homophobia was coined in the early 1970s by George Weinberg. "In Weinberg's formulation, society itself was phobic or sick, while the homosexual, to the extent he was able to free himself from the ever present phobia, was healthy." (Daniel Wickberg, "Homophobia: On the Cultural History of an Idea" in *Critical Inquiry* Vol. 27, No.1 (2000), p. 47.) This original perception of 'suffering' from homophobia has quite a different ring to it than contemporary understanding, where the homosexual, in comparison to the heterosexual subject, remains fixed within the terminology of deviance and illness. The changing connotation illustrates that meaning is constantly in flux, which necessitates a thorough investigation of influential discourses on those who produce texts.

RESEARCHING THE WAR

THE SILENT WAR

Quentin Crisp's *The Naked Civil Servant*, published 1968, does not contain any typical references to the war such as the Blitz[9], or London's endurance characterised by its people coming together to fight a common enemy. Instead of retelling the horrors of war, Crisp polemically focuses on its positive side effects, specifically the rising number of art students, which the war seemed to produce, guaranteeing his employment as a model. His recollection of the time reads like an antithetical war story, indicated by his style of narration that challenges the mainstream parlance of inevitable devastation: "Perhaps drawing was a pleasant distraction from the bombs before which some people tended to go to pieces." (135) Disengaged from the danger of air raids, notable in his formulation "people *tended* to go to pieces", Crisp's comprehension of wartime is mostly shaped by the pleasure of having a job and of playing a part in the flourishing production of paintings as a reaction to the destructive force of bombs. His lightheartedness and involvement in art stands in direct contrast to how the war has been represented in scholarly research from the second half of the 20th century until the 1990s. During this period, it was assumed that the horrors of the time could not find aesthetic expression, that "[w]ar and culture are posited as antithetical"[10]. This antithesis has led to the presumption that there is virtually no literature written during the war years. In *Women's Fiction of the Second World War*, Gill Plain re-states this perception when saying: "The Second World War opened to the sound of silence, and the fragmented voices that later arose never achieved the cohesion of a single identifiable literary movement."[11] Plain's latest work, *Literature of the 1940s*, accounts for this silence by evaluating how authors such as Elizabeth Bowen perceived the changing "parameters of 'war writing'"[12]: "In every form, from the direct statement that the acts of war are inde-

---

9 Petra Rau explains: "In Britain, 'the Blitz' stands for the prolonged aerial attack on cities and ports over nine months from September 1940 to May 1941". For further information see Rau (2016), p. 4.

10 Mark Rawlinson, *British Writing of the Second World War* (Oxford: Clarendon Press, 2000), p. 9.

11 Gill Plain, *Women's Fiction of the Second World War: Gender, Power and Resistance* (Edinburgh: Edinburgh University Press, 1996), p. 1-2.

12 Gill Plain, *Literature of the 1940s: War, Post-war and 'Peace'* (Edinburgh: Edinburgh University Press, 2013), p. 8.

scribable, to metaphorical conceits of impossible reversals and unimaginable juxtapositions, there is an epic history of writers' acknowledgement that war defies representation."[13] Plain concludes that the perception of the non-literary war was not fashioned retrospectively and retroactively by scholars, but derived from authors themselves, who found it difficult to narrate the war – to put language to the unspeakable. Instead of literature, cinema was "the characteristic form of the 1940s, and new media was similarly dominant in the reporting of war and its aftermath"[14]. Radio served as a vital medium and brought news of the war to remote corners of the nation. It follows that the Second World War is constructed as a medial rather than a literary period, in contrast to the First World War's embedment in fictionalisations.[15]

Angus Calder's *The People's War* published in 1969 is clearly informed by the prevailing perspective of his time that the Second World War was a largely non-literary period. He claims that "very few memorable works of fiction or drama emerged during the war itself"[16], because if writers continued to find the time to practice their profession, they most often wrote propaganda or contented themselves with brevity in short stories, documentaries or poems. Calder's assertion details that it is particularly *novels* and *drama* that was thought to be absent from consciousness. Similar to Plain's evaluation that the cinema was a popular form of aesthetic expression, shorter literary texts, in addition to letters and diary entries, were continuously produced throughout the war – sometimes with more vigour than during peacetime resulting from the separation of lovers or married couples and from the distance between sons or fathers and their families. Kristine A. Miller's study on *British Literature of the Blitz* affirms that "[a]t no other moment in history have so many British citizens felt compelled to write so extensively about their daily lives and ideas"[17]. Her findings resonate with Calder's revision of the Second War as a non-novelistic rather than a non-literary period.

13 Plain, (2013), p. 8. Plain later refines this statement by stating: "In spite of the war's disruptive influence, the decade produced some rich and rewarding fiction." p. 23.

14 Plain, (2013), p. 4.

15 "Dem 'literarischen' Ersten Weltkrieg steht dann der '(massen-)mediale' Zweite Weltkrieg gegenüber." Zeno Ackermann, *Gedächtnis-Fiktionen: Mediale Erinnerungsfiguren und literarischer Eigensinn in britischen Romanen zum Zweiten Weltkrieg* (Heidelberg: Universitätsverlag Winter, 2015), p. 19.

16 Angus Calder, *The People's War: Britain 1939-1945* (London: Pimlico, 1969), p. 513. Plain similarity argues that "it is the short story that demands to be recognised as the characteristic 'form' of the decade." Plain, (2013), p. 24.

17 Kristine A. Miller, *British Literature of the Blitz: Fighting the People's War* (Hampshire and New York: Palgrave Macmillan, 2009), p. 4.

Consequently, different forms of writing *were* produced during the war period, but scholarly research was slow to recognise their importance. This slow recognition is also evident in Plain's refined statement that "[i]n spite of the war's disruptive influence, the decade produced some rich and rewarding fiction."[18] However, it was not until the turn of the century, largely due to the expanding number of feminist investigations into the Second World War, that scholars such as Plain began to carefully revise the apparently silent canon of Second World War fiction.

Damon Marcel DeCoste's essay "The Literary Response to the Second World War" explains this misconception of the silent war to arise from the fact that "novelistic responses to that war do not fit the model for war writing bequeathed to literary scholars by the Great War"[19]. Whilst Calder's observation has corrected the non-literary war into the non-novelistic war, DeCoste asserts that novelistic texts were as much produced in the 1940s as during the First World War, but that the status of the author had changed drastically. His evaluation shows that there is not a lack of novelistic material to draw from, that war and culture are not mutually exclusive, but rather, that this material does not originate from the soldier as author and authority of the front. Unlike the First World War, literary responses to the 1940s parted with the 'soldier poet' to include a range of diverse voices unheard (of) or silenced in the recollections of the Great War.[20] Not only was the ideology of the fighting soldier protecting hearth and home shattered by the nightly endangerment of civil society, including his family, his authority for having seen the effects of the war at close quarters was also no longer needed for (re-)telling its stories. DeCoste concludes that "[r]ather than the testimony of infantrymen disillusioned by combat, British fiction of the Second World War offers us the war away from the front, and especially on the home front"[21]. This shifted authorship and setting originated from the influence of the Blitz on civilians and adds a new dimension to the wartime paradigm when making virtually everyone a prime witness.

Miller observes that "[b]efore 1943, more British civilians than soldiers had been killed or wounded; by the end of the war, civilian fatalities equaled almost 25 percent of military fatalities, while the number of wounded civilians was

---

18 Plain, (2013), p. 23.

19 Damon Marcel DeCoste, "The Literary Response to the Second World War" in Brian W. Schaffer (ed.), *A Companion to the British and Irish Novel 1945-2000* (Malden and Oxford: Blackwell Publishing, 2005), p. 7.

20 Ackermann, (2015), p. 19.

21 DeCoste, (2005), p. 4.

more than 33 percent of the number of wounded soldiers."[22] This large number of civilian casualties changed the parameters of war writings. Whilst the language of threat, devastation and suffering characterised the situation of the soldier in narratives during the First World War, it became more universally used during the Second World War. Being exposed to the Blitz, letters by civilians to husbands, fathers and lovers became as much testimony of violence, as the soldiers' experiences at the front. This proximity significantly "transformed [the] communication between soldiers and civilians"[23] as their respective rhetoric became almost indistinguishable. Consequently, the Second World War produced a greater variety of writings by people from the home front, but they were not acknowledged as literature by those critics who were searching for the kind of texts produced during and in response to the First World War. These prototype texts were mostly 'realist' representations of the war, or rather what readers and critics "expected it to be"[24]. Ann-Marie Einhaus contends that "[n]ot formal innovation but the 'correct' ideological stance on the war qualifies a text for inclusion in [the] cultural canon"[25]: "they have to tick the right boxes in what they say about the war: disillusionment, horror, camaraderie in the trenches"[26]. Einhaus' evaluation buttresses the theory that wartime writing is traditionally synonymous with soldier experiences as well as tightly linked with nationalism and propaganda. Due to the unprecedented scale of the Second World War these core qualities were shaken, which led to an uncertainty over the distinguishing markers of Second World War literature.

THE PEOPLE'S WAR

In addition to the confusion over a literary canon on Second World War literature caused by an enlarged authorship, patriotism and propaganda were received less euphorically during the Second World War than before. When at the beginning of the century men looked with excitement towards the opportunity of fighting for their country, the second generation of soldiers, who often remembered the disastrousness of the First World War, identified with their roles in the military more reluctantly. The scale of destruction at the home front additionally led to critical voices questioning Britain's leadership. In order to maintain con-

22 Miller, (2009), p. 2.

23 Miller, (2009), pp. 4-5.

24 Ann-Marie Einhaus, "Modernism, Truth, and the Canon of First World War Literature" in *Modernist Cultures* Vol. 6, No. 2 (2011), p. 299.

25 Einhaus, (2011), p. 298.

26 Ibid., p. 299.

trol, "[p]oliticians and the media emphasized the [apparently] unifying and levelling power of the Blitz" by claiming that the People's War would bring forth "changes in gender roles and class relations [which] might lead to post-war social reform"[27]. The speech "Westward, Look, the Land is Bright" given by Prime Minister Winston Churchill highlights these aspects:

> The sublime but also terrible and sombre experiences and emotions of the battlefield which for centuries had been reserved for the soldiers and sailors, are now shared, for good or ill, by the entire population. All are proud to be under fire of the enemy. [...] This is indeed the grand heroic period of our history, and the light of glory shines on all.[28]

The emphasis in the first sentence lies on the word 'sublime', which gives Churchill's speech an immediate sense of advocating something noble to the effect of not simply raising the cause he supports into higher spheres, making it just, necessary and beyond reproach, but also elevating the speaker himself. Neither the war nor Churchill can be exposed to criticism as it is an almost divine power that guides them. Thus, disguising the horrors of war, Churchill's style of speaking functions to vindicate a political power that leaves British citizens suffering. The word "sublime" is positioned at the beginning for emphasis and hovers as a modifier separated from its object until it is connected to the "experiences and emotions of the battlefield". That this battlefield is not exclusively sublime but also "terrible and sombre" is eclipsed by Churchill's syntax, which directs the focus to the beginning, rather than the middle, of the sentence. Yet, the "terrible and sombre" is not forgotten, it is acknowledged as a 'side-effect' without tarnishing the overall good of the war. Most importantly, the horrors are "shared [...] by the entire population", a unifying trope which constitutes the core of Churchill's message. It is no longer the soldier and the sailor, the male sex, who finds his honourable death on the faraway battlefield, but virtually everybody – women, children, old and young of all classes. The People's War on British ground becomes almost more significant than the front lines. "Proud to be under fire of the enemy", these citizens need to recognise their efforts and deaths as sublime, just like the soldier needs to accept the battlefield as his potential grave. To be sure that the people's suffering will not be in vain, Churchill pledges "the light of glory shines on all". It remains unclear what this glory constitutes of, but surely it will be sublime. Sonya O. Rose argues in *Which People's War*

27 Miller, (2009), p. 1.

28 Winston Churchill, "'Westward, Look, the Land is Bright,' Address Broadcast April 27, 1941" in Charles Eade (ed.), *The Unrelenting Struggle* (Boston: Little, Brown and Co., 1942), p. 93.

that this kind of rhetoric is a strategy "deployed to manage or organize the differences among people that have come to be sites of collective identity formation so that individuals see themselves as national beings regardless of their other loyalties and preoccupations"[29]. Churchill aims to unify Britons against a common enemy beyond class, gender or other differences.

However, rather than eliminating social distinctions, the Blitz brought them to light when people (most often women and children) waited in various kinds of shelters of varying quality depending on their social standing. Rau agrees that "[c]lass divisions remained visible and palpable throughout the war, which is why propaganda worked so hard to convince everyone that they had to be overcome if the war was to be won"[30]. Despite these efforts, individual war writings – letters, diaries, novels, short stories, etc. – demonstrate "an expression of imaginative freedom to disagree about the People's War"[31]. These texts represent the fracturing of British society and people's diverging attitudes towards the war. Miller concludes that "the imaginative representation of vastly different blitz experiences was an essential part of wartime life across social strata in British culture"[32]. It follows that there are rich accounts of and about the Second World War that negotiate individual perspectives of a collective event to subvert the dominant narrative of the People's War.

Crisp's response to the Government's propaganda is initially enthusiastic when he exclaims: "though some of the buildings [in London] had been ruined, most of the people had been improved. Everyone talked to everyone – even to me." (152) His allegory between ruined buildings and improved people illustrates a strange aestheticization of wartime, and he unwittingly recites People's War rhetoric when saying that despite bombed out and collapsed houses indicating the horrors of war, solidarity appears to be growing among Britons. Their lessened aversion against Crisp startles but delights him: it seems that despite its atrocity, the war has improved his life.

However, Crisp realises that his initial evaluation of change was premature because "[i]t was only superficially and only by day that strangers were friendly" (153). This statement displays Crisp's disappointment in discovering that the

29 Sonya O. Rose, Which People's War?: National Identity and Citizenship in Britain 1939-1945 (Oxford: Oxford University Press, 2003), p. 9.

30 Rau, (2016), p. 6.

31 Miller, (2009), p. 11.

32 Miller, (2009), p. 11. For further information see Calder, (1969) and Angus Calder, *The Myth of the Blitz*, [1991], (London: Pimlico, 1992). Similar to Miller, he analyses how people's personal lives were much too diverse to assume a coherent contribution to and belief in a People's War.

People's War was an increasingly failing fabrication. Differences were not overcome that easily, neither regarding class, let alone gender and sexuality. At one point, Crisp is severely beaten up in a train for no other reason than his effeminate looks, revealing how prejudices of various kinds continued to prosper. Consequently, whilst at times positive in their description of war circumstances, individual accounts such as *The Naked Civil Servant* remain to be infused with "conflicting discourses" [33], both welcoming and criticising the People's War, which contributes to the difficulties when trying to establish a coherent canon of Second World War literature.

THE GENDERED WAR

Whereas People's War propaganda sought to unite British citizens by declaring an end to social and gender differences, the military was paradoxically built on a stereotypical segregation of gender. Karen Schneider's *Loving Arms* shows that "[t]he assumption that war literature is properly written by and about men stems from the widespread if not altogether accurate identification of war as an essentially male activity and aggressive masculinity as an ontological condition"[34]. However, the following chapters will show that masculinity as such is a far less stable concept than the military portrays it to be, and that the potential of what Eve Kosofsky Sedgwick has coined "homosocial desire"[35] challenges the military's heteronormative self-image. The historian Allan Bérubé, who devoted his career researching and interviewing homosexual veterans of the Second World War, explains that in order to countermand any narratives that might threaten the masculine ideology of war, the US army and Navy developed screening processes to 'spot' homosexuals – a practice that had been unheard of during the First World War.[36] The detection of deviating sexualities within the military followed

33 Miller, (2009), p. 12.

34 Karen Schneider, *Loving Arms: British Women Writing the Second World War*, [1997], (Lexington, Kentucky: The University Press of Kentucky, 2015), p. 4.

35 Eve Kosofsky Sedgwick, *Between Men: English Literature and Male Homosocial Desire* (New York: Columbia University Press, 1985).

36 Allan Bérubé, *My Desire for History: Essays in Gay, Community, and Labor History* (Capel Hill: The University of North Carolina Press, 2011), p. 90. Carol Cohn also argues that the "U.S. armed forces have had policies prohibiting homosexuals from serving only since the beginning of World War II." Carol Cohn, "Gays in the Military: Texts and Subtexts" in Marysia Zalewski and Jane Parpart (eds.), *The 'Man Question' in International Relations*, [1997], (Boulder, Colorado: Westview Press, 1998), p. 129).

the assumptions that homosexuality was an illness that was thought to negatively influence the performance of men during battle.[37] Such a categorical discharge of a group of men was only possible because homosexuality was considered to be a 'core identity'. This 'argument' is a relatively recent phenomenon that is aptly summarised by Michel Foucault:

> the psychological, psychiatric, medical category of homosexuality was constituted from the moment it was characterized [...]. Homosexuality appeared as one of the forms of sexuality when it was transposed from the practice of sodomy onto a kind of interior androgyny, a hermaphrodism of the soul. The sodomite had been a temporary aberration; the homosexual was now a species.[38]

Foucault argues that "the practice of sodomy" – by which he means sexual acts between men – was transformed by "psychological, psychiatric [and] medical" discourse into "a kind of interior androgyny" – a fixed, sexual identity. Whereas ancient Greek culture did not perceive sexuality in dualistic terms, but differentiated men based on gender, the late 19th century paved the way for a more rigid classification that turned 'acts' into 'identities' and "the homosexual [became] a species". Anne Fausto-Sterling details that "physicians began to publish case reports of homosexuality – the first in 1869 in a German publication specializing in psychiatric and nervous illness. As the scientific literature grew, specialists emerged to collect and systematize the narratives"[39]. The cartoon "Constructing Sex and Gender: A political, Religious and Scientific History" (Figure 1) printed

37 This 'argument' was still in use in 1993 when Bill Clinton lifted the prohibition on gay men serving in the military. In addition to the assumption that "gays in the military would undermine good order, discipline, and morals" (Cohn, 1998, p. 130) a newly evoked fear over their security among their homophobic peers was brought up to enforce their exclusion. Consequently, gay men are not simply unwelcome because of their alleged incompetence "but because heterosexual men do not want to serve with them" (Cohn, 1998, p. 135). The prevailing issue of HIV/AIDS and the apparent endangerment of the heterosexual soldier through blood transfusion or coming into contact with a wounded gay men, presented another line of 'argument' for "pro-ban sentiments" (Cohn, 1998, p. 131).

38 Michel Foucault, *The Will to Knowledge: The History of Sexuality Volume I*, [1976], (London: Penguin Books, 1998), p. 43.

39 Anne Fausto-Sterling, *Sexing the Body: Gender Politics and the Construction of Sexuality* (New York: Basic Books New York, 2000), pp. 13-14.

in Fausto-Sterling's *Sexing the Body* illustrates that homosexuality has been constructed differently at various periods in time.[40]

Figure 1: "Constructing Sex and Gender: A Political, Religious and Scientific History..."

Building on the argument that the late 19th century brought forth a significant change in the perception of same-sex erotisation, Carol Cohn observes that this shift "from punishing individual sexual acts" to "identifying and excluding a category of person" helped to judge homosexuals "as inherently unfit"[41] to join the

40 Fausto-Sterling, (2000), p. 11.

41 Cohn, (1998), p. 130.

military during the Second World War. Because homosexuality was understood as an identity rather than an act, a whole group of people could now be discharged. The newly arisen 'problem' with homosexuality, however, concentrated not on sexuality *per se*, but on those men who were "*openly* gay in the military"[42] and able to challenge the institution's demonstration of hegemonic masculinity and heterosexuality. Bérubé rightly concludes that these "screening[s], needless to say, identified only obviously effeminate men, many of whom were not gay"[43]. There is no absolute number of cases but relying on Alfred Kinsey's *Sexual Behavior in the Human Male*[44] and converting his findings onto the U.S. military, Bérubé calculates that between 650,000 and 1.6 million serving men were homosexual.[45] In consequence, this large number of serving homosexuals inherently challenges homogeneous wartime narratives habitually representing heteronormative soldier heroes.

Quentin Crisp's recollection of his discharge suggests that similar screening processes focusing on gender to detect homosexuality were practised in Britain[46]:

---

42 Cohn, (1998), p. 130.

43 Bérubé, (2011), p. 90. For further information see Kathy J. Phillips, *Manipulating Masculinity: War and Gender in Modern British and American Literature* (Basingstoke: Palgrave Macmillan, 2006), especially chapter three "World War II: No Lace on His Drawers".

44 Alfred C. Kinsey, *Sexual Behavior in the Human Male*, [1948], (Bloomington and Indianapolis: Indiana University Press, 1975).

45 Allan Bérubé "World War II" in B. R. Burg (ed.), *Gay Warriors: A Documentary History from the Ancient World to the Present* (New York: New York University Press, 2002), p. 226.

46 Unfortunately there appears to be no equivalent study to Bérubé's on the British military, but according to the BBC the number of homosexual men fighting for Britain ranged around 250,000. The website "WW2 People's War: An Archive of World War Two Memories – written by the public gathered by the BBC" bases its projections on the "1990-91 National Survey of Sexual Attitudes and Lifestyles which found that six per cent of men report having had homosexual experiences". BBC, <http://www.bbc.co.uk/history/ww2peopleswar/stories/36/a2688636.shtml> [last accessed: 06/10/2016]. For an account on gay soldiers in the Canadian army during the Second World War see Paul Jackson, *One of the Boys: Homosexuality in the Military during World War II*, [2004], (Montreal and Kingston: McGill Queen's University Press, 2010).

> My appearance was at half-mast. I wore no make-up and my hair was hardly more than hooligan length. [...] [B]ut of course my hair was still crimson from having been persistently hennaed for seven years and, though my eyebrows were no longer in Indian file, it was obvious that they had been habitually plucked. These and other manifestations of effeminacy disturbed the board deeply. [...] I was told, 'You've dyed your hair. This is a sign of sexual perversion.' (117)

It is Crisp's outward appearance, especially his hair, which initially "disturbed the board deeply", leading them to conclude that Crisp is homosexual. Even this moderate display of femininity performed by a male body challenges the supposedly dualistic gender order.[47] Worse still, Crisp demonstrates that he is not ashamed of his sexuality or gender performance. By renouncing inferiority, Crisp provokes the military board whose conservative views cannot allow for sex and gender variance. He is perceived as a threat that needs to be discredited as a sexual pervert for the military board to handle their considerable irritation over finding their world-views challenged by a person they perceive as absolutely disgraceful. Marginalised as sexually deviant, the danger is redirected into another discourse, that of medicine and psychoanalysis, which can deal with Crisp without challenging the stereotypic gender order of the 'normal world'. After this point it is no longer of interest whether or not Crisp would be physically fit to join the military, the mere fact that his gender performance does not conform to military masculinity is sufficient to reject him and thus deny him a "glorious and convenient death" (119). When fighting and dying for one's nation means performing hegemonic masculinity, Crisp realises from his detached, sarcastic perspective that the nation at war was more prepared to let him live in effeminacy than reward him with a death that bestows masculinity upon him.

Not only men's lives were changed in the military or due to their discharge, women, too, saw transformations when they became active members of the war as nurses, ambulance drivers, members of the Women's Royal Naval Service (WRNS, more commonly known as Wren) or fire watchers.[48] Since the home

47 I use the term dualistic according to Paechter's definition: "A dualistic relation is one in which the subordinated term is negated, rather than the two sides being in equal balance." Carrie Paechter, "Masculine Femininities/Feminine Masculinities: Power, Identities and Gender" in *Gender and Education* Vol. 18, No.3 (2006), p. 256.

48 Miller states: "In the past, soldiers had fought and died on the battlefield, while civilians had watched and waited at home. The Blitz transformed the relationship between home front and front line by forcing civilians to fight like soldiers and soldiers to watch and wait like civilians: now everyone was fighting and everyone knew the danger that threatened loved ones." Miller, (2009), p. 5.

front became the chief narrative of death and survival during the Blitz, the British Government could not afford to maintain the myth of the soldier protecting his homeland whilst the female population was awaiting his return. A subsequent speech by Churchill highlights the changing role of women at the home front and pledges that their fighting during the war will continue to find recognition in the future.

> This war effort could not have been achieved if the women had not marched forward in millions and undertaken all kinds of tasks and work for which any generation but our own – unless you go back to the Stone Age – would have considered them unfitted [...]. Nothing has been grudged, and the bounds of women's activities have been definitely, vastly, and permanently enlarged.[49]

The military term "marched" situates women directly into the war discourse and, similar to the excerpt on the People's War, highlights civilian efforts as equally important as front line battles. The speech is thus immediately characterised as People's War rhetoric by parading the home front alongside the battlefield. Churchill's use of the definite article in "the women" has a simultaneously unifying and degrading effect: it emphasises women as a group and constructs solidarity among those who "marched forward in millions" to work together and to defend their country. It also treats women like objects when using the impersonal article "the". This female unity as an indefinite force to be reckoned with is fashioned in order to overcome class distinctions and to promulgate the Second World War as horrible yet beneficial in its facilitation of social change. Moreover, Churchill claims that "any generation but our own [...] would have considered [women] unfitted" to defend Britain at the home front. Narcissistically praising the courtesy of his generation, women's (presumably) altered social position is tightly linked to the generosity of men like Churchill, who have permitted this change to happen for the duration of the war. That his words are not seriously supportive of emancipation is clear when he claims that "[n]othing has been grudged". Because it is simply not true that "*nothing* has been grudged", as will be illustrated in the analysis of the mannish lesbian Kay in *The Night Watch*, Churchill's emphasis becomes implausible. Building on this note of doubt, his assertion that "the bounds of women's activities have been definitely, vastly, and permanently enlarged" appears similarly weak. Striking is that these "bounds of women's activities" are not equal to men's but have been "enlarged". 'Enlarged

49 Winston Churchill, "The Women of Britain" in Charles Eade (ed.), *Onwards to Victory: War speeches by the Right HON. Winston S. Churchill* (London: Cassell and Company Ltd., 1944), p. 285.

to what?' one immediately wants to ask. Churchill leaves this question unanswered and instead speaks of "a far more complete equalisation of the parts to be played by men and women in society"[50], which is as revealing as women's "enlarged" activities, leaving open the question: why not complete equalisation?

From the end of the 20th century, literary studies began to consider how Churchill's promises might be reflected in wartime writings by disregarding conventional narratives of the male soldier at the front, to instead focus on women's voices and female experiences. Works like Gill Plain's *Women's Fiction of the Second World War* and Karen Schneider's *Loving Arms* contribute to a continually growing body of feminist writing aimed at reclaiming a male dominated past.[51] Schneider seeks to expose the symbiotic connection between war as a masculine endeavour and "gender-encoded ideology"[52] more broadly. Her evaluation deliberately breaks with male-centred analyses of war literature when focusing on fiction written by female authors, featuring female protagonists who tell a story of war from a female perspective. She claims:

> if we are to know an 'other' story of war – if we are to denaturalize the gender-encoding implicit in war and its stories, if we are to consider their ideological power for individuals, cultures, and humanity at large, if we are to understand without illusions the seduction of loving arms, then we must hear the war stories women tell.[53]

Schneider's analysis of works by Stevie Smith, Katharine Burdekin, Virginia Woolf, Elizabeth Bowen, and Doris Lessing renders visible other wartime voices and seeks to reveal the ambivalence with which women of the time perceived the war: caught between patriotism, nationalism, pacifism and their role as female novelists. Due to the enlarged scope of possibilities for women, including transformed feminine fashion and behaviours, gender norms where simultaneously more relaxed yet increasingly patrolled by a Government that feared the emancipation of its subordinated subjects. Schneider concludes that "[b]ecause of the war's double threat to the stability and legitimacy of its own sex-gender system, Britain's patriarchal hegemony made every attempt to (re)assert its political and

50 Churchill, (1944), p. 224.

51 For an account on women's private correspondences and their perception of the war's influence on their lives see Jenny Hartley, *Millions like Us: British Women's Fiction of the Second World War* (London: Virago, 1997) and Phyllis Lassner, *British Women Writers of World War II: Battlegrounds of their Own* (London: Palgrave Macmillan, 1998).

52 Schneider, (2015), p. 3.

53 Ibid., pp. 5-6.

narrative authority over the feminine (feminized) Other."[54] Whereas Plain carefully suggests that "[w]ar can be understood in metaphorical terms as a transcendental deconstructor, with the power to overshadow, disrupt and displace all other discourses"[55], Schneider articulates the many ways in which conventions regarding gender not only prevailed, but became reified at a time where stability was hard to come by otherwise. She argues that the common narrative of subordinating the feminine is rehearsed and strengthened in the greater conflict between Britain and Germany when two "patriarchal nations [are] quarreling about which is the better man, which can force the (feminizing) surrender of the other"[56]. Schneider's polemic but insightful remark exposes the ever-present gender-game as a determining factor at times of peace, but more so during war.

Contradicting her earlier assertion that war is a "transcendental deconstructor" that "overshadow[s], disrupt[s] and displace[s] all other discourses", Plain ultimately agrees with Schneider when claiming that "[t]he patriarchal system [...] stands firm despite the chaos of war"[57]. Whilst doubting that the war altered dominant gender roles, Plain concedes that it brought forth an alteration in the distribution of masculine power.[58] This means that instead of replicating the "hegemony of masculinity" as conducted by First World War literature, narratives of the Second World War often concern themselves with the "hegemony of masculine *power*"[59]. In Plain's account, masculinity was no longer just performed by men but also by women. Regardless of this relaxation in the performance of gender norms, Plain evaluates women's writing of the Second World War to reveal how they were "asked to assume temporarily the *semblance* of masculinity – to act like men, but to remain constantly aware of their femininity"[60]. The war did not liberate women from their imposed femininity, nor did it attribute a lasting masculinity to their bodies. It only allowed for brief alterations of heteronormative conventions for the sake of winning the war. Both Plain and Schneider thus point towards the difficult position British women had to adopt during the war and the force with which parameters of 'decent gender' prevailed.

That Crisp who believes himself to be "indistinguishable from a woman", is challenged by a policeman for his effeminate outfit, exemplifies the ambivalence with which wartime society perceived and greeted altered gender norms. His ap-

54 Schneider, (2015), p. 26.

55 Plain, (1996), p.22.

56 Schneider, (2015), p. 26.

57 Plain, (1996), p. 26.

58 Ibid., p. 26.

59 Ibid., p. 27, [emphasis original].

60 Ibid., p, 28, [emphasis original].

pearance demonstrates what Judith Butler decades later will come to famously call 'gender performativity' which "revolves around [...] the way in which the anticipation of a gendered essence produces that which it posits as outside itself"[61]. Gender performativity is not a conscious decision or a translation of a gender essence but "a repetition and a ritual, which achieves its effects through its naturalization in the context of a body"[62]. The body becomes the surface on which the socio-historical as well as cultural regulation of subjects is marked in terms of (non-)conformity. According to Butler, any claim for an inner core or gender identity is a misleading conception deriving from the fantasy of sex-gender coherence, meaning the deceptive ideology that one's gender automatically follows one's sexed body: biological women are seen as feminine whilst biological men are regarded as masculine. Butler continues arguing that the discursive power structures that render a subject intelligible produce gender as a mechanism of control and regulation.

A subject's wish for recognition is followed by the consequential threat of qualifying the opposite as the Other, the "less-than-human"[63]. The power relations that regulate, who becomes a recognisable human are also those that promulgate a normative system to punish those who "misbehave"[64]. The relation between the human and the less-than human puts the discourse of power into a delicate but ultimately asymmetrical balance in which elements of norm and Other are mutually dependant and at the same time transgressive over time and space. "As a result, the 'I' that I am finds itself at once constituted by norms and dependant on them but also endeavours to live in ways that maintain a critical and transformative relation to them."[65] Accordingly, subjects are constituted to perform gender without recognising it as a performance and, at the same time, need to make these performances visible in order to change them. "[T]o intervene in the name of transformation means precisely to disrupt what has become settled knowledge and knowable reality, and to use, as it were, one's unreality to make an otherwise impossible or illegible claim."[66]

In perceiving himself as "indistinguishable from a woman", Crisp makes such a claim and challenges the assumption of sex-gender coherence to disclose the perception of gender identity as illusionary. His cross-dressing is not a per-

61 Judith Butler, *Gender Trouble: Feminism and the Subversion of Identity*, [1990], (New York and London: Routledge Classics, 2006), p. xv.

62 Ibid., p. xv.

63 Judith Butler, Undoing Gender (London and New York: Routledge, 2004), p. 2.

64 Butler, (2004), p. 25.

65 Ibid., p. 3.

66 Ibid., p. 27.

formance on stage but a felt identity, and thus parodies what is thought to be the property of women – namely femininity. Surprisingly, the policeman keeps relatively calm despite Crisp's daring gender trespass. Only upon Crisp's witty response – "Are you blaming me because everybody else is so eccentric?" – does the policeman raise his voice, clearly feeling threatened by Crisp's confrontational frankness. However, the policeman's outrage does not primarily concern Crisp's feminine appearance or his homosexuality, but his audacity to imply that women have become *voluntarily* eccentric – that 'ordinary people', too, may come to question the rules of gender identity. His exaggerated response to Crisp's observation of 'female eccentricity' indicates that the *unashamed* association of men's clothes with female bodies was intolerable for wartime society because women were, according to Plain, only allowed to perform masculine power as long as their femininity remained unquestioned. The policeman's terror at the thought of masculine women, compared to his relative disinterest in Crisp's effeminacy highlights the hypocrisy of the gender system.

Moreover, Crisp's military papers clearly state that he is "suffering from" and not "glorying in" sexual perversion, which reflects the contemporaneous perception of homosexuality and effeminacy as simultaneously perverse and malaise. The medical discourse highlighted in the military papers depicts Crisp as an unfortunate figure burdened by an illness and contrasts him from women who *voluntarily* part with femininity by wearing trousers. The *Naked Civil Servant* therefore shows that a woman positively taking to displays of masculinity and savouring in men's clothing was less acceptable than Crisp's public demonstration of his 'homosexual illness'. How, then, are women fictionalised at a time where they were required to 'do their part' for the cause of winning the war, which involved getting their hands dirty, whilst needing to constantly preserve their femininity? Can a narrative such as Waters' *The Night Watch* challenge the paradigm of female femininity when inscribing a contemporary mindset of gender performativity into the discourse of the 1940s, or does the depiction of Kay as a mannish lesbian reiterate the narrative of masculine warfare? These questions shall be addressed in the last chapter of this study in an analysis of queer bodies, space and time.

The Retrospective War

Crisp does not only challenge the gender order of the 1940s when observing the transformations of women's clothing, he also questions the dominant position of heterosexuality in war writings by insinuating that (at least some of) these women were "butch" (152) lesbians surfacing the streets of London since gender regulations slackened. Although coming slowly into common parlance in the United States during the war, it was not until the 1950s that 'butch' became more widely used to denounce a masculine woman in Britain. The contemporary meaning of 'butch' as "a lesbian of masculine appearance or behaviour"[67] was fashioned in the 1960s and possibly informed Crisp's usage of it when writing and publishing his auto-biography in the late 1960s. *The Naked Civil Servant* is thus a memory informed by different discourses, not only giving insight into a life of a self-affirmed homosexual rejected by the military, but also into his retrospective construction of this period. War novels reflecting first-hand experiences of male soldiers are thus once more disengaged from their authenticity claim when searching for a war story from the vantage point of 1968.

Despite a steadily growing canon, and Plain's insight that "the war lived on in the mind of the nation even as many looked forward to the prospect of a new Britain"[68], both she and Schneider (among others) continue to retrieve and investigate narratives of the time instead of incorporating contemporary perspectives into their studies in order to enable a more diverse reflection. Zeno Ackermann criticises that scholars too often look for the war's commemoration in wartime itself instead of exploring more contemporary material.[69] He explains that this phenomenon is specifically British and stands in opposition to German, French or American scholarship, where commemoration of the Second World War generates greater critical attention.[70] Ackermann further criticises that when studies do concentrate on the memory of the war by drawing on retrospective and retroactive accounts, literary negotiations are often mentioned for the sake of completeness rather than for their rich and diverse contents and ability to critically question the cultural memory of the Second World War. One such study is Juliette Pattinson and Lucy Noakes' *British Cultural Memory and the Second World War*. Their take on "learned historical memory"[71] intriguingly traces commemo-

67 "Butch, n.1." *OED Online*. Oxford University Press, September 2016. Web. 20 September 2016. Paul Barker deploys another theory involving the American Airforce: American soldiers brought words such as 'butch' as well as 'crouse', 'blow-job' and 'naff' to wartime London. For more information see Paul Barker, *Polari – The Lost Language of Gay Men*, [2002], (London and New York: Routledge, 2003), p. 35.

68 Plain, (2013), p. 7.

69 Ackermann, (2015), p. 21. He polemically calls this being trapped in the gravity centre of the war and its culture. Original: „Gefangensein im Schwerkraftzentrum des Kriegs oder der Kriegskultur." p. 29.

70 Ibid., p. 21.

71 Juliette Pattinson and Lucy Noakes, *British Cultural Memory and the Second World War* (London: Bloomsbury, 2014), p. 2 and p. 4.

ration as an individual as well as public phenomenon that is always selective, interpretative and a narrative creation that involves forgetting as much as recalling. Historical, political, cultural and economic discourses are as relevant for the creation of collective memory as personal involvement. The constant cultural and medial evocation of the Second World War after 1945 leads Pattinson and Noakes to argue that later generations have adopted "the memories as their own"[72] in slogans such as 'Keep Calm and Carry On' and Sara Ahmed claims that "[t]he very failure of individual memory is compensated for by a collective memory"[73]. Both statements emphasise that collective memory emerges from the past to serve a communal purpose in the present. By doing so, the 'memory' of the Second World War is a contemporary product and not a 'truthful' representation of events, because it is re-negotiated and re-interpreted in each appropriation. It is also characterised by erasures and amnesias of the unsavoury past such as the Japanese success in Burma, or the disastrous battle of Dunkirk, which obscure the taintless victory of the British nation. Novels like Walter Baxter's *Look Down in Mercy* (1951) challenge this constructed memory by portraying an English officer in Burma fighting for his life against the Japanese, and Mary Renault's *The Charioteer* (1953) remembers the horrors of Dunkirk in the depiction of a soldier named Laurie Odell, who was severely injured during an attack leaving him burdened with a permanently stiff knee. Whilst bringing into conversation various forms of medial commemoration that shape the construction of the war's legacy on British culture, Pattinson and Noakes pay little attention to such fictional negotiations of pain and despair that begin to re-shape a collective memory of the war in Britain.

More inclusive works with extensive literary material are Victoria Steward's *The Second World War in Contemporary British Fiction* and Eva M. Pérez Rodríguez's *How the Second World War Is Depicted by British Novelists since 1990.*[74] The incorporation of largely disregarded fictions about the Second World War written by novelists who did not personally experience the war widens its conventional reception beyond mainstream premises. Stewart's focus lies on the issue of secrecy, and how commemoration and retrospective wartime novels continue to negotiate and reveal war secrets. She argues that secrecy was not only used during combat as a means to conceal information from the enemy,

72 Pattinson and Noakes, (2014), p. 2.

73 Sara Ahmed, *Strange Encounters: Embodied Others in Post-Coloniality* (London and New York: Routledge, 2000), p. 77.

74 Stewart, (2011); Eva M. Pérez Rodríguez, How the Second World War Is Depicted by British Novelists since 1990: The Passage of Time Changes Our Portrayal of Traumatic Events (New York: Edwin Mellen Press, 2012).

it also, perhaps with more far-reaching effect, influenced the immediate post-war period and how the war was henceforth remembered. The possibility that many stories have not yet been told, whether due to their military delicacy or because they did not comply with contemporaneous dominant discourse, calls into question our trust in the knowledge we believe to have of the past.

Stewart consequently incorporates Sarah Waters' *The Night Watch* (2006) into her analysis in order to negotiate the discrepancy between "what was known then and what is known now"[75], because Waters looks into the past through a different lens, one which is often disinterested in recollecting collective memory in favour of focusing on issues disregarded by novels of the time. Like Quentin Crisp's homosexual auto-biography, Waters' lesbian war story "disrupts this homogeneity by incorporating less familiar aspects of the war into [the narrative], and in the process, ask[s] why these have come to be concealed or neglected"[76]. The question why certain texts have become collective memories whilst others have been disregarded is the central issue of Stewart's work and inserts into my own study.

Pérez Rodríguez's work on *How the Second World War Is Depicted by British Novelists since 1990* takes a perspective similar to Stewart's when tracing the impact of the war on later generations of various nationalities. Accordingly, retrospective war novels do not simply glimpse into the past but also question "the economic, political and social systems that shape their world" in the twenty-first century. Like Steward, Pérez Rodríguez values the implication of homosexuality as a way of calling to attention aspects of war writings conventionally forgotten in dominant discourse, and she seeks to disclose what British identity meant in the 1940s and how it is represented through a contemporary mindset. In doing so, she also concentrates on *The Night Watch* and its challenging of "a conventional chronology"[77], expressed in Waters' backward narrative beginning in 1947 and working its way back to 1941, which simultaneously reveals the disorder of the war years, and modern British society's confusion over its place in the world. The post-war depiction of the characters Helen and Viv working as matchmakers for example, is read by Pérez Rodríguez as "a reflection on the contemporary degree of social upheaval"[78] in Britain because the characters' non-conforming relationships place them in opposition to the heteronormative couples they want to bring together. This paradox shows that whilst advocating gender and sexual diversity in contemporary Britain, heteronormative standards continue to domi-

75 Stewart, (2011), p. 2.

76 Ibid., p. 2.

77 Pérez Rodríguez, (2012), p. 3.

78 Ibid., p. 31.

nate social life. Retrospective war novels can therefore not only call into question Britain's collective memory of the Second World War as traced by Stewart but may also inscribe a contemporary discourse of homosexuality into the past in order to address current social and political issues. The value and challenge of retrospective war writings is therefore twofold: simultaneously correcting the image of the soldier poet by implementing untold aspects of the war, whilst reflecting on and infiltrating a modern consciousness into the past that questions the present. Consequently, in analysing retrospective narratives it needs to be carefully considered at what point a (homosexual) past is being created to serve a present (political) purpose.

Adam Fitzroy's *Make Do and Mend* (2012) illustrates this challenge more extensively than *The Night Watch*, as some scenes are very explicit in their display of sexual intercourse, which betrays its modern basis in sexual liberation. The protagonist Harry Lyon serves as a submarine officer until an accident causes severe injuries to his lungs and the death of two of his men. Unfit for active service, Harry recovers at his childhood home called Hendra where he makes the acquaintance of Jim Brynawel – a farm worker and pacifist who performs alternative service. Their bond soon becomes more intimate but is temporarily cut off when Harry has to go to Liverpool to work for military intelligence. In Liverpool Harry encounters a rampant homosexual subculture, which hardly conceals its promiscuity and he describes the room he rents to have "served rather different functions before the war" (174). Such euphemistic language is quickly abandoned when Harry concedes that he is living in former "knocking-shop" facilities (174). While the first impression suggests a decidedly modern consciousness where sexuality is hardly (if at all) censored, a comparison to Walter Baxter's *Look Down in Mercy* reveals that the term "knocking-shop" (*LD* 23) was already present and in use in 1951 when the novel was published. It follows that rather than infiltrating a liberal mindset into the 1940s, Fitzroy rehearses the language of the time. However, when Harry has oral sex with an acquaintance named Clive, *Make Do and Mend* is so explicit as to leave no doubt over its contemporary context: "Now he participated fully, licking and sucking and leaving his throat open do be plundered, finally accepting the spasming ejaculation as if through a feeding tube directly into his stomach, bypassing his brain and his emotions altogether." (179) This quote is representative of many more of its kind and emphasise *Make Do and Mend* as a novel from the 21st century. Fitzroy's varying style of dramatising intercourse shows that modern novels use the language of the time and garnish it with current parlance to create a hybrid version of the past.

This section has focused on the critical terrain regarding Second World War fiction, from the immediate post-war claims of not having produced any literary work, to its retroactive and retrospective negotiation, shows that critics have repeatedly engaged themselves with the past. The following will trace similar efforts regarding gay and lesbian scholarship in order to disclose the complicated history of homosexual liberation as well as the amnesia regarding the past that succeeded the Stonewall riots in 1969.

STONEWALL AND GAY LIBERATION

June 28, 1969 has become the benchmark for the gay liberation movement, which was provoked when police raided the Stonewall Inn, a nightclub in New York City located on Christopher Street (hence the German adaptation of Christopher Street Day) known for its gay and lesbian scene.[79] During these regular raids, the police never encountered or even anticipated resistance from customers whom they regarded as having low morals, but little violent potential due to their fear of legal forces or of being publicly 'outed.' Similar to Crisp at the beginning of that century, men dressed as women were most severely scrutinised that night and forced to undress to identify their 'true' sex. Contrary to the police's expectations, however, visitors of the Stonewall Inn did not oblige to the order, but began to perform exaggeratedly in the streets, celebrating instead of hiding their effeminacy. Having nothing to lose, these men as well as other customers of the Stonewall Inn and bystanders attracted by the noise began to fight the police with beer cans and stones turning the raid into a riot. The following nights saw similar scenes, which led to escalating demonstrations and calls for liberation and legal rights among lesbians, gays, bisexuals, trans*[80] people and intersexuals, later to be named LGBTQI[81] community. Further uproars were happening in Europe, especially in Britain, where the Gay Liberation Front (GLF) was formed to organise resistances and to publicly demonstrate against homophobia

79 Elizabeth A. Armstrong and Suzanna M. Crage, "Movements and Memory: The Making of the Stonewall Myth" in *American Sociological Review* Vol. 71, No. 5 (2006), pp. 724-751.

80 I use the umbrella term "trans" with an asterisk rather than differentiating between transgender and transsexual people in order to include a variety of gender identities and those who are pre or post surgery or feel no need for medical assimilation.

81 Current activism uses the lable LGBTQI+ in oder to signify the openness of this classification.

throughout the 1970s.[82] In the commemoration of the Stonewall riots, June 28, 1969 thus marks the beginning of a new mindset where homosexuality was no longer considered a perversion or curse and being gay, lesbian, bisexual, trans* or other turned into a cause for pride. At this point, the formerly dismissive and disrespectful term 'gay' became common usage among the LGBTQI community "as a badge of positive self-identification"[83]. It forged the turning of an "internalized [...] negative image[...] of homosexuality and homosexuals"[84] into an affirmative gay consciousness.

The second half of the 20th century became vital for gay and lesbian scholarship grounding their research in experiences following the Stonewall riots. In this new legal environment culminating and manifesting into contemporary queer studies, various disciplines covering philosophy, sociology, psychoanalysis, anthropology, and literary studies converged in the interest of making visible structural reiterations of homophobia within heteronormative societies. Existing feminist studies were revived and complemented with new aspects on identity, sexual fluidity and gender embodiments. This new way of thinking profited from and contributed to poststructuralist theories that called into question the former school of structuralism sought to order the world on a comprehensive scale to grasp its depth. Social critics such as Michel Foucault (among others) challenged the structuralist approach for its focus on and creation of hierarchical binaries like signifier/signified, but also man/woman, public/private etc. In determining these binary positions, structuralists tried to perceive the essence of "'meaning', 'truth', 'subjectivity', 'freedom', 'power', and so on"[85], whereas poststructuralists pressed for a rethinking of these concepts as inherently constructed within a set of power relations. Foucault argued that these power relations and systems of knowledge form the discourse in which 'truth' is engendered and becomes naturalised.[86] Similar to Butler's theory on gender performativity, Foucault determines that there is no 'core truth' but only production and re-production of truth-

82 Chris Waters, "The Homosexual as Social Being in Britain, 1945-1968" in Brian Lewis (ed.), *British Queer History: New Approaches and Perspectives* (Manchester: Manchester University Press, 2013).

83 Les Brookes, *Gay Male Fiction Since Stonewall: Ideology, Conflict, and Aesthetics* (New York and London: Routledge, 2009), p. 8.

84 Claude J. Summers, *Gay Fictions: Wilde to Stonewall: Studies in a Male Homosexual Literary Tradition* (New York: Continuum, 1990), p. 16.

85 Nikki Sullivan, A Critical Introduction to Queer Theory (New York: New York University Press, 2003), p. 39.

86 Michel Foucault, *Discipline and Punish: The Birth of the Prison*, [1975], (London: Vintage Books, 1995).

effects – of knowledge that appears to be genuine whilst being a cultural fabrication. This process becomes disguised as universal knowledge through socio-historical discourses that turn the idea of, for example, heterosexuality, into something perceived as 'normal' and 'natural', whereas homosexuality becomes the Other.[87] This process does not make heterosexuality 'natural' and 'normal' *per se* since it "is a (historically and culturally specific) truth-effect of systems of power/knowledge" that engender its currently dominant social position.[88] In order to deconstruct this system of truth-effects, poststructuralism concentrates on the analysis of difference, non-compliance and struggle by focusing on dynamic processes between subjects and/or groups. While poststructuralist approaches to the subject differ among themselves, they share "a rejection of the belief that the subject is autonomous, unified, self-knowing, and static"[89].

Within this atmosphere of rethinking and change, gay liberation and gay scholarship was formed, but poststructuralist notions of an unstable and more importantly not autonomous self significantly hampered efforts of liberation. Moreover, Foucault's assertion that power does not reside in an elite group able to wield it against others, but builds on structures that afflict and enable everybody, took away a great deal of potential agency for gay liberationists. Nikki Sullivan nicely summarises the futile situation: "since resistance is not, and cannot be, external to systems of power/knowledge, then an oppositional politics that attempts to replace supposedly false ideologies with non-normative truths is inherently contradictory"[90]. If there is no single power-possessing group to resist and if any attempt of changing dominant order reifies new power hierarchies, how could the LGBTQI community possibly become liberated without themselves becoming drawn into the swirl of deceptive power formations? Within this climate of striving for change and theorising increasingly more complex ways to understand social structure, post-Stonewall activism faced many obstacles.

Unlike wartime researchers who took to re-evaluating the image of the silent war by analysing unfamiliar works of female novelists, LGBTQI theorists seldom looked into the unexplored literary past to make more powerful claims for their futures. This reluctance is partially caused by to inner conflicts following the Stonewall riots over the place of homosexuality within heteronormative society, which made genealogical efforts secondary. Les Brookes explains:

87 Foucault, *The Will to Knowledge* (1998), p. 43.

88 Sullivan, (2003), p. 39.

89 Ibid., p. 41.

90 Ibid., p. 42.

> The subculture of the early 1970s was in fact a battlefield: on one side were those who had no great quarrel with the social order, while on the other were those who wished to see it razed to the ground. The former were keen to show their allegiance to heterosexist norms, seeing such loyalty as evidence of their right to social inclusion [...]. The latter group, on the other hand, were so determined to break free of these norms that relationships of more than a night's duration were condemned as showing abject deference to the heterosexist ideal of lifelong partnership.[91]

Brookes' study *Gay Male Fiction Since Stonewall* evaluates the role of literature in the construction of a gay consciousness and people's negotiation of identity. In order to do so, he taps into the historically important and contradictory standpoints of radicalism and assimilation of the 1970s and asks: "In what way does gay male fiction since Stonewall engage with the longstanding conflict in gay culture and politics between [...] the need for integration into the wider social scene on the one hand and the need to assert an independent identity on the other?"[92] This pressing question includes an often ambivalent standpoint and mixture of both sides, which defies clear-cut positions or answers, thus infesting its literature with tensions and controversies. Brookes acknowledges that these tensions are not an exclusively post-Stonewall phenomenon but have a long history "stretching back to that period in the late nineteenth century when homosexuality first became conceptualized"[93]. *The Naked Civil Servant* not only illustrates Brookes' claim that homosexuals formed communities long before the Stonewall riots, but also that these were ridden with ambivalences over their place in society similar to later generations. While presenting himself as openly homosexual through his effeminacy, which suggests a radical attitude towards heteronormative society, Quentin Crisp nevertheless "regarded all heterosexuals, however low, as superior to any homosexual, however noble" (69). His criticism is not only self-reflexive but primarily directed against the homosexual subculture that disguised their sexualities and engaged in "teasing flirtations" with women which amount to "masquerade[s]" when the "admiration or respect or love aroused were really for some other man of the same name" (87). After having been excluded from homosexual bars several times for his open display of effeminacy and his critique on assimilated gays, Crisp concludes that "[h]omosexuals were ashamed. They resented not being in the mainstream of

91 Brookes, (2009), p. 2.

92 Ibid., p. 4.

93 Ibid., p. 12. For further information see Foucault, *The Will to Knowledge* (1998), p. 43 and the Cartoon "Constructing Sex and Gender: A Political, Religious and Scientific History..." Figure 1.

life" (87). Crisp's experiences indicate that the struggles between radicals and assimilationists have a long-standing history and the lingering dispute among homosexuals over their place within society explains why the newly formed gay community after 1969 was not particularly interested in refurbishing a past (literary or otherwise) when their future seemed so uncertain.

Despite the diverse and fundamental struggles accompanying the period, there were efforts to fabricate a homosexual tradition. In 1971, two years after the Stonewall riots, Rictor Norton filed a motion to teach a course entitled "The Homosexual Literary Tradition" at Florida State University.[94] After passing the first round of approval, the faculty eventually rejected the seminar for being too outspoken – their preferred title was "Friendship in Literature"[95]. In his paper "The Homosexual literary Tradition: Course Outline and Objectives" Norton retrospectively reflects on the course, which he was only allowed to give on a non-credit basis. In consideration of his students who were confronted with such a subject matter for the first time, Norton (consciously or not) confirms a positive gay subject position in order to ease the mind of his students (and his own?) when stating:

> During the first few days of the course, treat the subject of homosexual love in a fairly light-hearted manner. Remember that guilt and anxiety rarely appear in homosexual literature until the late nineteenth century, and don't become the major theme of *Angst* until after 1914.[96]

My aim is neither to refute nor to validate his claim, but to call to attention how students came to encounter the topic in the immediate post-Stonewall period. Feeling the newness of public attention, gay scholars such as Norton began to transfer a positive and possibly assimilated image of homosexuality into the past in order to calm down protests. In her critical study *Feeling Backward: Loss and the Politics of Queer History*, Heather Love similarly argues that "[e]arly work in gay and lesbian studies" "responded to the history of violence and stigmatization by affirming the legitimacy of gay and lesbian existence"[97]. In the course of this self-validation, academia produced accounts of historical and homosexual figures such as Alexander the Great or Sappho from Lesbos – what Gregory

94 Rictor Norton, "The Homosexual Literary Tradition: Course Outline and Objectives" in *College English* Vol. 35, No. 6 (1974), p. 674.

95 Ibid., p. 674.

96 Ibid., p. 677.

97 Heather Love, *Feeling Backward: Loss and the Politics of Queer History* (Cambridge and Massachusetts: Harvard University Press, 2007), pp. 1-2.

Woods calls "lists of praiseworthy inverts"[98] –, but these efforts remained strictly set within the bounds of discovering historical gay-affirmation rather than struggles or denials.

Michael Bronski's *Pulp Frictions* uncovers a broader picture to explain why pre-Stonewall novels have either become forgotten or restricted to a small number of familiar names such as Radclyffe Hall, E. M. Forster, Gore Vidal or Christopher Isherwood.[99] The example of Norton's efforts into teaching a homosexual literary tradition demonstrates that a more positive gay consciousness became established, and this positive outlook had to be manifested, despite conflicts within the community. Bronski calls this the "'Is it good for the gays?' argument", which questions whether gays and lesbians are represented in literature as "heroic, likable, or even neutral? Or are they presented in ways that draw upon injurious and untrue stereotypes that reinforce pre-existing prejudices?"[100] With this activist form of interrogation, pre-Stonewall novels were read within a post-Stonewall mindset which meant marginalising or even falsifying their impact during a time characterised by obscenity laws and censorship. Censorship is, according to Butler, "that which is directed against persons or against the content of their speech"[101]. She continues stating that "censorship appears to follow the utterance of offensive speech: speech has already become offensive, and then some recourse to a regulatory agency is made."[102] This "regulatory agency" that decides over which texts became censored in Britain, was the board acting according to the Obscene Publications Act of 1857. It "amalgamated the previous common law offence of obscene libel to make to publication and sale of obscene writing a legal offence and extended the power of the police to target publishers"[103]. Since the definition of what constitutes 'obscene writing' was extremely

98 Gregory Woods, *A History of Gay Literature: The Male Tradition* (New Haven and London: Yale University Press, 1998), p. 7. Woods gives further examples of historical figures "with Uranian temperament" such as "Michel Angelo [sic], Shakespeare, Marlowe, Alexander the Great, Julius Caesar, or among women, Christine of Sweden, Sappho the poetess", p. 4.

99 Michael Bronski, *Pulp Friction: Uncovering the Golden Age of Gay Male Pulps*, [2003], (New York: St. Martin's Griffin, 2013).

100 Bronski, (2013), p. 10.

101 Judith Butler, *Excitable Speech: A Politics of the Performative* (London and New York: Routledge, 1997), p. 128.

102 Ibid., 128.

103 Rachel Potter, "Introduction" in David Bradshaw and Rachel Potter (eds.), *Prudes on the Prowl: Fiction and Obscenity in England, 1850 to the present* (Oxford: Oxford University Press, 2013), p. 2.

broad, many authors and publishers faced prosecution, because their texts allegedly "deprave[ed] and corrupt[ed] the minds and morals of those who are open to such immoral influences"[104]. Benjamin Hicklin composed this ambiguous definition, commonly known as the 'Hicklin ruling', which was not only very far-reaching, but also highly subjective in qualifying at what point "the minds and morals" of some people become offended. Michael Warner rightly claims that 'obscene' is "a word designed to shame dissenters into silence"[105]. He concludes that "it enlists the government in the politics of shame, making sure that nothing challenging to the tastes of the majority will be allowed to circulate"[106]. Censorship laws thus function to preserve an alleged universality of 'norms' and 'moral standards' that echo the "tastes of the majority". These laws disguise that the supposedly universal standards are deeply embedded in a patriarchal and nationalistic system that arbitrarily shames a spectrum of acts raging from violence to sodomy.

Censorship laws impaired novelists in the freedom of speech, which needs to be taken into account when judging the value of pre-Stonewall novels. For instance, the evaluation of Radclyffe Hall's *The Well of Loneliness* (1928)[107] as a prominent example of gloominess and "sufficiently self-hating to be almost palatable to certain types of anti-homosexual readers" [108] exposes how a contemporary discourse can be obtruded onto a text from 1928. By the time Hall published *The Well of Loneliness*, the Obscene Publications Act of 1857 was still in operation and the novel subsequently banned for indecency in 1928. Such rulings did not decrease after the Second World War, but became even more common. Alan Travis observes that compared to 39 prosecutions for indecency in 1935, the number rose to 132 almost two decades later in 1954, and "111 people were founded guilty of publishing obscene libels compared with only 39 in 1939"[109]. The rapidly rising number of censored texts resulted from an increasing "[f]ear of Americanization"[110] after the Second World War, prompted by a "dread of

104 Definition of 'obscenity' by Benjamin Hicklin in 1868, known as the 'Hicklin ruling'. Potter, (2013), p. 2.

105 Michael Warner, *The Trouble with Normal: Sex, Politics, and the Ethics of Queer Life* (Cambridge and Massachusetts: Harvard University Press, 1999), p. 12.

106 Ibid., 13.

107 Radclyffe Hall, *The Well of Loneliness*, [1928], (New York: Anchor Books, 1990).

108 Woods, (1998), p. 205.

109 Alan Travis, *Bound and Gagged: A Secret History of Obscenity in Britain* (London: Profile Books, 2000), p. 94.

110 David Bradshaw, "American Beastliness, the Great Purge and its Aftermath (1946-1959)" in David Bradshaw and Rachel Potter (eds.), *Prudes on the Prowl: Fiction*

transatlantic contamination as the popularity of American films, music, comics, and pulp fiction gathered pace"[111]. The infiltration of British culture with "American fictional imports"[112] that were considered 'immoral' according to the vague definition of the 'Hickling ruling' also increased efforts to cleanse national texts from 'depravations'.

Interestingly, whereas Hall's novel caused upheaval at the beginning of the 20th century for being too outspoken and controversial, modern perceptions focus on its largely depressing and restrained tone. This discursive transformation in answering to an unchanged text illustrates that modes of assessment are constantly in flux and not grounded in stability. Whilst "there was an almost systematic lack of frankness in approach to sexual matters"[113] until the passing of a new Obscene Publications Act in 1959, modern narratives are saturated with what used to be censored. Michel Warner observes that "[p]leasures once imaginable only with disgust, if at all, become the material out of which individuals and groups elaborate themselves"[114]. His argument that former "disgust" will turn into pleasure, explains the repeated misreadings of pre-Stonewall literature: whereas novels such as *The Well of Loneliness* were allusive in the discussion of silenced desires, modern culture demands self-affirming clarity. The discrepancy between these expectations illustrates why the arguably depressing depiction of the protagonist Stephan and her struggle to live as a masculine woman cannot speak to a modern version of "Is it good for the gays?": Stephan, and Hall in creating her, faced very different obstacles than contemporary gay communities as well as novelists. When judging *The Well of Loneliness* according to a post-Stonewall mindset, it is removed from its legal and cultural context. What follows from such a reading is the assumption that pre-Stonewall novels depict sad, self-hating characters, who do not fit the new gay spirit of the liberated refusing nostalgic gazes into this depressing past.

Heather Love persuasively argues that despite severe criticism, *The Well of Loneliness* is one of the most read and analysed texts representing female homosexuality. This enduring popularity derives from a sense of fascination with and inspiration from the text (whether positive or negative) that "compels readers in

and Obscenity in England, 1850 to the present (Oxford: Oxford University Press, 2013), p. 138.

111 Ibid., 139.

112 Ibid., 139.

113 David Kynaston, *Family Britain, 1951-57*, [2009], (London: Bloomsbury, 2010), p. 552.

114 Warner, (1999), p. 12.

a way that brighter stories of liberation do not"[115]. Despite this merit, gay and lesbian scholarship remained largely critical of Hall's and other 'damaging' novels. Even texts that did not portray homosexuals as explicitly burdened characters came under critique, for they renounced the place of outlawed desire in society or homosexual existence altogether when homosexual characters "appeared repeatedly in novels of the period as the *almost* unthinkable other"[116]. In vague and alluding language these narratives make "homosexuality hover indeterminately between that which may be recognized – the novel asks the reader to recognize it – and that which the 'good' narrator hardly knows"[117]. Such hesitant representations fit the new gay consciousness just as bad as explicitly negative accounts.

However, since obscenity laws were still in operation during the Cold War period, novelists often *had* to encode homosexual contents in allusive language. Drewey Wayne Gunn and Jaime Harker elaborate on this:

> Those [authors] who chose to be more open [...] often wrote about [homosexuality] in appropriately depressing ways in order to escape the charges of obscenity and immorality. Though the number of novels with happy endings published between 1906 (*Imre*) and 1959 (*Sam*) is greater than is usually thought, it became a literary truism that homosexual men and women were filled with self-hatred and led miserable, unhappy lives that ended in bodily violence or death, often by suicide, unless they converted to heterosexuality.[118]

In agreement with this evaluation, Michael Bronski emphasises: "It is really a myth that all these pre-Stonewall novels end in total misery. We seem to want to see the 1940's and 1950's as a time of unmitigated queer-hating, without social, political or emotional nuance."[119] Bronski gives ample evidence for his thesis that a vital and often positive subculture continued to flourish in response to the Second World War, despite the growth of institutionalised violence against homosexuals in its aftermath. Bérubé similarly argues that the roots of a greater homosexual (literary) consciousness can be found during the Second World War

115 Love, (2007), p. 3.

116 Sinfield, (1989), p. 68.

117 Sinfield, (1989), p. 68.

118 Drewey Wayne Gunn and Jaime Harker, "Introduction" in Drewey Wayne Gunn and Jaime Harker (ed.), *1960s Gay Pulp Fiction* (Amherst and Boston, Massachusetts: University of Massachusetts Press, 2013), pp. 3-4.

119 Michael Bronski, "The Shock of the Old: Christopher Bram Chats with the Author of *Pulp Friction*" in *The Gay & Lesbian Review Worldwide* Vol. 10, No. 2 (2003), p. 32.

where homosexual men formed a network of friendship groups through which they "discovered and contributed to the rich gay nightlife – parties, bars, and nightclubs – that flourished in the war-boom cities"[120]. With the exception of Baxter's *Look Down in Mercy*, all narratives discussed here give insight into this subculture, whether dauntingly critical as Renault's *The Charioteer*, invitingly supportive as Waters' *The Night Watch*, or flamboyantly sexual as Fitzroy's *Make Do and Mend*. These varieties call into question Claude J. Summers' assertion that "the subculture centered around bars is often depicted very negatively in gay fiction"[121]. Furthermore, the novels place Bérubé's findings concentrating on the U.S. military on a greater scale by suggesting that for Britain, too, "[t]he experiences of homosexuals serving in World War II led to their greater awareness of their numbers, and writers began to treat homosexual themes more freely in the 1940s and 1950s"[122]. Not without reason does Bérubé conclude:

> A later generation of gays would point to the famous 1969 bar fight at Greenwich Village's Stonewall Inn as the beginning of gay liberation. But the current spirit of resistance and solidarity predates the 1960s. It was born under fire during World War II and the Cold War.[123]

Bérubé criticises that due to the scale of the war and its long-term effects on society, economy and its unfathomed destruction, the memory of the early roots of a gay liberation was lost. I will argue that this memory is not lost but disregarded and subsumed under mainstream stories of both popular war literature and contemporary gay literature which concentrate on more recent themes such as the Stonewall riots, the outbreak of AIDS, and the development of a gay consciousness and its abjection.[124] Even in literature designed to address people's experiences beyond heteronormative standards, certain issues have become more thoroughly discussed than others, and homosexuality during the Second World War has not been researched as thoroughly as the gay liberation movement or its setback during the AIDS epidemic. This is significantly noticeable in the relative lack of research material to draw from, especially regarding the British canon.

120 Bérubé, (2002), p. 230.

121 Summers, (1990), p. 23.

122 Gunn and Harker, (2013), p. 3.

123 Bérubé, (2011), p. 112.

124 For further information see: Calvin Thomas, *Masculinity, Psychoanalysis, Straight Queer Theory: Essays on Abjection in Literature, Mass Culture, and Film* (New York: Palgrave Macmillan, 2008). Or Monica Pearl, *AIDS Literature and Gay Identity: the Literature of Loss* (New York and London: Routledge, 2013).

Whereas Renault's *The Charioteer* and Waters' *The Night Watch* have received a fair amount of critical attention and become increasingly read in conjunction, Adam Fitzroy's *Make Do and Mend* is arguably absent from academic scholarship. It is particularly striking that Walter Baxter's *Look Down in Mercy* has not been given more far reaching acclaim considering that he was friends with E. M. Foster, who recommended his work to Christopher Isherwood. Commenting on Baxter's second novel *The Image and the Search* (1953)[125], Foster writes in a letter to Isherwood:

> Walter Baxter's new novel has much progressed – it sounds completely different from its predecessor and I am longing to read it. We meet or correspond regularly. He has just read Maurice and is terribly upset by its sadness but was drinking all the time he read. I hope to see him this week again. I hate him being sad. I shall read the 'new' chapter to him and see how he feels then.[126]

The familiarity with which Foster speaks of Baxter indicates their close friendship, which makes the neglect of Baxter's work all the more curious. Foster must have trusted Baxter to keep the knowledge of *Maurice* (written between 1913 and 1914 but posthumously published in 1971) secret. Whereas Foster was afraid of releasing a novel that dealt with the issue of homosexuality head on, Baxter's *Look Down in Mercy* was composed *and published* at a time when Foster did not dare to do the same. Their friendship compared to their different degree of publicity illustrates how little attention non-heteronormative war writings have gained and how arbitrary the selection of works for public celebration seems to be. This last point gains more traction with view to the enthusiastic review of *Look Down in Mercy* in *Time* magazine from 1952: "In an uncommonly good first novel, Author [sic] Walter Baxter tells the story of an ordinary British captain and how his codes and courage crack wide open under the strain of retreat, ambush and torture in Burma in World War II."[127] In an obituary of Fergus Provan, Baxter's long-term partner, the *Independent* wrote in 1997 that Baxter's "novel *Look Down in Mercy* (1951) was hailed, like Gore Vidal's *The City and the Pillar* (1948)[128], as a pioneering study of gay relationships in a hostile and

125 Walter Baxter, *The Image and the Search* (London: Hutchinson, 1953).

126 Richard E. Zeikowitz, *Letters Between Forster and Isherwood on Homosexuality and Literature* (New York: Palgrave Macmillan, 2008), p. 153.

127 *Time*, "Books: Man Under Pressure" <http://content.time.com/time/magazine/article/0,9171,816164,00.html> [last accessed: 24/08/2016].

128 Gore Vidal, *The City and the Pillar*, [1948], (New York: Vintage Books, 2003).

indifferent world"[129]. Lastly, an essay by Henri Peyre published in an article on "The Most Neglected Books of the Past Twenty-Five Years Selected by Writers, Scholars and Critics" values *Look Down in Mercy* as a "very remarkable English novel[…], even [a] truly great novel[…]" that has "not been acknowledged as such by the majority of American [and I want to add British] critics"[130]. When scholars and book critics from different fields and periods agree on the literary merit of Baxter's work, why then did it not receive more far-reaching acclaim?[131] Bronski explains that "gay liberation was a youth movement whose sense of history was defined to a large degree by a rejection of the past. [...] The idea that some books were not 'good for the gays' is closely tied to why they are not better known today and why they were lost to gay history."[132] However, what happened after the "youth movement" matured and developed into queer theory?

QUEERING THE PAST

While the immediate post-Stonewall period was preoccupied with legitimating LGBTQI existence and experience, the late 20th and early 21st century saw a turn toward a queer consciousness that "attempt[ed] to counter stigma by incorporating it"[133]. In an influential essay on "the usefulness of 'queer'", Shane Phelan argues that "'queer' is to the 1990s as 'gay' was to the 1970s, a mark of pride, a throwing off of closets and politeness, and a bid for an autonomous culture"[134]. Unlike the positive re-claiming of the term 'gay' by activists in the 1970s, "queer was adopted in the late 1980s [...] because it evoked a long history of insult and abuse – you could hear the hurt in it"[135]. In *Feeling Backward*, Heather

129 *Independent*, "Obituary: Fergus Provan", <http://www.independent.co.uk/news/people/obituary-fergus-provan-1247639.html> [last accessed: 24/08/2016].

130 Henri Peyre, "The Most Neglected Books of the Past Twenty-Five Years Selected by Writers, Scholars and Critics" in *The American Scholar* Vol. 25, No. 4 (1956), p. 492.

131 This question can, of course, be broadened to include a critique on the largely 'white' tradition of gay and lesbian writers gaining scholarly acclaim. For an intriguing debate on this issue see Brookes, (2009), pp. 193-194.

132 Bronski, (2013), p. 12, p. 11.

133 Love, (2007), p. 2.

134 Shane Phelan, "The Shape of Queer: Assimilation and Articulation" in *Women & Politics* Vol. 18, No. 2 (1997), p. 57.

135 Love, (2007), p. 2.

Love argues that "[t]he emphasis on injury in queer studies has made critics in this field more willing to investigate the darker aspects of queer representation and experience and to attend to the social, psychic, and corporeal effects of homophobia."[136] However, it took until 1990 before a single case study devoted itself to Anglo-American fiction with homosexual contents "written in the advent and aftermath of the [Oscar] Wilde scandal of 1895 and in the period following World War II, but before New York's Stonewall riots of 1969"[137]. Summers' *Gay Fictions: Wilde to Stonewall* is acutely aware that it is indebted to the Stonewall riots for making its investigations possible, but nevertheless maintains that the liberal spirit of the late 1960s finds its roots almost a century earlier. Summers' study sets out to "explore [...] the necessary preconditions to gay liberation", which rest on the Criminal Law Amendment Act adopted in Britain in 1885 criminalising all same-sex behaviour.[138] While designed to harass and prosecute homosexuals, the law generated a first sense of self-affirmation among people, who shared the fate of victimisation based on their deviating sexuality. Their increasing visibility enhanced open hostilities and homophobia, and the Oscar Wilde trial became a public cause for both conservative heterosexuals and newly inspired homosexuals who began to resist their stigmatisation and developed a kind of collective consciousness. Summers concludes that, as an effect, fictional representations of homosexuality were becoming more numerous and more daring, notably Wilde's own texts. In him, Summers sees the first prominent figure of gay liberation and his literary negotiations of "self-realization, the yearning for escape from moralistic prohibitions, the desire to recover an Arcadian past in which homosexuality is valued and respected, and the depiction of divided selves"[139] are equally deployed by later novels. By drawing a parallel between Wilde's writings and post-Stonewall fiction in form and content, Summers begins to establish a literary genealogy.

However, in Summers' reading of Renault's *The Charioteer*, Bronski's 'Is it good for the gays?'-paradigm becomes once more apparent. Although accounting for Renault's effort to fashion "a portrait of homosexual love as potentially elevated and dignified", Summers' evaluation of *The Charioteer* as a "'homosexual problem novel[...]'"[140] is more a reflection on his assessment of the Cold War as a bleak period for homosexuals facing harassment and stigmatisation, than an analysis of the novel, which is much more diverse in its treatment of

136 Ibid., p. 2.

137 Summers, (1990), p. 12.

138 Ibid., p. 17.

139 Ibid., p. 20.

140 Summers, (1990), p. 26.

homosexuality. His further claim that "[t]his guilt and self-doubt [of the period] is apparent in *The Charioteer*" [141] positions the protagonists' struggles exclusively as a result of their sexuality, and forgets the narrative's setting in the Second World War, which provides a second important narrative strand and reason for the characters' challenging negotiations of their sexuality and masculinity within the military. The remarkable freedoms the protagonist Laurie experiences in the military hospital are overshadowed by Summers' enhanced interest in the characters' alleged self-doubts and self-hatred.

Regardless of these oversimplifications deriving from the objective of *Gay Fictions* to "place the fictions within their appropriate ideological context"[142], Summers' study gives vital insight into the development of homosexual representations in literature when detecting a displacement of influence from the late 1940s onwards. His examinations show that "[w]hile the first wave of serious gay fiction in English is the outgrowth of the early homosexual emancipation movement and the Wilde scandal, the second wave is part of the post-World War II literary boom, and *it is predominantly American rather than British*."[143] This shift is not only evident in Summers' own work on American authors such as James Baldwin and Gore Vidal as examples of this new kind of literature, but also in Joseph Bristow's chapter on censorship in *The Cambridge Companion to Gay and Lesbian Writing*. Whereas detailing the exact circumstances of the trial of Hall's *The Well of Loneliness* in 1928, Bristow leaves unmentioned the interim period until 1979, when *Gay News* was prosecuted under the blasphemy law.[144] He concludes that "[f]or over twenty years, Hall's *Well* was not republished in Britain, and in the intervening period a number of works that had homosexual content were seized and destroyed"[145]. One of these books that were withdrawn shortly after publication is Walter Baxter's second novel *The Image and the Search* (1953) leading Baxter to permanently terminate his career as a

141 Ibid., p. 26.

142 Ibid., p. 12.

143 Ibid., p. 23, [my emphasis].

144 For more information on novels with homosexual contents written after the Second World War see Sonya L. Jones, *Gay and Lesbian Literature Since World War II: History and Memory*, [1998], (New York: Routledge, 2014) and Anthony Slide, *Lost Gay Novels: A Reference Guide to fifty Works from the First Half of the Twentieth Century*, [2003], (New York: Routledge, 2003). Neither study includes Mary Renault's *The Charioteer* (1953) or Walter Baxter's *Look Down in Mercy* (1951).

145 Joseph Bristow, "Homosexual Writing on Trial: from *Fanny Hill* to *Gay News*" in Hugh Stevens (ed.), *The Cambridge Companion to Gay and Lesbian Writing* (Cambridge: Cambridge University Press, 2011), p. 30.

writer.[146] Vital scenes in Baxter's *Look Down in Mercy* have also been altered, but neither novel is mentioned in Bristow's account of censorship thus illustrating the lack of attention given to British writings with a homosexual content in the 1950s and 1960s.

Gunn and Harker's *1960s Gay Pulp Fiction* also focuses on the American literary canon and observes that, like British novels with a homosexual subject matter written before Stonewall, American gay pulp fiction of the 1960s has disappeared from public as well as academic consciousness. They explain that gay pulp fictions of the 1970s and 1980s "were essentially dismissed as erotica or pornography"[147]. Whilst "in the 1970s [pulps] served as little more than masturbatory aids, their quality degenerate[ed] even further in the 1980s when publishers tried to compete with videotapes as erotic stimuli"[148]. This dismissive attitude towards gay pulp fictions derives from the fact that "critics [had] no sense of a need to examine such seemingly marginalized literature"[149]. Additionally, the gay liberation movement made 'mainstream publishers' more daring and "literature [notably not pulp fictions] by, about, and for gay and lesbian readers became publicly celebrated for the first time"[150]. Whereas before, the publishing of homosexual literature bore severe risks of becoming prosecuted under obscenity laws, the public celebration of Foster's *Maurice* (1971) or Isherwood's *A Single Man* (1964), among others, permanently changed the public perception of these novels. Gunn and Harker conclude: "As such writers successfully blurred the division between mainstream and marginalized literature, theirs and similar works furthered the roles that 1960s gay pulps had performed."[151] Consequently, in the

146 In his diaries of the sixties Christopher Isherwood writes about Baxter that he "has become a rather tragic self-pitying drunken figure with a philosophy of failure. What use was success, [Baxter] asked. Oh yes, he *could* write again if he wanted to, but it would mean giving up drinking, smoking and sex – and was it worth it? The only thing that interested him, anyway, was to record some of his very early sex experiences; and those couldn't possibly be published ..." Isherwood's description shows how gravely the censoring of *Look Down in Mercy* (1951) and the banishment of *The Image and the Search* (1953) distressed Baxter. He felt like his writings could only ever encounter resistance from a public that was not prepared to read about homosexuality. Christopher Isherwood, *The Sixties: Diaries Volume Two 1960-1969* (London: Chatto and Windus, 2010), p. 120, [emphasis original].

147 Gunn and Harker, (2013), p. 16.

148 Ibid., p. 15.

149 Ibid., p. 15.

150 Ibid., p. 14.

151 Gunn and Harker, (2013), p. 14.

course of establishing a modern queer consciousness neither 1960s American gay pulps nor non-conforming and little-known British novels of that and earlier periods have become equally celebrated.

Following this outline of war literature and gay and lesbian fiction and their respective negotiation within academia, this study pursues to focus on various objectives: firstly, challenging wartime writing as a heteronormative endeavour by implicating a homosexual subject matter. Secondly, engaging with the Second World War as a memory that is repeatedly negotiated in retrospective fictions to enable a re-telling of events from a marginalised subject position. Thirdly, retrieving pre-Stonewall novels from their place of banishment in order to renegotiate a literary amnesia that succeeded efforts of gay liberation and emancipation. The next section will clarify my approach to Walter Baxter's *Look Down in Mercy* (1951), Mary Renault's *The Charioteer* (1953), Sarah Waters' *The Night Watch* (2006) and Adam Fitzroy's *Make Do and Mend* (2012), as well as the methodological procedure of discussing these novels.

FEMINIST NARRATIVE THEORY: APPROACH AND OUTLINE

In order to clarify my use of terminology, I wish to begin this section by defining key terms like 'fiction' and 'narrative' as well as their distinctions and characteristics with regard to a homosexual subject matter. Norman W. Jones' *Gay and Lesbian Historical Fiction* dissects the term 'historical fiction' to characterise *fiction* set at a time different from the author's.[152] This is contrasted to nonfiction histories as *narratives* "which more clearly denote [...] nonfictional as well as fictional stories"[153]. Linda Hutcheon equally states that "both historians and novelists *constitute* their subjects as possible objects of narrative representation"[154] –

152 Norman W. Jones, *Gay and Lesbian Historical Fiction: Sexual Mystery and post-Secular Narrative* (New York: Palgrave Macmillan, 2007), p. 29.

153 Jones, (2007), p. 30.

154 Linda Hutcheon, *A Poetics of Postmodernism: History, Theory, Fiction* (New York and London: Routledge, 1988), p. 111, [emphasis original]. In the 1970s Hayden White developed the understanding of history as subjective rather than empirically and universally true. Building on White's claim, Natasha Alden summarises that "the truth about the past lies not in a rationally organised, empirically based sequence of static facts taken from a stable reality, but in the chaotic dialogue between competing narratives." Natasha Alden, *Reading Behind the Lines: Postmemory in*

a definition which is acutely aware of discursive and ideological influences on authors of both historical fiction and nonfiction histories. In light of this, "historical fiction novels offer intellectually valid ways of exploring history – sometimes more intellectually honest ways than totalizing, endpoint-oriented nonfiction history writing"[155]. According to Jones it is *because of*, not despite, "the muddiness of historical fiction", that it bears potential for correcting an often homogeneous and reductive historicization of the past.[156] In this way, Jones takes up feminist criticism regarding *his*torical reconstructions and reveals the measure by which they erase not only female voices but also accounts on homosexuality or subordinated nationalisms. These issues are not detached from dominant reconstructions but mingled within them in a reciprocal connection. Rau translates the value of reconstructing aspects of an unknown past into the present when stating that "its margins, blind spots, codes, and clichés, its hyperbole and omissions, are of an unplumbed complexity that might help make sense of where Britons think they are today"[157]. It follows that retrospective narratives not only help to re-imagine untold queer stories, but also to uncover a nation's current self-understanding and, more specifically, its attitude towards marginalised subject matters such as homosexuality.

Brookes' definition of 'gay male fiction' as "fiction by self-identified nonheterosexual men, who may or may not choose to call themselves gay" is an example for inflicting a contemporary mindset onto earlier periods. [158] Although responsive to the identity struggles within the gay community when allowing for variance in authors' self-identification as gay or otherwise, and despite the understandable urge for "a convenient shorthand term"[159], specifying 'gay male fiction' with the authors' sexuality in mind homogenises and categorises writings along constructed parameters. Brookes' inclusions of a *potential* heterosexual readership does not convincingly soften the implications inherent in his definition, which not only excludes novels with homosexual contents produced by heterosexual authors, but also restricts novelists to their gender and sexuality as if their experiences gives them sole authority to represent male homosexuality. Similar to the soldier poet as the preferable author of wartime fiction, narrowing the scope of 'gay male fiction' to novels by "self-identified nonheterosexual

Contemporary British War Fiction (Manchester and New York: Manchester University Press, 2014), p. 9.

155 Jones, (2007), p. 28.

156 Ibid., p. 33.

157 Rau, (2016), p. 28.

158 Brookes, (2009), p. 8.

159 Ibid., p. 8.

men" disregards writings by (lesbian) women such as Mary Renault whose novel *The Charioteer* features male protagonists entangled in a homosexual love triangle. According to Brookes' definition, Renault's work is an (almost) impossible conundrum. Claude J. Summers gives a much more nuanced definition of his title and subject matter *Gay Fictions* to variously mean:

> the fictional representation of male homosexuals by gay male and lesbian writers; the evolution of concepts about homosexual identity; and the construction, perpetuation, revision, and deconstruction of fictions (including stereotypes and defamations) about homosexuality and homosexuals.[160]

Without denominating solely gay or lesbian authors or a homosexual readership, but instead alluding to pressing themes of identity and a deconstruction of the familiar, Summers finds a much broader basis for the term 'gay fictions' which, unfortunately, turns it into a blurry and unfeasible concept, making the shorthand an umbrella term.

In contrast to both Brookes' and Summers' efforts of incorporating 'gay' as a badge for self-affirmation, Quentin Crisp continued to use the less glorious terms 'homosexual' and 'homosexuality' even whilst living and publishing in New York City at the peak of gay liberation. His ambivalence in identifying with this new movement which caused many young gays and lesbians to dissociate themselves from him even before he infamously called the outbreak of AIDS a "fad"[161], shows that even the post-Stonewall area was less homogeneous than the category 'gay male fiction' suggests. Consequently, I will refrain from using the term 'gay male fiction' not only due to my inclusion of female authors, or the anachronism when using the term 'gay' for a Second World War setting, but more broadly because the current understanding of 'gay male fiction' is either too reductive or too broad in its conceptions of authors, readership and subject matter. A more accurate classification, if one so desires, is to think of Renault's *The Charioteer* (1953) and Baxter's *Look Down in Mercy* (1951) as wartime fictions based on personal experiences as nurse and soldier respectively, negotiating the increasing visibility of homosexuality during the war. Their counterparts

160 Summers, (1990), p. 1.

161 Crisp had used the words 'fad' in the context of the increasing AIDS epidemic in Chicago 1983 during his one-man-show after someone had asked him about his opinion regarding the quickly spreading disease. His reaction and the consequent hostilities brought against Crisp is recalled in his second biographical film adaptation *An Englishman in New York* (2009), Dir. Richard Laxton, DVD, Momentum Pictures.

in the 21st century, Sarah Waters' *The Night Watch* (2006) and Adam Fitzroy's *Make Do and Mend* (2012), are historical fictions as identified by Jones, that retrospectively and retroactively construct these stories of homosexuality during the Second World War. Instead of involuntarily disseminating a modern ideology and consciousness into the past, I will speak of novels and plots negotiating homosexual tendencies, characters, desires or subcultures. Sometimes I will also be referring to the word 'queer' in order to denote a more contemporary mindset.

In her doctorate thesis *Wolfskins and Togas: Lesbian and Gay Historical Fictions, 1870 to the Present*, Sarah Waters argues (self-reflexively) that "historical fiction tells us less about the past than about the circumstances of its own production – reveals, if nothing else, the historiographical priorities of its author, or its author's culture"[162]. Similar to Linda Hantcheon, Waters thus draws attention to the importance of the author as well as to the context of writing and publishing a text. Whilst Roland Barthes' "The Death of the Author"[163] and Michel Foucault's "What is an Author?"[164], rendered the role of the author insignificant, feminism, black activism and other marginalised groups rightfully insisted on its prominence. In *Sexual Politics*, Kate Millett challenges the anonymity and death of the author proclaimed by Foucault and Barthes, when examining the sexist subtext of literature deriving from a male author position.[165] According to Millett and feminists pursuing her work such as Waters, it matters who is telling a story and in which context it has been produced because knowledge of authors and their background allows for perceiving a text in a more specific socio-historical context.

In recent years critics like Susan Lanser[166] and Robyn Warhol have defended what they call '(queer and) feminist narrative theory' "[b]ecause the term 'narratology' still connotes for many a theoretical approach cut off from questions of

162 Sarah Waters, *Wolfskins and Togas: Lesbian and Gay Historical Fictions, 1870 to the Present* (London: University of London, 1995), p. 8.

163 Roland Barthes, *Image Music Text, Essays Selected and Translated by Stephen Heath* (Fulham: Fontana Press, 1977), pp. 142-148.

164 Michel Foucault, "What is an Author?" in James D. Faubien (ed.), *Aesthetics, Method, and Epistemology: Volume two, Essential Works of Foucault 1954-1984* (New York: New Press, 1998), pp. 205-222.

165 Kate Millett, "Instances of Sexual Politics", *Sexual Politics*, [1970], (Urbana and Chicago: University of Illinois Press, 2000), pp. 3-22.

166 Susan Sniader Lanser, *Fictions of Authority: Women Writers and Narrative Voice* (Ithaca and London: Cornell University Press, 1992).

history and context"[167]. This history and context plays an important role for queer and feminist literary critics because a marginalised subject position cannot be grasped if, as Foucault determines, one's "task of criticism is not to bring out the work's relationships with the author, not to reconstruct through the text a thought or experience, but rather to analyze the work through its structure, its architecture, its intrinsic form, and the play of its internal relationships"[168]. Such a sole emphasis on form and structure of the text disguises the often damaging dominant culture that influenced the author and their work. Consequently, Warhol concludes, "[f]eminist narrative theory [...] tries always to frame its analysis with as much socio-historical context as can be known for the author and readers in question"[169]. In such a reading, literature creates a reciprocal conjugation with culture, simultaneously being influenced by it and being an active part in its formation.[170]

By incorporating auto-biographical knowledge of the authors under discussion (as far as available) and by considering censoring practices especially during the 1950s, my approach to the novels follows Warhol's 'feminist narrative theory'. My reading of Renault's *The Charioteer* is especially influenced by the author's political views as they reveal most thoroughly why her novel cannot be perceived as an inherently negative representation of homosexuality. Her privileged position as a white European living in South Africa hesitant to engage in anti-apartheid protests betrays her own often conflicting moral and social attitudes, which she fictionalises in *The Charioteer*. Homogenising Renault's work as a "homosexual problem novel[...]" as proposed by Summers[171], marginalises the merit of dramatising her troubled and incoherent thoughts on the subject matter. Whilst Summers acknowledges that "Renault challenges the sexual ideology of the 1950s by sketching her characters as individuals responding to universal human dilemmas and by her insistence on the preeminent value of self-knowledge", he cannot refrain from constantly qualifying such positive evaluations by pointing at the "guilt and self-doubt", "the gay subculture as pathological" and the "conception of homosexuality as a personal failure"[172]. The following chapters will show that whilst Summers' is right to read *The Charioteer* as

167 Robyn Warhol et. al., *Narrative Theory: Core Concepts and Critical Debates* (Columbus, Ohio: The Ohio State University Press, 2012), p. 9.

168 Foucault, "What is an Author" (1998), p. 207.

169 Warhol, (2012), p. 10.

170 Alan Sinfield, *Literature, Politics and Culture in Post-war Britain* (Oxford: Blackwell, 1989), p. 36.

171 Summers, (1990), p. 26.

172 Ibid., p. 26.

"mirror[ing] the homophobia of its day", the conclusion that this yields to the characters' "guilt and self-doubt" lacks textual foundation. Neither the protagonist Laurie nor his lover Ralph actively loath themselves for being homosexual but criticise society's narrow-mindedness. In fact, with the exception of Baxter's *Look Down in Mercy*, the exaggerated signs of suffering due to sexual deviance as detected by Summers, are predominantly noticeable by their absence. And when scenes of despondency emerge, they need to be considered within the context of the Cold War as a period of heightened homophobia that made publication for writers of homosexual fiction all the more difficult.[173]

To better compare and contrast the novels' approach with regard to how homosexuality is represented, and in what way the intersecting fields of gender, sexuality, nationalism, patriotism and propaganda work to induce conformity into national citizens, I will merge readings of each text in every chapter. The chapter on "Re-Negotiating the Homosexual Problem Novel" will engage with the overarching question of how the novels approach the complex issue of homosexuality during the Second World War. In order to reveal the influence that publication practices during the 1950s had on both Mary Renault and Walter Baxter, I am focusing on methods of self-regulation and official censorship respectively. Whereas Renault inscribes an appropriated medical view on homosexuality into her novel in order to suggest a homophobic sub-tone, Baxter's writing is ridden with incongruities regarding the vastly different versions for the American and British readership. I will reveal the hypocrisy of censorship practices that disguised homosexual passion in the British edition, but explicitly referenced non-consensual intercourse between the protagonist Kent and his mistress Helen. Due to the homophobic discourse at the time of publication, allegedly 'obscene' scenes between men were deleted, or defended through a psychoanalytic sub-narrative in order to avoid complete censorship.

Modern narratives such as Waters' *The Night Watch* and Fitzroy's *Make Do in Mend*, in contrast, are more liberal in the depiction of homosexuality. However, despite making use of such freedoms in the explicit description of same-sex

173 I believe that Summers' evaluation of Cold War paranoia causing self-doubt in homosexuals is too sweeping. He claims that "[t]he popular consensus that homosexuals were immoral, emotionally unstable, and untrustworthy justified their punishment and stigmatization, and unavoidably engendered guilt and self-doubt in gay people themselves." Summers, (1990), p. 26. Whilst this causal connection between external projections of homophobia onto homosexuals, who internalised their own abjection might well be true for some people of the time, it cannot be uncritically translated onto *The Charioteer* considering the number of characters who actively defend their desires.

conduct, Fitzroy's novel reveals an assimilated attitude of homosexuals living in heteronormative society. Whereas Laurie in *The Charioteer* and Kent in *Look Down in Mercy* disturb dominant knowledge simply by the fact of secretly engaging in forbidden sex acts, Harry and Jim in *Make Do and Mend* are, troublingly, relegated to and controlled by society's margins. This marginalised storyline becomes most obvious at the end of the novel when Harry and Jim stay at a remote farm hut, whereas Harry's brother Jack and his wife Kitty enjoy their public marriage with the whole village wishing them well. Displayed in the epilogue of the novel, the homosexual characters are literally 'Othered' compared to the heterosexual couple. Unlike the otherwise activist writing in *Make Do and Mend* when Baxter exaggerates homosexual promiscuity, Waters' *The Night Watch* approaches sexuality in less excessive language and concentrates on rewriting an invisible lesbian past. The novel is preoccupied with the issue of retroactively retrieving history when its narrative structure proceeds from 1947 to 1944 and ends in 1941. This backward narration as well as the characters' observation that the past is more interesting than the future functions as a self-reflexive comment, not only on Waters' writing, but on the perception of pre-Stonewall narratives as bleak and self-loathing.

The next chapter on "Nation, Masculinity and War" concentrates on how the novels represent nationalistic efforts to convince men to die for their country and how these are built on the power of myth[174] – that of the Unknown Soldier according to which men who fight heroically will become immortal and praised in narratives of national glory. In *Long Shadows* Petra Rau elaborates on the term 'myth' by saying:

> Myth should not be understood as fabrication or fiction, nor is it mendacity. Rather, it functions to disguise its own mechanics [...]. Myth lingers because it simplifies a very complex set of circumstances into a much more straightforward and emotionally resonant *fact* that appears to need no explanation.[175]

174 For an excellent evaluation of the means and merit of myth see Ackerman, (2015), pp. 14-15. He asserts that what Calder's *The Myth of the Blitz* (1992) describes as 'myth' can better be grasped as a powerful discourse that was institutionalised through various agents under guidance of the state. Original: "Was hier mit dem traditionale Überlieferungszusammenhänge und bündige Narrative evonzierenden Begriff des „Myth" gefasst wird, wäre präziser als mächtiger Diskurs zu beschreiben, der in einer bedrohlichen historischen Situation durch eine breite Koalition von Akteuren unter staatlicher Leitung und mit Hilfe moderner Medien institutionalisiert wurde." p. 14.

175 Rau, (2016), p. 6, p. 7, [emphasis original].

I will simultaneously discuss the myth of the People's War and that of the Unknown Soldier to carve out the manipulative role of the nation in guiding men into battle and determining their reputation as masculine or cowardly. The inclusion of two narratives by male authors – Walter Baxter's *Look Down in Mercy* and Adam Fitzroy's *Make Do and Mend* – will help to challenge the perception that male writing largely contributes to the dominant reiteration of (soldier/heroic) masculinity when they disclose the public image of *the* male soldier as equally deceptive as *the* female nurse. The insight of the changing parameters of war writings deriving from the importance of the home front will be expanded upon by analysing the nation's relentless oppression of men when turning them into soldiers, which discloses the traumatic experience of having to perform in a manner befitting masculine ideals. Through repeatedly hesitating or actively challenging national narratives designed to induce conformity, homosexual characters open scope for retrieving and re-negotiating the Second World War as a damaging period for men's self-worth. Whereas Waters' lesbian character Kay in *The Night Watch* bravely saves the city, Kent in *Look Down in Mercy* is repeatedly rendered motionless by the threat of war and his responsibilities as an officer. These differences between the characters call to attention the arbitrariness of bestowing 'strong' masculinity on male bodies and 'weak' femininity on women.

The last chapter on "Queering Space, Body and Time" therefore engages with Waters' portrayal of Kay as a mannish lesbian performing (female) masculinity – a more masculinist version of Halberstam's female masculinity. The analysis highlights Kay's female complicity within the patriarchal power structure when she subordinates her girlfriend Helen whilst claiming a more phallic version of what Plain has identified as "the *semblance* of masculinity"[176] performed by fighting women. I have positioned this analysis after the chapter on "Nation, Masculinity and War", because Kay's heroism as an ambulance driver complements my reading of male characters' failure to live up to the damaging ideal of hegemonic masculinity during war. I will expand on this reading of injurious masculinity for men by examining homelessness at the front as well as at the home front in order to disclose the spatial restrictions that the characters face and fear. Moreover, the destruction of buildings results in a sense of non-belonging which symbolises the characters' difficult position within a society that seems totally transformed through the war. At the same time as contributing to the horror of the time, the demolition of houses enables a re-reading of gender

176 Plain, (1996), p. 28, [emphasis original].

norms when uncovering hidden societal scripts regarding the gendered politics of home as a domestic space that stereotypically restraints female bodies.

After having outlined the general aim and approach of this thesis, the following chapter will engage with an analysis of how homosexuality is depicted in the novels and how the dramatisation of outlawed desires changes according to varying censorship practices. Whereas Renault and Baxter, writing and publishing in the early 1950s, encountered diverse challenges to their work, Waters and Fitzroy enjoy a liberal publishing market that allows them to approach homosexuality during the war more freely. I will firstly disclose how *The Charioteer* (1953) and *Look Down in Mercy* (1951) circumvent censorship by using euphemistic language, inscribing a medical discourse or changing significant scenes, to then examine how historical fiction like *The Night Watch* (2006) and *Make Do and Mend* (2012) take liberties in approaching the past. Rather than revealing differences and oppositions between novels of the time and contemporary re-writings, I will look at the continuation of a thematic emphasis on the characters' individuality and their resistance in accepting stigmas and stereotypes associated with their sexual desires. In doing so, I challenge various presumptions regarding both world war fiction, and gay and lesbian historiography: firstly, the propagation of a heterosexual war that excluded homosexual men from service. Secondly, the dominant narrative of the homosexual subject in the first half of the 20th century as a burdened individual who despises himself for his sexual proclivities. Thirdly, the assumption that historical fictions are upbeat re-writings of a depressing past that project affirmation into a time that renounced homosexual existence. My analysis will show that whilst the novels are diverse in their treatment of homosexuality, they collectively challenge the dominant image of a heteronormative Second World War.

“People’s Pasts [are] so Much More Interesting than Their Futures” –

Re-Negotiating the Homosexual Problem Novel

ENGAGING WITH THE LITERARY PAST

In her doctoral thesis *Wolfskins and Togas: Lesbian and Gay Historical Fictions, 1870 to the Present*, Sarah Waters stresses the “value of gay and lesbian historical romances in their affirmation of the transhistorical tenacity of outlawed desires”[1]. Self-reflectively mirroring this statement, Waters’ character Kay claims that “people’s pasts [are] so much more interesting than their futures” (106), which shows *The Night Watch*’s (2006) conscious investment in and interpretation of past times in order to retroactively inscribe lesbian desires into a consciousness of heterosexual *his*tory. In “Lesbian postmemory: haunted ‘history’ in *The Night Watch*”, Natasha Alden similarly argues that

> there is a potentially unlimited scope for postmemorial identification between the affective community of lesbians now and at any point in history, albeit with the significant proviso that this [theory] is aware of its own limitations of current preconceptions and conceptions of identity categories.[2]

Both Waters’ and Alden’s statements insinuate that contemporary queer narratives (in contrast to future orientated post-Stonewall gay and lesbian activism) try to establish and create a genealogy between historical subjects and modern consciousness, in order to strengthen the claim for a legitimate place within soci-

1 Sarah Waters, *Wolfskins and Togas: Lesbian and Gay Historical Fictions, 1870 to the Present* (London: University of London, 1995), p. 12.

2 Natasha Alden, *Reading Behind the Lines: Postmemory in Contemporary British War Fiction*, (Manchester: Manchester University Press, 2014), p. 179.

ety and against homophobic assaults. Setting out to re-work and reclaim the ghostly history of lesbian narratives and to broaden lesbian history beyond Sappho of Lesbos[3], Alden positions Sarah Waters in line with earlier lesbian novelists and asks whether *The Night Watch* is "pastiche? Homage? [Or] [m]etafictional intervention into the historical record?"[4] She assumes that Waters "playfully subvert[s] some of the more conservative mores" of the Second World War period to offer a less depressing view of the homosexual past.[5] While I agree that *The Night Watch*'s representation of lesbianism in the 1940s is largely upbeat, I take issue with Alden's broad dismissal of earlier novels as depicting "crippling self-hatred and fear" that "seems to be a universal condition"[6]. Her evaluation of Mary Renault's *The Charioteer* (1953) needs particular revision as it is too rigidly informed by what Michael Bronski critically calls the "Is it good for the gays?" question deriving from immediate post-Stonewall activism.[7]

Scholars who were influenced by the gay liberation movement of the late 1960s and early 1970s approached novels written and published before Stonewall with a certain kind of expectation that systematically eliminated representations of self-loathing, homophobia and victimisation. This phenomenon can be observed in the conflicting perception of Renault's novels: whereas her earlier works set in the 1940s and 1950s such as *The Charioteer* did not find extensive recognition, the turn to historical fiction set in ancient Greece where sexuality was less victimised, has significantly increased her reputation as a serious writer. These historical novels have become part of the expanding canon of gay and lesbian fiction because they represent homosexuality not as a burden, but as a fluid identity that is embedded in Greek culture.[8] The resulting discrepancy in recognition and celebration signals a variation of Bronski's criticism: novels like *The Charioteer* depicting homosexuality in less cunning ways, have been misread and misunderstood by critics brought up in the post-Stonewall consciousness of affirmation. Lisa Lynne Moore calls this the "ethos of celebration" – the tenden-

3 Sappho of Lesbos was an ancient Greek poetess, who wrote about love between women. Her texts are symbolic for a lingering lesbian consciousness.

4 Alden, (2014), pp. 185-186.

5 Ibid., p. 181.

6 Ibid., p. 185.

7 Michael Bronski, *Pulp Friction: Uncovering the Golden Age of Gay Male Pulps* (New York: St. Martin's Griffin, 2013).

8 Recall that Greek culture did not categorise homosexuals but differentiated between masculinised (top) and feminised (bottom) sex acts.

cy to hype some texts for a certain purpose whilst forgetting or misreading others even by the same author.[9]

Drawing closer to other equal rights movements such as Second Wave Feminism, queer studies and queer activism from the late 1990s onwards "has focused on negative aspects of the past in order to use them for positive political purpose"[10] in the present. In contrast to gay and lesbian scholarship educated in and operating according to the spirit of gay liberation, queer theorists constantly work against homogeneity of research, against the establishment of a coherent historiography and against a consistent theorisation of sexual desire or gender embodiment (amongst many other fields of interest). In order to re-work certain aspects deriving from early gay and lesbian research, Heather Love explicitly turns to the oppressive elements in literary texts and seeks to uncover the "gap between aspiration and the actual"[11]. Allowing for political criticism, she challenges the affirmative turn of the 1970s as "wishful thinking" that misjudged a homosexual literary tradition.[12] This chapter investigates the other end of Love's research by critically evaluating, how pre-Stonewall texts such as Renault's *The Charioteer* have been (falsely) perceived as negative representations of homosexuality. Contemporary scholars such as Alden share this critical perception of pre-Stonewall fiction, which homogenises these novels' complicated and heterogeneous fictionalisation of same-sex love in the 1940s. Novels like Waters' *The Night Watch* that have been perceived as queer, in contrast, are celebrated for "making affective connections [...] across time", as Carolyn Dinshaw terms the ability of fashioning a relationship with the past.[13] In the following, I will trace the deceptiveness of reading pre-Stonewall novels as damaging, whilst celebrating contemporary texts as upbeat. For a more comprehensive understanding, the hypocrisy of censorship needs to be taken into account when analysing novels of the 1950s in order to understand how publication processes influenced authors and their texts.

Renault's *The Charioteer* (1953) and Baxter's *Look Down in Mercy* (1951) show that social critique is not absent from their novels: it is subversively inscribed in minor characters rather than explicitly portrayed in protagonists. Texts

9 Lisa Lynne Moore, "Lesbian Migrations: Mary Renault's South Africa" in *GLQ: A Journal of Lesbian and Gay Studies* Vol. 10, No. 1 (2003), p. 23.

10 Heather Love, *Feeling Backward: Loss and the Politics of Queer History* (Cambridge and Massachusetts: Harvard University Press, 2007), pp. 18-19.

11 Love, (2007), p. 4.

12 Ibid., p. 4.

13 Carolyn Dinshaw, *Getting Medieval: Sexualities and Communities, Pre- and Postmodern* (Durham and London: Duke University Press, 1999), pp. 11-12.

written before Stonewall are thus not unilateral representations of a homophobic discourse but multiplicitous in their depiction of homosexual lives. Re-assessing these novels in more detail and in contrast to contemporary fictions like *The Night Watch* (2006) and *Make Do and Mend* (2012) will illustrate a shared rejection of a collective identity in favour of a multi-dimensional and often conflicting approach to homosexuality. This is not to say that there is an uncomplicated genealogy between novels of the 1950s and contemporary fiction. I am not advocating what David Halperin calls "homosexual essentialism" – an idealism that is "thoroughly disqualified by its implication in the various strategies of elitism and exclusion that identity politics often carries with it"[14]. Instead, there seems to be a lineage of novelistic resistance to collectivism and shared identity in favour of individuality. Consequently, in this chapter I attempt to read the novels against the grain of self-loathing and misery, to show their surprising continuity of privileging the personal over the (sub-)communal that overcomes social burdens.

Natasha Alden distinguishes various sources that have seemingly impacted Waters in her writing in order to fashion a literary tradition between *The Night Watch* and earlier lesbian texts. According to her findings, the most influential sources are: Barbara Bell's auto-biography *Just Take your Frock Off: A Lesbian Life* (1999), Nevil Shute's *Requiem For a Wren* (1955), Radclyffe Hall's short story "Miss Ogilvy Finds Herself" (1934), and Mary Renault's *The Charioteer*.[15] In an interview with Lucie Armitt, Waters herself highlights the importance of this background material:

> [...] I'm imagining a reader who will 'get' the lesbian stuff [...], I probably situate my lesbian stories in something bigger, like an echo chamber. There are hints at other lesbian texts or traditions of representation – but that's something that most of my readers won't necessarily pick up on.[16]

14 David M. Halperin, *How to do the History of Homosexuality* (Chicago and London: University of Chicago Press, 2002), p. 16.

15 Barbara Bell, *Just Take your Frock Off: A Lesbian Life* (Brighton: Ourstory Books, 1999), Nevil Shute, *Requiem For a Wren*, [1955], (München: Random House, 2010), Radclyffe Hall, "Miss Ogilvy Finds Herself", [1934], (New York: Random House, 2013).

16 Lucie Armitt, "Interview with Sarah Waters" in *Feminist Review* No. 85, Political Hystories (2007), p. 117.

In order to clarify this context of lesbian history apparently lost on "most" readers, I will briefly summaries Alden's reading of the most influential texts and their adaptation in *The Night Watch.*

Bell's *Just Take your Frock Off* provides a general account of how lesbian women lived during the Second World War. Her recollections influenced Waters' representation of opportunities for women such as driving, liberty in clothing and hairstyle. Bell's depiction of lesbian affairs during the Black-Out are echoed in Waters' illustration of Julia and Helen's first sexual encounter in London during the Blitz – in a public street concealed by darkness. Additionally, Bell emphasises the reluctance of looking into the future when saying "[i]t was the swarm and swirl of wartime. The immediate future was unknown. You didn't plan for the future." (79) Waters dramatises this reluctance to make plans through her backward narration, which shatters progressivity and a sense of futurity. Alden's reflections on *Just Take Your Frock Off* terminate here, and she ignores that Bell's auto-biography does not solely focus on lesbian opportunities during the war, but also stresses the atrocities of the home front:

> Seeing a dead body or a few bodies with pieces off them lying about, you don't store it up. [...] You had a good cry and then, next day, it all happened again and you stopped having a good cry, you took it. [...] You just thought – well, this is war, get on with it. (79)

Waters' novel similarly recounts the struggle to continue fighting and the characters', especially Kay's, traumatic confrontation with death on a daily basis. *The Night Watch* cannot simply be read as a lesbian novel, it is as much a passionate representation of battling and surviving the war. Bell's auto-biography is equally more than an account of her life as a lesbian, because she was also a policewoman during the Blitz, a teacher, a volunteer worker for disabled children and she supported many men and women infected with HIV/AIDS. Reducing her life story or Waters' novel to a sexual identity falls short of the myriad of the other features and issues they address. All novels discussed in this study repeatedly show that their characters are as much influenced by the Second World War as by their sexual preferences. They reveal diverse ways of coping with stigmatisation at a time that offered simultaneously more freedoms for and greater supervision of homosexual desires. Alden overlooks these issues when exclusively concentrating on Waters' adaptation of Bell's experiences of "how life changed for gay people [in positive ways]"[17]. In doing so Alden ignores scenes of contemplation and dismay in *The Night Watch* and Bell's moving description of how the war overshadowed newly found opportunities.

17 Alden, (2014), p. 193.

Nevil Shute's novel *Requiem For a Wren* is an example of this pessimism arising from wartime tragedies. The protagonist Alan Duncan returns home to Australia several years after the war has ended and learns that the family's housekeeper has committed suicide. Investigating the case, Alan discovers that the woman was his late brother's (Bill) girlfriend, whom he had tried to contact after Bill's death. From this point onwards, the housekeeper's life is retrieved making the reverse style of *Requiem For a Wren* reminiscent of Waters' backward narrative. Alden concludes that Waters' modification of this reverse narrative form "unsurprisingly" manages "to do much that [fiction of the time] can't in its depiction of gay life and gay sexuality"[18]. Leaving open what Waters' retroactive narration exactly does that earlier novels did not, Alden hastens to argue for the liberal approach of *The Night Watch* in the depiction of gender and sexuality expressed in the mannish lesbian Kay. Comparing Kay to Radclyffe Hall's protagonist in the short story "Miss Ogilvy Finds Herself", Alden sees a parallel between Miss Ogilvy and Kay who both feel passed over after the war. Watching their lives go by when looking out of a window and observing the outside world from a distance, neither Miss Ogilvy nor Kay manage to handle the return to 'normality' emerging with the establishment of peace. Unlike Miss Ogilvy who "is found dead at the end of the story", Kay "is simply left over", which leads Alden to conclude that Waters' novel "steers clear of fantasy and whimsy"[19]. Although Waters' tone is indeed sober for the most part of the text, particularly Kay falls into dramatic displays of her misery after the war. During a conversation with her friend Mickey, for example, Kay insinuates that she would not mind if the house she is living in collapsed over her head: "How much longer are you going to stay there, Kay? Till the day it collapses, I hope!" (106). Kay's apodosis "I hope" emphasised with an exclamation mark, indicates that she has no plans of moving out of the house although it is not safe to stay there. This image of the unsafe house is recalled when Mickey tries to persuade her to accept that the war is over and that Helen, Kay's former girlfriend, has left her for another woman. Kay replies to Mickey:

> '*Get over it.* What a funny phrase that is! As if one's grief is a fallen house, and one has to pick one's way over the rubble to the ground on the other side ... I've got lost in my rubble, Mickey. I can't seem to find my way across. I don't think I *want* to cross it, that's the thing.' (108)

18 Alden, (2014), p. 190.

19 Ibid., pp. 190-191.

Speaking of her heartache in metaphors of rubble not only references the war when Kay was an ambulance driver, and the collapse of her flat where she used to live with Helen, it also highlights her investment in the past. To Kay, the war and her lost relationship intermingle as rubble that keeps her from moving on. The tragedy that resonates in her poetic language emphasises Kay's grief and stands in contradiction to Alden's analysis of Waters' style of writing as "steer[ing] clear of fantasy and whimsy". In fact, Kay is highly dramatic in communicating what little her life is worth to herself, which seems only a few steps away from suicide as depicted in Hall's "Miss Ogilvy Finds Herself". Moreover, the sudden termination of the narrative on Kay's story precludes a resolution of her case. The last mention of Kay shows her in a little room in the unsafe house listening to the landlord and looking at her former 'engagement ring' symbolic of her lost relationship with Helen. This scene fixes her to the past when "[s]he put [the ring] on her slender finger; and closed her fist, to keep it from slipping" (171). Alden omits this significant re-taking of the ring as well as Kay's unstable emotional state three years after her splitting up with Helen, in order to justify her claim that *The Night Watch* is less invested in "[l]oss and regret"[20] than lesbian texts of earlier periods. The depiction of Kay clearly shows that heartache and misery are not absent from *The Night Watch* and that Kay regards her past as an oasis to which she wants to return. The last section of this chapter will further elaborate on Waters' approach to the past as an incongruous re-writing that infiltrates sorrows and joy alike, which makes *The Night Watch* not simply a compelling read but allows for more diverse analyses of historical novels and their recreation of homosexual experiences before Stonwall.

Alden's analysis concludes that "to a reader who *does* recognise [the intertextual allusions to Bell, Shute and Hall], the effect is, indeed to situate [*The Night Watch*] in a bigger context of lesbian history, and to give it added weight as a re-imagining of what might have been"[21]. However, by arguing that *The Night Watch* "playfully subvert[s] some of the more conservative mores of the time, to offer a (qualifiedly) more utopian view" of homosexual life, Alden obscures the merit and legacy of these incorporated texts.[22] Her evaluation of novels written before Stonewall seems influenced by the assumption that it was a thoroughly oppressive time for homosexuals fostered by Cold War paranoia, which apparently finds unchallenged representation in literature. Her undiscussed list of "universal condition[s]"[23] and frequently inscribed vindications

20 Alden, (2014), p. 191.

21 Ibid., p. 183 [my emphasis].

22 Ibid., p. 181.

23 Ibid., p. 185.

of homosexuality in pre-Stonewall fictions include: "abjection", "secrecy", "shame", "self-loathing" and the "recourse to sexology or Freudian analysis of how [characters] had been 'warped' into perversity"[24]. Judging pre-Stonewall texts in such negative ways imposes a contemporary mindset onto them that disdains the accomplishment of publishing texts with a homosexual content during the Cold War in the first place.

This premature judgement is specifically distinct when Alden compares *The Night Watch* to Mary Renault's *The Charioteer* and concludes that "Waters does not need to construct the kind of elaborate defence of her gay characters that Renault does."[25] Renault's defence of her characters occurs, according to Alden, in a medical discourse following a tradition of psychoanalytic rhetoric fashionable during the 1950s.[26] Caroline Zilboorg criticises such readings where *The Charioteer* "has often been wilfully misread by critics eager to see it as a case study in abnormal psychology"[27]. It thus seems vital to closely analyse Renault's use of psychoanalytic references, which undeniably exist throughout the novel, in order

24 Alden, (2014), p. 193.

25 Ibid., p. 197.

26 It is vital to remember that the psychoanalytic rhetoric of the 1950s differs greatly from Freud's founding studies at the turn of the century. Whereas Freud was interested in the many layers of psychic development, radical psychoanalysis that followed his approach became decidedly more orthodox and psychoanalytic research was later dismissed as heteronormative with the family at its centre. Connell summarises that "[t]he course towards adult heterosexuality, which Freud had seen as a complex and fragile construction, was increasingly presented as an unproblematic, natural path of development. Anything else was viewed as a sign of pathology – especially homosexuality. [...] Psychoanalysis as a practice increasingly became a technique of normalization, attempting to adjust its patients to the gender order." Connell, *Masculinities*, [1995], (Cambridge: Polity Press, 2016), p. 11. This growing conservative attitude within psychoanalysis is the reason for why it is often (and often rightfully) dismissed as essentialising, heteronormalising and stigmatising.

27 Caroline Zillborg, *The Masks of Mary Renault: a Literary Biography* (Columbia, Missouri: Univesity of Missouri Press, 2001), p. 107. In the "Afterword" to her novel *The Friendly Young Ladies* (1944), Renault herself pledges that "defensive stridency is not, on the whole, much more attractive than self-pity." Regardless of her critical words, *The Charioteer* is saturated with moments of "defensive stridency", which demonstrates the author's reluctance to admit to her own investment in mechanism of literary self-regulation. Renault, "Afterword" from 1984 in Mary Renault, "Afterword" *The Friendly Young Ladies*, [1944], (London: Virago Press, 2014), p. 322.

to evaluate if and to what degree *The Charioteer* is what Claude J. Summers terms a "homosexual problem novel[...]"[28].

MEDICALIZATION OF HOMOSEXUALITY: LITERARY SELF-REGULATION

Psychoanalysis was developed in the 19th century as a method of treating mental illness and comprehending the complex workings of the unconscious. Sigmund Freud coined the term psychoanalysis to describe the therapeutic techniques exercised in various case studies. One major field of research concerned itself with sexuality and the question of how humans develop certain sex drives. In *Three Essays on the Theory of Sexuality* Freud asserts that the 'polymorphously perverse child' "displays a mixture of the character-traits belonging to his own and to the opposite sex"[29], thus compelling the child to negotiate between heterosexual and homosexual desires. Freud's interpretation relies on his assumption that humans are prone to bisexuality which necessitates a transformation of diverging desires into heterosexuality. More specifically, in a psychoanalytic model to describe the complex and abstract workings of the psyche, every infant is thought to go through various stages in its early life with the phallic stage (3-6 years) being the most important for the development of 'gender appropriate' sexuality. For boys, the key moment within this stage is said to be 'castration anxiety' where he gets caught playing with his genitals and learns his parents' (in most cases mother's) disapproval and threat of cutting off his penis. In combination with the boy's visual image of a naked female body or his witnessing of sexual intercourse between adults, he realises the abstract possibility of castration. Comparing and contrasting the castrated female body with the power and penis-possessing male body, the young boy allegedly abandons his former rivalry with the father for his mother's love, and comes to identify with the male role model, which leads to a resolution of the Oedipus complex into 'gender appropriate' masculinity and cross-gendered sexual desire. Freud claims that if this process is not or not fully performed, for example due to the absence of the father, the child may later find his sexuality to deviate from the 'norm'.

In *The Charioteer*, the young protagonist Laurie Odell is plunged into oedipal crisis when witnessing his father leaving the family. The exact mentioning of

28 Claude J. Summers, *Gay Fictions: Wilde to Stonewall: Studies in a Male Homosexual Literary Tradition* (New York: Continuum, 1990), p. 26.

29 Sigmund Freud, *Three Essays on the Theory of Sexuality. Complete Psychological Works*, Standard Edition, [1905], (Vol. VII, 1955), pp. 219-220.

Laurie's age, five years and ten month, functions to indicate that he is on the brink of outgrowing Freud's neurotic phallic stage when tragedy strikes. Lying in bed, Laurie tries to conceptualise the noises outside his bedroom door and his own awakening – meaning the double entendre of him being unable to sleep and his rising homosexual consciousness indicated by the chapter's closing words: "what he remembered best was having known for the first time the burden, prison and mystery of his own uniqueness" (13). Instead of stereotyping Laurie's homosexuality as an illness, he perceives it as unique, which introduces the character's positive self-perception and unwillingness to be ashamed of himself. Laurie observes another dimension – a man whistling in the streets. "The noise had an absolute foreignness, like the note of a jungle bird. It had no link with humanity." (7) Except for his male sex, the figure outside is unknown and the noise he is making is as foreign to Laurie as his nightly restlessness. Described as not "linked with humanity", the noise is abjected and relegated to the borders of society. First heard at his parents' separation and symbolic of his sexual deviation, the sound metaphorically accompanies Laurie for the rest of the text. It will become clear that this negative depiction of homosexuality is not sustained throughout the novel and that the core aim of *The Charioteer* is to establish a link between homosexuality and humanity.

Operating in the sexological rhetoric of the time[30] – "burden", "prison", "mystery" "uniqueness" "foreignness" – it seems plausible why critics such as Alden or Summers conceive *The Charioteer* as a "homosexual problem novel[...]"[31], particularly considering that Freud's analysis of castration anxiety is dramatised in Laurie's feelings upon realising that his father will actually leave him: "The *absolute impotence* of childhood crushed him like a weight of the pyramids." (11) [my emphasis] Laurie's weak identification with his father is devastated through this strange sense of castration: he "loved and admired, *without respecting his father*" (9) [my emphasis]. This lack of respect for the father figure derives from his softness towards Laurie and stands in contradiction to his stereotypical male role as the head of the household: "he took things easily, and whether he decided to answer a question or not, never rebuked one for having asked it" (10). Although this sensitivity, conventionally attributed to the mother, is welcomed by Laurie, it seems not encourage his heterosexual development and identification with the male gender, which allegedly relies on displays of masculinity and distance from femininity.

30 For further information on terminology and scholarly research on homosexuality in the 1950s see Heike Bauer and Matt Cook (eds.), *Queer 1950s: Rethinking Sexuality in the Postwar Years* (Palgrave McMillan, 2012).

31 Summers, (1990), p. 26.

Laurie's mother also challenges stereotypical displays of femininity: "Laurie knew that his father had to obey his mother just as he had, under the penalty of exile from love." (9) Mrs Odell's power to subordinate and infantilise the father refutes gender clichés within the family and leads towards a psychoanalytic explanation for homosexuality according to which the disruption of family norms is the cause for 'sexual inversion'. However, Laurie's feeling of impotence or castration has not been initiated when seeing his parents in intimate display, but during their breakup. Zilboorg rightly calls this the "witnessing of the *reverse* of the primal scene"[32], which indicates Renault's ironic appropriation of what she identifies as Freud's "dogmatic and inadequate"[33] explanation for sexual deviation.

Beyond its psychoanalytic tone, the first chapter is rich with a perpetual amazement and the young boy's childish incomprehension: having learned and accepted that only illness can keep one awake after bedtime, Laurie logically concludes that he "would probably die" (8) because of his sleeplessness. Consequently, when Laurie "perceive[s] that his father didn't think he would die" (11) the worst conceivable threat is averted. Combined with his naive and hyperbolic approach to being awake after ten o'clock – "the mountains of the moon, the burial-place of the elephants: white on the map" (7) – the introductory chapter is imbued with a constant sense of unfamiliarity and perplexity. However clear the psychoanalytic context might be, Laurie is preoccupied with himself first and foremost as a human being (regardless of sexuality) with 'normal' needs, desires and anxieties and he continues to be so throughout the novel. Instead of representing homosexuality as a case study, *The Charioteer* is much more invested in depicting variance and complexity, and the struggle of living a 'moral' life that involves none of the promiscuity Laurie will later come to identify with the homosexual subculture. I would therefore argue that Renault deploys a socially variable psychoanalytic account of homosexuality – the sexually deviating subject not as mentally ill and neurotic, but as an, albeit burdened, individual finding his place in the world of the 1940s. This reading is reinforced by Renault's own words in her "Afterword" to *The Friendly Young Ladies* (1944) when she criticises Radclyffe Hall's *The Well of Loneliness* (1928) for its "self-pity, and its

32 Zilboorg, (2001), p. 108.

33 Renault to Peter Wolfe, February 27, 1970, and December 7, 1971: "Responding to Peter Wolfe's psychoanalytic treatment of her work, the author [Renault] herself emphasized that she found Freud "often absurdly dogmatic and inadequate to the totality of human experience" and indicated that Laurie is "naturally homosexual" rather than sexually compromised as a consequence of a broken home." Cited in Zilboorg, (2001), p. 108.

earnest humourlessness [which] invites irreverence"[34]. Renault keeps wondering how Hall "could bring herself to sound so woebegone a note"[35]. In view of these provocative words, it would be misleading to read *The Charioteer* as a similarly depressing representation of male homosexuality.

The text challenges its readers to look beyond the obvious scenes of homophobia and oppression in order to grasp a more complex situation of how to live as a homosexual during the Second World War. Consequently, Renault's references to the Oedipus complex are fashioned in order to appropriate and modify the medical approach to homosexuality by using its very own language. This is most explicit in Laurie's inability to spell "psychology" (14) when writing a paper in college. Vaguely familiar with the term, Laurie is unsure "where the *h*" (14) belongs, indicating a growing distance to the concept. This linguistic uncertainty demonstrates Butler's argument that "speech exceeds the censor by which it is constrained"[36]. Although the language of psychoanalysis constrains Renault's text and relegates it into a certain medical discourse that regards homosexuality as an illness, Laurie's inability (or reluctance) to correctly spell the concept that is supposed to limit him, demonstrates the power of language to subtly move beyond the realm of censorship. "If censoring a text is always in some sense incomplete, that may be partly because the text in question takes on new life as part of the very discourse produced by the mechanism of censorship."[37] The repeated self-regulation of Renault's writing by implicating a psychoanalytic defence for homosexuality discloses this very paradox observed by Butler: implicated in a system that prosecuted sexual indecency, *The Charioteer* simultaneously reifies this discourse in its self-regulation, and challenges it by finding space for escaping the grasp of the Obscene Publications Act of 1857.

Accordingly, Summer's analyses in *Gay Fictions: Wilde to Stonewall* is too sweeping to grasp the complexity of Renault's text: "Laurie's family situation in the stock psychiatric clichés of the 1950s is so obvious as to render trite and predictable what might have been an insightful study on the dynamics of mother-son bonding."[38] More promising is Zilboorg's argument that "Renault does not focus on 'mother-son bonding' because she is interested instead in locating Laurie within a specific social context and in exploring how he [...] will live with his

34 Renault, (2014), p. 322.

35 Ibid., p. 323.

36 Judith Butler, *Excitable Speech: A Politics of the Performative of Identity* (London and New York: Routledge, 1997), p. 129.

37 Butler, (1997), p. 130.

38 Summers, (1990), p. 162.

difference in a heterosexist society."[39] The term "focus" in Zilboorg's phrasing is significant: while it has been shown that Renault clearly offers a psychoanalytic reading of her characters, her *emphasis* lies on how to be a homosexual soldier during the Second World War. *The Charioteer* thus negotiates between the medical model that treats homosexuality as a psychic disease, and the characters' demand to be recognised as human beings.

Far from being written "in the stock psychiatric clichés of the 1950s", as Summers claims, Renault deconstructs familial stereotypes by depicting Mrs. Odell as calculatingly cool towards her son: "She loved him; but she was apt to offer or withhold her love in a system of rewards and punishments, as she had during his childhood." (64) Consequently, while their "mother-son bonding" may find its roots in a psychoanalytic framework, it is repeatedly modified throughout the narrative making it rich with references to identity formation and struggles of belonging, rather than representing Laurie as stagnating in his homosexuality. These variances are often superimposed by a focus on more obvious medical references such as the enduring bond between the male child and his mother: "When I'm grown-up, I'm going to marry you" (13). This is refined several years later by the teenage Laurie contending that his mother is "not going to die or get married" (272). Finally, when Mrs. Odell does marry the clergyman Mr. Straiker, Laurie is left "marked for life, as a growing tree is marked, by the chain that had bound him to her; but the chain was rusting away, leaving only the scar" (108). This highly symbolic and metaphorical description of Laurie as a tree that cannot grow properly because of a chain digging into its bark, reveals the protagonist's childlike dependency on his mother. Such depictions are read by Summers as signs of the "unnaturalness of the relationship of mother and son", allegedly culminating in Laurie declaring "his own intentions toward her"[40]. However, Mrs. Odell's marriage to Mr. Straike cuts the chain loose and releases Laurie from his role as the only man in her life.

Laurie's reaction upon receiving the news that Mrs. Odell is going to remarry shows that Summers' analysis is too simplistic because he fails to account for Laurie's wish to build a relationship of *confidence* with his mother that allows him to confess his homosexuality. At no point does the text seriously emphasise Laurie's "own intentions toward" her – his childish announcement to marry his mother was uttered at the age of five and is grounded in the traumatic experience of his father's leave-taking. Moreover, Laurie realises that "[b]efore she had abandoned him [due to her wedding], he had begun already to abandon her" (108) and he understands that

39 Zilboorg, (2001), p. 107.

40 Summers, (1990), p. 161.

the gulf of incommunicable things opened between them. Already it was unbridgeable. She would never now, as once he had dreamed, say to him in the silent language of day-to-day, 'Tell me nothing; it is enough that no other woman will ever take you from me' (108).

At this point in the novel, Laurie is already in hospital with a badly wounded knee as a consequence of the battle of Dunkirk. He clearly wants to confess his homosexuality to his mother but his naively imagined confidentiality remains unreachable. Laurie emphasises the finality of their separation metaphorically as a "gulf of incommunicable things [that] opened between them", which insinuates the profound depth of his distance to Mrs. Odell. When Laurie tries to bridge the gap that precludes their mutual honesty, he realises that his efforts are in vain. This comprehension is devastatingly reinforced upon meeting his soon-to-be stepfather Mr. Straike, which leads Laurie to sense the steadily growing estrangement to his mother for the first time. He is consequentially shocked by his mother's clumsy justification for why she did not bring his Tchaikovsky records when coming to visit Laurie in hospital:

His mother said, with a defensiveness which made her sound faintly reproachful, 'We didn't bring any of your *classical* records, dear, they'd be *sure* to get scratched in a place like this; and besides, Mr. Straike said he felt certain they wouldn't be popular with the men' (67) [emphasis original].

It is striking that Mrs. Odell speaks of "we" to include Mr. Straike. However, because Laurie is as yet unaware of his mother's new relationship, he does not catch the implication of the "we". Nor does he quite realise the importance of his mother listening to Mr. Straike's opinion that classical records would not "be popular with the men". Genuinely confused, Laurie struggles to comprehend the situation. Mrs. Odell's accentuation of "classical" and the overall defensive sounding argument betray her suspicion that records by an allegedly homosexual artist might expose Laurie as queer. This scene illustrates the complicated relationship between a closeted homosexual and his mother, which challenges Summers' argument that Renault "render[s] trite and predictable what might have been an insightful study on the dynamics of mother-son bonding"[41]. Contrary to this claim, *The Charioteer* precludes any straightforward reading of the relationship between mother and son by dramatising their co-closetedness.

41 Summers, (1990), p. 162.

In *Epistemology of the Closet*, Eve Kosofsky Sedgwick analyses the 'closet' – a metaphor for concealing one's sexuality – as a performative silence.[42] This means that an unexpressed and implied homosexuality regulates a person's conduct. Silence is not only performed by the homosexual but also by the people closest to him/her/them – in Laurie's case by his mother. Sedgwick claims that "no one person can take control over all the multiple, and often contradictory codes by which information about sexual identity and activity can seem to be conveyed"[43]. Keeping up his closetedness is thus much more complicated for Laurie in hospital than it used to be before the war. In school Laurie would play with the suggestiveness of homosexuality by joking: "I can't get him out of my head. Those long eyelashes. Would he look at me, do you think?" (18) This carefree attitude changes when trapped in the enclosed space of the hospital ward where every conversation can be overheard and every absence is noticed, which progressively shatters Laurie's confidence. While the rest of the hospital ward remains ignorant of Laurie's sexuality, he becomes increasingly aware of it, which is illustrated in a conversation between Laurie and his friend Reg concerning Laurie's unusual friendship with the hospital orderly and Quaker Andrew:

> Laurie went deep into his locker after a cigarette. […] 'That kid that does the ward at night, the young one, properly took to you, hasn't he?' 'Me?' said Laurie. He went back quickly into the locker again. 'Can't say I've noticed it specially.' 'What I'm getting at, Spud, you want to watch it. No offense.' 'Come again?' said Laurie into the locker. (87)

Laurie interprets Reg's statement that Andrew has "took to you" as a reference for his homosexual feelings towards "that kid", whereas Reg fears that talking to Andrew might seduce Laurie to become a pacifist himself. In order to conceal his embarrassment and insecurity during their ambiguous conversation, Laurie "went back quickly into the locker". The abstract concept of the closet is symbolised in Laurie's hiding to maintain the silence that protects him from harm. His fear of betraying signs of homosexuality is most obvious when he pretends to have missed Reg's advice to "watch it". Because Laurie cannot be sure what Reg refers to, he circumvents an answer. However, the mobility in the scene – moving in and out of the locker – bespeaks Laurie's restlessness and unease: he wants to escape the situation and the stinging suggestiveness of Reg's questioning. Believing that an open confrontation will restore his confidence that his secret is safe, Laurie boldly claims: "Don't worry, I guarantee that if any seduction

42 Eve Kosofsky Sedgwick, *Epistemology of the Closet*, [1990], (Berkeley and London: University of California Press, 2008), p. 3.

43 Sedgwick, (2008), p. 79.

goes on it'll be done by me. [...] He held his breath." (88) Laurie's agitation yields to stillness where even breathing is arrested. The tension that the statement provokes in Laurie is relieved when Reg (deliberately?) misunderstands: "That's all a lad like that wants, someone to make a man of him." (88) The abrupt termination of their conversation forecloses Laurie's response to Reg's telling statement. It remains unclear whether or not he is entirely unaware of Laurie's homosexuality, which only increases the ambiguity of their dialogue.

In such scenes Renault fashions solidarity between Laurie and the reader who shares the secret of Laurie's sexuality, whereas Reg and every other character of the hospital ward is excluded. Waters argues that "Renault's originality in *The Charioteer* was to ally her readers with, rather than against, the homosexual dissembler"[44]. Because the queer world which Laurie represents has infiltrated 'normal' society, every conversation or conduct is deprived of its implied heteronormativity. Consequently, those without queer knowledge become "the butt of the humour"[45] like Nurse Adrian, who fails to fully grasp Laurie's incomprehensible babbling whilst awakening from narcotics:

> 'I don't deserve it, you know. If you knew all about me, you wouldn't be good to me like you are.'
> 'Hush, you've had an operation, you must keep quiet.' [...]
> 'You don't think I'm like that, do you?'
> 'Of course not, it's just the anaesthetic.'
> 'Going through a phase is different, I mean people do. It isn't anything.' (39)

Only under the influence of narcotics does Laurie display the stereotypical discourse of self-loathing and pity. Even then, the double entendre of Laurie talking about his homosexuality and Nurse Adrian's blatant ignorance rings a humoristic tone. The scene seems to push the limits of plausibility – how much more clear does Laurie need to be before Reg and Nurse Adrian take off their heteronormative goggles and perceive Laurie for who he is? How far can the dramatisation of ignorance be pushed before the text loses credibility?

Even the most glaring allusions to homosexual desire are being overlooked by heteronormative characters to illustrate society's ignorance and to unsettle the authority of dominant knowledge. It follows that the novel can convincingly employ a plotline where Nurse Adrian develops romantic feelings towards Laurie because to her the wounded soldier is an attractive, masculine and heterosexual bachelor. When Laurie tells Nurse Adrian that he will soon be relocated to an-

44 Waters, (1995), p. 218.

45 Ibid., p. 218.

other hospital, she begins to cry because she does not want to see him go. Unsure how to react, Laurie embraces her, which plunges him into unfamiliar terrain:

> He could no more have kept from kissing her than he could have kicked a lost puppy back into the street. [...]
> What's the matter with me? He thought. At first, he wouldn't admit to himself that it was happening: it was disruptive, undermining all the established decencies and securities of his life. Then suddenly he felt delighted with himself. After this nothing would ever be exactly the same, one's limitations would never seem quite so irrevocably fixed. [...]
> She knew nothing, she had scarcely even preconceptions; he had only to find himself the right kind of emotional pose, which as she trusted him wouldn't be difficult, and he could make use of her to almost any extent. She would be very useful, invaluable indeed, and after all, it was what she wanted. [...]
> She doesn't think me different, except as the person one loves is always different. No one need ever think that again. I could tell her the truth sometime, perhaps. If I put it nicely she wouldn't know what it really meant. She'd probably think it very romantic. Or perhaps she need never know at all.
> One would have to be tactful, not let her think she'd rushed one into it. Perhaps one could say ... (249-251)

Whilst shocked at first, Laurie soon begins to realise that a relationship with Nurse Adrian would significantly change his life and he momentarily betrays all of the "established decencies and securities of his life" by kissing her. Laurie perceives the possibility of a heteronormative life as generally attractive: "One's limitations would never seem quite so irrevocably fixed" and "[n]o one need ever think that [he is different] again". However, "[o]ne would have to be tactful" if one was to eventually come clean about the truth. Laurie's repeated self-identification as "one" indicates his actual distance to the whole idea of heterosexuality. Although potentially imagining married life, he cannot betray his personal convictions. In addition to his own reasons for dismissing the thought, Laurie is sympathetic with the nurse, who would ultimately be the one "paying for all this" (250). This scene demonstrates Laurie's deep-rooted desire to live a 'moral' life, which precludes deceiving himself as well as others. By suddenly terminating his ponderings, registered in the interruption ("..."), Laurie consciously decides to continue fighting for a life as a homosexual. The novel does thus not represent the common discourse of marriage for the sake of becoming recognised as a heterosexual and 'normal' individual. *The Charioteer* manages to remain authentic in its depiction of homosexuality as a desire that lived in the shadows of heteronormativity and the respective scenes successfully illustrate that dominant standards are inherently fragile.

Due to these diverse discourses surrounding Laurie's homosexuality, his mother's reluctance to bring his classical records is likely to carry a deeper meaning. The deliberateness of her action suggests not only that Laurie is a closeted homosexual, but that his mother partakes in the symbolic performance of silence, which signals a co-closetedness between the characters. I characterise co-closetedness as a shared moment between mother and son where both may or may not know about the latter's sexual deviance, which leaves them in a position of co-dependency. Sedgwick similarly argues that "[t]he pathogenic secret itself, even, can circulate contagiously *as* a secret: a mother says that her adult child's coming out of the closet with her has plunged her, in turn into the closet in her conservative community"[46]. While Sedgwick sees a causal connection between a child's coming out process and a mother's consequent closeting, *The Charioteer* emphasises its synchronicity: from the moment that Laurie recognises his sexuality, Mrs. Odell becomes part of the silence that constitutes the closet. This interdependence between mother and son leaves Mrs. Odell with the potential of tampering with Laurie's chance of coming out to her: if silence was broken due to the public playing of Tchaikovsky records, her own closetedness, and therefore her good reputation and upcoming marriage with a conservative clergyman, would be endangered. She thus has a keen interest in moderating, navigating and restricting Laurie's desire to reveal himself to her. Mrs Odell's initiative challenges Sedgwick's claim of parental closeting as a *cause* of the child's outing. Whereas Sedgwick's asserts that the "adult's child coming out of the closet [is the reason for] plung[ing] [the mother], in turn into the closet in her conservative community", Mrs Odell cannot be plunged into the closet when she already lives in it. Consequently, while benefiting from the silence surrounding co-closetedness, Mrs. Odell would be forced to take a stand if her son was to leave this space of silence. If she allows Laurie to confess his homosexuality to her, she would need to respond – either by keeping silent out of embarrassment and shame, which would betray the loyalty to her child, or in accepting his otherness and any possible consequences. In order not to be put into this impossible situation, Mrs. Odell ensures that no sincere intimacy occurs between her and her child. It follows that rather than entrapping Laurie and Mrs Odell in the narrative of mother-son-bonding, Renault has Laurie realise his growing distance to his mother.

By positioning Laurie's first experiences with the homosexual subculture directly after realising that his bond with his mother is broken, the text resolves the

46 Sedgwick, (2008), p. 80.

Oedipus complex: no longer striving for his mother as the ultimate love-object, Laurie – the tree formerly marked by a chain – is free to develop and grow. His subsequent immersion into the queer world seems to be a counter-performance to the conservative lifestyle aspired to by his mother when marrying the clergyman Mr. Straike. Like a teenager, Laurie has to rebel and experience his freedom before he can conceptualise what he really wants in life.

If, as Alden argues, Laurie's "longing to be accepted by society prevents him from accepting his sexuality for nearly the entire duration of the book"[47], Laurie would neither plunge into the homosexual subculture, nor blithely admit to his love for Andrew in an imaginary letter to his mother. At this point, Laurie can still conceptualise a confidential understanding with his mother, and although the letter is a product entirely of his fantasy, it lays bare Laurie's true feelings for the young Quaker and signals his acceptance of his homosexuality. It is a glimpse into his psyche, which heteronormative discourse denies him to make public.

> Darling Mother,
> I have fallen in love. I now know something about myself which I have been suspecting for years, if I had had the honesty to admit it. I ought to be frightened and ashamed, but I am not. Since I can see no earthly hope for this attachment, I ought to be wretched, but I am not. I know now why I was born, why everything has happened to me ever; I know why I am lame, because it has brought me to the right place at the right time. I would go through it all again, if I had to, now that I know it was for this.
> Oddly enough, what I feel most is relief, because I know now that what kept me fighting it so long was the fear that what I was looking for didn't exist. (57)

Despite never identifying Andrew as the love-object in this letter, the reader easily infers whom Laurie is talking about, because this scene is positioned immediately after his first encounter with Andrew in the hospital. Their conversation had ended with Laurie saying "Oh, by the way ___" (56). The unfinished sentence marks a desire to continue their conversation, which is denied to Laurie by the confined space of the military hospital where a prolonged talk between a soldier and a Quaker conscientious objector raises suspicions. The letter functions to complete Laurie's sentence and to disclose his stirring emotions. Addressing the letter to his "Darling Mother" sets a tone of softness and trust, which emphasises my reading of Laurie's wish to confide in Mrs. Odell. Instead of attempting to declare his own love for her, as Summers argues, Laurie imagines telling her the truth about his sexual leanings. This hopeful atmosphere of sharing his thoughts is continued until Laurie fears that his fantasy might invol-

47 Alden, (2014), p. 196.

untarily be projected onto the paper as written words. For the first time, Laurie realises that he cannot easily overcome the silence that governs his relationship to his mother because society would not allow him to disclose his outlawed love. His anxiety to reveal himself is symbolic of the social pressure to conform and not reminiscent of Laurie's alleged self-loathing. He is very conscious of what he "ought" to feel – "frightened and ashamed", "wretched" – but instead he is relieved to have discovered his true sexuality. His first sentence "I have fallen in love" shows not only a youthful lack of concern over admitting to his feelings, but also joy over having found out "something about myself which I have been suspecting for years". Encountering Andrew and falling so quickly and hopelessly in love with him is part of Laurie's self-discovery, which he registers as a positive turn towards self-fulfilment. Having known of his "own uniqueness" (13) since he was a little boy and having had homosexual friendships, Laurie now realises that what he has so far experienced was adolescent and immature compared to his feelings for Andrew. He even believes that he was destined to be injured during the war only to meet someone to connect with. The last sentence reveals that Laurie, if he ever truly fought his sexuality, was worried about finding true love instead of being ashamed for what he is.

This complex relationship between Laurie, his mother, his stepfather, Andrew and later Ralph in combination with Renault's appropriation of a psychoanalytic context shows that *The Charioteer* cannot be easily judged as non-affirmative or dramatising repentance as Alden argues. Her reading of the novel is too homogeneously influenced by a contemporary consciousness that lacks diversity in the judgement of the text and omits the publication conditions during the Cold War era. It is important to recognise that by alluding to homosexuality as a psychic condition deriving from failed identification with a male role model, *The Charioteer* was partially vindicated and protected from being censored in Britain. Butler calls this self-regulation a form of "implicit censorship"[48] which means that "the power of the censor is not exhausted by explicit state policy or regulation"[49]. At the same time as being self-censoring, Renault's novel circumvents obscenity laws by utilising the gaps that "[e]xplicit forms of censorship"[50] unconsciously produce. Stating "*what it does not want stated*", official boards of regulation "are exposed to a certain vulnerability precisely through being more readily legible."[51] Because the Obscene Publications Act of 1857 controlled how sexuality was presented in texts – "passion fine, 'sex' or titillation [especially in

48 Butler, (1997), p. 130.

49 Ibid., p. 130.

50 Ibid., p. 130.

51 Ibid., p. 130, [emphasis original].

homosexual acts] far from fine"[52] – authors like Renault were able to adjust their writings accordingly.

Despite its psychoanalytic self-regulation, *The Charioteer* was still daring and explicit enough to be refused by Renault's publishers Morrow in New York, who were influenced by McCarthyism and its homophobia. David Sweetman argues that "[t]he idea of a homosexual love story involving soldiers and pacifists must have seemed to the editors at Morrow like a scenario for their worst Cold War nightmare."[53] This reluctance to print *The Charioteer* illustrates that Renault was not as free to write about homosexuality set during the Second World War as novelists are today. Infiltrating certain stereotypes into her writing was therefore necessary for Renault's novel to get published – and as her American editors demonstrate, even that was not always sufficient.[54]

THE HYPOCRISY OF CENSORSHIP

The Charioteer was not the only novel that encountered resistance during publication. Walter Baxter's *Look Down in Mercy* (1951) was changed for an American readership to end on a note of confidence rather than in suicide. The discrepancies between the two versions give insight into the complicated world of writing against the grain of heteronormativity in the context of the Cold War. Whereas Renault teases her readership to find gay-affirmation in the allusive language of the text to circumvent censorship in Britain, Baxter's novel is generally more direct in is display of homosexuality and does not shy away from representing an officer in highly compromising terms. The following analysis will highlight the hypocrisy of censorship when certain acts of homosexuality as well

52 David Kynaston, *Family Britain, 1951-57*, [2009], (London: Bloomsbury, 2010), p. 552.

53 David Sweetman, *Mary Renault: A Biography* (London: Chatto & Windus, 1993), pp. 145-146.

54 In passing, David Sweetman acknowledges a significant detail in Renault's life that is often neglected in analysing her texts: Renault and her partner Julie needed money because the significant sum of $150,000 that Renault had earned when *Return to Night* had won the MGM Award, was spent. Sweetman concludes that "[n]ow that the money had run out Mary must write, Julie must work." Sweetman, (1993), p. 135. It is thus plausible that in order to guarantee publication and to come out of debt, Renault took precautions and deliberately infused her text with homophobic stereotypes so that it became published and a broader audience would be inclined to buy the novel.

as tender touches between male bodies are excluded from the British version, whereas non-consensual sex between the protagonist Kent and his mistress Helen remained un-censored in both editions. A comparison between the British and American edition of *Look Down in Mercy* will on the one hand clarify the pressure brought against authors of homosexual fiction in the 1950s, and on the other hand highlight the lingering patriarchal attitude that pardoned raping women. To begin with, I will examine the two vastly different endings that are both printed in the 2014 edition of *Look Down in Mercy*. Without further knowledge of other changes, the American version seems implausible as it parts with Baxter's otherwise largely realistic and burdensome style of writing.

After drinking heavily in an attempt to conceal his attempted suicide as an accident, Baxter's protagonist Anthony Kent sits on the window-sill in both endings. The British version unfolds as follows:

> His face was running with sweat and his arms shook; as he straightened his body to get back into the room the ledge of wood broke and he fell forward across the window-sill. His hands clawed at the woodwork behind him, but he could only touch it with the tips of his slippery fingers, and then he knew that he would fall. As his body began to plunge towards the drive he held his arms in a grotesque attitude as though to break his fall and he cried out; but not in mercy. (*MD* [1951], 273-274)

This ending is consistent with the rest of the narrative, featuring a weak man out of touch with his feelings and indecisive in his actions. The fated killing of the protagonist is a mixture not only of personal failure as an officer and heterosexual man, but also of continuous misfortune recognisable in his failed attempt to crawl back into the room and save himself. The use of words such as "clawed" and "grotesque" indicates homosexuality as 'unnatural' and creature-like, which dehumanises Kent making his death not only inevitable but also just. The British version has no sense of a happy ending and shows Kent moments before his death as a 'reasonable' homosexual who cannot/ should not cry for mercy. In contrast, the alternate version for the American market paints a different scene:

> His face was running with sweat and his arms shook; as he straightened his body to get back into the room the ledge of wood broke. He pushed violently with his arms and toppled backward, striking his head on the stone floor. He lay quite still on his back, his arms outstretched.
>
> (19)
>
> [...]

> But in spite of the wretchedness of his physical condition Kent was filled with happiness; the unbelieving happiness when the near miracle occurs at the last moment. [...] He knew he had solved nothing and he persuaded himself there was nothing to solve, all he had to do was to go on living and be with Anson. He resolved to try and be brave and to try and be good; to do more, he told himself, was not in his power. (*MD* [1952], 275-276)

Unlike the British ending, which depicts Kent as a grotesque creature, the American version emphasises his humanness in outstretched arms indicating openness rather than insecurity. His homosexuality seems to no longer be the cause of his troubles and his attempted suicide, but the reason to continue living. This ending is only consistent with the rest of the novel when reading the American version, which has been altered at other points as well to emphasise Kent and Anson's affair as simultaneously sexual and affectionate. Without knowledge of other passages from the American edition, the thoroughly transformed Kent, who refrains from worrying when repeatedly emphasising that he had tried to the best of his abilities to be the man society wants him to be, sounds implausible and inconsistent. Baxter additionally parts with his otherwise realistic narrative when deploying the concept of almost divine luck that saves Kent: "He had no idea that the failure of his attempt was inevitable" (276). When the British ending prohibits Kent from crying for mercy to substantiate his fate as self-imposed, the "inevitable" rescue of him in the American version paints homosexuality in a more positive light. Gregory Wood's introduction to the 2014 re-print edition cleverly circumvents to account for this change of mind by only stating that both endings are "ambivalent" (ix) – an observation to which I subscribe, given that we neither find Kent actually dead nor know of his plans concerning Anson, his batman and lover. Wood's further observation that "One [ending] is unhappy and the other happy" (ix) is equally plausible. However, his reluctance to "go into detail about this" (ix) and to instead emphasise the author's alleged unwillingness to depict a definite ending does not resolve any questions regarding their vast opposition. More enlightening is reading both versions through the lens of Michael Bronski's claim that 1950s novels were much less morbid in the United States than stereotypes suggest.[55] A less burdened and more optimistic portrayal of Kent in the American version suggests that Bronski's observation holds true. However, the delayed publication of *The Charioteer* in the United States seems to refute this assumption of more liberal American censorship. Obviously, there is no categorical truth to the convention of publishing and censorship in the 1950s but regardless of this discrepancy, it is revealing to look at further scenes

55 Michael Bronski, "The Shock of the Old: Christopher Bram Chats with the Author of *Pulp Friction*" in *The Gay & Lesbian Review Worldwide* Vol. 10, No. 2 (2003), p. 32.

from *Look Down in Mercy* that have been altered in the American edition of 1952 in order to gain insight into the time's arbitrary set of prejudices.

Comparing key scenes to the British version published a year earlier reveals a deep-rooted homophobia that required euphemistic language for the chaste British readership. Generally speaking, the American version is more voyeuristic about Kent's and Anson's sexuality and lingers to express tender kisses and touches. The British version suffices, like Renault's novel, to hint at physical contact between the characters and never makes their relationship sexually explicit. The more expressive language in the American edition significantly alters the reader's understanding of Kent's increasing sorrows throughout the novel. For instance, one scene in the British edition shows Kent and his batman in embrace to keep warm during the night – a conduct that does not appear as particularly controversial considering that the platoon is resting outside in the cold night, exhausted after a long and arduous march:

> [Kent] put his arms round Anson and pulled him closer. They lay still for a moment and then Kent lifted his shoulder from the ground and Anson put his arms round him. Kent was dimly aware that although his body might demand more, he himself did not: it was sufficient that they should rest in each other's arms, no longer hearing the firing or the man who had begun to scream again. (*MD* [1951], 152)

Expressing nothing more than mutual comfort, the text's most daring trespass contains Kent's faint realisation that "his body might demand more". True to his conditioning as a white, middle-class, heterosexual and married man, Kent withstands his somatic impulses and escapes further disgrace. This scene is the sole explanation for Kent's increasing self-doubt and his life-threatening actions to demonstrate his masculinity in heroic conduct that follow this passage: "he wanted to prove something to himself and to Anson, but what it was he did not know" (*MD* [1951], 152). Kent seems to feel the need to compensate for his body's stirring desire, even though his and Anson's behaviour displays hardly more than camaraderie in extreme circumstances. Consequently, Kent's reaction is vastly exaggerated and lacks credibility.

The considerably more explicit American version reveals a different situation where Kent and Anson share a kiss:

> [Kent] put his arms round Anson and pulled him closer. They lay still for a moment and *then their mouths met.* Kent lifted his shoulder from the ground and Anson put his arms round him. *They lay pressed closely together and* Kent was dimly aware that although his body might demand more, he himself did not: it was sufficient that they should rest in

each other's arms, no longer hearing the firing or the man who had begun to scream again. *They lay together for a long time and then Kent carefully moved his hand from beneath the blanket and brushed Anson's hair back from his forehead.*
'Let's try and get some sleep,' he whispered again, and felt Anson nod his head slightly. Very carefully, as though he was afraid someone might hear, he moved his body until he could lay his head on the soft pad of muscles below Kent's shoulder. Kent put his arm back beneath the blanket, their hands met and their fingers interlocked. (*MD* [1952], 169-170) [my emphasis]

The parts in italics signal the additions of the American version. The first two – "then their mouths met" and "they lay pressed closely together" – illustrate a different dynamic between the men. Their innocent embrace has turned into a kiss and they are described as clinging to each other like lovers. Whereas the British edition can still justify Kent's behaviour in terms of extreme military circumstances, the American version leaves no doubt that their relationship is sexual, and its depiction of intercourse becomes increasingly explicit. The latter addition of Kent touching Anson's hair expresses an initiative in Kent that seems startling to the readership of the British version, where the protagonist is characterised as restrained and passive until drunkenness loosens his inhibitions. The altered text illustrates a much more determined Kent who still feels that homosexuality is "utterly disgraceful and criminal" (1951:152; 1952:169), but whose emerging feelings for Anson overpower any feared consequences. Knowing this, it seems far more consequential that Kent feels the need to prove his manliness in heroic actions to himself as well as to Anson, in order to countervail the threat of emasculation that stereotypically accompanies homosexual conduct.

In contrast to the American edition, the British version does not obviously trespass conventional military camaraderie that legitimatises a certain degree of intimacy between men. However, a closer look reveals that the display of male conduct deconstructs the military as an institution of what Eve Kosofsky Sedgwick calls lingering "homosocial desire"[56]. Both editions show Kent at a military ball spending "most of the evening in the bar set aside for officers and sergeants, watching the men dancing with their women and with each other, gossiping on and on about the company with the persistence and inanity of a man in love" (15). This scene uses stereotypical markers of femininity to describe Kent. He persistently engages in gossip and disobeys conventions of male rationality when being inane. Culminating in a description of him as "a man in love", Kent displays exaggerated female emotions and the lack of control therein. As Brian

56 Eve Kosofsky Sedgwick, *Between Men: English Literature and Male Homosocial Desire* (New York: Columbia University Press, 1985).

Pronger argues the "essence of manhood lies in its *difference* from womanhood"[57] – a difference that is violently devastated because of Kent's conduct. Moreover, placing this scene in a masculine space like the bar for officers and sergeants, challenges Connell's assumption that "the military and government provide a fairly convincing *corporate* display of masculinity"[58]. By depicting Kent's gender performance as bordering on femininity, the narrative shows that masculinity is prone to becoming undone even within institutions like the military. When additionally emasculating the *bar* – an allegedly highly masculine space – *Look Down in Mercy* substantiates a critical stance regarding the fixity of gender norms. Implicitly the novel also suggests that *because* the military was a 'male only' institution during the Second World War, men such as Kent were able to disguise their sexual desires. Sedgwick calls this social interaction between men "homosocial desire" which "describe[s] social bonds between persons of the same sex" that may often "be characterized by intense homophobia, fear and hatred of homosexuality"[59]. In addition to this, "homosocial desire" "hypothesize[s] the potential unbrokenness of a continuum between homosocial and homosexual – a continuum whose visibility, for men, in our society, is radically disrupted"[60]. Sedgwick emphasises that men are often unaware of the lingering "continuum between homosocial and homosexual" – meaning the potential transformation of male bonding into homosexual desire. *Look Down in Mercy* dramatises this paradoxical position by depicting the military as a space that facilitates male bonding and the possibility for it to turn into homosexual desire. Paul Hammond intriguingly argues that the expression of feelings among men "blurs the very distinction [between a homosexual and a homosocial context] which the British army still patrols"[61]. This means that despite its all-male environment, the British military had an interest in keeping its reputation unfettered by homosexual suspicions. Consequently, the British editors of *Look Down in Mercy* took good care to delete any scenes that exceed conventional male wartime bonding such as the drunken talkativeness of Kent at the military dance. Nonetheless, it remains obvious, even to the readership of the British version, that Kent is very attracted to the opportunity of engaging with men in a setting that raises no suspicions over his heterosexuality.

57 Brian Pronger, The Arena of Masculinity: Sports, Homosexuality, and the Meaning of Sex (New York: St. Martin's Press, 1990), p. 71.

58 Connell, (2016), p. 77.

59 Sedgwick, (1985), p. 1.

60 Sedgwick, (1985), pp.1-2.

61 Paul Hammond, *Love Between Men in English Literature* (New York: St Martin's Press, 1996), p. 225.

Although Kent and Anson's first sexual encounter is printed in both editions, the fictionalisation of their shared intimacy differs drastically, and the toned-down display in the 1951 version accords with the rest of the narrative and leaves a lot of blanks for the reader to fill in:

In the darkness of the bedroom they stripped off their clothes swiftly, laying them on the floor at their feet, noiselessly taking off their boots [...]. Lying down side by side on the bed they encircled each other with their arms [...]. (*MD* [1951], 207)

The American version goes into more detail:

[...] *and their mouths met.* In the darkness of the bedroom they stripped off their clothes swiftly, laying them on the floor at their feet, noiselessly taking off their boots [...]. Lying down side by side on the bed they encircled each other with their arms [...]. *A gentle, almost unintentional movement began, and their muscles crushed their bodies together.* (*MD* [1952], 233)

As before, the most explicit references to intercourse are deleted from the English edition. In the American version Anson and Kent's sexuality is depicted as simultaneously tender and rough, intentional and accidental, beyond both their rational understanding. The emphasis on "their bodies" shows that Kent's former superiority over his desire did not last and now his "muscles" control his movements. Their parting, too, is depicted in different terms. Small and tender gestures such as "[*h*]*e gently rubbed his unshaven face against Kent's*" (*MD* [1952], 235) and "[*h*]*e smiled and touched Kent's fingers through the* [*mosquito*] *net*" (*MD* [1952], 235) are missing from the English novel. By editing out these non-verbal signs of affection, the English version loses a sense of intimacy that trespasses mere physicality. Evidently, English editors did not simply object to expressive displays of love making between men, but also to signs of emotional attachment that would challenge a reading of Kent as a lonely man in the military craving human contact. Considering these conservative views on homosexuality, it seems deeply troubling that the English edition had no difficulty depicting Kent raping an innocent woman named Helen Dean.

Kent and Helen meet during the military ball, mentioned previously. Kent's conversation with Tarrant and other officers is interrupted by Doctor Rowland, who shows up to "talk about the sexual behaviour of women in general and Eastern women in particular" (21), indicating the novel's repeated and pronounced racism against Indians, which Kent himself shares and advocates. Generally uninterested in the topic of female sexual behaviour, Kent chooses the less dreary convention of dancing with Helen, one of Doctor Rowland's nurses. During their dance Kent remains silent and inattentive whereas Helen leads the conversation until addressing the officer directly, who responds: "I'm sorry, Miss – er … what did you say?" (16) When in the scene quoted earlier, talk connected to pleasure and positive social interaction between men drinking at a bar, it is now associated with female triviality in conversation and Kent's reluctance to follow it. Instead of talking to his partner, Kent feels the "surreptitious attention" (16) his dance with Helen is causing. Not disclosing what this attention exactly constitutes, the text instead highlights Kent's indifference towards Helen whom "[h]e had almost forgotten" (16). That Kent's silence is caused by his lack of interest is misunderstood by Helen, who fills it with wild fantasising: "she wondered if he had been watching her for some time, and had had rather too much to drink in order to pluck up courage to be introduced to her" (16). Helen's interpretation of Kent's behaviour is so innocent and naive that she comes across as weak and unconfident.

These destructive dynamics between the characters are even more obvious when Helen *stops* talking: "She knew that the dance would be over in a few minutes and she stopped talking in order to see if he would ask her to reserve another dance for him later on." (17) Helen's silence is a counter-performance to her talkativeness designed for Kent to express his interest in her, but Kent "found her unattractive, her voice, her thin body and her colouring" (17). He shallowly reduces Helen to her racialised and female body because he has failed to get to know her personality when not listening to her during their dance. Their conversation is a display of expectations and the immediate devastation thereof. Until encountering actual war action in Part Two, the novel reads like a parody that brings to the fore the destructive social conventions that govern heterosexual courting – the innocent and dull female who tries to win the heart of the indifferent yet desirable man. This is most obvious when Helen envisions a future date with Kent: "there aren't any English girls in Sialpur, he might easily want to see me again" (17). Conscious of her Eurasian heritage, Helen feels insecure, which does not, however, prevent her from re-immersing into pointless hoping. Again, the depiction of Kent stands in contradiction to Helen's expectations: "But Kent was bored and only wanted to return to the bar." (17) In no way does Kent share Helen's dream of a future meeting and instead seems to plan his escape.

After their first dance, Kent and Helen meet again onboard of a ship that brings them to Burma. By now, the other officers have perceived that Helen is "rather sweet on" (33) Kent and wants to accompany him to another dance: "And Kent tried to protest his innocence, but at the same time he was pleased that she was thought attractive, and that he should be suspected, however jokingly, of having an affair." (34) Kent enjoys the attention his relationship with Helen is causing, because it distinguishes him as heterosexual and masculine. During the dance he consequentially demonstrates an exaggerated interest in her by "calling her 'darling' in a voice just loud enough to be heard by Maguire, who sat next to him" (38). Helen, in turn, never stops to think that "the word 'darling' might be meaningless" (38). This scene displays the same characteristics as before when Kent performs a social role that is misinterpreted by Helen as true intentions: "She genuinely believed that Kent was falling in love with her; she knew that she was in love with him. By the end of the evening Kent was almost drunk and had forgotten that he was only playing a part." (38) When alcohol disables rational thinking and dissolves inhibitions, Kent loses control over his act and becomes intimate with Helen in her cabin.

At first, their desire is mutual and Helen "clung to him, kissing fiercely with closed lips" (38). Kent perceives the kiss as "uncomfortable and stupid" (38) because it "doesn't fool anyone, and he pushed his tongue until her lips suddenly parted" (38). Kent's realisation that their kissing "doesn't fool anyone" indicates that he is still performing the act of heterosexuality but does it badly because he feels no true desire for Helen. Nor does the memory of his wife Celia, "her photograph or her handwriting" "stir[...] him physically" (30). Fantasising about "the first night they [he and Celia] had slept together" "no longer move[s] him", and "for several months he had been completely sexless, except now and then for some fantastically improbable dream that he preferred to forget as soon as possible" (30). The "improbable dream" that must be forgotten immediately illustrates Kent's stirring homosexual desires for Anson who becomes increasingly important for the officer. When the intimate bond with Anson grows, Kent's desire for women in general and for Helen in particular diminishes. In order to compensate for this trespass, he becomes more demanding and takes a forced initiative towards Helen who initially responds with pleasure and "her breath quickened" (38):

> Half drunk and thinking herself in love she was defenceless. Had Robert done such a thing she would have been beside herself with outrage modesty, even if they had been formally engaged. But it was impossible for her to judge Kent's action, she was afraid that if she tried to disapprove it would only underline her difference from other women that he knew. (39)

The shadow of patriarchy, where the white male subject claims universal power over the female, is already visible in this prelude to the rape scene when the emotional and weak woman "thinking herself in love" yields to the male demanding intercourse. The added element of race complicates this scene because it subordinates the Eurasian Helen to the Caucasian Kent. Interestingly, Helen's reluctance if Robert (a fellow Eurasian in love with Helen) had tried to sleep with her would have placed her in a more traditional Caucasian female role than her behaviour towards Kent does. Renault's *The Charioteer* emphasises female, especially English, "modesty" with reference to Nurse Adrian: "She was sexually backward as is scarcely any female creature except the English girl of a certain upbringing: nothing she wanted was clear to her but love" (249). Both texts highlight female preoccupation with finding love as their major goal in life. Whereas the "English girl of a certain upbringing" is naïve and sexually inexperienced, the racially visible and marked Helen misinterprets Kent's forwardness as a sign for his experience with permissive white women. Scared to "underlin[e] her difference from other women that he knew", Helen surrenders her resistance and gives in to "his touch" (39). Her rising pleasure, however, challenges her status as a racialised woman "who [is her] own violation, who [is] logically inviolable because marked *as* sexual available without sexual agency"[62]. In Wendy Brown's analyses, racialised female bodies are not supposed to enjoy the touch of the white man and claim sexual agency in such enjoyment. This argument substantiates Sara Ahmed's reading of racialised bodies as investing "skin colour with meaning, such that 'black' and 'white' come to function, not as descriptions of skin colour, but as racial identities"[63]. When racialisation involves the body in the process of investing meaning onto it, Helen's body defies its status through sexual pleasure. Kent's reaction is consequential: "So you like it, Kent though, and suddenly he was disgusted with himself and then angry and vicious against Helen." (39) Kent re-directs his disgust over his forced heterosexual initiative towards Helen, which unloads itself in him violating her, thus re-establishing the boundaries between white male power and racially marked femininity devoid of agency.

> He kissed her again with his open mouth, wet with gin, and when he thought that she was responding sufficiently well without warning slid his hand down the front of her dress and cupped her naked breast in his hand. [...]
> She was frightened now and protested, trying to hold his hands away from her body and whispering: 'No, Tony, my dearest, please no.' But he went on, kissing her with a semblance of passion until her struggles ceased. He thought her gasps of pain were pleasure, too drunk and too indifferent to wonder whether she was a virgin. (38-39)

62 Wendy Brown, *States of Injury: Power and Freedom in late Modernity* (New York: Princeton University Press, 1995), p. 170.

63 Sara Ahmed, "Racialized Bodies" in Mary Evans and Ellie Lee (eds.), *Real Bodies: A Sociological Introduction* (New York: Palgrave, 2002), p. 46.

The double moral standard in the practice of censoring during the 1950s could not be any more evident in this scene: whilst homosexual intercourse was considered 'indecent behaviour' from which the innocent English readership needed to be sheltered, non-consensual heterosexuality was apparently so commonplace that it did not even require concealment in allusive language. The detailed description of the naked female body – "naked breast" – reducing Helen to her sexual parts, in combination with the depiction of Kent forcefully "kissing" Helen, evidences that heterosexual intercourse, however brutal, is protected from censorship. The conventional objectification and victimisation of women is so entrenched in patriarchal society that sexual assault becomes too ordinary to provoke objections.

Helen is no longer able to claim sexual agency when she is desperately "trying to hold his hands away from her body" (39) and becomes overpowered by his "indifference" (39) towards her. She turns into a body which serves to pleasure the white man's needs, and to silence his ever-growing fear of not sufficiently performing in a heterosexual and masculine manner. Helen's representation as weak and hardly able to pronounce protest – only in a whisper and only disguised in endearing language – substantiates the text's unconcern for her. The image of the exploited and colonised female body is abundantly clear especially when considering the light-dark dynamics that frame the scene.

Before the rape, Kent switches off the lights and plunges the room into darkness. With their vision impaired, no threatening gazes can be exchanged and the focus lies on touch and scent. This is further highlighted in Helen's wish to *stay* in the darkness when Kent is leaving, for fear of revealing that the illness is "reflected in her face, [that] her hair [is] disarranged and [her] lipstick smeared round her mouth" (39). Unwittingly, Helen relieves Kent from visually encountering the consequences of his action, thus not only protecting herself from shame, but foremost leaving his masculinity and patriarchal rights towards female bodies unchallenged. The next chapter will clarify that while violence is part of performing hegemonic masculinity, chivalry prohibits men to physically abuse women. Consequently, by raping Helen, Kent has forfeited rather than substantiated his right to perform masculinity. Through staying in the dark, Helen shelters Kent from recognising this mistake. Moreover, the characters' perpetual use of endearments such as "[d]arling, I must go" (39), "Tony, darling" (39) and "Tony, my dear" (40) works in similar ways: Helen gives the impression that she still relishes Kent who gladly accepts her offer to remain oblivious to his action. Unwilling to let the despicable act surface their consciousness, both characters continue in their enactment of fondness for each other.

Throughout the novel, Kent repeatedly seeks Helen's company in order to counteract his increasing feelings for Anson. The following scene succeeds Kent's raping of Helen and mirrors two things: Kent's desire to comprehend his sexual assault against Helen as a mutual exchange of affection, and his need to return to this memory in order to countervail his emerging homosexual feelings.

> All the time he had been in hospital he had tried to feel desire for Helen; whenever she came into the ward to spend her few moments of freedom with him he would hold her hand and watch her face, trying to relive the drunken moments on the bed, trying to graft the desire he had then felt on to the present moment. His cold behaviour toward Anson had all been part of the pattern he was trying to weave, but nothing seemed to go right, he could not understand what was happening, he only knew that he was deeply frustrated and unhappy. (193)

Unsuccessfully, Kent tries to actively transform his feelings for Anson into desire for Helen by showing indifference towards the former and recollecting a past intimacy with the latter. Daringly for its time of writing, this scene implies that homosexuality cannot be 'treated' and re-converted into heterosexual desire, even when built on memories of intercourse. Consequently, Kent takes a more radical step when planning to share another night with Helen. To increase the symbolic meaning of inviting her to his quarters, he asks Anson to personally deliver his message, and to accompany the nurse to Kent's bungalow. Unanticipated by Kent, Anson and Helen bond over their shared interest in the officer: "it had been a relief for both of them to talk about him, and although there was only time to touch on the merest superficialities it had served as a link between them" (195). Whatever detail these "merest superficialities" have revealed to them is unclear, but when Kent sees them at ease with each other, he is bewildered and excluded from their intimacy. His discomfort is elevated when Helen says goodnight to Anson: "Kent saw them smile at each other as though they shared a secret. It made him feel uneasy" (196). Kent is no longer able to control the situation and becomes increasingly insecure in Helen's company. The nurse, however, misinterprets the situation once more and believes that Kent is longing for his wife and feels guilty over betraying her. Helen tries to comfort Kent but "to her horror his eyes filled with tears that spilled over before he could hide his face" (198). "And [then] Kent gave up the unequal struggle and cried, because he had had too much to drink, because she had said that she understood, and he knew that was impossible, mourning [...] for his dead love and the unknown terrors of the new" (198). In this key passage, Kent is represented as desperate, yet finally able to admit to himself (but not to Helen) that he is in "love" with a man and that his former "love" for his wife or for Helen is a "dead" one. He is terrified of what this implies, but no longer capable of fighting his feelings. Helen, too, is terrified but for a different reason: a man overcome by emotions is too overwhelming for her to comprehend. Raised in a society that excludes emotions from the realm of masculinity and replaces them with an allegedly undying desire for sex, Helen takes action:

> Helen had made her decision but found it was too difficult to put into words. She stood up and held out her hand and he took it in his with a questioning look. She smiled at him, reassuringly, nodding her head slightly and he stood up. Still holding his hand she led him through the lounge and into the bedroom. (199)

This scene unfolds almost in 'slow-motion' where every bit of movement is emphasised as a huge change in Kent and Helen's relationship of dependency. Moral censorship on female sexuality prevents Helen from articulating her thoughts and to dissolve what the "it" is that cannot be "put into words". Even when the "it" is linked to the bedroom there is still no clear explanation for the meaning of the "it" since Kent misinterprets Helen's movements as a preamble for goodbyes "on to the veranda" (199). Only when "she had shut the door" does he realise "what she intended" (199). The "it" is here dissolved by Kent's emerging understanding and the connotation of a shut bedroom door as determining the most intimate of spaces. Lee Edelman and Lauren Berlant pointedly unmask this space as shielding the heterosexual sex act[64] that is conventionally initiated by the male, transforming the private bedroom as "a place where men have assumed their right to sexual intercourse"[65], and where women have been fixed in their reproductive roles. Such an assumption fails to prevail in this instance as it is Helen – a female – who takes initiative. By acting contrary to heteronormative conventions, Helen re-genders the bedroom space and transfers autonomous femininity into it. She is the active part who *leads* Kent towards the bedroom, which troubles notions of female passivity in general and her former depiction as the victim of rape in particular. It is her reassuring smile and her slight movements that seduce Kent to trust and follow her. In holding his hand as a way of comfort, yet also to guide him almost like a mother would with her children, Kent is not only emasculated by her but also infantilised.

64 Lauren Berlant and Michael Warner, "Sex in Public" in *Critical Inquiry* Vol. 24, No. 2 (1998), p. 555.

65 Nancy Duncan, "Renegotiating Gender and Sexuality in Public and Private Spaces" in Nancy Duncan (ed.), *BodySpace: Destabilizing geographies of gender and sexuality* (London and New York: Routledge, 1996), p. 131.

Standing out and contrasting with previous scenes, is the utter silence that surrounds them. When before, Helen was represented as the communicative part – to conceal nervousness during the dance or verbalise resistance in the cabin – she is now speechless upon her imminent plan to sleep with Kent. For the first time he cannot interpret sounds in his favour as he had done when he raped Helen thinking that "her gasps of pain were pleasure" (39). Through being silent, Helen claims a new form of power that overpowers the officer.

A sudden shift in Helen's confidence occurs when the narrative reveals that neither she nor Kent truly desire the unspeakable "it": "In silence and *against both their wishes* they took off their clothes and crept under the mosquito net, then they clung to each other in the darkness like children" (199) [my emphasis]. When before Helen was striving to be Kent's mistress, she now realises that her desires have never been real, that she wanted to be with Kent in order to elevate her own status beyond markers of race. Both Helen's and Kent's fate is manifesting, which is expressed in a tragic gesture of the characters clinging to each other's bodies and realising that their efforts are in vain because intercourse will do nothing but graven their pain. It appears as if Helen and Kent begin to acknowledge their destinies as racially and sexually marked subjects respectively. In sharing the plight of abjection, Kent and Helen find a moment of false consolidation that betrays their integrity.

Several weeks later, after having survived the worst of his journey out of Burma, Kent meets Helen one last time to find her taking care of Robert:

> 'Robert?' Kent asked, puzzled. 'Robert who?'
> 'Johns. You know who I mean, he's been a hospital orderly with me for a long time. At least, he's a warrant officer now,' she added proudly. 'You used to tease me about him.'
> 'No, I can't seem to place him, Helen. Did I meet him with you?' [...]
> 'No, you wouldn't know him, he's a Eurasian.' There was no trace of bitterness in her voice, and when she said 'Eurasian' she lifted her chin slightly. (247)

In this final encounter between Kent and Helen, she realises that as an English officer, Kent would not have bothered to recognise Robert's existence let alone remember him. Preoccupied with his "white man's burden" (8)[66] – a demonstra-

66 In the poem "The White Man's Burden: The United States & The Philippine Islands" from 1899 Rudyard Kiplan praises imperialist missions where the 'white man' sets out to colonise foreign lands inhabiting people "Half devil and half child" (l. 8). As a euphemism for imperialism, "The White Man's Burden" captures the racist discourse of colonialism. Kent's usage of the phrase in *Look Down in Mercy* underlines his own racism towards the Indians and Eurasian whilst aiming to substantiate his current situ-

tion of Kent's deep-rooted racism – Kent has never cared about anyone but himself, least of all about a Eurasian orderly. When Helen realises Kent's utter indifference towards Robert and her heritage more broadly, she "lifted her chin": a sign of pride and solidarity to help the man who has been worshipping her despite Helen's disrespectful behaviour towards him. Simultaneously, she comes to understand that Kent will not linger to help her and Robert retreat – that he is once again more worried about his own survival than anyone else's. Her altruism in helping Robert whilst knowing that she will be left alone to face the enemy positions Helen as the novel's most courageous character, putting Kent and the soldiers of war to shame. Helen proves that gender, race and class do not determine a person's decision and that fabricated norms are only cages for those who are prepared to linger behind bars. On this positive note the novel ends its story of Helen, who is positioned as a strong, brave and independent woman, free to choose for whom to die.

RESISTING BLACKMAIL – RESISTING STIGMATISATION

The unrevised representation of Helen's fate as a victim of rape in contrast to the censoring of homosexual conduct shows the double-standard of publishing practices during the Cold War. Helen's new-found pride as a Eurasian woman does not compensate for the fact that the scene of rape explicitly references, and thus condones violence against women, whereas tender kisses between men are censored in the English edition of *Look Down in Mercy*. Moreover, Kent's constant self-doubts and his disrespectful treatment of Helen in order to prove his heterosexuality seem to substantiate Alden's and Summers' negative evaluation of novels written in the 1950s as representations of burdened individuals perpetuating stigmatisation and homosexual trauma. However, Baxter's novel is not as straightforward as it seems. In his introduction to the 2014 edition Woods identifies Kent's inconsistent personality: "Kent is both a hero and a coward, a saver

ation as a 'burden' because he is not yet in direct combat and deprived of the chance to "search your manhood" (l. 29). Rudyard Kipling, "The White Man's Burden: The United States & The Philippine Islands", in Rudyard Kipling (ed.), *Rudyard Kipling's Verse: Definitive Edition* (Garden City, New York: Doubleday, 1940).

66 Kristine A. Miller, *British Literature of the Blitz: Fighting the People's War* (London: Palgrave Macmillan, 2009), p. 3.

of lives and a killer, a homophobe and the lover of a man."[67] Considering this accurate description, it seems deceptive to judge Kent as thoroughly compromised due to his questionable deeds, and assessing the novel as "not good for the gays" would overlook its complexity as well as its inscriptions of paradoxical bravado against homophobic culture, illustrated when Kent commits a murder that saves him from being outed.

A mischievous character named Goodwin turns into Kent's personal rival when Anson becomes the officer's batman, whereas Goodwin, who was first friends with Anson, is left a lonely outcast. Without a friend to keep him company, Goodwin falls into a habit of roaming the deserted villages by himself whenever he has a day off. At one point he encounters a bombed-out house with a safe lying outside. He manages to open the safe and finds "twenty-five medium-sized rubies" (221). This treasure would make him a rich man, but in order to keep the rubies, Goodwin needs to leave the army immediately. He consequently approaches Kent and demands to be given a note that allows him to be transported out of Burma by train. Because Goodwin begins to suspect an unnatural bond between Kent and his batman when he catches Anson coming to the barracks very late one night, he feels superior to his officer. His suspicions are fostered by his knowledge over Anson's sexual preferences: "Anson and me were muckers for a long time, I know all about Anson, thank you very much." (227) Although the term 'mucker' only denotes comradeship in the conventional sense[68], the characters seem to interpret the term to imply more than friendship. When Kent ponders its meaning, he explicitly states that it "means *more* than mere friends; he sometimes wondered exactly what it did cover" (20) [my emphasis]. Consequently, Goodwin and Kent share a specific understanding of the term 'mucker' that clarifies Anson's sexual preferences as queer and his association with Kent reinforces Goodwin's suspicion that the commanding officer is equally queer.

Goodwin's titillating knowledge provides ground for blackmail: "if you don't [give me a note] I'll tell everyone I can about you and Anson. [...] I'll tell them what you are, nothing but a bloody nancy boy!" (227) "[M]aybe I can't prove anything but you know it's the truth" (228). Goodwin strengthens his allegedly superior knowledge by calling Kent a "nancy boy" with an exclamation mark for emphasis. The derogatory phrase "nancy boy" means "an effeminate

67 Gregory Woods, "Introduction" in *Look Down in Mercy*, [1951], (Richmond: Valancourt Books, 2014), p. ix.

68 The *OED* defines 'mucker' as a military terms used in British English to describe a "close companion or friend; a person with whom one regularly socializes or teams up" "mucker, n.1." *OED Online*. Oxford University Press, June 2017. Web. 9 September 2017.

man or boy; a homosexual man"[69], which emphasises Goodwin's deployment of an explicitly homophobic insult. In *Excitable Speech*, Judith Butler claims that the person who performs a speech act, such as Goodwin's "nancy boy", is imagined to wield sovereign power. This is done "to the extent that the speaker of hate speech is understood to effect the subordinating message that he or she relays"[70]. Consequently, when Goodwin evokes a speech act that has its roots in homophobic language, he not only makes use of its current meaning but also "recalls prior [speech] acts" in order to position his accusation – "nancy boy" – into a wider narrative of homophobic insults.[71] Because hate speech is citational, and homophobic hate speech is informed by particular previous discourses around such speech, the subjects resorting to these preceding acts, put themselves in relation to them. As Butler argues, "this means that the subject has its own 'existence' implicated in a language that precedes and exceeds the subject, a language whose historicity includes a past and future that exceeds that of the subject who speaks"[72]. Due to his own deviating sexuality expressed in his former relationship with Anson, Goodwin's blackmail towards Kent is ultimately ineffective. He is trying to make use of a power settled in homophobia, which he is not capable to evoke convincingly.

Kent's reaction to Goodwin's blackmail additionally demonstrates Butler's assertion that being called a "nancy boy" is an "address [that] constitutes a being within the possible circuit of recognition and, [as in this example] outside of it, in abjection"[73]. Language is not only injurious in multiple ways but can also be enabling for the subject who has been made the object of hate speech. It is therefore not exclusively the initiator of language, who actively performs, but also, unforeseen by the speaker, the receiver, who is brought into being through the address. Butler argues that:

> one is not simply fixed by the name that one is called. In being called an injurious name, one is derogated and demeaned. But the name holds out another possibility as well: by being called a name, one is also, paradoxically, given a certain possibility for social existence, initiated into a temporal life of language that exceeds the prior purposes that animate that call.[74]

69 "Nancy boy, n." *OED Online*. Oxford University Press, June 2017. Web. 21 August 2017.

70 Butler, (1997), pp. 80-81.

71 Ibid., p. 20.

72 Ibid., p. 28.

73 Ibid., p. 5.

74 Ibid., p. 2.

It is this double effect of language that, on the one hand, degrades Kent as homosexual, but, on the other hand, catapults him out of the closet into the realm of the abjected, which gives him agency to react, whereas the closet keeps him unintelligible and passive.

Julia Kristeva's *Powers of Horror* is essential for theorising the abject as a social position that oscillates between object and subject but cannot quite assimilate into either: "what is abject is not my correlative, which providing me with someone or something else as support, would allow me to be more or less detached and autonomous"[75]. The abject is "the jettisoned object"[76] which *confuses* and *shatters* meaning by lying outside a certain set of rules. This "place of banishment"[77] enables the abject to unsettle dominant discourses merely by its existence as abject. Shunning the abject is a consequence of its power to collapse learned and absorbed behaviours – its ability to turn meaning into meaninglessness. This is not to assess abjection as more positive than the closet – ultimately, an outed homosexual is increasingly exposed to various kinds of harassment. However, despite its difficult social position, an outed subject opens grounds for reaction and defence, which is evident in Kent's response to the blackmail. His only way of not falling into "a bottomless gulf of disgrace yawning at his feet" (227), is to keep "his head and [find] out exactly how much Goodwin [knows]" (227).

Kent's temporary need for action challenges Sedgwick's claim that

> in many, if not most, relationships, coming out is a matter of crystallizing intuitions or convictions that had been in the air for a while already and had already established their own power-circuits of silent contempt, silent blackmail, silent glamorization, silent complicity.[78]

Sedgwick argues for the interdependence between blackmail and coming out, where the force of harassment compels the subject to move from the 'private' environment of the closet to the insecure but less restricting realm of the public. Kent however, only momentarily harnesses the relative autonomy of an outed homosexual, to extinguish the source of the threat by shooting Goodwin in the face, thus not simply killing him, but symbolically muting all future hate speech: "He raised the revolver slowly until the muzzle was level with Goodwin's mouth

75 Julia Kristeva, *Powers of Horror: An Essay on Abjection* (New York: Columbia University Press, 1982), p. 1.

76 Ibid., p. 2.

77 Ibid., p. 2.

78 Sedgwick, (2008), pp. 79-80.

and pointed slightly upwards. [...] Goodwin started to speak: 'Put that thing down, you gutless nancy.' Still smiling Kent fired." (228-229). "[H]e would rather be suspected of murder than homosexuality" (228). While the last statement substantiates the officer's own homophobia and disgust over his deviating sexuality, Kent's action rings a tone of bravado to not allow himself being blackmailed. His struggle to admit to his homosexual feelings and learning to live with them is dramatised in such a compassionate way that the reader is paradoxically persuaded to identify with this highly compromised protagonist although he is committing a murder.

In *The Charioteer*, Ralph, too, becomes involved in a form of blackmail when he is expelled from school for indecent behaviour whilst holding the position of Head of School. Although it can be argued that this is a less stereotypical case of blackmail than in *Look Down in Mercy*, it nevertheless clarifies the predicaments homosexuals may be exposed to in a homophobic society. Little is known about the real reasons for Ralph's expulsion at the beginning of the novel, but Laurie instantly declares Ralph's innocence despite all rumours. While his own motivation for defending Ralph is outwardly camouflaged in an advocacy of justice deriving from his conviction that Ralph is not to blame, it becomes clear that by helping Ralph, Laurie is unconsciously arguing his own case: "He felt suddenly, the enormous release of energy which comes when repressed instincts are sanctioned by a cause." (20) While Laurie is incapable of openly arguing against the discrimination of homosexuals, he instead channels his frustration in the defence of Ralph, whom he deeply admires. This reaction is contrasted by Ralph's when he unresistingly accepts the expulsion.

Much later in the novel it is explained that Ralph and Hazell (the boy who was responsible for Ralph's expulsion) had an affair. Their fallout was over a physical punishment of Hazell executed by Ralph in his function as the Head of the School. When Hazell ejaculates as a consequence of the pain inflicted by Ralph, he reveals himself not only as a homosexual but also, in Ralph's terms, as being "sick" (180). However, instead of shaming and blaming Hazell for his dismissal, Ralph critically recalls his own reaction to the situation:

> I'd have liked to see him dead, so long as I hadn't got to touch him. I suppose he saw it. It may be he went to Jeepers out of revenge, but I don't think so. I think he was scared, and it made him a bit hysterical. He told it reversing the point of the final episode, if you see what I mean. I didn't see very much future in arguing about it. (180)

Ralph's allusive style of speaking circumvents clarity, which indicates that he still feels uncomfortable about the incident. His ambiguous sentence "[h]e told it reversing the point of the final episode" means that Hazell, hurt over Ralph's dismissive reaction towards his sadomasochistic leanings, told the headmaster a story that depicts Ralph as "sick" rather than himself. Despite the fact that he would be in the right, Ralph sees himself as unworthy of defence because he perceives his own reaction towards Hazell's proclivities as inconsiderate. He reflects that "a perfectly normal person wouldn't have been so angry. [Hazell] was sick, after all." (180) Unfamiliar with these details of Ralph's bond with Hazell and their subsequent dispute, the schoolboy Laurie can only see his hero being treated unfairly and plans to come to his rescue. He suggests a 'counter-blackmail':

> What we want is more of a sort of psychological war. Now the whole thing about Jeepers is that he's terrified of scandal. It's himself he has cold feet about, really, and his job. [...] We'll just all go along to him in a body and say the whole House is immoral, one and all, and we've come to confess like Hazell did. Then he won't sack anyone, he'll fall over himself to hush it up. (22)

Laurie's response exposes the weakness of the hegemonic system: instead of being incontestable and indisputably prevailing, the dominant order is itself vulnerable to blackmail. However, Butler rightly asserts that for a "threat to work, it requires certain kinds of circumstances, and it requires a venue of power by which its performative effects might be materialized."[79] This "venue of power" does not lie within the reach of Laurie but is associated with the school and its administration. Consequently, his threat is rendered ineffective even before it is actively performed because Laurie's fellow students are not prepared to risk their reputation over Ralph. Similar to Goodwin's failed attempt of blackmailing Kent, Laurie cannot harness the potential he sees in a collective upheaval against the school.

These two cases show that, whilst being a compelling option to gain certain privileges, the concept of blackmail is highly unstable as it entails a set of potentials that cannot be controlled by a single party. Another character from *The Charioteer* named Alec pinpoints this deceptive power of blackmail and highlights that homophobia is the root of struggle that needs countermanding. He refutes any conclusion that assumes his homosexuality as damaging, and instead blames society for its unfair stigmas. In a passionate monologue Alec claims:

> It's a matter of what your self-respect's worth to you, that's all. [...] In the first place, I didn't choose to be what I am, it was determined when I wasn't in a position to exercise

79 Butler, (1997), p. 12.

> any choice and without me knowing what was happening. I've submitted to psychoanalysis; it cured my stutter for me, which was very useful as far as it went. [...] But I don't admit that I'm a social menace. [...] I'm not prepared to accept a standard which puts the whole of my emotional life on the plane of immorality. I've never involved a normal person or a minor or anyone who wasn't in a position to exercise a free choice. I'm not prepared to let myself be classified with dope-peddlers and prostitutes. Criminals are blackmailed. I'm not a criminal. I'm ready to go to some degree of trouble, if necessary, to make that point. (199)

This scene clarifies why *The Charioteer* was a daring text to be published at a time where homosexuality was more forcefully criminalised and medicalised than before. The recurring issue of psychoanalysis, which played a major part in the medical discourse 'treating' homosexuality, is qualified as ineffective in Alec's argument when he states that "it cured my stutter for me, which was very useful as far as it went". The usefulness of psychoanalysis is reduced to treating a speech disorder, because it fails at 'curing' its actual target. As mentioned before, psychoanalysis functions as a broad framework in the novel that is constantly challenged and appropriated through sarcastic references such as Alec's.

Passionately, Alec prompts fellow homosexuals to reflect on "what your self-respect's worth to you" (199). He does not want to be judged as a homosexual, and rejects any kind of identity that fixes him into the category of "menace", "immoral" or "criminal". Homosexuality is something that 'just happened' to Alec; it is intrinsic of what constitutes his personality, which he does not want to deny but neither allows himself to be reduced to. Zilboorg rightly claims that Alec is "arguing for more than being left in peace that requires remaining hidden, closeted"[80]. He pledges "for the affirmation of the emotional wholeness of huge numbers of people"[81]. Arguing against the blackmailing of homosexuals, Alec concludes that "[c]riminals are blackmailed. I'm not a criminal." (199) By establishing a difference between homosexuality and criminal conduct Alec shows strong self-affirmative streaks. Except for Ralph, who judges his reaction towards Hazell as a justification for his punishment, each character resists being blackmailed for their tendencies.

To Alec homosexuality is not a sickness but a variation of an arbitrary norm that disguises itself as a standard. Ralph experiences this standardaised version of sexuality in similarly critical ways when he describes his short period of 'going straight':

80 Zilboorg, (2001), p. 115.

81 Ibid., p. 115.

'I did two years of women, when I first went to sea.' [...]
'Did you?' said Laurie. 'Why?' [...]
'I didn't want to give [fellow sailors] anything on me. Besides, when I found I could if I gave my mind to it, I thought I might become *naturalized*, so to speak.' (182-183) [my emphasis]

He continues:

Funny thing, you know, it didn't feel at all like going straight. More like trying to cultivate some fashionable vice that never quite becomes a habit. [...] I happened to meet someone [...]. All I can remember thinking is 'Thank the Lord, back to *normal* at last.' (183) [my emphasis]

This scene is predominantly interesting in its usage of the terms "naturalized" and "normal". Brian Pronger states that "to say something is natural is to make a judgment; what we are really saying when we say that a phenomenon is natural is that it fits our view of the world – a view that is the product of tradition"[82]. This means that there is no 'natural' sexuality but only a standard that continues to be perpetuated by certain conducts following a tradition. What is assumed to be 'biologically natural' – that is heterosexuality – transforms into a standard that appears to be 'normal': an assimilated social behaviour according to cross-gender erotic desire. Michal Warner concedes that "[n]early everyone, it seems, wants to be normal. And who can blame them, if the alternative is being abnormal, or deviant, or not being one of the rest of us?"[83] By seeking female companionship, Ralph reveals his wish to fit into the standard narrative of normalised society. When he says "I thought I might become *naturalized*", Ralph hopes to "blend, to have no visible difference and no conflict"[84]. For a period of two years, he adheres to this premise of normalization/naturalization when he withstands any homosexual tendencies. However, his failure to maintain relationships with women indicates that the standard of 'normal' and 'natural' is void for subjects who diverge from dominant conventions. When Ralph is becoming conscious of his true desires, social norms and their apparent universality are put into question. This illustrates what Warner titles *The Trouble with Normal*: the realisation that what is thought to be 'natural/normal' (heterosexuality) is 'abnormal' for homosexuals. Ralph's temporary attempt of living in a heterosexual re-

82 Pronger, (1990), pp. 50-51.

83 Michael Warner, *The Trouble with the Normal: Sex, Politics, and the Ethics of Queer Life* (Cambridge and Massachusetts: Harvard University Press, 1999), p. 53.

84 Ibid., p. 60.

lationship shows the pressure on homosexuals to conform to dominant standards and mirrors the homophobic discourse of past (and present) times. His reluctance to continue on this path, on the other hand, signals strength and the will to find self-fulfilling love. Moreover, Ralph's recollection of this period in his life, and the awareness with which he reflects on it, reinforces my claim that *The Charioteer* does not represent homosexuals as thoroughly burdened and suffering individuals. Instead, Ralph shows a remarkable ability to analyse himself and to conceptualise his desire, whilst making a conscious decision to take the more troublesome path when following his homosexual desire.

More daringly still, Alec renounces in his monologue quoted previously the stigmatisation of homosexual men seducing innocent young boys when saying: "I've never involved a normal person or a minor or anyone who wasn't in a position to exercise a free choice". Similar to Ralph, who talks of becoming 'normalised', Alec assumes dominant society to be 'normal'. His essentialist argument does not keep him from demonstrating the inherent arbitrariness of standards when he criticises the presumption that homosexuals assault children – a stereotypical accusation that Laurie, too, becomes aware of when he soothes a young boy in hospital, who is fretting over the sound of airplanes and bombs. Laurie realises that being in the boy's bed holding him in his arms might be understood in very different ways than intended, and that this would destroy the "perfect innocence between them" (308). Depressed, he continues thinking that "[i]t wouldn't take so very long for that kind of consciousness to settle under one's skin." (308) Both Laurie and Alec are acutely aware of the stigma that accompanies their sexuality, but refuse to identify with its negative stereotypes. The difficulties in living their lives as homosexual men thus derives from the prejudices brought against their desires and is not, as Alden previously argued, a reflection of their damaged psyche resulting from deep-rooted self-hatred. Because pre-Stonewall novels are evidently less activist than a modern gay consciousness would like them to be, they become oversimplified and reduced to obvious scenes of contemplation, blackmail and dismay.

Adam Fitzroy's *Make Do and Mend* (2012) demonstrates a contemporary, post-Stonewall desire to re-write the past in more uplifting terms. The novel displays the slowly developing relationship between the protagonist Harry Lyon and the farm labourer Jim Brynawel. Towards the end of the novel, Jim is suspected of murder and in police custody because he does not want to clarify his whereabouts during a time of absence from the Hendra estate. The village vicar and a close friend of the Lyon family named Philip, explains Jim's underlying concerns:

> 'Of course I understand his reasons; homosexual acts are just as illegal as murder, and in some people's eyes the penalty should be no different, but the fact remains that very nearly the only way for Jim to establish his innocence of one crime is to admit to having committed another – which he won't do because it would mean implicating you.' (237)

This scene and the resolving of the murder case in general, places no emphasis on either the victim or the suspect, but on the fact that by revealing that Jim has stayed with Harry in Liverpool, his and Harry's homosexual relationship would become exposed. Harry's reaction to Jim's silence betrays the novel's modern consciousness as well as the protagonist's apparently unconscious derogative use of language: "he's a dear, silly, loyal man, and it looks as if we're going to have to save him from himself" (237). Although meant as a term of endearment, calling Jim a "dear" but "silly, loyal man" emphasises Harry's higher class compared to a farm labourer who loyally fulfils his duties. Harry thus maintains a certain standard that depicts him as superior to his lover. At the same time as undermining a subversive discourse, Harry confronts the solicitor Mr Pugh with his homosexual relationship, whose reaction is surprisingly temperate:

> 'You mean that for a period of some thirty-six hours you were continuously in one another's company – even during the hours of night?'
> 'Yes.' Harry did not elaborate, but nor did he retreat from his position.
> 'Very well. Did anyone see you together during any part of this time?' (250)

As the vicar has rightly identified, homosexual acts where punishable at the time, and Harry's blithe admittance that he and Jim have spent several nights in each other's company situates him and the novel into modern discourse. Moreover, Harry and Mr Pugh's conversation presents the solicitor as open-minded, liberal and anti-homophobic, which seems to contradict the prejudices experienced by Ralph, Laurie and Alec in *The Charioteer* and by Kent in *Look Down in Mercy*. These anachronisms are equally present in the reaction of Harry's brother Jack upon receiving the news that Harry is a homosexual: "bloody hell, Harry, I've been treating the poor man [Jim] as if he was an ordinary labourer" (239). Not only is Jack completely unconcerned by Harry's sexual preference, he finds fault in his own treatment of Jim. Instead of being abjected, Jim becomes elevated above the status of labourer through his relationship with Harry. It seems doubtful that this retroactive and retrospective representation convincingly captures homosexual life in the 1940s, but what it shows is a contemporary gay and lesbian consciousness that feels oppressed by a stigmatised and stigmatising past that leaves little scope for critique on the social system. The active re-writing of this period reveals the need to fashion a genealogy that is free from burdened individuals who can only chose between being outed or becoming murderers when their secret is threatened.

Unlike narratives from the 21st century, pre-Stonewall novels had to disguise critique in more elusive and allusive language. This is particularly evident in *Look Down in Mercy* when Anson reflects on Kent and his first intimate encounter: "it was wrong of course and disapproved of by the vast majority of people, but then so were many things; people, he thought, always disapproved most of what they didn't want to do themselves" (153). Anson evaluates that "the vast majority of people" are homophobic because they do not share homosexuals' desire for male bodies. In Anson's view, intolerance is based on ignorance, but that does not make him despise his feelings for Kent. Rather, Anson displays an indifferent attitude towards the judgment of other people, because they "*always* disapproved" and there is no point getting worked up about it. A further comparison to Harry in *Make Do and Mend* clarifies the astonishing lucidity and sobriety with which Anson perceives sexual deviance. Harry says: "I admit this sort of thing isn't really supposed to happen – it never is, between men – but believe me it does, all the bloody time, and you soon learn to treat it with respect." (186) Both novels refrain from actually naming outlawed sexual preferences and refer to them as a "sort of thing" (*MD*, 186) and "it" (*LD*, 153). *The Charioteer* often adopts military language when addressing homosexuals as "refugees" (*TC*, 305), and *The Night Watch* calls lesbianism "the whole grisly 'L' business" (*TNW*, 274). United in a reluctance of linguistic clarity, the contemporary novels pledge as much hesitance as novels of the time to do justice to their historical setting. *Make Do and Mend* and *Look Down in Mercy* both allude to the time's prejudices and stigmatisation of differences, but Anson more clearly qualifies homosexuality as "wrong" (*LD* 153) rather than simply not "supposed to happen" (*MD* 186) in Harry's display. Harry's challenge to "treat it with respect" (*MD* 186), too, diverts from Anson's attempted explanation that people "disapproved most of what they didn't want to do themselves" (*LD* 153). Clearly, Fitzroy's text speaks from a contemporary mindset that is impatient with discrimination and intolerance. This attitude is most obvious when the vicar, Philip, characterises Harry as a "sensible, well-rounded individual" (*MD* 291), whereas his homophobic and misogynic brother Thomas lacks any noble qualities. This reversal of who and what constitutes a 'sensible individual' – a homosexual is privileged over a conservative heterosexual – substantiates *Make Do and Mend* as a contemporary narrative. Yet, it needs to be recognised that strong self-affirmative roots can be found in the much earlier consciousness of *Look Down in Mercy* when Anson ponders his and Kent's homosexuality in "quite uncomplicated" (*LD* 153) ways.

Moreover, scenes in which characters such as Kent or Laurie show resistance make *Look Down in Mercy* and *The Charioteer* such compelling reads and trouble any straightforward analysis that evaluates them as "homosexual problem novels"[85]. Baxter manages to keep the reader engaged *because* Kent is far from content with his life and his homosexual awakening. A very significant pedagogical value of endurance despite setbacks is inscribed in the text that probably spoke to many homosexual men of the time, especially ex-servicemen who themselves experienced the exceptional circumstances of wartime and faced similar obstacles in their lives. The protagonist's path shows that becoming aware of homosexual desires during the Second World War was possible and the characters Anson and Goodwin illustrate that the odds of homosexuality were higher than the military was prepared to admit. Kent's reaction towards the challenges that come with navigating and negotiating his desires for a man is, admittedly, minted with shortcomings and his murder of Goodwin as well as his sexual assault against Helen preclude a thoroughly positive reading of him. This might account for why the novel is not better known today and the corresponding paucity of critical attention – it is simply not convenient for a modern gay consciousness.

However, characters of both *Look Down in Mercy* and *The Charioteer* criticise society's intolerance, which shows that none of the pre-Stonewall novels discussed here have a categorically negative or positive opinion of homosexuality or represent the whole of their characters as burdened individuals. Instead, it is striking that in earlier novels minor characters such as Anson or Alec often operate as the 'voice of tolerance' or express passionate critique concerning a prejudice society. In this way, novels of the 1950s incorporate challenges in more concealed ways than contemporary representations, which makes them easily misjudged as "not good for the gays". Reader responses to Renault's *The Charioteer* strengthen this argument and show that the novel was perceived as a passionate representation of a largely privatised subject matter. It helped, for instance, a schoolmistress to cope with her friend's suicide: stating that *The Charioteer* "must have lifted the hearts of many who have come up against that problem and its effect", the schoolmistress praises the novel whilst disguising its controversial topic as "that problem and its effect"[86]. Her reluctance to be more explicit, even in a 'fan-letter' to a writer of homosexual fiction illustrates that different forms of sexuality where not named. Renault's relative explicit fictionali-

85 Summers, (1990), p. 26.

86 Sweetman, (1993), p. 149.

sation of this unutterable subject matter reveals the daringness of *The Charioteer* within the context of the early 1950s. Another letter by Gerald Heard, a friend of Christopher Isherwood's, states: "The dialogues are really amazing – as Isherwood said to me, how can an author who must in many respects be 'above the battle' and outside that particular circle of Purgatory understand it so well?"[87] Renault's readership obviously did not share the modern consciousness of gay-affirmation against which Alden judges *The Charioteer*. Heard speaks of the "battle" to simultaneously mean the Second World War, and the conflict between deviating sexuality and heteronormative society. Equally symbolic is the term "Purgatory" – it denotes the hostile environment of the 1950s whilst also suggesting a troubled attitude towards the homosexual subculture that determined many men's (and women's) lives.

Sarah Waters rightly argues that "Renault seeks a model of homosexual conduct, asking not, What is a homosexual?, but, How might one be a decent homosexual"[88]. This question is explicitly addressed by Ralph, who states that "[i]t's not what one is, it's what one does with it." (131) Distinctly, Ralph is *not* troubled by his deviating sexuality, but struggles to find his way to negotiate it within 'normal' society and in tension with its promiscuous subculture. Laurie is admittedly less self-confident when saying: "We sign the warrant for our own exile, he thought. Self-pity and alibis come after." (308) However, the certainty of his homosexuality is not denied – he has signed onto it – but how to perform it and remain 'morally superior' to the flamboyant subculture proves troublesome for both Laurie and Ralph. In order to give Laurie and Ralph something to hold onto, Renault appropriates Plato's *Phaedrus* as a strategy of finding an uplifting love and harmony of the soul, which will be the focus of the following section.

"TEMPER TANTRUM AND JEALOUS SPATS": FASHIONING HOMOSEXUAL RELATIONSHIPS

As Renault's title suggests, *The Charioteer* is saturated with references to Plato's dialogical text *Phaedrus*. Laurie is first introduced to the text by Ralph, who gives him his copy upon being expelled from school. Before presenting the book to Laurie, Ralph warns him that "[i]t doesn't exist anywhere in real life, so don't let it give you illusions. It's just a nice idea." (32) As if to prove his point, the chapter ends with a secretive kiss or an embrace between the characters, indicat-

87 Cited in Sweetman, (1993), p. 149.

88 Waters, (1995), p. 220.

ed, as is characteristic of Renault's allusive writing, by an ellipse: "Come here a moment. ... Now you see what I mean, Spud." (33) Clearly unconvinced by the ideal of Platonic love that is of the mind and not physical, Ralph leaves the plot for now to let Laurie find out his own convictions. The following will analyse Laurie's relationship to both Ralph and Andrew in order to more fully comprehend the external factors that influence homosexuals in their desire to build and maintain a lasting relationship. Not only is Laurie's outlawed desire scrutinised by society, his self-imposed moral standards fashioned after Plato's *Phaedrus* also preclude him from enlightening Andrew about his homosexuality. The *Phaedrus* thus promises a world Laurie is highly attracted to, but which remains out of reach for him.

In Plato's *Phaedrus* Lysias makes an inductive argument for why love is a disadvantage as it maddens the soul and defies reason. Several years after his last encounter with Ralph, Laurie recounts Lysias' speech to Andrew in hospital: "a lover who isn't in love is preferable to one who is. Being less jealous, easier to live with, and generally more civilized." (102) Lysias' model of non-love is illustrated in the depiction of the homosexual subculture that is informed by Renault's own experiences in South Africa, where she associated with many homosexual ex-service men. Sweetman writes that "Mary [Renault] rapidly realized that these young men longed for stable, enduring relationships, yet often found it impossible to create one. She became accustomed to temper tantrums and jealous spats, to broken hearts and threats of suicide."[89] Renault's long-time girlfriend Julie Mullard, who lived with her in South Africa, directly links their homosexual company to Renault's representation in *The Charioteer*, stating that if "Mary" had not "got to know [homosexual ex-servicemen] on very close terms, she would never have been able to write *The Charioteer*"[90].

Renault's dramatisation of these experiences is most evident at a party where her alter-ego Laurie (note that the names Renault and Laurie are almost anagrams) encounters "[*n*]*ous autres*" (305). Nikolai Endres sums up the party as providing a ground for "bitchiness and backbiting, cattiness and camp, pettiness and pretense, drama and desire" – it is a "gay world of immediate consummation and instant gratification, where love is endlessly deferred in the guise of sex"[91]. Laurie stands at a crossroad where he can either renounce this effeminate and flamboyant lifestyle, which would mean turning his back on his childhood idol

89 Sweetman, (1993), p. 129.

90 Zilboorg, (2001), p. 105.

91 Nikolai Endres, "Horses and Heroes: Plato's Phaedrus and Mary Renault's *The Charioteer*" in *International Journal of the Classical Tradition* Vol. 19, No. 3 (2012), p. 154 and p. 155.

Ralph, who latently associates with "[*n*]*ous autres*" or immerse into it. Laurie uses a style of speaking influenced by the military to describe the undesirable hold the homosexual subculture is beginning to have on him: "You get swept along the road with the refugees, till you find you've been carried through the gates without noticing, and you're behind the wire for the duration." (305) Juxtaposing war and homosexual subculture in his rhetoric of "refugees" and "wire", Laurie insinuates that both endanger the human soul. He stigmatises effeminate homosexuals and implicitly makes them responsible for a homophobic society:

> [t]hey [effeminate homosexuals] were specialists. They had not merely accepted their limitations, as Laurie was ready to accept his [...]. They had identified themselves with their limitations; they were making a career of them. (132)

It is not only obvious that "they" "have no life apart from being homosexuals"[92] as Peter Wolfe rightly perceives, but that Laurie is not willing to identify with them. Laurie's aversion is highlighted in the incessant use of the third person plural "they" and his distinct dis-identification notable in the emphasis on his name: "Laurie was ready to accept his". Not only is the protagonist a first person among the rest, he is a name within an anonymous mass and whilst accepting his homosexuality, Laurie is not willing to be associated with those "specialists". In *The Night Watch*, Waters depicts her character Duncan in strikingly similar ways. In prison, Duncan and his cell-mate Fraser encounter the 'prison queens' – a group of homosexuals who impersonate femininity like drag queens onstage. When Fraser implies that his sexual preference puts Duncan in close proximity to these effeminate homosexuals, he loses his temper:

> [Stella] makes me sick. They all do, all that crowd. They don't want to go to bed with girls, but they make themselves like girls. They make themselves worse than girls! They need doctors! I hate them. (432)

Duncan's anger, signalled in short, aggressive sentences, culminating in his cry for doctors, is reminiscent of Laurie's perception of the homosexual subculture. Both characters take the discourse of heteronormativity when they imply the need to medicalise homosexuals. In Duncan's outburst the anonymous group "they" is once more contrasted to Duncan's "me" and "I". Duncan and Laurie feel insulted by the flamboyant homosexuals and are angry over being lumped together with "them".

92 Peter Wolfe, *Mary Renault* (New York: Twayne Publishers, 1969), p. 114.

Their aversion towards effeminate men also illustrates the dichotomy between masculinity and femininity. Connell[93] argues that hegemonic masculinity is based on gender performances, which vary according to situation, time and relation to others whilst nevertheless perpetuating itself as an ideal version men ought to enact.[94] It is therefore highly undesirable for men to deviate from hegemonic masculinity whereas "[d]istancing oneself from stereotypical femininity" is, according to Carrie Paechter, "a claiming of power"[95]. Unlike masculinities, femininities "do not confer cultural power, nor are they able to guarantee patriarchy"[96]. This is due to the fact that there cannot be a hegemonic femininity, "because being in a hegemonic position is also about being in a position of power"[97]. This relates to the dilemma that hegemony and patriarchy mutually inform male dominance and female subordination. Accordingly, female gender performances that most severely distance themselves from hegemonic masculinity, are not considered hegemonic at all but hyperfeminine – "a form of dramaturgical, glamorized femininity"[98] often related to drag queens like Stella, whose "cheeks were rouged, and her lips as red as a girl's" (231). Traditionally the use of make-up and neat hair-style derives from a wish to please men, which amplifies Butler's argument that the dualistic relationship between masculinities and femininities originates from "compulsory heterosexuality"[99]. She argues that "[t]he heterosexualization of desire requires and institutes the production of discrete and asymmetrical oppositions between 'feminine' and 'masculine,' where these are understood as expressive attributes of 'male' and 'female'"[100]. It is not only men's fear of being considered feminine but also their assumed heterosexual desire for it which connects masculinity and femininity in a dualistic position. Homosexual desire is based on similar distinctions between masculinity and femininity where the person performing the former (independent of biological sex)

93 Connell is a transgender woman whose transition from male to female was completed after the first publication of *Masculinities* in 1995. Due to various changes of first names, I will refer to Connell by their last name whenever possible and use 'they' and 'them' to indicate gender fluidity.

94 Connell, (2016), p. 77.

95 Carrie Paechter, "Masculine Femininities/Feminine Masculinities: Power, Identities and Gender" in *Gender and Education* Vol. 18, No. 3 (2006), p. 257

96 Ibid., p. 256.

97 Ibid., p. 256.

98 Ibid., p. 255.

99 Judith Butler, *Gender Trouble: Feminism and the Subversion of Identity*, [1990], (London and New York: Routledge Classics, 2006), p. 24.

100 Ibid., p. 24.

finds pleasure in the latter and vice versa. While Waters' prison queens clearly perform gender in unconventional ways, their hyperfemininity and desire for masculine men paradoxically fixes them according to a conventional system of dualistic genders without changing masculine or feminine qualities. This suggests that heterosexual desire might be the origin of dualistic gender erotisation and performance, but it is not exclusively responsible for its perpetuation.

Laurie's and Duncan's disidentification with the homosexual subculture demonstrates Mimi Schippers' argument that "gay men claim their status as 'real men' by defining their embodiment of a gay identity in relation to [an] inferior feminine form – as a 'straight gay' in relation to effeminate gay men"[101]. While probably not all gay men perform in the way suggested by Schippers, Duncan and Laurie clearly understand themselves as 'straight' rather than 'effeminate' homosexuals. The threat of emasculation is thus as operative on homosexual men as it is on heterosexuals, which highlights emasculation as a powerful mechanism in monitoring the great majority of male bodies regardless of sexual preference. Consequently, Laurie and Duncan use the dynamic between 'us' and 'them' not simply to differentiate their homosexuality from heteronormative society, but more distinctly, to signal themselves as 'morally superior' to the great mass of effeminate homosexuals, who deceive allegiance with masculine standards.

Quentin Crisp's auto-biography *The Naked Civil Servant* (1968), introduced at the outset of this study, alters this perspective when he admits that "homosexuals didn't like me" (87). Crisp's implied 'they' comprises those homosexual men who pass as heterosexuals such as Laurie and Duncan. This group "did not look forward with pleasure to living in a world where the facts about their abnormality would be common knowledge" (87). He explains further that being "outrageously effeminate" (87) constituted the ground for hostility brought against him by fellow queers. *The Charioteer* and *The Night Watch* change the parameters of Crisp's experience: whereas Crisp stresses his effeminacy as unique among homosexuals, these novels dramatise it as common. Whilst Laurie and Duncan stand alone as morally superior protagonists fighting association with the "specialists", Crisp experiences his flamboyancy as exceptional. Consequently, the novels use a highly stigmatised and fabricated group image in order to position their heroes in contradiction to the Other, and to substantiate them as morally superior. Rightly, Alden observes that Laurie's "difference from the effete, histrionic homosexual men, and [his] horror at them [...] is extremely

101 Mimi Schippers, "Recovering the Feminine Other: Masculinity, Femininity, and Gender Hegemony" in *Theory and Society* Vol. 36, No.1 (2007), p. 97.

strongly emphasised"[102]. While I agree that Laurie feels disconnected from the homosexual subculture, Duncan feels no less threatened by the 'prison queens', a detail Alden conveniently overlooks in order to strengthen her overarching argument that past representations of homosexuals are more depressing than contemporary re-writings. Contrary to Alden's claim, both Laurie *and* Duncan display an aversion against collective displays of a homogeneous identity that stigmatises homosexuals, which not only highlights their focus on individuality, but also a textual continuity of addressing it. When Alden sets out to establish Waters lineage with gay and lesbian authors of the past and her appropriation of material, a more fruitful endeavour might be to emphasise Waters' thematic revision of Renault's reluctance to fictionalise a protagonist who surrenders to a damaging image of his desire by uncritically participating in an eccentric subculture.

The homosexual world of sex and promiscuity, criticised by Laurie and Duncan, relates to Lysias' concept of non-love in the *Phaedrus*. Believing himself to be above this permissive subculture, Laurie refuses to identify with this world that "suffers from halves and unbalanced charioteers and roped off wings"[103]. He is searching for a more exhilarating love, and upon hearing that Ralph is expected to join a party, Laurie's hope for it subconsciously reawakens when he ponders: "It was *madness* to have come" (115) [my emphasis]. Informed by the first speech in the *Phaedrus* where love is a form of madness overthrowing the rational mind, Laurie's statement implies a lingering and persuasive love for Ralph. Dressed in the semantics of madness, the text disguises Laurie's true feelings, even from himself. As yet unaware of Socrates' model of the tripartite soul where love is never absolute but multiple and unsteady, Laurie's intellect can only grasp love in terms of Lysias' binary argument. It follows that whilst capable of explaining the first speech of the *Phaedrus* to Andrew, Laurie's recollection of Socrates' response is fractured and concentrates on rhetoric: "Only as the whole thing hangs on the definition of love, [Socrates is] able to turn it inside out in the refutation, which is the highlight of the piece. It —" (102). Emphasising Socrates' move towards a deductive argument to challenge Lysias' claim that love is madness and madness is bad, Laurie breaks into silence. He is incapable of recalling the abstract concept of Socrates' pure love where the soul is split in three pieces: one white horse (self-control), one black horse (desire) and a charioteer (reason). In Greek mythology, only the gods have perfect harmony of the tripartite soul and can live in heaven. The charioteer of the earthly human, however, struggles to keep the horses in lockstep as the black horse is easily distract-

102 Alden, (2014), p. 195.

103 Endres, (2012), p. 161.

ed and disobedient. It does not nourish the soul but feeds the body with pleasure. Fleeting of nature, this pleasure satisfies only the black horse, but leaves the white horse and the charioteer in disharmony. This is why Lysias' non-love, the satisfaction of the body in promiscuous intercourse, is not good for the soul. Platonic love pursuits of a harmony between all parts of the soul and claims that this can be achieved by finding your reflection in the beloved. Laurie reads from his version of the *Phaedrus*: "*... he sees himself in his lover as if in a mirror, not knowing whom he sees*." (100) [emphasis original] When the soul finds harmony, it becomes one with the beloved. Slightly modified, Renault's *The Charioteer* embodies the white horse in Andrew, the black horse in Ralph and Laurie becomes the charioteer, who tries to negotiate his love for them. Having experienced his first kiss with Ralph at school, Laurie's attraction to him is from the outset predominantly physical whereas his conversations with Andrew in the hospital kitchen are intellectual and devoid of bodily desire. Zilboorg rightly argues that Renault's novel illustrates a model of Platonic love where "physical homosexual union is to be refigured as intimate but 'pure' companionship"[104]. Far from renouncing bodily pleasures altogether, Plato's myth is illustrated as a moral choice for Laurie to "fulfil his erotic desires while behaving admirably with worthy companions"[105]. Consequently, the obstacles between the innocent Andrew and Laurie's striving for a harmonic soul that involves the mind *as well as* the body are too grave to ever be overcome. Rapidly Laurie becomes aware that "[t]he lovers of the innocent must protect them above all from the knowledge of their own cruelty" (101). Identifying himself as "the lover" and Andrew as "the innocent", Laurie pledges not to seduce his beloved. He reinforces his good intentions in a conversation with Ralph:

> I think [Andrew] quite likes me, and he mustn't ever know. It would spoil his life, and there's no need. [...] It's much more important he should be all right. [...] The thing about him is, he wouldn't know how to run away from it. (223)

Laurie shoulders the responsibility of concealing his love for Andrew whilst suspecting the young Quaker's own sexual deviance. Unwilling to force self-awareness onto his friend, whom he fears will not be able to handle such knowledge, Laurie suffers heartache in his stead. Consequently, Laurie and Andrew's conversations are for the largest part of the text minted with double discourses. Andrew's innocence and literal understanding of Laurie's careful hints and suggestive language give the text a humoristic, yet tragic, touch. During

104 Zilboorg, (2001), p. 111.

105 Ibid., p. 111.

their first meeting, for example, Laurie tries to evaluate the situation and Andrew's sexual preferences by reference to Tchaikovsky's alleged queerness. But Andrew keeps misunderstanding:

> 'I read somewhere once, Tchaikovsky was queer.' [...]
> 'Was he? I hadn't heard. He was never actually shut up surely?'
> 'No, it never came out. Though I believe' – [Laurie] saw his mistake, and with a painful jolt caught himself up just in time. 'Not mad, you know. Just queer.' [...]
> 'I find all Russians slightly mysterious'. (56)

Familiar with the implication of the term 'queer', Laurie does not stop to think that Andrew might perceive it in very different terms as a mental illness. Realising his mistake "just in time", Laurie tries to be more explicit. His short chopped off sentences – "not mad, you know. Just queer" – betray his own inexperience in flirting and he fails to clarify things for Andrew. In the end Laurie is convinced that Andrew has no understanding of sexuality on a great scale, let alone of homosexuality in particular. After this failed attempt to establish confidentiality, the characters' friendship develops in a perpetual sense of unease trumped by mutual yet innocent affection.

In a different situation, Laurie has to carefully explain why Anson's suggestion to roll up in a rug to keep warm whilst sitting outside is not a sensible idea.

> 'You must think,' Laurie managed, 'that I've a horrible mind. The trouble is, I've got a pretty good idea what the Staff Sergeant's is like.'
> 'Yes,' said Andrew. He swallowed. 'Luckily you thought. Sorry.'
> 'That's the army for you.'
> 'I shouldn't really have been as dumb as that […].' (172)

Similar to playing his classical records in the hospital ward, the two men rolling up in a rug is suspicious beyond measure, and Laurie's acute awareness of the madness of Andrew's suggestion takes his breath away for some time before he can "manage" an explanation. Unable to fully pronounce the reason for his objection, Laurie flounders and saves himself by alluding to the strict conduct of the military hospital. He leaves distinctly open if "the Staff Sergeant" would suspect indecent behaviour between the men, or if his objection would concern Andrew's pacifism in combination with his association with a soldier. As a conscientious objector, Andrew's friendship to the soldier Laurie often breeds more resentment than the fact that they are of the same sex. This is evident when they encounter Mrs. Chivers – an old woman who allows the hospital patients to relax in her garden. Laurie and Andrew call this garden their "private Eden" (73). In Christian belief, the Garden of Eden is a paradisiacal place of innocence and the use of it in this context underscores the characters' innocent relationship and sanctifies Laurie's homosexuality. Upon realising that Andrew is not a soldier but a conscientious objector, Mrs. Chivers transforms into a "serpent" (73) and breaks into a torrent of hatred: "Get away with you out of my garden, it's no place for the likes of you." (79) Her anger originates not from Laurie's homosexuality, of which she is ignorant, but from Andrew's pacifism, which clearly indicates the Second World War as a time where society was preoccupied with the war and often disinterested in people's sexualities as long as it remained hidden from public discourse. Behind this backdrop, it becomes clear why Laurie's comrades remain unaware of his homosexuality even when it appears to be obvious: the war directs their attention to more pressing matters than sexuality. The nurses even call Andrew and Laurie "David and Jonathan" (209) – a reference to homoeroticism – but no-one seems to suspect their bond to go deeper than mere friendship.[106]

After several more strained conversations between Andrew and Laurie, the charioteer realises that however great his love might be for Andrew, their friendship will continuously be "falsified by what had been left out" (305). True to his convictions that preclude sexual openness with Andrew, Laurie indulges in the experienced Ralph, who fosters Laurie's latent desire of finding a relationship that is not only of the mind, but also physical. Similar to their kiss at the beginning of the novel, Ralph and Laurie's first sexual encounter remains inexplicit and marked by a spare line in the text.[107] Afterwards, Laurie is troubled by his

106 One scene implies that Laurie's friend Reg might be less unaware of Laurie's homosexuality than he pretends to be. After a private conversation in the hospital bathroom, Laurie holds the door open for Reg to leave, but Reg hesitates: "Oh, no, but *no*, [Laurie] thought in helpless protest: it really was, at last, too much; suddenly it collapsed into an outrageous joke. He stood in the doorway and rocked with laughter. 'But it's —' he gasped, He gazed at Reg and imagined him creeping coyly out after a discreet delay, like a *femme galante* at a house-party. It was excruciating." (213) Reg's reluctant behaviour and Laurie's interpretation thereof suggests that Reg might know of his friend's sexuality and fears that the other patients might judge their friendship as suspect. Laurie is annoyed and disappointed in his friend, who is more worried about what people think of him than about his loyalty to Laurie. However, the novel never mentions any further scenes that might reveal the extent of Reg's actual knowledge beyond Laurie's own interpretation.

107 Renault comments in her "Afterword" to *The Friendly Young Ladies*: "I have always been as explicit as I wanted to be [...]. If characters have come to life, one should

actions whilst Ralph is sound asleep. Laurie compares his sexual desire, which had gradually stirred in him since meeting Ralph at the party, to "animals [that] move toward water over miles of bush" (291). Disturbed by the loss of control over his mind when giving into his desiring body, Laurie feels remorse over his animalistic action. Worse, now that he has experienced the pleasure of intercourse, "he knew, and must go on knowing" (291) for the rest of his life that he cannot fulfil all of his desires on a mental basis. In consequence, he now realises that his friendship with Andrew is foredoomed. Despite these regrets, there is a conciliatory tone to the passage when it ends with Laurie slightly touching Ralph's fair hair: "Ralph's eyes opened. They were smiling, and with fear Laurie saw in how deep a happiness, too silent and too deep, eating like rust the core of his defenses." (292) Ralph's smile conquers Laurie's wall of self-protection and he realises that the homosexual subculture with which he does not want to associate, and which constitutes the "it" (223) Andrew will not be able to run away from, is not determining each of his sexual romances – that a homosexual has more choices than sexual abstinence or promiscuity.

However, the gay subculture – the black horse, the desiring body – are not so easily tamed and struggle back when Bunny (impersonating his ex-lover Ralph) discloses Laurie's true feelings and sexuality to Andrew in an act of vengeance for losing Ralph to Laurie. Overwhelmed and confused, Andrew rushes to London where he takes up dangerous ambulance service – possibly to kill himself and his painful awareness that Laurie's homosexuality is a reflection of his own feelings. When Laurie travels to London to ease his friend's heart, Dave (Andrew's father figure) advises him to leave the boy in peace. Taking Dave's advice, Laurie only leaves his copy of the *Phaedrus* behind. Ultimately, Laurie's sacrifice is self-reflective – the incessant need to live as a 'moral' homosexual and to prove to himself, to the homosexual subculture and to heteronormative society that neither will determine his fate, has left Laurie bereft of the one person who could have shared his ideal of Platonic love. In the *Phaedrus*, Socrates concludes that harmony of the soul can be achieved when the lover and the beloved are one in their reflections: but Laurie never achieves to see himself in Andrew because he cannot sacrifice the boy's innocence. Instead, he betrays his convictions when he returns to Ralph and gives in to the black horse. In the last paragraph of *The Charioteer* it says:

> Quietly, as night shuts down the uncertain prospect of the road ahead, the wheels sink to stillness in the dust of the halting place, and the reins drop from the driver's loosened

know how they will make love; if not it doesn't matter." Renault, "Afterword", (2014), p. 324.

hands. [...] They are far, both of them, from home, and lonely, and lengthened by their strife the way has been hard. Now their heads droop side by side till their long manes mingle; and when the voice of the charioteer falls silent they are reconciled for a night in sleep. (347)[108]

The Charioteer displays no happy ending considering that "both of them [were far] from home, and lonely" (347). Laurie has not managed to fulfil all of his desires and both Laurie and Ralph feel lonely in each other's company. The charioteer has lost control of the horses and "loosen[s]" his grip at which the horses embrace "for a night in sleep". Laurie and Ralph share *one* night together which indicates that their love is not eternal. Aptly Endres questions: "Ralph and Laurie are reconciled for a night in sleep, but what does the morning after hold?"[109] Considering this vague ending, I partly disagree with Summers, who contradicts his earlier reading of *The Charioteer* as a "homosexual problem novel[...]" when concluding that Renault's novel is ultimately "optimistic, and in its optimism it is subversive of the 1950s sexual ideology that would condemn homosexuals to unhappiness"[110]. Laurie's dissatisfaction in his relationship with Ralph challenges Summers' positive reading. Instead, *The Charioteer* movingly demonstrates the fate of homosexuals, who try to live 'moral' lives in a society that scrutinises their desires. Laurie is destined to become Ralph's lover for now because Andrew is not yet ready to face the truth. However, they "reconciled for *a* night in sleep": the novel leaves open what might happen in the morning. Possibility and chance are not devastated through closure, and the novel's sad ending is not finite, which is indeed "subversive of the 1950s sexual ideology".

Fitzroy's *Make Do and Mend* (2012) appears to be a contemporary revisiting of the *Phaedrus* myth and a remodelling of Renault's hesitant ending, where the modern version of Laurie (Harry) enlightens the contemporary Andrew (Jim) and they live 'happily ever after'. Moreover, *Make Do and Mend* exaggerates Renault's display of the homosexual subculture in the figure of Clive Campbell-Ainslie – an antagonist who represents the dark side of both homosexuality and the black market. "[Clive] would barter sexual favours for goods with [sailors], and later on would barter those self-same goods for different sexual favours with

108 Renault paraphrases Plato's *Phaedrus* in this scene. This is formally indicated by not italicising this paragraph which distinguishes it from other quotes directly taken from the *Phaedrus*. Endres analyses other scenes and compares them to Plato's text in order to reveal where Renault takes liberties to divert from the original. For more information see Endres, (2013), p. 161.

109 Endres, (2012), p. 161.

110 Summers, (1990), p. 170.

other people [...] the black market had never been quite so black." (182) Whereas in Renault's party chapter the seedy element of the "underground" (*TC* 199) gathers to exchange sexual favours for moments of company, Clive transfers sexual promiscuity into economic use. In both depictions Lysias' non-love is clearly privileged, but Clive more forcefully focuses on rationality to process transactions – to him, only a non-love can provide economic profit.

Harry is accustomed to these transactions and willing to perform them in order to buy Christmas presents for the women working at his farm. When Clive demands his 'pay', the text gives insight into how black the black market has become: "Don't undress, Clive instructed him, coldly. You won't be here long enough. I'll just have your mouth this time, I think." (178) The black market can be read as an allegory to the black horse in Plato's *Phaedrus* and when Harry gets involved in it, he plunges to the ground. In a commanding tone, Clive not only emasculates and objectifies Harry he also fractures his body when saying "I'll just have your mouth". When *The Charioteer* depicts homosexual promiscuity as morally condemnable, *Make Do and Mend* dramatises its threat to the soul as well as to the body – a modification that might be informed by the knowledge over the HIV/AIDS crisis, which so distinctly revealed the real physical threat homosexual men would come to encounter. No longer bodily whole, Harry becomes almost a machine: "Moving dispassionately, as if deploying some soulless piece of equipment, Clive positioned Harry on the bed, his head hanging back over the edge, and stood over him feeding him hot, stale flesh." (179) Harry's head seems separated from his body and becomes the sole emphasis of Clive's impassionate transaction. The text continues in great detail to describe Clive's expression of power over Harry, climaxing in the depersonalising of the characters by focusing on the institutions they represent: "the RAF, fucking the Navy" (179). Harry reflects that wearing different uniforms satisfies Clive even more because subordination is always most effective when more than one factor combines. Harry is emasculated, objectified and bodily fractured, all of which can be transferred onto the Navy and its oppression by the RAF. As the initiator of this subordination Clive feels vastly empowered.

While "[a]t first it was all usage and being used" (179), Harry cannot sustain self-control over his own desiring body. Gradually he begins to enjoy Clive's seduction and identifies with his own objectification and bodily destruction. The expressive language – "accepting the spasming ejaculation as if through a feeding tube directly into his stomach" (179) – borders on pornography and locates *Make Do and Mend* most definitely as a novel of the 21st century, where texts are no longer censored for indecency. Despite this apparent difference to *The Chari-*

oteer where Renault stays far away from making sexual contact explicit, Harry echoes Laurie's remorse after sleeping with Ralph when he realises that:

> a cerebral, academic man [like Jim] who lived a life of the mind would surely be unwilling to subject himself to the vagaries of carnal desire. Indeed, it would probably be better to forget about Jim altogether [...]. Harry's world, regrettably, contained more facsimiles of Clive than it ever would of Jim. (180)

The similarity between Laurie's and Harry's protective attitudes towards their innocent lovers is remarkable. Even their conclusion to renounce their attraction in order to save Andrew and Jim is identical at this point. However, *Make Do and Mend* opts for a different solution to the *Phaedrus* dilemma and has Harry and Jim reconcile in the end. Ultimately, self-knowledge is bliss to Harry and ought to be encouraged because he and Jim "could be closer if [Jim] was willing to allow it" (164) – a thought that would never cross Laurie's mind. Whereas *The Charioteer* portrays self-knowledge as an unnecessary burden on Andrew, *Make Do and Mend* considers it a positive path towards self-fulfilment. Consequently, Jim takes initiative and says to Harry: "I need to know, once and for all, who I really am; I need you to show me, if you can." (189) Jim's repetition of the first person "I" emphasises his personal desire for knowledge and protects Harry from being charged as a seducer. Whereas Laurie actively restrains Andrew's development and maturity, Fitzroy's character demands to become enlightened. At this point, the narratives diverge as Harry, unlike Laurie, becomes able to envision a relationship that satisfies bodily and mental pleasures with his beloved.

Harry and Jim's first sexual encounter betrays none of the dirty-mindedness explicit in Clive when the text stays clear from detail and suffices in describing a kiss: "And Harry turned his face up towards Jim's, pulling him closer, and the kiss happened somehow although he was never sure exactly how." (189) Clearly differentiating their love-making from Clive's promiscuity, Harry and Jim's relationship seems to envision the harmony of the tripartite soul. *Make Do and Mend* does not have the charioteer reconcile with the black horse as in Renault's novel, but risks the moment of self-awareness to allow for Harry to attain a more innocent yet equally physical love. Having momentarily turned his back on morality, Fitzroy's charioteer does not need to sacrifice himself, but highlights that Harry "had been immeasurably improved by knowing Jim" (294), which illustrates Socrates' argument that the lover sees himself in the beloved for the benefit of both. Concluding on a modern note of equality, Harry pledges that the "gender of the partner" (295) is irrelevant for finding true love.

Regardless of Harry and Jim's satisfaction with their situation, I claim that *Make Do and Mend* is compromising in a different way – not in terms of self-pity or by settling for the black horse, but in its depiction of homosexuality as heterosexuality's abjected Other relegated to the border of society. The novel ends in an epilogue where Jim and Harry celebrate their happiness and the marriage of Harry's brother Jack to Kitty, one of the women working at Hendra. After the ceremony, Harry and Jim go to the remote farm where Jim lives and find it cleaned with a fire waiting to be lit and a note saying:

Dear Jim and Harry [...]
There was enough mixture left over to make an extra little cake, which we thought you might appreciate – and you'll find a bottle of Thomas's [sic] champagne chilling in your sink (We've got the other one with us!) Promise to drink our health tonight, and we'll promise to drink yours ...
All our love,
Your affectionate brother and sister
Jack and Kitty Lyon. (294) [emphasis original]

While the rest of the village is unaware of Jim and Harry's love, Jack and Kitty know and receive it in an uncharacteristically positive way given that the novel is set during the Second World War. Apart from that, it seems significant that this scene is displayed in the epilogue making it literally 'other' to the rest of the novel. The letter suggests that Harry and Jim's romantic intimacy is a distorted image of Jack and Kitty's public wedding, emphasised in the smaller cake and the leftover champagne. Jim and Harry stay on the remote farm, in the little cottage where their difference does not affect 'decent' citizens whereas the newlywed couple "set[s] off for the railway station" with "[m]ost of the village [...] scatter[ing] flower petals as they went" (290). In contrast to Jack and Kitty's open display of their love, Harry and Jim remain hidden. While *Make Do and Mend* represents homosexuality in modern terms as a choice, the separation of Jim and Harry's romantic evening from Kitty and Jack's marriage in form and content perpetuates homosexuality as a deviance that needs to be assimilated into heteronormative discourse in order to control it. Wendy Brown argues:

The very invocation of tolerance [...] indicates that something contaminating or dangerous is at hand, or something foreign is at issue, and the limits of tolerance are determined by how much of this toxicity can be accommodated without destroying the object, value, claim or body. Tolerance appears, then, as a mode of incorporation and regulating the presence of the threatening Other within.[111]

Instead of filling the text with double discourses to destabilise dominant language and knowledge as done in *The Charioteer*, Fitzroy's novel represents a neat space for homosexuality. By appearing as an uncloseted couple, Jim and Harry pose no threat to heteronormative society, as they become distinguishable into new categories and a different discourse that cannot threaten 'the norm'. No longer indefinable, people can finally lay to rest their issues with Harry being unmarried and Jim being a stranger within the village. Fizroy's ending has an unsatisfactory tone of re-establishing order and the dominance of 'civilised society'. Whereas characters such as Laurie try to live within homophobic society and constantly erode its alleged superiority simply by being a stranger within, Jim and Harry are relegated to the borders – to the rural farm hut where they get fed with leftovers. The characters' sexuality seems to determine their lives in the most fundamental way so that they become utterly reduced to it.

Unlike Harry and Jim, Laurie is primarily a human being before he is a homosexual, a soldier, a cripple, a son and a lover. This combination of identities makes *The Charioteer* a much more compelling, authentic and liberating read than *Make Do and Mend. Look Down in Mercy*, too, becomes enthralling because Kent cannot resist his desires at a time and in a position that could endanger his life. The emotional setbacks and his cruel attitude towards both Helen and Anson persuasively narrate the struggle of living a secret. There is never a truly positive or negative affect on the reader regarding the novels of the 1950s, but always a mixture of both and many more. In this way *The Charioteer* and *Look Down in Mercy* compare to Waters' *The Night Watch*, which also depicts characters who are aware of their homosexuality whilst trying to live with and beyond it. Consequently, Alden's conclusion that "*The Charioteer* is the story of Laurie's progress towards entering a relationship with a man; [whereas] *The Night Watch* is the story of individual women for whom sexual orientation is only one part of their identity" seems questionable.[112] Both novels as well as Baxter's narrative resist any form of essential identity shared by one group. Instead, the most contemporary novel, *Make Do and Mend*, seems to reduce its characters to their sexuality.

111 Wendy Brown, *Regulating Aversions: Tolerance in the Age of Identity and Empire* (Princeton: Princeton University Press, 2006), p. 27

112 Alden, (2014), pp. 197-198.

THE INVISIBLE STRUGGLE: REFURBISHING A GHOSTLY PAST

I have thus far analysed why novels of the 1950s cannot be categorised as homophobic or self-damaging according to a contemporary mindset. This debate was evoked by Alden's critical evaluation of pre-Stonewall novels, especially Renault's *The Charioteer*, and her reading of Waters' *The Night Watch* as a more positive appropriation of the past. I shall now return to *The Night Watch* in order to evaluate the novel's investment in and refurbishment of the invisible homosexual past by means of examining the characters Duncan and Kay, who both struggle to find their place in post-war London and develop an attachment to bygone times. Waters resolves their plight in two ways: depicting Duncan's homosexual identity formation and consequential liberation from Mr Mundy (his former prison guard), whereas Kay stays firmly attached to the memory of the war years. Figuratively, *The Night Watch* seems to suggest that there is not one 'true' approach to historiography – that our perception of the past is always imbued with a contemporary consciousness. Transferred to the perspective of a queer historiography, this might imply that there is more than one queer story to be told that opens vast readings of a colourful and not singularly oppressing past. A refurbishment of gay and lesbian figures or a genealogy between pre- and post-Stonewall writers will therefore always be troubled by incongruities. These frictions, as dramatised in the varying character developments of Duncan and Kay, need to be recognised by the gay and lesbian community in order to reclaim a past that is heterogeneous and might not unproblematically suit a contemporary (political) self-understanding.

The Night Watch begins in 1947 when the war is over and people have disposed of their wartime identities and returned to 'regular' life. At this point in the novel, the reader is unaware of the characters' pasts because Waters' backward narrative, beginning in 1947 and ending in 1941, compels the reader to constantly revisit and re-evaluate the text and its characters. Through its form and narrative structure, *The Night Watch* challenges any perception of a stable identity and instead reveals that fluidity and transformation constitute life. In this way, the novel dramatises modern queer theory[113], where the concept of a stable

113 The term 'queer theory' was initially coined by Theresa De Lauretis in 1990 in the course of a conference held at the University of California. She also used the term in the accompanying issue *Differences: a Journal of Feminist Cultural Studies*. In her "Introduction" De Lauretis explains that "'Queer Theory' conveys a double emphasis – on the conceptual and speculative work involved in discourse production, and

identity is challenged in favour of identity formation. Thomas S. Weinberg defines identity formation as "a dynamic social process that involves a variety of possible sequences of stages through which a person passes while seeking to construct a credible and acceptable definition of his self"[114]. By thus moving away from static identity politics that seek to gather and categorise diverse sexualities under umbrella terms, queer theory has established fluidity and diversity in society. However, Leo Bersani rightly asserts that "by rejecting the whole concept of identity – we risk participating in the homophobic project that wants to annihilate us"[115]. Consequently, when arguing for a character's identity constructed on the basis of sexuality, we need to distinguish between heteronormatively *assigned* identities following the essentialist notion of a knowable and unchangeable self, and a non-heteronormativly *negotiated* self-understanding that seems to, albeit still controlled by discourse, refuse stability in the terms assumed by patriarchy. Duncan's identity formation illustrates that characters can come to reject a conscious perpetuation of a heteronormative identity by accepting their difference. When Duncan liberates himself from social standards, he also begins to conceptualise a life free from Mr Mundy, a former prison guard who took Duncan in and symbolises Duncan's imprisonment in the past.

Although no longer behind bars, Duncan persistently identifies as a social outcast. The official verdict for his imprisonment in 1941 was attempted suicide to escape military service, but his homosexuality, which was also punishable by law, remains a latent factor for his fate. After the war Duncan has moved from the prison into a candle factory "for invalids and charity cases" (18-19) where the sound of the "whistle" (82) determines his day. The reference to medical disorder in connection with the factory and Duncan's occupation at such a place is significant. The war and post-war years were a period of disorder not only dis-

on the necessary critical work of deconstructing our own discourses and their constructed silences." (iv) 'Queer' was intended to "mark a certain critical distance from" (iv) the distinct terms 'gay' and 'lesbian' or their juxtaposition in 'gay and lesbian', 'lesbian and gay' in order to "avoid all these fine distinctions in our discursive protocols, not to adhere to any one of the given terms, not to assume their ideological liabilities, but instead to both transgress and transcend them – or at the very least problematize them." (v) Theresa De Lauretis, "Queer Theory: Lesbian and Gay Sexualities An Introduction" in *Differences: a Journal of Feminist Cultural Studies* Vol. 3, No. 2 (1991), pp. iiix–viii.

114 Thomas S. Weinberg, *Gay Men, Gay Selves: The Social Construction of Homosexual Identity* (Virginia: Irvington Publishers, 1983), p. 1.

115 Leo Bersani, *Homos* (Cambridge and London: Harvard University Press, 1995), p. 42.

tinguishable in architectural damage, but also written on the male body. Whereas the bodies of returning soldiers were shattered by the war, Duncan, who never saw combat, is physically healthy but characterised by a childlike dependency on Mr Mundy. The constant narration of Duncan as "a boy like him" (127) projects infantile innocence and naivety onto him and hampers his ability to live an autonomous life. Having existed in a routine outside of his making since the beginning of the war, Duncan feels anxiety over any hint of freedom and is wary of the consequences "waiting for him at home" – referring to Mr Mundy. Consequently, even as a free man the prison continues to constitute Duncan's existence because he subordinates to a former prison guard and to the factory routine.

Duncan's obsession with the past is substantiated in his collection of old objects that the war takes from bombed out houses and scatters over London for Duncan to find and carefully place on the shelves in Mr. Mundy's house. Katharina Boehm reads these objects as symbolising a "desire to connect with the past in a creative and fanciful manner"[116] without appropriating it into the terms of the present. Boehm follows Bill Brown's "thing theory"[117] and claims that

> The object in its irreducible thingliness becomes a middle ground, or a third term, that enables the imaginative negotiation of relations between past and present while safeguarding the autonomy of the past against the cultural preoccupations of the present."[118]

While this reading is intriguing in its focus on the object as an autonomous thing, and Boehm's perception of the mutual touch between subject and object integrates with my reading, I believe the consequences for Duncan and his role as collector to go further than Boehm suggests. Instead of just connecting with the past, Duncan is trapped by it, which is equally highlighted by Fraser, Duncan's former prison cellmate, during a conversation with Duncan's sister Viv:

> I think he has got stuck. I think, he's made himself be stuck, as a way of – of punishing himself, for all that happened, years ago [...]. I think Mr Mundy is taking very good care to keep him stuck; [...] I don't think anyone else is doing anything to, as it were, unstick him. All that fascination of his with things from the past, for instance. (126-127)

116 Katharina Boehm, "Historiography and the Material Imagination in the Novels of Sarah Waters" in *Studies in the Novel* Vol. 43, No. 2 (2011), p. 247.

117 Bill Brown, "Thing Theory" in *Critical Inquiry* Vol. 28, No. 1 (2001).

118 Boehm, (2011), p. 247.

Fraser's constant repetition of the word "stuck" lays emphasis on Duncan's immobility which, in the end, he directly identifies with his obsession with abandoned or lost objects from the past. The additional reference to Mr Mundy who "keep[s] him stuck" and Viv who does not try to "unstick him" reveals Duncan's dependence on other people and substantiates his constant perception as a "boy" – all of which indicating that Duncan is not living in the present but continues to be stuck in the past of which his objects are symbolic.

Fraser not only points out Duncan's desperate situation, he also involuntarily triggers a sense of desire in Duncan to free himself from his past and his objects. After their random meeting at the factory, the former prison mates renew their friendship, but when Fraser fails to show up one evening, Duncan is left insecure and devastated. In consequence of his friend's absence, Duncan parts with his usual bedtime routine, which ordinarily involves "looking over the pots and jars and ornaments, the teaspoons and tear-bottles, picking them up and delighting in them all over again; thinking about where they'd come from and who'd owned them before" (162). This routine agrees with Boehm's reading and emphasises Duncan's attitude towards his objects as things telling their own story of the past vastly different from the present and knowable only through imagination and touch. "But he looked at it all, tonight, without much interest." (162)

> He briefly picked up the bit of clay pipe he'd found on the beach by the riverside pub, that was all. He put his pyjamas on slowly, buttoning the jacket, then tucking it tidily into the trousers. He cleaned his teeth, and combed his hair again – combed it differently this time, making it neat, putting a parting in it like a child's. He was very aware, as he did all this, of Mr Mundy waiting patiently in the room next door; he pictured him lying very still and straight, his head propped up on feather pillows, the blankets drawn up to his armpits, his hands neatly folded, but ready to pat the side of the bed, invitingly, when Duncan went in … It wasn't much. It was almost nothing. Duncan thought of other things. There was a picture, hanging over Mr Mundy's bed: a scene of an angel, safely leading children over a narrow, precipitous bridge. He'd look at that until it was over. He'd look at the complicated folds in the angle's gown; at the children's large, innocent-spiteful Victorian faces.
>
> He put down his comb and picked up the bit of clay pipe again; and this time touched it to his mouth. […] He opened his eyes – and at once met his own gaze in the mirror. His hair was combed in its neat white parting, his pyjama jacket buttoned up to the chin; but he wasn't a boy. (162-163)

The relationship between Duncan and Mr Mundy alludes to ancient Greek culture where men are said to spend some time of their lives involved with other men of younger age.[119] Instead of identifying these men as homosexuals, "truth and sex were linked, in the form of pedagogy, by the transmission of a precious knowledge from one body to another; sex served as a medium for initiations into learning."[120] Homosexual sex acts did consequently not determine a sexual identity, but rather a person's gender identity: "In ancient Greece, males who engaged in same-sex acts changed, as they aged, from feminine to masculine roles."[121] Since Duncan is the boy, he is emasculated compared to the older and arguably more mature Mr Mundy. During intercourse, Duncan looks at the Victorian painting to distract himself from the old man's obscene touch "until it was over". The "it" that is "almost nothing" and in any case "wasn't much", reveals Duncan's inability to properly reflect on his relationship of dependence with Mr Mundy. The painting, which is the only thing Duncan can recall from their intimate moments, transforms the old man into a two-faced angel – at once kind and helpful when giving Duncan a place to stay (or "safely leading children over a narrow, precipitous bridge"), but also ridden with "complicated folds" unnoticed by the carefree observer. The Victorian children are equally troubling in their symbolic significance: they may stand for the relationship between Duncan and Mr Mundy, where the former is the innocent young boy and the latter the spiteful old man expecting sexual favours for his kindness and hospitality.

In the end it is the "clay pipe" and its touch on Duncan's mouth which liberates him from his attachment to Mr Mundy. The "it" that Duncan did not dare to name earlier is no longer anonymous but directly associated with the old man whom Duncan sends "to hell" (163). Whereas the objects on the shelf of Mr Mundy's old childhood bedroom entrap Duncan in the past, touching the clay pipe that reminds him of Fraser with whom he had found it, liberates him from his boyishness. This transformation is enhanced through his reflection in the mirror and the awareness that the boy, who Mr Mundy sees in him, is not the man Duncan wants to be. "He was twenty-four, and could do what he liked." (163) Suddenly, "[t]he world seemed full, to him, of extraordinary new things" (165). Duncan is no longer entrapped by the past through his collection of old objects, but open for "new things" and ready to move into the future. He manages to break free from these things through the indirect touch of Fraser – a touch which sustainably alters Duncan's self-perception and "[h]e messed up the parting in

119 Anne Fausto-Sterling, *Sexing the Body: Gender Politics and the Construction of Sexuality* (New York: Basic Books New York, 2000), p. 14.

120 Michel Foucault, *The Will to Knowledge: The History of Sexuality: 1*, [1976], (London: Penguin Books, 1998), p. 61.

121 Fausto-Sterling, (2000), p. 14. For further information revisit Fausto-Sterling's cartoon (Figure 1).

his hair." (163) Although Duncan is free to gaze into the future to fashion an independent life, Waters' approach to the past is not always resolved by turning towards the future. In fact, the backward narrative structure itself seems to foreclose a reading of progressivity in order to more decisively reclaim an invisible lesbian history.

Terry Castle criticises that the refurbishment of a homosexual past is not equal for men and women. In contrast to homosexual men like Duncan, lesbian woman often remain "in the shadows, in the margins, hidden from history" dominated by the male homosexual who, despite his marginal social position, contains in his male body the potential for masculine power.[122] In her work on *The Apparitional Lesbian*, Castle further states that "[t]o try to write the literary history of lesbianism is to confront, from the start, something ghostly: an impalpability, a misting over, an evaporation, or 'whiting out' of possibility"[123]. In this way, the male homosexual tradition has "both subverted historical master narratives and substantially overlapped with them"[124]. Positioned simultaneously in conflict and in marriage with patriarchal structures, "masculine privileges"[125] remain situated within the male homosexual realm of power or wedded to performances that idealise masculinity. It follows that while male homosexual historiography can "confidently and nostalgically [look] to the homophile communities of classical Greece, ancient Rome, Persia and Renaissance Europe", lesbian scholars in their "search for lesbian originals" are confined to the poetess Sappho of Lesbos.[126] Mary Renault's character Ralph Lanyon pointedly lists a number of historical figures who are, but for one exception, male: "Plato, Michelangelo, Sappho, Marlowe; Shakespeare, Leonard, and Socrates if you count the bisexuals" (178). It is evidently easy enough to search for and find prominent male homosexuals, but lesbian desire often remains invisible.

Waters' novel not only criticises the difficult contemporary perception of lesbianism as well as its historic invisibility, she also emphasises the psychological impact invisibility, or being differently visible, has on subjects. At the beginning of *The Night Watch*, Kay is described as "haunt[ing] the attic floor like a

122 Terry Castle, *The Apparitional Lesbian: Female Homosexuality and Modern Culture* (New York, Columbia University Press, 1993), p. 2.

123 Castle, (1993), p. 28.

124 Laura Doan and Sarah Waters, "Making Up Lost Time: Contemporary Lesbian Writing and the Invention of History" in David Alderson and Linda R. Anderson (eds.), *Territories of Desire in Queer Culture: Refiguring Contemporary Boundaries* (Manchester: Manchester University Press, 2000), p. 12.

125 Ibid., p. 12.

126 Ibid., p. 13.

ghost or a lunatic" (4), which places her in line with Castle's analysis of lesbian invisibility. The flat in which Kay lives "was nothing to her but a place in which to sleep or to lie sleepless" (5). When everyone else is beginning to rebuild homes, Kay has become emotionally homeless and walks the streets of London aimlessly and lonesome, not noticing and unnoticed by other people crossing her path. Kay has become an invisible lesbian, struggling with the return of peace-time heteronormativity, because "the apparent freedoms of wartime are not sustained with the return of peace" [127]. Kay is no longer recognised as a strong woman since the ground on which she is standing now is different from that of the early 1940s. No longer claiming the public streets of London as her workplace, Kay has no purpose in life and no position that awards her with recognition.

In contrast to Kay, her ex girlfriend Julia Standing becomes the apparitional and assimilated lesbian after the war when she dresses up in feminine fashion for a photograph to promote her latest novel. Wearing make-up and lipstick, she turns out looking rather "*marriageable*" (146) [emphasis original]. Julia's heteronormative visibility illustrates the paradoxical position of lesbians in society: when being recognised as "marriageable", Julia's lesbianism becomes invisible. In contrast to both Kay and Julia, Helen looks "like pressed meat" (47), "*like a lovely onion*" (51) [emphasis original]. Helen, who used to date men before meeting Kay and Julia, portrays bisexuality as the most damaging social position that resides between lesbianism and heterosexuality. Her insecurities are reinforced when Julia, her current partner, begins spending more time with her publisher Ursula, whom Helen describes as looking "neat, moneyed, tailored" (56), not at all like a "lovely onion". Battling her jealousy of this woman who successfully combines the distinct spheres of heterosexuality and lesbianism in her appearance, Helen wishes she could transform her inner torments and ambiguous social position into intelligible marks on her body:

> For a burn or a cut might be shown, might be nursed, might scar or heal, would be a miserable kind of emblem; would anyway be *there*, on the surface of her body, rather than corroding it from within (153) [emphasis original].

Helen tries to use her body as a space for protest but fails to do so because "the slicing was too precise" (155) and "[t]he edges of flesh were already closing" (155). Unable to produce a cut that signifies the depth of her emotions, Helen is overpowered by her own body. This moment of attempted self-destruction re-

127 Victoria Stewart, The Second World War in Contemporary British Fiction: Secret Histories (Edinburgh: Edinburgh University Press, 2011) p. 128.

calls a long and tragic history of self-inflicted injuries by people who cannot find their place in society.

Whereas the initial representation of Kay as a ghost substantiates the narrative of invisible lesbianism, *The Night Watch* develops a more diverse picture when Kay voluntarily stays attached to the war years. Waters thus re-writes the negative implication of the invisible lesbian and invests Kay with positive feelings towards the past in order to emphasise the relevance of lives like hers. When visiting her friend Mickey after the war, Kay is shown to repeatedly recall the war when she used to enjoy herself with a group of lesbian friends. Yet, it turns out that the gin slings she recalls drinking with them during happier times had instead been gin gimlets. "The fact that she'd misremembered before – misremembered to the extent that she'd been able to picture Mickey actually cutting up the lemons, squeezing out the juice – made her uneasy." (109) Kay's 'memory' of real lemons during war bespeaks the nostalgia with which she recalls that time when she was still happy with her girlfriend Helen. That Kay already begins to forget what had happened only two years ago additionally shows that looking back is always a form of narration and becoming aware of this has an uneasy effect on those who misremember. A sense of truth is turned into fiction, and the mind's capacities are put into question.

Kay's appeal to women is equally gone with the emergence of peace. During one of her laborious walks, Kay tries to flirt with a girl – "[t]he girl, however, wasn't much good" (34) because she does not understand Kay's small talk as flirtatious. The girls careful dress code and her high heels present a constant site for comment to Kay who wonders, how the girl "can go so fast, in heels so high" to which the girl replies "carelessly" (34): "One gets into the habit, I suppose" (34). The girl's "careless" response suggests that she does not question why she is wearing high heels but regards it as possibly the latest trend after years of grovel on the streets and austerity where flat shoes were a necessity. Kay's emphasis that the shoes were not ordinary high heels but "heels *so* high" further suggests that the girl is wearing especially high ones, hinting towards the impending Barbie image of femininity that would become increasingly established and popular within the next centuries.[128] This indicts femininity as a manufactured product in the competitive system of heteronormative reproduction during the post-war period where few men returned and many women had survived, which boosts the sexual economy of the post-war era. The selection process was in favour of men who had a large number of potential mates to choose from, making women a product to be judged as 'good' or 'bad'. Critically, Iris Marion Young summarises this habit on the "disciplines of the feminine" to "mask or

128 Manufacture of first Barbie in 1959.

subordinate the raw facts of embodiment, to make the body 'pretty' by constraining fluid flesh, masking its organic smells with perfumes, painting skin, lips, eyes, and hair that have lost their nubile luster"[129]. Furthermore, the girl's generalisation that "*one* gets into the habit" indicates that women in general followed fashion for exceptionally high-heels. With this careless generalisation, the image of women following trends for the sake of appealing to men, who will, like Kay, notice that the shoes are "good for the shape of the legs", has emerged. Kay's voyeurism in this scene reinforces her desired gender performance as modelled on male masculinity, rather than female masculinity that partakes in the subordination and objectification of women as will be discussed in the fourth chapter.

However, the girl was "not understanding, not understanding at all", (35) and fails to recognise Kay's advances as flirtatious. Regardlessly, Kay starts a conversation with her in which she persistently, almost pathetically, tries to get the girl's attention. The girl's naïve misunderstanding is a reflection of Kay's failing masculine power, which is underlined by the number of men returning home from the front making 'boyfriends' and 'husbands' terms and concepts to be reckoned with again. In 1944 the attitude towards men had been different, which proved to be a blessing for Viv as it allowed her to keep the shameful imprisonment of her brother Duncan to herself because "[t]hese days, [...] no one asked after brothers, boyfriends, husbands – just in case." (247) Kay's explicit interrogation about the girl's boyfriend registers a shift in mood and manner, and renders Kay's advances ineffective when men, as the 'legitimate' mates of women, return from the front. Kay is no longer able to successfully claim the role of man and her lesbian desire remains unrecognised by the girl.

The parting scene between Kay and the girl substantiates how gender and sexuality are returning to heteronormativity after years of exceptional circumstances.

> She went on faster, to the edge of the kerb, looked quickly to left and to right, then ran across the road. Her high-heeled shoes were pale at the instep; they showed, Kay though, like the whitish flashes of fur you saw on the behinds of hopping rabbits.
> She hadn't said 'Goodbye', 'So long', or anything like that; and she didn't, now, look back. And they turned down a street and were lost. (34-35)

Kay's observation that the girl's "high-heeled shoes were pale at the instep" and looked "like the whitish flashes of fur" of rabbits are telling in several ways: firstly, the pale instep signals the girl's inner paleness when following fashion

129 Iris Marion Young, *On Female Body Experience: "Throwing Like A Girl" and Other Essays* (Oxford University Press, 2005) pp. 5-6.

trends to please men. She has lost personality and instead has become part of the machinery that endlessly produces dependent women. Secondly, she is moving away from Kay like a rabbit on the run which shows that Kay's appeal on women is fading because women have returned to conventional relationships with men. Thirdly, the image of the rabbit as an animal preyed on completes this renewed patriarchal system in which women are the 'prey of men' and lesbian desire returns into invisibility. In the end Kay is left standing on the street looking after the girl thinking that she was "lost". The scene ends in a double entendre, superficially indicating that the woman is no longer in sight for Kay, but more tellingly suggesting that she is a lost cause – that she is too far gone in the conventions of society and lost for Kay to show her alternatives.

Through such scenes where Kay's present contradicts her glorious past, *The Night Watch* turns the gaze into bygone times in order to emphasise lesbian autonomy during the war, which troubles arguments regarding their categorical invisibility. When Alden asserts that the gay and lesbian past is ridden with self-loathing, Waters' Kay questions this argument by expressing the very opposite. This is additionally evident in her attitude towards watching movies in the cinema:

> Sometimes I sit through the films twice over. Sometimes I go in half-way through, and watch the second half first. I almost prefer them that way – people's pasts, you know, being so much more interesting than their futures. Or perhaps that's just me ... (105-106)

Kaye Mitchell comments that this scene "encodes a subtle pessimism – if 'interest' is always a backwards movement, then what of hope, progress, development?"[130] This pessimism is, of course, part of Kay's character and challenges Alden's reading of *The Night Watch* as a thoroughly positive display of homosexuality. It is also, however, an incorporation of the narrative form as such. Disrupting time as a continuing force, Kay thinks in the parameters of Waters' writing where the present precedes the past. Kay's habit of watching the second half of a film first can be read as a meta-narrative to self-reflexively mirror Waters' narrative structure. Almost a *mise en abyme*, Kay's judgement of people's pasts being (in the present *continuous* form) most interesting also evaluates her own past as more interesting than her present and future. Constantly deconstructing time, the reader is left in an uncanny state of un/knowing – raised in the logics of progressive time and encountering its permanent undoing. In this way, the past

130 Kaye Mitchell, "'What does it feel like to be an anachronism?' Time in *The Night Watch*" in Kaye Mitchell (ed.), *Sarah Waters: Contemporary Critical Perspectives* (London, Bloomsbury, 2013), p. 94.

becomes less rigidly fixed and made available to be reinvented and retold to incorporate nostalgic and retrospective gazes, as well as progressive ones into the future. Waters' text reminds of the possibility of re-encountering that which seems fixed to imagine a different queerstory. When Kay can be represented against convention as nostalgically gazing into the past, the past might not be as oppressive as Alden conceives it to be, which makes the future a less compelling concept. It can thus be argued that Waters' reverse chronology is not simply a disruption of progressive time but a judgement of it – a critique of society's relentless forward movement. Rachel Wood nicely summarises that *The Night Watch* is "attending to a history of isolation, sadness, and exclusion that contemporary history makers might wish to evade"[131].

Literary representations of homosexual lives before gay liberation offer a discerning perspective into society and must be considered by contemporary critics in their own right. Equally important is the critical evaluation of modern novels such as *Make Do and Mend*, which has been shown to be more content with the abjected position of homosexuals than Renault's *The Charioteer*. Waters' *The Night Watch* enunciates a hybrid version where the past might be arresting, but where it is also facilitating modes of living that are not destined towards futurity. Whereas this chapter addressed the many ways of representing homosexuality, the following analysis will concentrate on the depiction of the Second World War in the context of such outlawed desires. I will challenge the assumption that war is a heteronormative endeavour that perpetuates nationalism, patriotism and hegemonic masculinity by disclosing that the novels share a collective reluctance of praising the war. In fact, despite their discrepancies in form and content, the novels largely agree upon the ruthlessness of combat and criticise the national leadership for manipulating men into battle.

---

131 Rachel Wood, "'Walking and Watching' in Queer London: Sarah Waters' *Tipping the Velvet* and *The Night Watch*" in *Journal of Lesbian Studies* Vol. 17, No. 3-4 (2013), p. 315.

"We Have to Do the Things They Tell Us" –

Nation, Masculinity and War

LITERATURE AND NATIONAL PROPAGANDA

National propaganda in all of its forms, from official speeches to fictional narratives, gains importance at times of crisis when more subtle means of control, such as state-enforced laws, become insufficient vehicles of surveillance. Particularly during the Second World War, cultivating a collective British identity and sense of belonging became vital conditions for warding off the threat coming from continental Europe. Benedict Anderson in *Imagined Communities* argues that the myth of the Unknown Soldier plays a central role in the construction of national identity and in assimilating men into a nationalistic discourse when turning them into soldiers.[1] The novels discussed here negotiate and challenge this myth by depicting male characters which refuse to lay down their life for the nation. Whilst Adam Fitzroy's *Make Do and Mend* (2012) questions the authenticity of the People's War by dramatising the long standing tension between Wales and England (thus plunging into a debate on Britishness versus Englishness), Sarah Waters' *The Night Watch* (2006) illustrates institutionalised nationalism in form of prison routine and the inmates' disobedience to claim the war as *their* war. "We have to do the things they tell us" (481) is one of the characters' weary recognition moments before he commits suicide to escape serving in a People's War that is, in reality, led by "a load of government men[...]" (481). Mary Renault's protagonist Laurie Odell is similarly disillusioned in *The Charioteer* (1953). His conflict with his stepfather and clergyman Mr. Straike demonstrates the church to be an institution of nationalistic convictions. Finally, Walter Baxter's *Look Down in Mercy* (1951) demonstrates the struggles of a heteronormatively conditioned officer, who becomes aware of his feelings for another

1 Benedict Anderson, Imagined Communities: Reflections on the Origin and Spread of Nationalism, [1983], (London and New York: Verso, 1991).

man, which puts the military as a masculine institution representing the ideals of the nation into crisis. Kent's inability to perform heroically in battle is only overcome when he allows his homosexual feelings to surface. Baxter's novel thus drafts an alternative version of performing wartime masculinity that is informed and complemented by femininity.

This chapter investigates the lingering implication of norms concerning gender and sexuality within nationalist ideologies which People's War propaganda tried to subsume. I will uncover the tight link between the creation of nation-states and patriarchal power structures organising gender by looking at the various ways in which characters try to circumvent the system of masculinist power bestowed upon their male bodies. I argue that the novel's characters may come to symbolically represent the British nation as Unknown Soldiers and in doing so reify the myth of immortality through mortal bodies. At the same time as being complicit, these characters often resist fully identifying with the myth and thus challenge its overarching authority. These frictions and paradoxes contribute to the wariness and the author's often discernible uncertainty over how to represent the war. In order to more fully grasp the novels' approach, I will question when and why nationalistic propaganda becomes compelling for characters and, more importantly, at what point it disintegrates. Through this disintegration, homosexual war narratives can significantly broaden the canon of war literature by challenging dominant perceptions of military masculinity as tough and heroic, and of conscientious objectors as weak and effeminate.

Narratives grounded in masculine heroism or other legends of bravado function to (re)create and sustain the elusive and illusive nation. Anderson carves out national immateriality by defining the nation as "an imagined political community"[2] where people do not personally know each of their national neighbours, yet where each citizen envisions themselves as belonging to the same community. Anderson's emphasis on the nation as an *imagined* and therefore phantasmal community leads scholars such as Antony Easthope to lament the lack of theorising the nation "as collective identity" in favour of "promulgat[ing] merely another version of nation as unreal"[3]. This criticism oversimplifies Anderson's connotation of the term imagined: he does not deny the physical reality of nation-states and their economic, political and institutional capacities. Instead, Anderson questions any logical substance that precedes the creation of nation-states. In *Strange Encounters: Embodied Others in Post-Coloniality* Sara Ahmed clarifies Anderson's conception as an "approach [that] allows us to recognise that the

2 Anderson, (1991), p. 6.

3 Anthony Easthope, *Englishness and National Culture* (London and New York: Routledge, 1999), p. 8.

boundaries of nations are not simply geographical or geopolitical (though they take both these forms), but also discursive"[4]. She further argues that

> [t]he imagination of the nation as a space in which 'we' belong is not independent of the material deployment of force, and the forms of governmentality which control, not only the boundaries between nation states, and the movements of citizens and aliens within the state, but also the repertoire of images which allows the concept of the nation to come into being in the first place.[5]

Despite the geopolitical and institutionalised reality of nation-states, they remain essentially fictitious. In order to compensate for their insubstantiality, nations need a "repertoire of images" that creates and reifies national belonging. These images do not simply work to distance the nation from other nations but also to establish a hierarchy among citizens by denoting some as 'friends' and others as 'strangers'. Nationalism is thus a complex process of differentiation between nations and among national citizens that requires tropes of identification. Texts enhance a sense of national belonging and lay "the bases for national consciousness"[6]. Because of this dependency on images and texts, Anderson is right to claim that nationalism cannot be grasped by looking for an authentic centre or a single origin because, as Geoffrey Bennington agrees, "we undoubtedly find narration at the centre of nation: stories of national origins, myths of founding fathers, genealogies of heroes"[7]. The repetition of these founding and heroic stories determines a sense of naturalisation, making the nation-state's centre forever obscured through myth. Consequently, "[t]he nation is a reification, a conceptual abstraction, but through representations and rhetoric it appears to exist in a concrete form."[8]

National propaganda of a People's War was a vital image for inducing conformity among national citizens during the war in order to strengthen an imagined community. It helped the national leadership to disguise the monitoring of gender conformity by promulgating the war as genderless, classless and sexless

4 Sara Ahmed, *Strange Encounters: Embodied Others in Post-Coloniality* (London and New York: Routledge, 2000), p. 98.

5 Ibid., p. 98.

6 Anderson, (1991), p. 44.

7 Geoffrey Bennington, "Postal Politics and the Institution of the Nation" in Homi K. Bhabha (ed.), *Nation and Narration* (London and New York: Routledge, 1990), p. 121.

8 Sonya O. Rose, *Which People's War?: National Identity and Citizenship in Britain 1939-1945* (Oxford: Oxford University Press, 2003), p. 7.

to highlight the United Kingdom as *one* nation that fights the threat of invasion. Mark Rawlinson argues in *British Writing of the Second World War* that texts spanning various genres of fiction, letters, propaganda, documentaries and diary entries (often unconsciously) perpetuate the narrative of the People's War. He asserts that "[w]artime literature is both critical of the content and vehicles [that legitimate the war], and fully implicated in the reproduction and invention of alternative justifications of violence."[9] In such replications that vindicate war violence, writers become part of the machinery that disseminates People's War rhetoric. George Orwell's *The Lion and the Unicorn: Socialism and the English Genius* is an example of such a text that simultaneously criticises the division of Britain's people, and praises their solidarity in times of crisis. Despite emphasising Britain as "the most class-ridden country under the sun" that is "notoriously two nations, the rich and the poor", and recognising his language as offensive when using "the word 'England' oftener than 'Britain'", Orwell maintains that "somehow these differences fade away the moment that any two Britons are confronted by a European"[10]. Perceiving themselves as a "family", Orwell continues, there is a "tendency of nearly all [British] inhabitants to feel alike and act together in moments of supreme crisis"[11]. Whilst representing Britain as a complex nation where people hold diverse and often conflicting social positions, Orwell's *The Lion and the Unicorn* illustrates Rawlinson's argument that texts can come to support and spread the myth of the People's War, regardless of their inherent incongruities. By calling Britain a "family" whose inhabitants "feel alike and act together", Orwell advocates solidarity against so-called Nazi Germany. He points out that any differences among Britons subside in the event of jeopardy. These rhetorical abstractions insinuate a greater focus on issues of identity, predominantly national identity during war, and the need to create a narrative that unites people around a collective goal. Writing is thus a major means of establishing and maintaining a grand narrative of a shared identity when people such as Orwell disseminate nationalistic opinions to be read by large numbers of people. In times of crisis, such representations that proclaim a cohesive nationalistic identity increase and manipulate people into subordination to the national Government.

---

9 Mark Rawlinson, *British Writing of the Second World War* (Oxford: Clarendon Press, 2000), p. 3.

10 George Orwell, The Lion and the Unicorn: Socialism and the English Genius, [1941], (The University of Adelaide: eBooks@Adelaide, 2014) <https://ebooks.adelaide.edu.au/o/orwell/george/lion_and_the_unicorn/> [last accessed, 18/07/2017], chapter 3.

11 Ibid., chapter 3.

Kristine A. Miller's *British Literature of the Blitz* "challenges the mythology that Rawlinson and others describe by approaching the literature not as a coherent collective defence of the war but as an expression of imaginative freedom to disagree about the People's War"[12]. According to Miller, wartime writings represent diversity rather than homogeneity and often challenge authenticity claims within People's War propaganda. Quentin Crisp's *The Naked Civil Servant* (1968) illustrates Miller's opposition to a categorical argument that views accounts of the war as either supportive or antagonistic. Crisp perceives the war as simultaneously thrillingly exceptional when liberating people's sex lives, yet as exasperatingly conservative in the monitoring of gender norms. Since the number of soldiers and sailors on British soil grew, intense male friendships and even homosexual conduct became more frequent. However, Crisp was discharged from military service due to his effeminacy, and he was repeatedly violently assaulted for transgressing gender norms. Crisp's contradicting experiences illustrate Miller's compelling thesis that "[b]ecause People's War ideology simultaneously magnified and masked existing problems within the social system, different civilians imagined the People's War in very different ways."[13] Sarah Waters' character Julia uncovers this very paradox of "magnify[ing] and mask[ing] existing problems" when she states: "I hate this passion for uniforms, too. Uniforms, armbands, badges. I thought the military impulse, as it's grown up in Germany, was what we were against!" (273) Uniforms as a collective style seems ironic at best: whilst outwardly levelling people and confirming their shared interest in winning the war through signalling patriotism, they disguise not only Britain's proximity to their enemy, but also the exclusion of those not wearing uniforms. In *Make Do and Mend*, Harry also points out that uniforms can come to increase differences among people when he observes that his sexual transaction with Clive translates into "the RAF, fucking the Navy" (179). Julia's and Harry's reflections are grounded in the narratives' modern vantage point that enables Waters and Fitzroy to narrate the war "within a more comprehensive set of existing narratives and images"[14]. Because with hindsight there comes a greater understanding of events, the once "blissful clarity"[15] of mythic images begins to fade. Whereas "accounts of the Blitz written in the 1940s demonstrate a keen awareness of their relationship to the dominant cultural ideology of a

12 Kristine A. Miller, *British Literature of the Blitz: Fighting the People's War* (London: Palgrave Macmillan, 2009), p. 11.

13 Ibid., p. 11.

14 Ibid., p. 4.

15 Barthes, (1973), 143.

People's War"[16], modern re-writings stand on less restraining ground. Despite this greater distance to the events, which allows for a more critical perspective, it seems significant that all novels share a more or less pronounced reluctance to identify with the war as a People's War. Their perspective reveals the lingering scepticism described by Miller and suggests that more than half a century later, there still seems to be wariness over the ideologies propagated by Prime Minister Winston Churchill. Moreover, the rehearsal of doubt uncovers the uncertainty over how to deal with the Second World War retrospectively – how to handle a past that was so destructive that it continues influencing the present. The confusion of the 1940s is often expressed through incongruities when depicting characters which simultaneously oppose and propagate the war.

Interestingly, the homosexual protagonist Harry in *Make Do and Mend*, who repeatedly criticises his brother Thomas for his conservative and nationalistic attitude helps to perpetuate the myth of the People's War most effectively by writing reports for the British Broadcasting Corporation (BBC). Harry has been asked to meet up with Hywel Vaughn, the brother of Thomas' wife Joan, to write about the routine at the front. Hywel outlines the basic idea of these reports:

> [Joan will] have mentioned that I'm a producer for the BBC? The fact is, I'm also on attachment to the Ministry of Information, and my contribution to the war effort is to make the people who are staying at home feel personally involved on as many fronts as possible. I've been asked to find personnel from different services to give talks about their lives, and that's why Joan thought I should approach you. Nothing too grim, obviously – accommodation, food, routine, the occasional funny story – just to give the families an idea of what their boys experience every day. (150-151)

This representation of the BBC demonstrates Bennington's thesis that "we undoubtedly find narration at the centre of nation"[17]. Hywel explicitly outlines what sort of identity the BBC wants to narrate and transmit: one that is nationalistic and British, indicated by its *British* Broadcasting Corporation production, but one that is also global when covering "as many fronts as possible". It is meant to be positive and to describe a rose-tinted routine of soldiers "just to give the families an idea of what their boys experience every day". Death and fear as well as other war atrocities will find no space in the report because they are "too grim". Asking Harry to create this sort of narrative is highly ironic considering that he is only available because he is on convalescent leave due to bad injuries

16 Miller, (2009), p.4.

17 Bennington, (1990), p. 121.

incurred during the war. This irony is enhanced by Harry's formulation a few weeks later: "he was intending to visit Hywel Vaughn in Bristol [for a spell check] before the war claimed him again" (161). The term "claimed" clearly determines the powerful hold the war has on soldiers and that service is not just about "accommodation, food, routine [or] the occasional funny story". Regardless of this, Harry is eager to write about his experiences, obviously unaware that in doing so, he glorifies the national war effort.

Walter Baxter's *Look Down in Mercy* (1951) depicts the exact opposite to Harry's eagerness to narrate his experiences when the protagonist Toni Kent is shown to struggle writing a letter to his wife Celia. Unlike Harry who enjoys sharing his experiences and thus contributes to the myth of the People's War, Kent is more reluctant: "He hated writing letters but one had to do it, and of course one wanted to do it." (7) Kent's self-description as "one" signals disidentification with the role of husband composing a love letter to his wife and indicates his increasing emotional indifference towards Celia. It also universalises soldiers at the front as a group that faced the difficulty of putting their experiences into words appropriate to People's War propaganda. These letters were meant to contain the sort of stories Hywel wants Harry to write for the BBC: "Nothing too grim, obviously" (150-151). Kent is thus left with a limited scope of things to write about and circumvents this challenge by focusing on the home front:

> You don't say very much about the bombing, my sweet. I suppose you are trying to avoid adding to the white man's burden, but nothing you could say or not say would make me worry more than I do. And I feel so phoney too, living out here in the lap of luxury, literally thousands of miles away from the nearest shot being fired in anger and with nothing more dangerous to cope with than being poisoned by the mess cook. But it's no good grumbling I suppose, there's nothing I can do about it and as you can imagine the Army could scarcely care less about my personal problems. (8)

Kent's mentioning of the Blitz on Britain in 1940 and 1941 illustrates the paradigm shift regarding wartime narratives of the Second World War: whereas the First World War and its literary negotiation was dominated by soldier experiences from the front, the scale of the Second World War made civilians as much witnesses of wartime atrocities as soldiers. Kent's account represents this new emphasis on the home front where "[s]urrounded by the dead and dying, many civilians began to feel that they were fighting as soldiers in a People's War"[18]. In contrast to such atrocities, Kent lives in the "lap of luxury" at the beginning of

18 Miller, (2009), p. 3.

the novel, far away from gun fire and bombing. His apparent concern for Celia and his alleged dissatisfaction with his "phoney" lifestyle, however, is not meant sincerely. This becomes obvious when comparing his written words to his internal ponderings accompanied by actions that symbolise a deep satisfaction with his current situation.

Kent talks of a "personal problem" to insinuate that he would prefer to fight and die in the war as any good national citizens would. To substantiate his regrettable sense of safety, Kent states humorously that the only thing that could cost him his life is the military food. His fear of "being poisoned by the mess cook" is a blatant lie, as Kent has his own private chef to order about: "'Dinner in ten minutes, Ahmed, I'm going to have another drink and look at the paper. Bring the bottle and some more ice.'" (10) Moreover, Kent is in no hurry to see any frontline action when he "slump[s] into a long wicker arm-chair and lazily pull[s] a newspaper off the table" (10). The authenticity of his letter is further compromised when he laments the shortage of officers, whilst silently embracing his "novel and delicious sense of importance; having another officer in the company could only diminish that feeling" (9). Kent refrains from disclosing these true thoughts to Celia not simply because letters were read to ensure that no information would pass to the enemy[19], but because Kent finds the savouring of his luxurious lifestyle "embarrassing" and "difficult to express" (9). According to the laws of the People's War, Britons were glad to defend their country and Kent cannot confess that he is an exception to this rule. He is aware that his attitude does not conform to wartime propaganda disallowing military personnel to embrace moments of safety. Consequently, his letter to Celia taints his true feelings in favour of demonstrating a false allegiance to nationalism and patriotism.

Kent's and Harry's contradicting participation in producing propaganda shows that those who, like Harry, are generally wary of the war can come to unconsciously spread its ideologies through creating stories of praise, whereas oth-

19 In Make Do and Mend Harry's brother Freddie writes a letter to his family at Christmas from Germany whilst being a prisoner of war: "*we had sausage and sauerkraut for Christmas dinner and the Red Cross sent enough plum cake for everyone. Church parade in the morning, good Scottish chaplain and plenty of lusty hymns to keep us warm. In the afternoon we had a concert, with people singing and reciting poetry and rather a good comic turn, and then someone got on the piano and we sang until we were hoarse.*" (137) [emphasis original]. This cheerful representation of German imprisonment is highly doubtful and obviously informed by conducts that require soldiers to present their situation as bearable according to Red Cross standards. Only Freddie's closing words "I've had enough adventures for a while!" (138) [emphasis original] disclose Freddie's true feelings and the fear that accompanies war captivity.

ers like Kent, who are prone to the promise of glory, may fail to identify with the war.

In addition to People's War propaganda, the Unknown Soldier myth becomes another unifying trope to further collectivity:

> No more arresting emblems of the modern culture of nationalism exist than cenotaphs and tombs of Unknown Soldiers. [...] Yet void as these tombs are of identifiable mortal remains or immortal souls, they are nonetheless saturated with ghostly national imaginings.[20]

Nationalistic discourse fashions the myth of the Unknown Soldier in order to universalise the "ghostly national imaginings" of ancestral graves as "loom[ing] out of an immemorial past [...] glid[ing] towards a limitless future"[21]. This projection of a genealogy and an undisrupted continuity is vital for the survival of nation-states. Even though the "cenotaphs and tombs" are "void", they remain charged with meaningful projections that are turned into narration through repetition. However, Joanna P. Sharp remarks pointedly that the "Unknown Soldier is not entirely anonymous. We can all be fairly sure that the soldier is not called Sarah or Lucy or Jane ..."[22] Because the metonymic Unknown Soldier could be any man (notably not a/ny woman), "who has laid down his life for the nation, the nation is embodied within each [fighting] man and each [fighting] man comes to embody the nation"[23]. The effect of the soldier risking his life in war is then the symbolic participation in and representation of national affairs, which enhances the sense of belonging to the imagined community. It follows that "symbols of nationalism are not gender neutral but in enforcing national norm, they implicitly or explicitly construct a set of gender norms"[24]. Literature about the Second World War is thus embedded in a specific narrative on gender that functions to portray soldiers as masculine representatives of the national war effort.

The military administration had a great interest in portraying the Army and Navy as highly masculine and heterosexual institutions and therefore intensified

20 Anderson, (1991), p. 9.

21 Ibid., pp. 11-12.

22 Joanne P. Sharp, "Gendering Nationhood: A feminist engagement with national identity" in Nancy Duncan (ed.), *BodySpace: Destabilizing geographies of gender and sexuality* (London and New York: Routledge, 1996), p. 99.

23 Sharp, (1996), p 99.

24 Ibid., p 98.

their efforts to exclude non-conforming individuals in order to guarantee pretence of control. Screening processes were invented to spot and discharge effeminate men.[25] The resulting assumption of the military as a homogeneously masculine institution has led to a scarce analysis of soldier masculinity during and after the Second World. In *Gender and Warfare in the Twentieth Century: Textual Representations*, Angela K. Smith polemically accounts for this lack of research into masculinity and warfare: "There is no need to extrapolate masculinity from man – in the soldier they become one."[26] Indeed, influential works such as Paul Fussell's *Wartime: Understanding and Behavior in the Second World War* compassionately represent the daily lives of soldiers, but do not analyse the challenging task of keeping up to masculine ideals fashioned by the military.[27]

In the ground-breaking study *Masculinities*, Connell destabilises various myths concerning male gender performance and develops a more diverse structure to explain how masculine power tries to retain its dominance. First of all, masculinity "is *not* a coherent object about which a generalizing science can be produced", which explains Connell's insistence on pluralising masculinit*ies* as variously constructed according to socio-historical moments and discourses.[28] Secondly, while bodies "in their own right as bodies, do matter" they do not determine masculine (or feminine) performance.[29] This envisions a liberating move from sex as the determining factor of gender performance to permitting male *and* female subjects to perform masculinity. Thirdly, "'[m]asculinity' does not exist except in contrast with 'femininity'" and intersects with issues of race, class, age and other social statuses.[30] The concept of patriarchy unites these varying markers that accompany the study of male gender performance and provides the ground on which masculinity builds.

Around 1970 the concept of patriarchy "came into whispered use"[31]. It describes a "system of gender domination" where men control the "governments,

---

25 Allan Bérubé, *My Desire for History: Essays in Gay, Community, and Labor History* (Chapel Hill: The University of North Carolina Press, 2011), p. 90.

26 Angela K. Smith, "Introduction" in Angela K. Smith (ed.), *Gender and Warfare in the Twentieth Century: Textual Representations* (Manchester: Manchester University Press, 2004), p. 4.

27 Paul Fussell, *Wartime: Understanding and Behavior in the Second World War* (New York and Oxford: Oxford University Press, 1989).

28 Connell, *Masculinities*, [1995], (Cambridge: Polity Press, 2016), p. 67. [my emphasis].

29 Connell, (2016), p. 51.

30 Ibid., p. 68.

31 Ibid., p. 41.

corporations, media", where men have "better jobs, incomes and command of wealth", and where men police "the means of violence, and the entrenched ideologies that push[...] women into the home and dismiss[...] their claims for equality"[32]. Hegemonic masculinity is the engine that attempts to keep this structure faultless – it gains its force from men's constant efforts of reaching an ideal gender performance and their inevitable failure. It is also "the configuration of gender practice which embodies the currently accepted answer to the problem of the legitimacy of patriarchy, which guarantees (or is taken to guarantee) the dominant position of men and the subordination of women"[33]. Hegemonic masculinity and patriarchy are thus two sides of the same coin since the former validates the latter's dominance and *vice versa*. Moreover, "violence on the largest possible scale is the purpose of the military; and no arena has been more important for the definition of hegemonic masculinity in European/American culture"[34]. This does *not* mean that a selected group of men (e.g. soldiers) are capable of performing their gender in such a way that they undisputedly fall into the category of hegemonic masculinity; indeed, it is impossible that a subject embodies all of its aspects. Connell's hegemonic masculinity is an *idealised concept* which needs to be understood as a blueprint for a version of male gender performance that is effectively unattainable but provides the model against which every other form of "'doing man' can be constructed and performed"[35]. Because the myth of the Unknown Soldier assimilates male bodies as the "essence of warfare"[36], homosexual soldiers who escaped discharge may come to idealise and perpetuate masculine identity during war despite their deviating desires. Analysing narrative negotiations of masculinity in connection to the nation at war facilitates a more complete understanding of the often contradictory social position of men within a patriarchal society. It also helps to disclose at what point the promise of hegemonic masculinity becomes unconvincing for homosexual men, who will never succeed in their pursuit of dominance within a heteronormative order. It is decidedly not my aim to rehearse narratives of stigmatisation when foregrounding homosexual characters who suffer under the pressure of command, but to reveal the damaging and often traumatising nationalistic structures that control and coerce men into battle. Homosexual storylines break with that standard and – facilitated through national crisis – enable a re-negotiation of gender and sexuality.

32 Connell, (2016), p. 41.

33 Ibid., p. 77, [my emphasis].

34 Ibid., p. 213.

35 Carrie Paechter, "Masculine Femininities/Feminine Masculinities: Power, Identities and gender" in *Gender and Education* Vol. 18, No. 3 (2006), p. 255.

36 Smith, (2004), p. 4.

Moreover, there is an ironic slippage inscribed in the propagated pride of the military as a highly masculine institution: through the coming together of large numbers of people of the same sex, deriving from the spatial division of soldiers at the front and women at the home front, homosexuals found companionship that peacetime did not offer to the same extent. Convincingly, Bérubé asserts that the spirit that led to the gay liberation movement in the late 1960s and 1970s "was born under fire during World War II"[37]. The increasing number of homosexual men serving in the military troubles its masculine self-image and calls into question the stability of national propaganda more broadly.

The following will critically analyse the novels' representation of wartime propaganda and the characters' growing sense of disidentification with such ideologies. *Make Do and Mend*, in particular, questions the ground on which the myth of the People's War rests when dramatizing how a collective British national identity is constructed at the expense of localised nationalities that become subsumed, subordinated and shattered.

ONE NATION FIGHTING A PEOPLE'S WAR?

Adam Fitzroy's *Make Do and Mend* (2012) portrays the life of Harry Lyon after a submarine accident that has damaged his lungs so badly that he is no longer able to serve as an active officer. The story begins when Harry returns to his childhood home Hendra – a farm and family estate that is managed by his brother Jack, and which represents Harry's former battles with his late father Sir Charles whose conservative attitude has driven his son to serve in the Navy. Two maids named Kitty and Blanche work and live in the Hendra house, and the farm labourer Jim Brynawel inhabits a farm hut on the estate. When encountering Jim for the first time, Harry is immediately captivated and the reader becomes aware of his homosexuality. When becoming more accustomed to the routine at Hendra and developing a relationship with Jim, Harry begins to disidentify with his former position as an officer and starts questioning the benefit of the People's War.

Whereas the myth of the Unknown Soldiers depends on the male body to "willingly" die to preserve a "horizontal comradeship" and "fraternity"[38], the myth of the People's War requires national unity among England, Wales, Scotland and Northern Ireland. In his speeches, Churchill praises Britons who "are

37 Bérubé, (2011), p. 112.

38 Smith, (2004), p. 7.

proud to be under fire of the enemy"[39] for their endurance and altruism in overcoming social differences. In order to guarantee good morale at times of national crisis, he promises the bereft people that "the light of glory shines on all"[40]. Churchill's emphasis on the effort of women who "marched forward in millions [to take up] all kinds of tasks and work"[41] traditionally performed by men, underlines his argument for a People's War where *everybody*, including women, get involved. Furthermore, Churchill and Government propaganda more broadly, pledged that the People's War would bring about social change and lasting equality between the sexes, in addition to the termination of tension between the individual countries on the British Isles. In the following, I will first trace the debate surrounding Englishness versus Britishness to subsequently analyse how Fitzroy's *Make Do and Mend* represents this lingering conflict by looking at Harry's growing identification with his home country Wales followed by the disassociation with his military association with Britain and the People's War. In doing so, my reading of the novel questions the authenticity of the Unknown Soldier myth facilitating an imagined community built on national unity. Since such a unity lacks credibility when Harry prefers a Welsh identity over national identification, both the myth of the People's War and that of the Unknown Soldier are represented as inherently flawed.

Robert Burden states that "Britishness seems to have been invented to extinguish the difference between the English, the Scots, and the Welsh" to place them under the rule of England disguised as Britain.[42] He continues by citing Linda Colley's argument that "Britishness was an invention 'superimposed over an array of internal differences in response to contact with the Other, and in response to conflict with the Other'"[43]. The Other stands in opposition to a group sentiment due to various markers covering religion, ethnicity, class, gender, but also national membership. For the exclusion of the Other, a definition of a collective national identity is needed that establishes a common sense of belonging

39 Winston Churchill, "'Westward, Look, the Land is Bright,' Address Broadcast April 27, 1941" in Charles Eade (ed), *The Unrelenting Struggle* (Boston: Little, Brown and Co., 1942), p. 93.

40 Ibid., p. 93.

41 Winston Churchill, "The Women of Britain" in Charles Eade (ed.), *Onwards to Victory: War speeches by the Right HON. Winston S. Churchill* (London: Cassell and Company Ltd., 1944), p. 285.

42 Robert Burden, "Introduction: Englishness and Spatial Practices" in Robert Burden and Stephan Kohl (eds.), *Landscapes and Englishness* (New York: Radopi, 2006), p. 16.

43 Ibid., p. 16.

in relation to and opposition with those who do not belong. However, debates concerning the conflict between Englishness and Britishness reveal a more complicated picture where England – sometimes reduced to London – is the locus of authority within the United Kingdom, which challenges a collective sense of national belonging.

The situation in Britain also illustrates Sara Ahmed's argument that Othering does not simply occur between nations but also within one nation.

> The proximity of strangers within the nation space – that is, *the proximity of that which cannot be assimilated into a national body* – is a mechanism for the demarcation of the national body, a way of defining borders within it, rather than just between it and an imagined and exterior other [emphasis original] [44].

Ahmed carefully distinguishes between defining the nation against external and against internal strangers. Internal strangers are "those who are not recognised as 'typical' of a nation"[45] and can come to threaten a collective national identity. However, these internal strangers are, just like external strangers, crucial for defining who 'we' are in response to, and opposition with, those who are different. In the case of Britain, such a negotiation of internal strangers is enhanced due to the multiplicity of 'sub-national identities' (English, Welsh, Scottish, Northern Irish) that become integrated into Britishness. Additionally, British is often used synonymously with English and *vice versa*, which indicates "the lordly English habit of subsuming British under English" [46] and demonstrates an Anglocentric hegemony. Such inner conflicts over the question of national identity destabilise the already vague sense of national unity. It follows that the United Kingdom presents a complex and conflicting situation that can be best explained by examining the various terms that are meant to denominate British identity.

The term Britain was first recorded by the Greeks to denote an offshore island that was home of the Celts. The Greek term was translated into the Latin word Britannia by the Romans and given to the Celts' island. In the fifth century AD, the Angles and Saxons came to the island Britannia and renamed it "Engla-land" [47] disregarding earlier terminologies. Subsequent attempts to unite the countries of England and Scotland since the 16th century were limited, until in 1707 "the Act of Union with Scotland" was signed and "the united kingdom of

44 Ahmed, (2000), p. 100.

45 Ibid., p. 100.

46 Krishan Kumar, *The Making of English National Identity* (Cambridge: Cambridge University Press, 2003), p. 1 and p. 4.

47 Ibid., p. 5.

Great Britain" was established.[48] The term Britain was quickly adapted as a shorthand for Great Britain and the adjective British became equally familiar. However, Kumar claims that today "[t]he majority of English, Welsh and Scots do not think of themselves as 'British'" but only use the term to "refer to their trade with other nations, their economy, their armed forces, their legal nationality, the inhabitants of the pre- and non-Anglo-Saxon cultures of the island called Britain".[49] To Britons, then, being British is a legal and economic position and not a denomination of "their social, cultural or personal life"[50]. Such personal identifications remain within the realm of the individual countries of England, Scotland, Wales and Northern Ireland. Fitzroy's *Make Do and Mend* demonstrates this discrepancy between a forced British national identity intensified through the myth of the People's War, and a more localised Welsh nationality marginalised into and subsumed under Britishness. The protagonist's account of his changing sense of identity from British to Welsh in addition to his homosexuality, demonstrates Harry's reluctance to symbolically reiterate both the myth of the Unknown Soldier and that of the People's War.

Several hints regarding the history of Welsh identity versus English superiority are given at the beginning of the novel, when Harry talks about "a Licence to Crenellate issued by King Henry IV" (12) and how "Cromwell's men" (12) destroyed part of the Hendra house. He also claims that the Lyon family is "supposed to be descended from King Edward III" (20). Later Harry is given a book entitled "*The Enigma of Owain Glyn Dŵr*" (175) [emphasis original] authored by someone named Rhys Montgomery. To most readers this information will not be particularly enlightening, but the repetition with which nationalistic figures and symbols are referred to suggests their relevance for the story. Towards the end of the novel a conversation between Harry and Jim picks up these threads and begins to mend them when Harry says: "You believe that Owain Glyn Dŵr might be buried on our land? [...] You're aware that Hendra was originally fortified *against* Glyn Dŵr, I suppose?" (200) [emphasis original] The story of Glyn Dŵr and the Lyon family's connection to the English crown seem to be the cornerstones that create a metanarrative about the history of Welsh identity. In order to fully grasp the historical background and how *Make Do and Mend* fictionalises it, the relationship between England and Wales needs to be briefly reconstructed from the 15th century onwards.[51]

48 Kumar, (2003), p. 5.

49 Ibid., p. 6.

50 Ibid., p. 6.

51 The following recollection of events is based on Robert Rees Davies' study *The Revolt of Owain Glyn Dŵr* and the website of the "Owain Glyn Dŵr Society" chaired by

Owain Glyn Dŵr or Owain Glyndŵr (1359- ca. 1415) was a Welshman whose success in fighting against English rule made him a national legend. In the Middle Ages Wales was entirely controlled by the English crown which constantly caused conflicts over land ownership and citizen rights. In 1400 Glyn Dŵr got involved in one of these conflicts and complained to the English Parliament that his land had been unlawfully taken by his neighbour. Instead of settling the dispute, the Parliament scorned the plea upon which Glyn Dŵr swore revenge against the English and was crowned Prince of Wales by his supporters. Adapting farm tools into weapons, Glyn Dŵr's men unexpectedly won several battles against the heavily armed English knights. For three years, King Henry IV repeatedly attacked Wales, but Glyn Dŵr and his men managed to defend their country.

Throughout their reign over the British Isles, English kings have granted loyal Welsh knights permission to fortify their property and to build castles in Wales. In return, these castles demonstrated English dominance on Welsh ground and bound the knights to serve the crown. In order to strengthen his power and to cast out the English for good, Glyn Dŵr began to attack these symbolically important castles and in 1404 declared victory over England. A year later, however, he was defeated in the battle of Pwll Melyn – Glyn Dŵr's brother was killed and his son was captured. From that point onwards, Glyn Dŵr's dominance dwindled, but he continued to fight the English and defended his remaining castles for five more years. Historic accounts of the period after 1409, when Glyn Dŵr had to go into exile to escape captivity, are scarce, but it is presumed that he died in 1415. To date, neither his body nor his grave have been found. This uncertainty over his death has increased the force of the legendary figure of Owain Glyn Dŵr. In *The Revolt of Owain Glyn Dŵr*, Robert Rees Davies argues that as the last Prince of Wales, Glyn Dŵr's death was turned into myth and that he "was, and has remained, exclusively and proprietorially Welsh"[52]. He thus illustrates Bennington's thesis that national narrations of founding fathers and heroic figures augment in people a sense of belonging together, of sharing a genealogy.[53] In order to understand the repeated references to such a national narra-

---

Adrien Jones and Eirwyn Evans. R. R. Davies, *The Revolt of Owain Glyn Dŵr* (Oxford: Oxford University Press, 1995); Adrien Jones and Eirwyn Evans, "Owain Glyn Dŵr Society" <www.owain-glyndwr.wales/> [last accessed: 21/12/2016]. For further information see the short film "Bloody Britain – The Welsh Rebellions" accessible through the "Owain Glyn Dŵr Society" website.

52 Davies, (1995), p. 325.

53 Bennington, (1990), p. 121.

tive, it is necessary to examine how and why *Make Do and Mend* dramatises the myth of Owain Glyn Dŵr.

The novel establishes that the Lyon family fought against Owain Glyn Dŵr in the Middle Ages. This is indicated when Harry claims that the Lyons are descendants of King Edward III who held the English crown from 1327 until his death in 1377. Not impressed by his royal ancestors, Harry sarcastically remarks: "The King and I are only sixteenth cousins at best" (20). Yet, the memory of the family's connection to royalty lingers on, and because this knowledge is shared by all characters in the novel, its relevance is substantiated. Another indication for a hidden storyline is Harry's seemingly arbitrary mentioning of the "Licence to Crenellate", making Hendra a "fortified manor house" but not a "castle" (12) – a dispute over status indicating the conflict between Harry and his brother Thomas Griffith-Lyon, which will be examined later. This "Licence to Crenellate" is the name of the document signed by the English King which gave permission to knights to fortify their land on Welsh ground. Having been given to the Lyon family, the Licence illustrates that, at the time of Owain Glyn Dŵr's fight for Welsh independence from the English crown, Hendra and the Lyon family were still positioned on the side of the English King and *against* their Welsh countrymen.

Two centuries after Owain Glyn Dŵr's death, Parliamentarians and Royalists fought over control of England in the English civil wars (1642-1651). The novel represents this historic event by stating that the Parliamentarians under the command of Cromwell took "the time and trouble to slight two of [Hendra's four towers]" (12-13). Here the second hint – Cromwell – seemingly randomly given at the beginning of the novel, becomes meaningful. Oliver Cromwell (1599-1658) led the English military against first King Charles I and later his son Charles II, which ended English monarchy and established the Parliament's direct influence on politics. *Make Do and Mend* fictionalises Cromwell's rebellion and implies that his attack on Hendra was not arbitrary but a result of the family's historic alliance with the English crown against which the Parliamentarians fought. The damage caused by Cromwell's men is significant for the story as it prevents the characters from using the entire house, making it an uncanny and uncertain element threatening to collapse and bury its inhabitants.

Laying emphasis on the decaying house and its history at the beginning of the novel distracts from the events of the Second World War, Harry's position as a Navy officer, and his life-threatening injuries caused by his submarine running aground. Instead, a more local story of Welshness is accentuated and steadily broadened in Harry's transformation from embodying the British nation at war, towards glorifying Welsh independence. As a naval officer, he adheres to British nationalism propagated to overcome regional boundaries and interests, which causes a loss of Welsh identity illustrated in Harry's unfamiliarity with his Welsh native tongue. When his loyalty to Britain is devastated because war is "wasteful" (212), Harry abandons his sense of Englishness grounded in his family's history and connection to the crown and begins to resurrect the myth of Owain Glyn Dŵr when travelling to Liverpool.

Whilst being aboard a train that brings Harry to his new office post in Liverpool, German bombers start their nightly attack. In the midst of the bomb fire, "a magnificent rolling bass" (157) begins to sing a popular Welsh Hymn called *Cwm Rhondda*. The disembodied "owner of the stirring voice" "strongly carry[s] the melody despite the chaos that reigned outside" (158). Only when the raid is over and the lights are switched on again does this voice reveal its embodiment in a "tiny, white-haired, elderly man in a shabby raincoat" (158). This figure is so at odds with the description of the strong voice that Harry believes it to be "a miracle in itself" (158). Initially, this passage does not appear to be more than the rallying of Welsh morale at times of distress, and the power of song to drown out the sound of the war. Yet, at the very end of the narrative, the scene is re-invoked and given a much deeper meaning when Harry links the strong voice and the encounter of its ill-fitted body to the myth of Owain Glyn Dŵr. By identifying the voice as the determining feature of the man, Harry projects his fantasy of a united and independent Wales onto the man's body and assures that "Glyn Dŵr is all around us" (296). Harry's exclamation asserts that the spirit of a free Wales lives within such voices, and that "the legend of Glyn Dŵr is the sort of thing that never, ever dies" (296). Davies argues that the memory of Owain Glyn Dŵr constitutes "an independent Wales, politically, ecclesiastically, culturally, and educationally"[54]. Harry's solidarity with this national legend therefore represents a strong sense of Welshness and a wish for independence from England.

Later in the story, the farm worker Jim Brynawel is revealed as the author of *The Enigma of Owain Glyn Dŵr*. Before the war, Jim was a historian who tried to solve the mystery of Glyn Dŵr's death. He assumes that the last Prince of Wales is buried at Hendra, which Harry refutes on grounds of his family's loyalty to the English King. Jim explains:

> Well, my research suggests that your distant ancestor Hugues de Lyon may have been one of several nobleman in the area playing both ends against the middle – as it were. If I'm right, he may be identifiable with a person named in the ballads as Huw Glascrow – which in rough translation would be 'Hugh the Blue-eyed'. He's described as having light-

54 Davies, (1995), p. 326.

coloured hair, which seems to indicate a Norman – rather than a Celtic – background; much like yourself, in fact. (200)

As a historian Jim wants to put the unsolved death of Glyn Dŵr to rest by suggesting that Harry's ancestor Hugues de Lyon may have provided cover for the Prince of Wales when he was fleeing from the English army. This implies treachery of Hugues de Lyon against the English King and would change the role of the Lyon family by transforming their supposed loyalty to the crown into support for Welsh independence. While this hypothesis seems entirely fictional – to my knowledge there exists no such theory based on historic accounts – Jim's proposition marks a profound wish for Welsh nationalism directed against English rule.

In the end Jim's theory is no longer pursued because Harry is "positive" (296) to have run into Glyn Dŵr on his train ride to Liverpool. Referring to the disembodied voice of the old man, Harry undermines the possibility of ever finding the grave of Glyn Dŵr because "he isn't really dead at all" (296). Searching for his grave is pointless "and even if you did succeed in finding it I'm sure you wouldn't find him" (296). Harry's position illustrates that the mystery of Glyn Dŵr's death is important for his prevalence as a national legend. His grave has to forever remain empty to be filled with significance and to proclaim the immortality of Welsh nationalism. Harry makes this explicit by saying: "You can bury a man, of course, but you can never really bury a dream – or not completely, at any rate, and certainly not forever." (297) This rhetoric illustrates Anderson's argument that "cenotaphs and tombs of Unknown Soldiers" are "void" of "mortal remains" but "nonetheless saturated with ghostly national imaginings"[55]. Because the grave of Owain Glyn Dŵr has never been found, his tomb is as empty as that of the Unknown Soldier, yet retrospectively filled with symbolic meaning of Welsh national identity. Desires for independence can be projected onto the figure of Glyn Dŵr *because* his death remains obscured by myth. Jim follows this thought and agrees that "Glyn Dŵr's a type" (296).

[L]ook at Evans Milk and Pritchard the builder – and look at Philip [...]. They're all the same, aren't they – tough little lifelong countrymen who'd give their last penny or their last drop of blood if they believed in the rightness of their cause? (296)

Reminiscent of Harry's projection of the disembodied voice onto the myth of Glyn Dŵr, Jim creates a collective Welsh identity, which is characterised in its people's endurance despite straining conditions. By envisioning Glyn Dŵr as a

55 Anderson, (1991), p. 9.

'type of person', Jim fashions an imagined community of Wales. This replaces English rule and a forced British identity with Welsh nationalism by projecting the myth of Glyn Dŵr onto individual Welsh bodies. The novel thus creates a shared knowledge of Welsh nationalism among its characters grounded in a myth that obscures the complicated and often positive bonds with England and uses the same imaginary strategies as People's War propaganda.

Polemically, Harry adapts the myth of Glyn Dŵr into the discourse of the Second World War by stating that "an army of Glyn Dŵrs" will continue to fight the enemy and that "if ever England is invaded, we'll know that without a doubt Wales will still hold on" (297). Harry's antagonism against the People's War is here most distinct when he differentiates between a Welsh "army of Glyn Dŵrs" and an unspecified English army. The possibility of England being invaded challenges Britain's propagated endurance and its unity in fighting for a common cause. In Harry's version, England and Wales are distinct countries that fight independently, whilst England is characterised as weaker than Wales to compensate for the history of oppression and subordination. Accordingly, *Make Do and Mend* does not simply reconstruct the Second World War, it also displays the dispute between England and Wales and the resurrection of Welsh nationalism since independence was lost in the Middle Ages. The propagation of a People's War during the 1940s is thus characterised as inherently flawed, because the centre of British patriotism was England and *not* a *united* Kingdom. It is then not only the Hendra house as an emblem of Englishness, which threatens to collapse, but also English rule on Welsh ground when the myth of Owain Glyn Dŵrs is resurrected to stand for a collective Welsh nationalism.

This battle between Welsh and British identity is paralleled in the dispute between Jim Brynawel and Harry's brother Thomas Griffith-Lyon. Thomas is a conservative character who represents the ideology of the People's War and consequently prohibits his family to associate with the conscientious objector Jim. Thomas' and Jim's different social and political positions are represented and reinforced in their last names. Thomas Griffith-Lyon is a composition of two surnames: 'Griffith' deriving from Middle Welsh and 'Lyon' from Latin meaning lion. 'Gruffudd' is the origin of the modern version Griffith and translates in its suffix -udd to 'lord'.[56] The meaning of the first element remains unclear, which leads to the commonly simplified translation of 'Griffith' as 'lord'.[57] Both names and their translation to 'lord' and 'lion' represent male strength and authority, with Griffith implying a direct link to the affairs of the nation, since a lord is

56 Basil Cottle, *The Penguin Dictionary of Surnames* (Harmondsworth: Penguin Publishers, 1967), p. 123 and p. 174.

57 Cottle, (1967), p. 123 and p. 174.

considered to be more influential in national and political affairs than a regular citizen. This recalls Harry's observation that the Lyon family are descendants of King Edward III. Double barrelled surnames additionally denote a higher social class in British English, which explains why Thomas diverges from social convention when he marries a widow and adopts not only her two children but also her surname Griffith to hyphenate it with his family name Lyon: it allows him to articulate and emphasise his self-assessment as a representative of the nation. Thomas' initiative challenges Nirmal Puwar's claim that "the universal figure of leadership and representative of humanity continues to be conceptualised in the shadow of the nation"[58]. In Puwar's formulation, the nation produces those who come to represent it, whereas the novel lays greater emphasis on the subject, Thomas, as the self-assigned embodiment and defender of the British nation. While the discursive power and the tales of nationhood remain undisputed in both formulations, the appropriation of Thomas' name shows greater agency and initiative when participating in the distribution of national power.

In contrast, the name Jim Brynawel translates from Welsh 'bryn' meaning hill, and 'awel' meaning windy or breeze, to 'windy hill'[59], which indicates simultaneously the geographic location of Jim's cottage and his involvement in building a windmill. The 'windy' part in Jim's name symbolises that there is some strange element to his character, which leads Thomas to question Jim's intentions and trustworthiness. Thomas' suspicions are grounded in Jim's unknown past as a historian and is fostered by the fact that Jim is keeping to himself instead of participating in village life. The name Brynawel signals Thomas' antagonism and fear towards suspicious subjects that, like wind, cannot be fully incorporated into and controlled by the nation. The characters' conflict illustrates Ahmed's argument that "[t]he recognition of others as being from the same nation, or as sharing a nationality, [...] involves an everyday and much rehearsed distinction between who does and does not belong within the nation space."[60] This question of whether or not Jim belongs "within the nation space", is one repeatedly asked by Thomas. Ahmed asserts that a conservative person such as Thomas would perceive "strangers [as] the ones who are encountered at the border, and whose proximity threatens the coherence of national identity"[61]. Thomas

58 Nirmal Puwar, *Space Invaders: Race, Gender and Bodies out of Place* (Oxford and New York: Berg Publishers, 2004), p. 34.

59 Evans H. Meurig and William Owen Thomas and Christopher Daviers, *Y Geiriadur Mawr: The Complete Welsh-English English-Welsh dictionary* (Llandysul: Gwasg Gomer, 1980), p. 59 and p. 36.

60 Ahmed, (2000), p. 99.

61 Ibid., p. 100.

approaches Jim in exactly this way, as a danger that needs to be excluded from the community. However, Ahmed continues arguing that "[n]ational identity emerges as a site of social conflict: there is a constant redefinition of who 'we' are through the very necessity of encountering strangers within the nation space."[62] Thomas ignores his own dependency on Jim in order to self-identify as a national citizen and tries to eliminate Jim, the stranger, and his pacifist thoughts by accusing him of murder – an inherently paradoxical accusation given that pacifism is defined as a resistance to violence.

Paranoid that someone might roam through the outskirts of the village, Thomas positions a "Boy Scouts troupe up on the hillside" (239) to spy. They find a dead body close to Jim's hut and conclude that Jim, who does not have an alibi, is "the only half-way decent suspect" (239-240). Harry, of course, is furious and blames Thomas' Boy Scouts for the situation:

> in Thomas's eyes Jim's pacifist leanings make him a target anyway, and I wouldn't be surprised if he'd sent them up the mountain in the hope of catching [Jim] out in some misdemeanour or other – all the time being conspicuously elsewhere himself, of course. To some men [...] just being different is enough to arouse suspicion. (242)

Harry elaborates that Thomas suspects Jim because of his pacifism, which makes him a general target in wartime and substantiates his outside position within the village. The vicar Philip agrees with Harry's negative evaluation of Thomas' action and clarifies that the unfounded accusation against Jim results from "all those public information films about 'traitors among us'" (235). Such propaganda to counteract treason stirs anxieties in people and elevates a constant monitoring and supervising of behaviour. The post office lady Mrs. Parry, for instance, reads private letters and passes information to the police (78). She is also terrified over not knowing the whereabouts of a German pilot who crashed in the hills during an air raid around Christmas: "They never found his body, did they? He could be anywhere, creeping around the valley at night looking for a chance to cut all our throats?" (102) Harry in contrast, "had little doubt the man was dead" (102). In the end it is revealed that Mrs. Parry's caution was appropriate. In a Germaphobic interlude the novel reveals that the pilot *had* survived the crash, and in need for a vehicle, he had cut the throat of a van driver who Thomas' Boy Scouts later found buried nearby Jim's hut. The interlocking of events that lead to the solving of the murder case illustrates the fabricated and entangled dynamics between 'friend' and 'stranger'. Thomas' unfounded suspicion of Jim further shows how easily characters, who are "different" become pre-maturely

62 Ahmed, (2000), p. 101.

judged and condemned, because "[a]ny male of apparently military age who was not in uniform was at risk of being seen as a 'bad citizen', even though there were men on the home front 'doing their bit' for the country."[63] Because fighting was the 'national norm' during the 1940s, conscientious objection was seen as disloyal to both the nation and to fellow men who risked their lives in battle. Jim's expressed pacifism contributes to Thomas' aversion, and when Harry tells his brother about his intentions of fixing a chimney with Jim's help, Thomas exclaims:

> 'Well, for Heaven's sake, Harry, don't allow the man to consider himself your equal, whatever you do. I realise that in a time of war social distinctions can become blurred, but nobody with a position to maintain could possibly associate himself with someone who refuses to do his duty to his country; there can be absolutely no honour in it. (52)

This scene focuses on the "blurr[ing]" of class distinctions during war and the struggle of those "with a position to maintain" to remain recognisable as more respectable. Thomas' attitude, however, places him in opposition to the People's War as a leveller of classes and challenges his nominally claimed representative position within the British nation. His emphasis on men's "duty" to serve their country is similarly ridiculed as he himself is not in the army because his job as a lawyer is regarded as 'too valuable'. Through his occupation, Thomas substantiated his higher class and discloses the People's War as a false narrative. Moreover, Thomas' constant fear that Jim Brynawel's pacifist attitudes might spread in the village and destroy its morale, illustrates the shaky foundation on which British nationalism rests:

> [Jim] had the unmitigated gall to turn up at a service of remembrance wearing a white poppy. White, I ask you; I'm beginning to think he's a fifth-columnist as well as a coward! Talk of peace will get him nowhere in a village full of patriots who have given their sons and brothers to defend their country; nobody around here takes any notice of those who spread gloom and despondency, thank goodness. (57)

The expressed relief ("thank goodness") with which Thomas responds to the unbroken patriotic mood of the village despite Jim's act of resistance is conspicuous. He is aware that the loss of "sons and brothers" can turn a favourable spirit sour, which threatens the war effort and weakens the nation as a whole. However, instead of campaigning for keeping up morale despite raids, losses and bombing as done in People's War propaganda, Thomas equalises the prospect of peace

63 Rose, (2003), p. 287.

with gloom and despondency. Contrary to historic reconstructions in which the sustainment of "morale despite the hardships imposed by war [...] emerges as something to be actively cultivated", Thomas is fully supportive of wartime inconveniences. This attitude works against the spirit of 'make do and mend', and positions Thomas in opposition to the novel's title. Consequently, Thomas has a twofold function within the text: externally representing British nationalism and a collective British identity promulgated to win the war, whilst unconsciously revealing the alleged unity among people as illusionary when emphasising class differences and the threat of pacifism. In depicting a nationalistic character who misunderstands and misrepresents the fundamental ideology of the People's War *Make Do and Mend* debunks the lingering disunity within Britain during the Second World War.

Despite his unwillingness to concede to the war as a straining time for people in the village, Thomas manages to correctly capture the ideology of the People's War as gender-neutral when saying that the village is "full of patriots". The choice of words indicates that the nation and the war effort are concealed as non-gendered, making women as much part of the war as men. Collectively, the village should rebuke Jim's pacifism and when a boy throws an egg at him for wearing a white poppy, Thomas' efforts seem momentarily successful. The white poppy was initially introduced by pacifists as an alternative to the red poppy, or remembrance poppy, which is a symbol in the Anglo-American culture for remembering the soldiers who died during the First World War. First established in 1921, the red poppy is still used in this way today, especially in Britain and Canada. The white poppy, however, symbolises not only mourning for the dead but also a political standpoint postulating peace. Jim's wearing of it illustrates a silent protest which circumvents Thomas' announcement that "[t]alk of peace will get him nowhere". While the patriotic village might decide to not listen to talks about peace, they are more inclined to notice a white poppy in the midst of a hundred reds.

However, Thomas' patriotism changes the symbolic meaning of both poppies significantly when the red poppy turns into a symbol for not simply remembering the dead, but for laying emphasis on the nation and its heroic effort in defending the country in the current war. The white poppy, respectively, becomes more than a symbol for peace – it turns into a sign for treason, because Thomas calls Jim a "fifth-columnist", which means "traitor" or "spy"[64] and thus uses national symbols in order to foster a patriotic spirit among the people, and to justify the exclusion of the already suspicious conscientious objector Jim from village

64 "Fifth column, n." *OED Online*. Oxford University Press, June 2017. Web. 21 August 2017.

life. Jim's behaviour is punished (verbally and physically by throwing an egg) because he represents a threat to the positive spirit in the village. Thomas can manage to control Jim only as long as his white poppy continues to stand alone in a sea of red, which in turn directs the village's anger over wartime shortcomings against Jim.

The significance of this scene is renewed in the context of the murder case when the solicitor remarks that Jim "is a pacifist and made something of an exhibition of himself by wearing a white poppy on Armistice Day" (247). Due to his previous actions, Jim seems to repeatedly arouse suspicions. Despite the fact that Jim's pacifism should rule him out of a murder, the solicitor questions Jim's character based on his aversion to the war. The paradox of suspecting someone of murder for postulating peace illustrates how wartime conduct is judged and interpreted along arbitrary norms.

Harry's response to the solicitor is characteristically forthright and indicates his growing disidentification with the People's War and with his professional occupation in the Navy: "Pacifism isn't illegal, you know; in fact I'm seriously considering joining him next Armistice Day and wearing a white poppy myself." (247-248). Similar to scenes of sexual frankness, Harry's challenge to the nation at war shows the slippages within historical fictions when opting for open resistance rather than silence and assimilation. Especially the solicitor's response: "That's your own business, of course" (248) seems rather inauthentic considering that this very behaviour has paved the way into prison for Jim. Clearly, it was not Jim's "own business" what to wear, but whereas Jim is constantly judged based on his position as an 'ordinary' farm labourer, Harry's higher class and reputation seem to protect him from antagonism, even when displaying open critique on the national leadership.

In the end, everybody who has judged Jim as 'lesser' is proven wrong when the narrative reveals that Jim is an academic with a doctorate title. Harry exploits the latter's newly recovered position when he formally introduces him as "Dr James Rhys Montgomery" (286) to Thomas, whose masculinity and class is in the next moment entirely subordinated: "I'd like you to meet my brother Tom." (286) Not only does Harry deliberately skip his brother's surname, which would have positioned him as almost equal to Jim due to its royal implication, he also calls him by his childhood nickname "Tom", which infantilises and subordinates him further. Moreover, Jim's discovered birth name, in addition to his doctorate title, works to lastingly change the gender and class dynamics between the men. The translation in *The Penguin Dictionary of Surnames* deciphers the name "Montgomery" as meaning 'hill' and 'Man Powerful' with an Old French and

Germanic origin.[65] With this background, Montgomery loosely translates to 'top of man power' and relates to Jim's former profession as a historian to imply that, before the war, his knowledge was considered a resource of high reputation – an interpretation that recovers not only his masculinity but also his upper-class upbringing.

The situation has thus become even more diverse: not only is Jim Brynawal the counterpart to Thomas Griffith-Lyon and an incalculable factor within the nation, his position as a conscious objector has also emasculated and downgraded him compared to his former profession as an academic. Under the name Jim Brynawel he is declassed, emasculated and considered to be dubious, but when resurrected as Dr. Montgomery his masculinity and class outranks Thomas'. The latter's accusation that Jim is a stranger within the nation is turned upside down, when Thomas himself becomes an outsider, who continues to scorn the conscientious objector whilst the rest of the village has changed their opinion of him. The novel seems to suggest that class and gender are unstable factors in a person's life, but, more importantly, that those who claim to represent the nation can come to forfeit this right when they misunderstand its structure, which turns them into stranger. Hence, *Make Do and Mend* creates a highly tangled, diverse and flexible epistemology of gender and class according to which social position and gender performance are absolutely dependant on circumstances.

OUTSIDERS INSIDE: IMPRISONING RESISTANCE

Whilst *Make Do and Mend* dramatises the inherent struggle between friend and stranger in the conflicting positions of Jim and Thomas, Sarah Waters' *The Night Watch* (2006) casts non-conforming characters who threaten the war effort behind bars. The prison is the institutionalised representation of Thomas' efforts to dispose of Jim, and functions to extract negative voices from ordinary society to protect the national war effort. This nationalistic sub-narrative becomes clear with view to the inmates' 'offences': Giggs and Atkin are deserters, Watling and Fraser are conscientious objectors, Stella is queer and the protagonist Duncan was convicted for attempted suicide to evade active service. Their crimes are thus characterised as a resistance to the war effort, and their exclusion functions not simply as a punishment for 'misbehaving', but portraits Sara Ahmed's intriguing observation that "as the outsider inside, the alien takes on a spatial func-

65 Cottle, (1967), p. 196.

tion, establishing relations of proximity and distance within the home(land)"[66]. The men are not simply removed from society but remain inside as outsiders who function to compare and contrast decent behaviour. The prison is the abjected and confined space within the universal nation and additionally a space where prisoners are made to encounter their own exclusion from the inside of prison walls and from the inside of society to which they have become "outsiders inside". The following section will firstly disclose the means by which order and control are established in the prison, to then focus on Duncan's queering of the prison space when fantasizing about his cellmate Fraser. Ultimately, it will be revealed that state control collapses under the homosexual desire of non-conforming subjects.

In order to contain and control unruly subjects, the prison displays mechanism of degradation that function to destroy the inmates' self-worth and attempts of critical thought. The press as an instrument of collective national identity, for instance, is banned from the prison to degrade its inmates and to increase their feeling of expulsion from the war effort. This strategy becomes more plausible with view to Anderson's theorisation that "print-capitalism" is "the embryo of the nationally imagined community" and vital for its citizens to know (of) their place within the nation-state's boundaries.[67] When Fraser holds up a cut-up newspaper, a discussion over the restrictive distribution of knowledge unfolds among the prisoners. Katharina Boehm states that:

> Emptied of the written word – of any information about the political events unfolding outside the prison walls – the newspaper is no longer a vehicle of knowledge but has been reduced to its materiality, a seemingly worthless pile of grubby paper.[68]

While I largely agree with this analysis that print media fails to distribute shared knowledge in prison, the narrative goes beyond such an obvious reading. Not only does the cut-up newspaper keep the prisoners from "hear[ing] about things from the world outside" (236) because that would "stir[...] [them] up" (236), it also re-directs Duncan's desires towards heteronormativity by reducing its message to emphasise family life. Duncan describes the cut-up newspaper as resembling "Christmas snowflakes made by children" only leaving "the family pages, the sporting pages, and cartoons" (235). This is an allegory of typical family life where the father reads the "sporting pages", the mother the "family pages" and

66 Ahmed, (2000), p. 3.

67 Anderson, (1991), p. 44.

68 Katharina Boehm, "Historiography and the Material Imagination in the Novels of Sarah Waters" in *Studies in the Novel* Vol. 43, No. 2 (2011), p. 248-249.

the child(ren) the "cartoons". Duncan's futile nostalgia for the family that promises traditional gender roles and male power, even for those men who do not fight as soldiers during the war, enhances his sense of exclusion. Consequently, Fraser's worry over "what they'll do to your [Duncan's] mind […] if you let them" (235) is a double entendre: the obvious message of withstanding prison methods that keep inmates from having critical thoughts, but also resisting the attempt of heteronormalising Duncan by advocating family life.

Boehm continues reading Duncan's situation in prison as allowing him "to repress unwanted memories of the outside world and grant[ing] him a certain measure of imaginative license"[69]. That Duncan does not mention Alec, his friend who succeeded in committing suicide, and hides the real reason for his imprisonment, indeed suggests that he is trying to keep his past and his memories from entering into the prison. Boehm's argument that Duncan "repress[es] unwanted memories of the outside world" is therefore not without credit: however, her claim of this giving him "a certain measure of imaginative license" remains problematic. In another argument with Fraser over dinner, Duncan is in fact resigned to his uselessness as a prisoner to the outside world when he claims that he does not "see the point of going on about things all the time" (235). While Boehm's assertion that Duncan tries to keep the outside world outside is again demonstrated, the outcome is not "imaginative license" but helplessness and resignation. The prisoners', especially Fraser's, constant talk about the events at the front agitate Duncan:

> We can't change anything. Why should we try? It's someone else's war, not ours.' […]
> 'Is it?' Fraser asked Duncan.
> 'It is,' said Duncan 'when you're in here. Just like everything else is someone else's too. Everything that counts, I mean: nice things, as well as bad –' (235)

The generalising terms "anything" and "everything" suggest a pessimistic mood in Duncan's talk: nothing can be changed from inside the prison, and outside life has no effect on the inmates, just like they have no effect on it. Fraser is unfamiliar with Duncan's past and cannot understand Duncan's pessimistic outburst. Only when uncovering the circumstances in which Alec dies, and how his opinion towards the war has lastingly influenced Duncan, can the latter's attitude in prison be fully understood.

When Alec receives the letter to join the military in 1941, he announces that "the war's not [the soldiers'] war but a load of government men's. It's not our war, either; we have to suffer in it, though. We have to do things they tell us."

69 Boehm, (2011), p. 149.

(481) Alec points at the power of the nation to order its citizens to fight in a war that is neither "their[s]", nor Alec's or Duncan's. Transferring his words into prison proposes an analogy between inmates and soldiers who both feel like the war is not theirs – the former because he cannot participate in the world outside and the latter because it is the nation that takes control and order over his life. Only when knowing Alec's account can the reader infer what Duncan means when he says that "[i]t's someone else's war" – a hidden but strong repetition of Alec's evaluation that it is not a People's War but specifically lead by "a load of government men [...]". This is modified in Duncan's speech by the word "someone" indicating singularity and hinting at Alec's identification of the nation with "*Mr Winston Churchill*" (485) [emphasis original] in his suicide note:

> '*To whom it may concern ...*' [Alec] looked at Duncan. 'Shall I put that? Or shall I put, *To Mr Winston Churchill*?'
> Duncan thought it over. '*To whom it may concern* sounds better,' he said. 'And it might be to Hitler and Goering and Mussolini then, too.' [emphasis original] (485)

Eva M. Pérez Rodríguez argues that "Alec and Duncan wish to commit suicide in response to the English government's decision to turn them into the murderers of others"[70]. Rightly, Pérez Rodríguez identifies the English government as the abstract institution that determines men's lives during a national crisis that was provoked by a small number of political leaders – the same leaders who now send men as soldiers to the front to fight for a cause with which they often fail to identify.

Duncan challenges this patriotic narrative of good (Britain) versus bad (so-called Nazi Germany) when he refuses to differentiate between Churchill, Hitler, Goering or Mussolini. To him, all of these men are responsible for his and Alec's desperate situation and whilst "*Mr Winston Churchill*" is the immediate reference point for Alec, Duncan's perception conflates the prime minister with the dictators of Germany and Italy – a powerful critique on the political leadership of Britain as indistinguishable from fascist leaders during the Second World War. Another inmate named Hammond picks up on Duncan's "someone" when stating: "It's someone else's fucking war, all right!" (235) Unlike Fraser, Hammond has understood Duncan's clumsy reference to Churchill, but since this nuanced critique is overheard by the rest of the prisoners, Duncan's argument loses is provocative power, so he attempts to be more explicit: "Just like everything

70 Eva M. Pérez Rodríguez, How the Second World War Is Depicted by British Novelists since 1990: The Passage of Time Changes Our Portrayal of Traumatic Events (New York: Edwin Mellen Press, 2012), p. 24.

else is someone else's too. Everything that counts, I mean: nice things, as well as bad –" (235). This explanation needs to also be compared with Alec's argument from three years before:

> They ought to let the stupid people fight, and everybody else – everybody who cares about important things, things like the arts, things like that – they ought to be allowed to go and live somewhere on their own, and to hell with Hitler – (481)

Once more Duncan echoes his friend's words and reinforces the strong connection he still feels towards Alec. Striking is the change from the domineering words "someone else's" in Duncan's version to "everybody who cares" in Alec's. Whereas Alec laid emphasis on the people who cared, Duncan anonymises these people further, no longer sure if there is anyone left who cares. Equally, when Alec in 1941 still knows of the "important things, things like the arts", three years later Duncan only remembers that there used to be "everything that counts" without quite knowing what these things are. Duncan's recollection is thus inspired by a memory where a group of people – people like those who have become prisoners – still had reason to fight against fighting by resisting to serve in the military. But this memory is fading, leaving Duncan with an inadequate and incomplete version of an argument, which has nevertheless notably and lastingly influenced his world views – despite the prison's efforts of reducing oppositional thoughts. It thus seems that the prison is little effective in regulating subjects when Duncan is free enough to inscribe a certain degree of critique over Britain's leadership in his formulations.

Moreover, the prison scenes repeatedly dramatise how the threat of inversion troubles Britons' self-image as impregnable. During air raids, when the wardens go into the shelters, the inmates are left behind to take care of themselves. Shouting and disorder, prisoners climbing on chairs and yelling encouragement to the pilots, visualise the lack of power the nation has over its citizens when the threat of invasion becomes physically palpable in rattling furniture and windows, fires or blasts. When a prisoner named Miller begins to sing, this mood of restlessness is momentarily silenced:

> *I hear your voice, I reach to hold you,*
> *Your lip touch mine, my arms enfold you.*
> *But then you're gone: I wake and find*
> *That I've been drea-ming...* (302) [emphasis original]

Singing of a lost love and dreaming of its prevalence, Miller queers the restless atmosphere of the prison by expressing emotions conventionally coded feminine. The song does not establish who the "I" and the "you" are, which potentially leaves open their sex and gender. Yet the qualities assigned to masculinity and femininity deciphers the "I" as male and the "you" as female when the former "hold[s]" the latter. This holding references stereotypical male strength and protection whereas the "touch[ing]" of lips indicates traditional female softness. Set in heteronormative terms, it is not simply the display of emotions which is troubling in Miller's song, but the fact that this relationship between a man and a woman is a product of the mind emphasising the inmates' exclusion from society. Atkin, another prisoner, cannot bear this moment of shared "longing" (302) and begins to counter Miller's song with another one sharply separating emotion from sexuality:

Give me a girl with eyes of blue,
Who likes it if you don't but prefers it if you do! (302) [emphasis original]

Give me a girl with eyes of black,
Who likes it on her belly but prefers it on her back! (303) [emphasis original]

Duncan notes that Atkin's song "sounded like something a serviceman would sing" (302), which immediately re-articulates masculinity in the prison by registering the song as military slang. Whereas the first lines are rather innocent despite shallowly focusing on female appearance, the second line of each stanza concentrates on sexual intercourse and the girl's alleged longing for and enjoyment of male penetration. Duncan notes that "[f]or almost a minute the two songs ran bizarrely together; then Miller gave in" (303). Atkin's vocalisation of military masculinity subordinates Miller's romantic image of heterosexual love, because instant sexual satisfaction is a more sought-after state than enduring relationships and soft emotions.

After the 'all clear' when the inmates have settled down, Fraser remembers the first song by Miller and he explains to Duncan: "I think I danced to this tune once. [...] I probably laughed at the bloody thing, then. Now – Now it seems strikingly apt, doesn't it? Christ! Trust Miller and a popular song to be so honest about longing." (302) Fraser captures the atmosphere of Miller's song to express "longing", which is exactly why Atkin countered it with a bawdy song. "Longing" is not appreciated among men in prison because it sheds too much light on emotions traditionally connoted feminine. Fraser, too, cannot accept his obviously romantic desires and transforms them into a misogynistic fantasy of seducing a "plain, stout, stupid, grateful girl" (305) thus rearticulating masculinity into Miller's soft lyrics. He continues:

> I'd have her, fully clothed. I wouldn't take off a stitch. I'd only loosen a button or two at the back of her dress – and I'd undo her brassière, while I was about it – and then I'd draw the dress and the brassière down to her elbows and get my fingers on to her chest. I'd give her a pinch. I might pull her about a bit – there wouldn't be a thing she could do if I did, for the dress – do you see? – the dress would be pinning her arms to her sides ... (306)

Fraser's fantasy betrays his profound need to prove his masculinity in a place that emasculates men who are not part of the war effort. He therefore fantasises about a girl instead of a woman, because girls are easier to charm and seduce due to their lack of experience. His wish for the girl to be "grateful" emphasises the fragility of his masculinity and his sub-conscious need for approval. Moreover, his incessant use of "I" signals superiority over his victim, but also reveals his need for self-affirmation. Beginning the narration with the utterly disrespectful phrase "I'd have her" establishes Fraser as the penetrator and denies the possibility of mutual pleasure by focusing exclusively on his needs. This is further illustrated when stating: "I wouldn't take off a stitch" – indicating that he wants to fully relish in his role as penetrator and not undress his victim to allude to the impression of 'conventional sex.' The girl becomes reduced to her sexual parts as well as the victim of objectification. Savouring this, Fraser constantly pauses (dashes) to meticulously explain the scene to Duncan. His focus on detail and the instructive tone is especially patronising in the end when Fraser explains to Duncan that he will enchain the girl with her own dress "pinning her arms to her sides". Fraser's rhetorical question ("do you see?") substantiates his need for Duncan to understand that he is in complete control of the girl, at least in his fantasy.

With this idea of performing sexual power in mind, Fraser puts his hand "to his cock; and after another moment he began, with a subtle, even motion, to stroke it" (306). Duncan, lying on the bunk underneath Fraser, queers this misogynistic account of heterosexual sex by also masturbating with the distinct difference of doing it whilst fantasising about his cellmate. Clinging to the wires of Fraser's bunk, Duncan's erection is a reflection of the male body above him. In this way, Duncan challenges the authority of compulsory heterosexuality and cross-gender erotisation when illustrating how "non-normative masculinity [...] undermine[s] the power of the discourse [prison] that seeks to control it"[71]. De-

71 Adele Jones, "Disrupting the Continuum: Collapsing Space and Time in Sarah Waters's *The Night Watch*" in *Journal of Gender Studies* Vol. 23, No. 1 (2014), p. 38.

signed to enforce heteronormative order, Duncan shatters the power of the prison by not simply romancing about men, but by turning Fraser's heterosexual discourse of sexual dominance over a girl into homosexual erotisation. In this way, Duncan's homosexual desires also challenge the prison's effort of trying to redirect him towards heteronormativity.

'THOU SHALT NOT KILL': NATIONALISM AND RELIGION

My analysis has thus far illustrated the outside position of men who do not participate in the war effort. Whereas *Make Do and Mend* exemplifies Jim Brynawel as a stranger within the village who is subordinated to Thomas Griffith-Lyon's nominally claimed authority, *The Night Watch* expels non-conforming men into the prison space. The stigma of emasculation follows such expulsions and functions to degrade conscientious objectors. In Mary Renault's *The Charioteer* (1953) the protagonists Laurie and Andrew subvert this dominant narrative when Laurie fails to feel pride in being a soldier and Andrew is not ashamed of being a pacifist. Additionally, Andrew's Quaker beliefs oppose Laurie's soon-to-be stepfather Mr. Straike, whose hostility towards non-fighting men reveals a discrepancy between the church and Christian values that disagree with the idea of war. As a vicar, Mr. Straike should represent these virtues, but his patriotic attitude in combination with his clerical position establishes the church as a hypocritical institution that perpetuates wartime nationalism and heteronormativity. The three characters' personal and ideological differences insinuate an opposition between institutionalised religion subsuming under wartime nationalism, and the personal enactment of Christian ideals according to which killing is a sin because every person should be treated with respect. The following will first examine how the church enforces gender norms, to then deconstruct the opposition of Mr. Straike as a vicar and Andrew's Quaker beliefs. Lastly, I will analyse Laurie's complicated situation as a homosexual soldier increasingly unconvinced by wartime nationalism, but equally bewildered by Andrew's moral integrity.

Anderson explains the proximity between nationalism and religion when he asserts that nation-states have "a strong affinity with religious imaginings"[72], because religious world-views are concerned with "the contingency of life". When the Enlightenment brought forth the "dusk of religious modes of thought", "the dawn of the age of nationalism"[73] was announced, because only an imagined

72 Anderson, (1991), p. 10.

73 Ibid., p. 10 and p. 11.

community could provide immortality in ways similar to religion. Nationalism and religion thus stand on similar ground and the following scene in which Laurie's mother Mrs. Odell marries Mr. Straike illustrates that the church enforces gender norms through marriage, which helps the British nation to maintain a semblance of order despite the chaos of the Second World War:

'… and, forsaking all other, keep thee only to her, as long as ye both shall live?'
In a round, announcing voice, Mr. Straike said, 'I will.'
The full realization of his physical presence hit Laurie like a blow. He stared at the floor and reminded himself that he was in church. But church had become a smell of hassocks and furnace coke and, ubiquitously, of Mr. Straike. It was an extension of him.
'Wilt thou obey and serve him, love, honor, and …'
Oh, God, make her say no.
'I will.'
He heard Aunt Olive behind him give a satisfied sigh.
'Who giveth this woman to be married to this man?'
'I do,' Laurie said. [...] He took a measured pace forward and handed his mother to Canon Rosslow to hand to Mr. Straike. He fell a pace back again. With a dry, empty relief, he realized that this was all. He had spoken his line; he could get back into the chorus. There was his place ready for him, beside Aunt Olive in the corner of the front pew. He moved toward it. (279)

Mrs. Odell's role in this scene represents conventional femininity that compels women into marriage by assuming their position as dependent and in need of guidance by men. Similar to the nation that fashions a collective identity among its citizens, the church, embodied in Mr. Straike, organises men and women into married couples by replacing Mrs. Odell's subjectivity with the role of 'wife'. Despite performing the traditional active part of masculinity when handing his mother to her husband, Laurie's position cannot be read as easily as his mother's. Movement is demonstrated here in two ways; in the active (Laurie) and the passive (his mother). Mrs. Odell is being handed from one man to the next until she arrives at her destination, which is Mr. Straike. Laurie, however, is taking "measured pace forward" and "a pace back again", which shows that movement, especially walking, does not come naturally to him like it should. His inhibited action is not only caused by his leg injury, but also by the physical presence of Mr. Straike. Two male bodies encounter each other here, where their physicality sets the terms on which they measure their own and each other's masculinity. Laurie, already feeling insecure about the limited mobility of his leg, sees himself as inferior to his stepfather, who represents a conservative attitude that scrutinises love between men due to his position as a vicar.

In contrast to her future husband, Mrs. Odell's life is less obviously embedded in a heteronormative structure. As a divorced woman and single mother, Mrs. Odell portrays a sense of (sexual) freedom, autonomy and self-determination, which the church, as an institution advocating traditions of gender roles, wants to see restricted in women. When, according to Linda Martin Alcoff, "women are defined in reference to men, as helpmates, wives, mothers, [and] caregivers of men", Mrs. Odell, who performs neither of these duties in a traditional way, is 'undefinable' and uncontrollable in patriarchal terms[74]. Order needs to be re-established and Laurie, as the cause of his mother's defection from the 'right path', has to symbolically as well as literally let go and give "this woman to be married to this man". By neither naming Mrs. Odell nor Mr. Straike but making them an anonymous couple of "this woman" and "this man", differences in sex and gender are emphasised, which substantiates and confirms the heteronormative character of marriage.

Consider the different emphasis during the ceremony addressing first Mr. Straike "... and, forsaking all other, keep thee only to her, as long as ye both shall live?" and then Mrs. Odell "Wilt thou obey and serve him, love, honor, and ..." (279). Mr. Straike's contractual obligation is to only stay faithful to his wife, whereas Mrs. Odell has to additionally "obey", "serve", "love" and "honor" him. This indicates a stereotypical understanding of marriage that is based on a submissive wife and an empowered husband. Mrs. Odell's abandonment of her house and home to move into Mr. Straike's vicarage substantiates her marriage as a means of control and re-establishment of traditional norms of femininity. Whereas her old home, a kind of "anti-home" as coined by Victoria Steward[75], is marked by her divorce and single parenting, her new accommodation represents an order of conventional gender roles, highlighted in its connection to the church.

At one point during the wedding, Laurie silently begs for her to reject Mr. Straike: "Oh, God, make her say no" (279). His choice of words needs deconstructing considering that the church is an extension of the Christian God, who in every bit stands for heteronormative matrimony. To hope that God would make Mrs. Odell turn down Mr. Straike is thus paradoxical and doomed to fail. Mrs.

74 Linda Martín Alcoff, "Feminist Theory and Social Science: New knowledges, new epistemologies" in Nancy Duncan (ed.), *BodySpace: Destabilizing geographies of gender and sexuality* (London and New York: Routledge, 1996), p. 25.

75 Victoria Stewart, *The Second World War in Contemporary British Fiction: Secret Histories* (Edinburgh: Edinburgh University Press, 2011), p. 144.

Odell's "I will" serves to underline this inevitable failure. Language is here instrumentalised as a performance: the words "I will" not only state agreement but actually perform the wedding: they are what Judith Butler terms after John Langshaw Austin 'illocutionary': "speech acts that, in saying do what they say, and do it in the moment of that saying"[76]. The power of illocutionary language lies not only in its inherent agency, but also in its ritualisation of the moment when spoken. Mrs. Odell's "I will" is not only the performance of the act of getting married, it also works to further ritualise the moment of heteronormative marriage. Hence, by performing an illocutionary speech act, Mrs. Odell moves into the anonymous discourse of heteronormativity, again becoming "this woman".

Moreover, the scene broadens Butler's argument by showing that illocutionary speech does not need to be composed of words in order to be intelligible. Aunt Olive "give[s] a satisfied sigh" after Mrs. Odell has pronounced the momentous two words that change not only the bride's life, but also that of her relatives. Aunt Olive's reaction shows that social disgrace does not necessarily only affect those people who brought it upon themselves through deviating actions or lifestyles, but also those who are connected to such non-conforming subjects. In communicating her relief as a "satisfied sigh", Aunt Olive participates in the ceremony and articulates the desirability for a woman to become a wife. While the sigh is not strictly speaking a speech act that "performs its deed" [77], it nevertheless becomes an expression that exceeds itself by legitimising the wedding and confirming the rightness and heteronormative significance of Mrs. Odell's "I will".

Laurie's homosexuality is contrasted to his mother's heterosexual wedding, which makes her deviating son an outsider in church and by extension expels Laurie from the new family. This is one reason why Laurie, narrating the story, drifts in and out of the ceremony and shuts out the formal voice of the church, whilst thinking of his mother and his relief over having come to the wedding despite hesitations. Such thoughts constantly disturb the authoritative voice marrying Mrs. Odell and Mr. Straike, which fragments the narrative flow and takes away some of the vows' overarching and regulating power. By asking himself "how she would have managed without him", Laurie remembers a time in their relationship where neither of them could have existed on their own. To him the past of having his mother to himself, and the present in which she is being claimed by another man, are intermingled, illustrating nostalgia and Laurie's la-

76 Judith Butler, *Excitable Speech: A Politics of the Performative of Identity* (London and New York: Routledge, 1997), p. 3.

77 Butler, (1997), p. 3.

tent oedipal relation to his mother. The sudden perception of the formal voice disturbs Laurie's thoughts and reminds of his forthcoming replacement by Mr. Straike. The narrative thus attracts the attention from Laurie's personal thoughts back to the heteronormative language of the wedding.

When Mr. Straike's "physical presence hit[s] Laurie like a blow" (279), Laurie is deeply unsettled by an awareness that the vicar is more than the earthly representation of God: "But church had become a smell of hassocks and furnace coke and, ubiquitously, of Mr. Straike. It was an extension of him." (279) Since the voice marrying his mother cannot be explicitly identified as the pastor's, it is strongly linked to Mr. Straike. As the town's vicar, he would logically be the extension or hand of the church (of God), but in Laurie's formulation the church becomes an extension of Mr. Straike. This does not simply make Mr. Straike speak in the name of God but embodies him *as* God making the disembodied voice His voice. Consequently, when Mr. Straike completes his union with Laurie's mother "[i]n a round announcing voice" stating "I will", he does not re-cite former wedding vows as Mrs. Odell has done but utters the ultimate wedding vow in which every citation finds its origin. Laurie's next movement is consequentially *away* from Mr. Straike, who embodies an ideology that scrutinises Laurie's homosexuality. He instead moves towards "[a]unt Olive in the corner of the front pew." With this retreat Laurie's masculinity is brought to the same level as aunt Olive's femininity, who was previously "behind" him whilst he was standing. Now he is sitting "beside" her. As this is the only description of bodies in spatial relation to one another, it emphasises not only Laurie as a moving body in a static scene but his movement downwards – literally in him sitting down next to aunt Olive and symbolically in the lowering of his masculinity. This scene illustrates "our inability of defining either masculinity or femininity except in relation to each other"[78]. Due to men's capability to mentally distance themselves from female gender performances, a dichotomous categorising is possible that proclaims rational acts as masculine and emotional conduct as feminine. It follows that Laurie's regular contact with female nurses enable him to model his masculinity in nuanced ways to differ from femininity. He consequently feels little threatened by potential emasculation, and remains calm when levelling his masculinity with aunt Olive's femininity. The depiction of aunt Olive crying, after all, distances her from Laurie's rational indifference to the seemingly romantic atmosphere of the wedding. In his acceptance of his place in the front pew, Laurie expresses ambivalence towards his mother's approaching conservative lifestyle as well as the nation's regulation of men through the threat of emasculation.

78 Paechter, (2006), p. 254.

This unimpressed attitude is similarly evident when Mr. Straike discredits his nickname Laurie as "a sissy name" (286). Immediately after the ceremony, his new stepfather deploys a parental role over Laurie by repeatedly calling him by his full name Laurence. The names Laurence and Laurie have very different connotations to Mr. Straike: Laurie being the "sissy" version of Laurence which automatically genders 'Laurie' as feminine and 'Laurence' as masculine.[79] In his persistence of calling him Laurence, Mr. Straike not only shows his disapproval of the nickname Laurie, he also, and more significantly, wields power over him by renaming and redirecting him towards heteronormativity. His attitude towards Laurie exemplifies Halberstam's claim that "fixity conferred by names also traps people into many different identities, racial as well as gendered"[80]. Butler similarly argues that "one is already claimed by the voice that calls the name"[81]. In calling Laurie by his birth name, Mr. Straike tries to claim authority over his stepson in order to coerce him towards gender appropriateness. Laurie registers unemotionally that "[h]e was being rechristened as a bracer". (286) The term "bracer" is puzzling here and needs evaluation. According to the *Oxford English Dictionary*, "bracer" most commonly means "[t]hat which clamps, binds, etc.; a cincture, bandage, brace" or "[t]hat which braces (the nerves); *hence* a tonic medicine" of which neither explanation sheds light on Mr. Straike's usage.[82] Another approach to the term is reading it as a verb deriving from 'to brace one-

79 Note the misogynistic implication of the abusive word "sissy". It is one of many examples where negatively evaluated femininity is applied to homosexual men in order to simultaneously degrade their masculinity and women's femininity. When found in contemporary usage, abusive connotations are often lost or remain unconscious, which highlights the importance of Butler's effort to emphasise that speech is always a citation of previous discourses making its implication different to its current usage.

80 Halberstam, *Female Masculinity* (Durham and London: Duke University Press, 1998), p. 8. In an interview with Sinclair Sexsmith for Lambda Literary Halberstam states: "So some people call me Jack, my sister calls me Jude, people who I've known forever call me Judith—I try not to police any of it. A lot of people call me he, some people call me she, and I let it be a weird mix of things and I'm not trying to control it." In order to do justice to the preferred gender fluidity that is also the object of Halberstam's professional work, I will refrain from gendering Halberstam. Sinclair Sexsmith, "Jack Halberstam: Queers Create Better Models of Success" (Interview from 2012) <http://www.lambdaliterary.org/interviews/02/01/jack-halberstam-queers-create-better-models-of-success/> [last accessed 11/08/2017].

81 Butler, (1997), p. 32.

82 "Bracer, n.1." *OED Online*. Oxford University Press, December 2015. Web. 23 February 2016.

self', which means "summoning up resolution for a task", or "to pull oneself together for an effort"[83]. By being called Laurence, Laurie is told to start 'being a man' and to pull himself together, which entails leading an independent life. This reading is reinforced when Mrs. Odell "had gone to change into her going-away things" (286), which is the last thing the novel ever says about her. Mr. Straike's "rechristening" of Laurie as Laurence can be understood as illocutionary, just like his mother's "I will" completing the church's aim for re-establishing Christian morality and normality in the family, which is (momentarily) successful: the 'unnatural' mother-son bond is broken and the deviating subject is expelled from his family. Laurie realises that Mr. Straike will be adopting a parental role as his stepfather just like the nation controls his life as a soldier. Religion and nationalism are thus combined in the character of Mr. Straike who tries to control the life of his stepson according to heteronormative parameters. This demonstrates a connection between church and nation following Anderson's proposition that nationalism builds and expands on religion because fundamental ideologies such as Christian values inform the establishment of nations as imagined communities to which the Unknown Soldier serves as a stabilising myth.

Moreover, when Mr. Straike learns that a group of Quakers, among them Andrew, work at Laurie's hospital, he reveals his deep-rooted nationalistic and patriotic convictions. In his view, religion is not a sufficient reason for not helping the war effort, which devastates his position as a clergyman further. Ahmed exposes that "[t]he construction of the nation space takes place alongside the production of national character as instances in which 'the nation' itself is fleshed out as *place and person*"[84]. By adopting a favourable position towards the war and a strict attitude against those men who refuse to fight, Mr. Straike – paradoxically a non-fighter himself – becomes the embodiment of nationalism. His role as vicar is only a distraction from his nationalistic attitude. During an argument with Laurie concerning conscientious objectors Mr. Straike claims:

> 'In fact, I well recall saying to your mother in [sic] the train that if conchies *must* be employed to wait upon war casualties, possibly in the hope of arousing some vestigial sense of shame, they might at least be kept where they need not affront the eye, in suitable activities such as scrubbing latrines, and so on.' (268) [Emphasis original]

83 "Brace, v.1." *OED Online*. Oxford University Press, December 2015. Web. 23 February 2016.

84 Ahmed, (2000), p. 99.

Mr. Straike's use of the passive voice ("be employed", "be kept") removes subjectivity from the argument to enhance its aspired persuasive power as 'collective truth'. He indicates superiority and forestalls any counter-arguments on Laurie's part by introducing his position with the words "[i]n fact". In combination with his emphasis on "well" recalling his words from some time ago, the conviction and intractability of his opinion is established, which follows his depiction as an intransigent character. The word "*must*", emphasised in italics, substantiates his aversion towards those men who refuse to fight, which is underscored by the derogatory use of the abbreviation "conchies" – not 'worthy' of being called by the technical term 'conscientious objector'.

By creating a long and entangled compound sentence, Mr. Straike tries to impress Laurie and to convince him of his superior knowledge on the subject in order to preclude protest. The use of punchy words ("shame", "affront the eye", "scrubbing latrines") and his emphasis on "*must*" distract from Mr. Straike's confusion over the point he wants to transmit. Aiming for acceptance without challenge, he does not realise that his argument is highly paradoxical thus nullifying its claim for validity: Mr. Straike wants non-serving men to feel ashamed of themselves for refusing to fight, which is induced in them by waiting on and physically/visually encountering injured men. At the same time, he demands that they stay out of sight of soldiers. In consequence, the sight of the injured should at once generate shame for the conscientious objector but equally "affronts the eye" of the soldier. The solution of making them "scrub [...] latrines" to effeminise them puts the affronting subjects out of sight for the soldiers, but also prevents them from having to encounter that which should shame them. Mr. Straike's argument is thus untenable and tautological. Additionally, he is not aware that "shared shame [is] a prime instrument for strengthening the sense of mutuality and community"[85]. The Quakers' conviction that fighting is morally wrong unites them and countermands the threat of shameful emasculation desired by Mr. Straike's speech.

Laurie responds sarcastically to his stepfather's illogical argument: "How did you guess? When I met my best friend he was doing that very thing [scrubbing latrines]." (268) In giving the 'conchie' a social status as his best friend, Laurie attacks the ground on which Mr. Straike's argument rests, namely conscientious objectors as anonymous obstacles to the war. Additionally, Mr. Straike's solution for them to scrub latrines to keep them out of sight has been proven ineffective because this activity seems as socialising as waiting upon injured soldiers. By pointing out Mr. Straike's reasoning as faulty and short-sighted, Laurie frees

85 Silvan Tomkins, *Shame and Its Sisters: A Silvan Tomkins Reader* Eve Kosofsky Sedgwick and Adam Frank (eds.), (Durham: Duke University Press, 1995), p. 156.

himself from both the increasing influence of his stepfather and the nation's desire to keep its soldiers away from conscientious objectors – a liberating move atypical for a soldier but in accordance with Laurie's disobedient character. Laurie continues challenging Mr. Straike:

> 'Oh, well,' said Laurie pleasantly, 'we all reacted to their arrival, of course. But actually, we found persecuting Christians awfully overrated. Perhaps we needed lions or something. Perhaps we ought to have tried burning them alive. Perhaps we just needed to be civilians and not soldiers. I wouldn't know.' (269)

In this highly sarcastic outburst Laurie addresses many metaphors of national power: "persecution", "lions", "fire" and "soldiers". National institutions persecute subjects for wrongdoings, the characteristics of the lion such as strength, fearlessness and power to destroy, are figuratively used to also describe the qualities of a nation. Fire is the symbol for burning abjected subjects in the Middle Ages initiated by the national leadership. The soldier, as has been established, is the embodiment and representation of national dominance. In judging all of these symbols as ridiculous in the dealing with conscientious objectors, Laurie scorns the nation and its ideologies. His use of the collective pronoun "we" includes his fellow hospital patients and soldiers and demonstrates that not he alone is of this critical opinion. Most interesting is the penultimate sentence "[p]erhaps we just needed to be civilians and not soldiers" to find an appropriate response to men who refuse to be the murderer of others that would satisfy Mr. Straike. Laurie implies that civilians have a much more hostile opinion towards conscientious objectors than those who actually fought. The suffering the soldier has seen during combat makes him lenient and understanding towards other men who have chosen a pacifist life, whereas civilians who stayed at home due to age or bodily infirmity do not know, or have forgotten, the horrors of war. This concretely positions Mr. Straike on the side of the civilian being too old to fight, and Laurie on the side of the soldier emphasising their personal difference as well as the discrepancy in their performance of masculinity. Since traditionally, soldiers are rewarded with heroic masculinity, the civilian Mr. Straike is subordinated to Laurie, and by claiming the moral high ground in the defence of conscientious objectors, Laurie erodes his stepfather's authority further. His evaluation that only "civilians and not soldiers" would share Mr. Straike's radical attitude towards non-fighting men, belatedly names the reason for the vicar's implausible reasoning displayed earlier: his lack of fighting experience makes him unfit to judge any war related issues including conscientious objection.

Make Do and Mend affirms Laurie's evaluation of soldiers as more lenient towards conscientious objector than civilians, when Thomas accuses his brother Harry of "condon[ing] the presence of a conshie" (53) (meaning Jim) to which Harry replies: "Simply because I *have* seen the war at close quarters [...] I don't believe a man should be bullied into killing another man if his conscience won't support it." (53) [emphasis original] A straightforward analysis of soldiers as representatives of patriotism and nationalism is thus challenged when novels differentiate between the rigid attitude of civilians and an understanding approach by soldiers. *The Charioteer* and *Make Do and Mend* demonstrate that civilians, who never directly encountered the horrors of the battlefield, come to ideologically superimpose the power of the nation, whereas the soldier sympathises with lenient and altruistic Christian values represented by the Quakers. Anderson explains that it is vital to distance these religious values "from their role in the legitimation of specific systems of domination and exploitation"[86]. Through the oppositional depiction of Andrew and Mr. Straike, *The Charioteer* differentiates 'traditional religious world-views' such as charity and compassion from the institution of the church. Whereas Mr. Straike is an emblem of collective national identity rather than of Christian virtues, Andrew's Quakerism is an individual representation of Christianity against nationalistic pressures to conform to and fight in the war. Laurie is positioned in between Mr. Straike and Andrew and seems confrontational to both extremes: as a homosexual soldier, he opposes traditional religious faith in heterosexuality, matrimony and procreation, but stands in equal distance to nationalistic attitudes and the myth of the Unknown Soldier as represented by Mr. Straike. Laurie has to constantly negotiate between these conflicting positions if he wants to find his place at a time characterised by extremes.

Laurie's reluctance to uncritically follow national narratives is initially broached at the very beginning of the novel after his father has left the family. He is lying in bed and his mother is telling him the story of St. George, a famous tale of the patron saint of England. The legend of Saint George glorifies courage, chivalry and heroism and is often adapted as a children's bedtime story emphasising the heroic action of Saint George when rescuing a princess from a dragon: "Then St. George pulled out his sword, and he said ... [Laurie's mother] paused, because this was the line on which Laurie liked to come in. But he had fallen asleep." (13) Laurie's failure to complete the nursery tale leaves the reader wondering what the hero might have said to the princess and signals a significant change in the protagonist: the parade of nationalism and glory has lost its fascinating hold on him. Caroline Zilboorg rightly emphasises that "Laurie can no

86 Anderson, (1991), p. 10.

longer fully accept the traditional national identity suggested in the nursery tale."[87] Before falling asleep, Laurie shuts out his mother's voice and perceives that "no one would ever look from these eyes but he: that among all the lives, numerous beyond imagination, in which he might have lived, he was this one, pinned to this single point of infinity; the rest always to be alien, he to be I." (13) This realisation of identity challenges the nursery story's projection of nationalism and heroism. Laurie pledges allegiance not to St. George, not to Britain, not to religion but to himself. His distance to master narratives of hegemonic masculinity and heroism during battle, increases throughout the novel until, after an argument with Andrew, he is no longer acknowledged as a soldier. In addition to his growing disidentification with the war, Laurie's friendship to Andrew starts losing its purity because of their conflicting points of view regarding the fate of a fellow hospital patient.

Having deceived himself for the better half of the text that Andrew's pacifism does not stand between them, Laurie comes to recognise their differences to be greater than expected, when he tries to take care of a fellow patient named Charlot, who is close to death. A French fisherman coming under fire during British retreat from Dunkirk, the heavily wounded Charlot ended up in the same hospital as Laurie. As the only person speaking French, Laurie befriends the fisherman. Because of this friendship, only Laurie can approach Charlot now that he is dying. Andrew, on the other hand, who is supposed to be in charge of the patient, cannot handle the situation and repeatedly calls for the Nurse to come and help. In his absence, Laurie tries to understand Charlot's incomprehensive muttering and perceives the words "*péché mortel*" (237) [emphasis original] which means 'mortal sin'. Laurie infers from this that "[h]e wants a priest" (237). Unable to get hold of "Father James" (238), Laurie suggests that Andrew should pretend to be a priest since Charlot no longer recognises his face and would not know the difference. Of course, Andrew dismisses this idea and explains his firm aversion against deceiving a dying person in this way. Laurie, sub-consciously aware that Andrew is right, loses his temper:

> 'Oh God. What difference does it make? He can't talk sense anyway. Just so he can go feeling it's all right.'
> 'You know we can't do it,' Andrew said. He stared at Laurie with a lost, exploring look.
> Laurie had a reasonless but terrible feeling of having been discovered and condemned. He tried to push it away, but his mind still felt shocked, bleeding and raw. 'But you don't believe those church things matter. So long as what he feels is right. You've always said so.

87 Caroline Zilboorg, *The Masks of Mary Renault: A Literary Biography* (Columbia, Missouri: University of Missouri Press, 2001), p. 107.

It isn't much to do for him.' [...] 'It's a responsibility neither of us has any right whatever to take.' Andrew's face had set with decision; Laurie felt that it had hardened against him. [...] With a sudden stab of nostalgia [Laurie] thought, Ralph would have understood.
'You're pretty hard, aren't you?' [Laurie] said.
Andrew had read in Laurie's eyes the will to hurt, his altered face showed it. It showed too that he knew that he was being punished partly for what he was and believed. He said, 'That doesn't mean anything. A thing's either right or it isn't.' (238-239)

Laurie and Andrew have had an understanding that the latter's pacifism and religion are personal ideals incompatible with warfare, but equally detached from the traditional institution of the church. Highly suspicious of the church, which Laurie associates with Mr. Straike, he is shocked about Andrew's assertion, and interprets Andrew's strict position as a betrayal of their friendship and as a sign of his friend's former dishonesty. Their conversation betrays a double discourse: the literal disagreement over Charlot's fate and the subliminal pronunciation of differences between the characters. Laurie's closeted homosexuality forecloses shared knowledge between the characters and obscures their communication, leading to Laurie's "reasonless but terrible feeling of having been discovered and condemned". The allusive style of writing complicates a clear reference to what Laurie might be "discovered and condemned" of. He seems to fear that ignoring moral conventions at the deathbed has revealed his sexual difference to Andrew. At the same time, he misinterprets Andrew's refusal to play the priest as a negative evaluation of his homosexuality, and thus confers his friend's words with meaning beyond Andrew's control.

Becoming conscious of their different social and ideological positions, Laurie thinks of Ralph who, as a homosexual officer, can relate to Laurie and would probably share his attitude in a crisis. The personal discrepancies between Andrew and Laurie, which until now had constituted their mutual attraction, determine their disagreement. Instead of admiring Andrew for his strength to withstand national pressures to join the military, Andrew's status as a conscientious objector becomes the ground on which Laurie can formulate his aversion, because the real reason for his struggles – his homosexual love for his friend – remains hidden from public discourse. Consequently, Andrew can perceive that he "was being punished *partly* for what he was and believed" [my emphasis]. The other part of Laurie's accusation remains unintelligible to him. Innocent of any sub-text, Andrew can only grasp him in terms of moral deceit. When Andrew defends his position by challenging Laurie "[d]on't you see, some things are too important to be tampered with" (239), Laurie feels the difference between them growing more profound and he realises that in "his gray hospital-orderly's coat

[Andrew] looked more like a soldier than Laurie did in his battle-dress. He was distinct and separate and far away. And strikingly good-looking." (239) Laurie begins to realise that even in comparison with a conscientious objector, his deviating lifestyle makes his attitude alien to heteronormative order. This is most severely expressed when Laurie compares his battle dress to Andrew's hospital uniform which paradoxically makes the latter a more convincing embodiment of the Unknown Soldier than the serving Laurie whose sexuality stands in direct contradiction to what he is supposed to represent. The disinterest in the nursery tale from the beginning of the novel, therefore, constitutes Laurie's life as a soldier: required to represent a collective national identity when his individuality rebels against such standards.

Laurie increasingly realises that every set of norms is failing for him – he neither identifies with wartime standards on masculinity and heroism, nor with Andrew's version of religious beliefs untainted by the conservative church grounded in gender norms and heterosexual wedlock. His constant struggles disclose the scripts of nationalism that circulate during the Second World War as deceptive when aiming for a collective identity that kills off individuality.

"MASCULINE, PATRIOTIC, MATURE AND CAPABLE"? – PERFORMANCES OF MILITARY MASCULINITIES

In Walter Baxter's *Look Down in Mercy*, (1951) Toni Kent suffers from the same burdens encountered by Laurie when his attraction to the batman Anson stands in contradiction to his role of commanding officer. Whereas Laurie is relatively unimpressed by potential emasculation when he is largely indifferent towards Mr. Straike's attempted rechristening, Kent is constantly afraid of losing privileges that position him as the nation's metaphoric Unknown Soldier – highly masculine and the ideal version of what Connell has coined hegemonic masculinity. In the "Introduction" to the 2014 edition of the novel, Gregory Woods indeed characterises Kent as "masculine, patriotic, mature and capable"[88] which would make him a stereotypical wartime protagonist representing the nation despite his deviating sexuality. Wood's automatic attribution of masculinity to the officer shows that bodies are made to stand for an identity – that a serving male body represents the nation even when his homosexuality contradicts its standardised myths. In contrast to Woods' assertion, I will argue that *Look Down in Mer-*

88 Gregory Woods, "Introduction" *Look Down in Mercy*, [1951], (Richmond: Valancourt Books, 2014), p. ix.

cy develops a much more complex character, who comes to challenge the myth of the Unknown Soldier when failing to act heroically, and who falls in love with another man. The novel reveals that the failure of hegemonic masculinity is grounded in the fact that men are either judged as too emotional and weak (Kent) or as too indifferent making them inhumane and savage (Goodwin, one of Kent's soldiers). Military masculinity modelled after hegemonic masculinity is thus a traumatic concept for men not only because it is unattainable, but because it leaves men in a constant state of anxiety over how their performance is perceived by others.

The following analysis will challenge Woods' judgement of Kent as "masculine, patriotic, mature and capable" by focusing on the protagonist's diminishing masculinity compared to other men, and the novel's development of an alternative version to masculine heroism that is informed by feminine emotions. It will also disclose that efforts of representing British masculinity as 'untarnished' by unnecessary violence in order to contrast it from the brutal enemy, are failing when Goodwin commits a vicious murder that brings him in close proximity to the savage Japanese.

In part two of *Look Down in Mercy*, Kent's latent reluctance to identify with the People's War discussed previously transforms into an inability to perform appropriate to his commanding position. Although at times carrying life-threatening responsibilities, Kent values his role as an officer because it entails reputation and honour. He is consequently devastated when in the midst of battle his professional incompetence comes to the fore and when he additionally falls in love with his batman Anson. At first, the bond between Kent and Anson rests on the latter's ability of making his officer "put aside the slowly accumulating burden of his responsibilities" (53). Despite identifying his position as a "burden", Kent is unwilling to resign his post (if that was an option), which illustrates Richard Howson's claim that "hegemonic characteristics must continue to be privileged over all others"[89]. The subject performing hegemonic masculinity needs to be rewarded in such a way that the potential danger of his action is marginalised and rendered insignificant. Rosi Braidotti calls this dualism of power "negative (potestas) in that it prohibits and constrains [but] also positive (potential) in that it empowers and enables"[90].

This paradoxical element of power is aptly demonstrated in Fitzroy's *Make Do and Mend* when Harry comes to realise that his position as a naval officer has

89 Richard Howson, *Challenging Hegemonic Masculinity* (New York: Routledge, 2006), pp. 60-61.

90 Rosi Braidotti, *Metamorphoses: Towards a Materialist Theory of Becoming* (Cambridge: Polity Press, 2002), p. 21.

earned him the white-enamelled gilt cross for Distinguished Service Order (DSO) whilst simultaneously killing his lover Michael in a terrible accident:

> 'I'd been on duty pretty much continuously for about a week when it happened,' Harry began. [...] 'Well, as one of the junior escorts, we had to wait our turn to enter harbour and be signalled a berth. [...] I decided to get my head down for a while. It should have been safe, it was nothing I hadn't done before, and I'd left instructions to be called if anything untoward happened. My First Lieutenant, however ... '
> Harry stopped then, suddenly aware of an obstruction in his throat. 'My First Lieutenant,' he began again, after a pause, 'countermanded my order. [...] In theory he should have been fine – he'd taken us into harbour on his own before and never had any problems – but those sandbanks are moving all the time[.] [...] The boat ran aground, and still Michael didn't send anyone to wake me; instead he decided to sort it out himself, along with our chief engineer, so that we could surface. [...] Anyway – by the time somebody did come to wake me they'd got most of the repairs done but the batteries were damaged, the engine-room had started filling up with fumes, and they'd both passed out. Two of us had to go in after them, but in the end it wasn't any good – Hutton and Michael both died.' (211-212)

Until quite late in the novel, the reader is unfamiliar with the exact circumstances of this accident, which obscures Harry's past as an officer and emphasises his present handicap and inability to perform active service. Only after this passage does the reader understand Harry's hesitations to enter into a relationship with Jim as it is the death of his former lover Michael and the impossibility of public grieving which have scarred him so deeply. Due to social conventions, Harry was only allowed to "mourn him as a comrade and not as a lover" (61). By telling his story, Harry begins to make up for this lack and liberates himself from the past to consider a new relationship with Jim.

Recollecting the accident in the past tense indicates a growing distance to it and enforces Harry's placement in the present as well as a potential future with Jim. His representation of events is factual and largely informed by military practice of reduction for transmitting information rather than emotional states. Harry continues his story in a clinical manner true to his military training even when realising "an obstruction in his throat" and needing to pause to regain self-control. This sober tone changes when the story is finished and Harry compares his former feelings for Michael to his growing affection for Jim: "But it seems to be so much more, somehow, this time – it isn't just a pleasant way to pass the time, but something I can't escape and shouldn't really try to. Inevitable, I suppose." (212) Parting with his military rhetoric based on clear and largely uninterrupted syntax to convey information, Harry now speaks hesitantly, which indicates insecurity over expressing his feelings for Jim. His confession that his present affection is stronger than his former feelings for Michael is disrupted by the word "somehow". No longer sure of what he wants to say, Harry is unable to put his emotions into words. This insecurity is climaxed when saying "[i]nevitable, I suppose". Designed as a short, punchy sentence, Harry's "I suppose" reverses the apparent inevitability of his love for Jim to substantiate his confusion over recalling the accident for the first time, and in doing so distancing himself from it.

Reluctantly he concedes that Michael's action "was wonderfully heroic, of course, but the line between heroism and stupidity is always such a narrow one, and I can't help thinking of it as an awful waste of a life. War is wasteful, though, isn't it?" (212) The juxtaposition of "wonderful" and "heroic" against the backdrop of hegemonic masculinity always comprising the possibility of death seems almost ironic yet substantiates the pleasure in acting heroically in battle. This thin line between "heroism and stupidity" is the engine that keeps the military running, but Harry no longer feels this tug to compel him into acts of heroism when he realises that war is not pleasurable at all but thoroughly "wasteful". His manner of speaking substantiates a discrepancy between the serving officer Harry representing the Unknown Soldier, and the homosexual Harry unfit for active service.

Although making a "big mistake" when falling asleep, Harry's attempted rescue of his comrades has guaranteed him the Navy's support, who awarded him with the white-enamelled gilt cross. This symbol of national service demonstrates hegemonic masculinity and openly displays not only service, but service of a special, life-threatening kind for the country. Repeatedly Harry is reduced to this award which functions to heterosexualise and masculinise him in the eyes of women, making him a desirable candidate for marriage. Consequently, whilst clearly accepting his homosexuality, Harry's association with the military remains undisputedly heteronormative – after all, a hero can never be openly homosexual.

During a conversation with Bettles, a member of the Women's royal naval service (WRNS, more commonly called Wren), Harry protests against her interpretation of the gilt cross by stating that "there are plenty of better-looking men about", to which Bettles returns that those would not be "decorated war-heroes who are baronets into the bargain" (104). In wearing the DSO, Harry is the embodiment of the Unknown Soldier and this status overrules shortcomings in physical appearance, health, gender performance and even homosexuality. Through the symbolic power of the DSO, Harry becomes a good-looking, capable, masculine, heterosexual man who is attractive to women. Not even his nephew Gareth Griffith-Lyon can take his eyes from the gilt cross: "His gaze had barely brushed Harry's face and was now fixated on the shining medal he wore." (57) Gareth's fixation on the cross instead of his uncle's face, whom he is meeting for the first time, suggests the profound significance of national symbols: "Traditions of ceremony, monument and national celebration have instilled national identity into the calendar and the landscape."[91] Harry's DSO functions in very similar ways and it withdraws subjectivity from Harry to project a mythic national identity onto his male body wearing the gilt cross. Deprived of personality, Harry-the-commanding-officer comes to be used by the nation to demonstrate its power against the enemy, and to perpetuate civilian enthusiasm for and fascination with the war.

Sarcastically, Harry understands his decoration as a distraction from the incident and the Navy's way of making "the best of a bad job – as usual" (56). Since "the Navy liked his officers to be gallant and resourceful in sorting out messes" (153), Harry's own proximity to death "had almost, but not quite, balanced out the fact that he was asleep in his bunk" (153) when tragedy struck. Because his injuries and lifelong disability does not quite compensate for the death of two men, the DSO functions as a further humiliation. Outwardly proclaiming honour and distinguished service, it is a reminder of Harry's personal and professional failure. Harry "wish[es] he could explain that he had done nothing to earn the white-enamelled gilt cross" (56) and complains that people such as Wren Bettles "were inclined to take them [decorations] out of context" (56). Yet he never does explain, and despite his sarcasm and open criticism, Harry continues to wear the gilt cross. While downplaying the accident as not "very exciting" (57) and "feel[ing] like a fraud" (56), the protagonist neither attempts to clarify under which circumstances he 'earned' the DSO. Similar to Kent in *Look Down in Mercy* who becomes increasingly uncomfortable with his commanding position, Harry claims unease when having to identify with the position ascribed to him by the nation. This contradiction between the characters' personal attitude versus their public behaviour questions Kent's and Harry's truthfulness when complaining about the burden of command. Suspiciously, neither character ever actively rejects their position, which substantiates the argument that hegemonic masculinity and the association with the Unknown Soldier are simultaneously oppressive and decidedly pleasurable for men who perform authoritative roles.

Similar to Harry, Kent has the strong desire to possess a power that is not only damaging and accompanied by burdens, but also highly pleasurable when wielding it against others, which is illustrated in the following scene where Kent

91 Sharp, (1996), p. 98.

relentlessly emasculates and subordinates a soldier called Goodwin.[92] Moments before encountering the Japanese enemy, Kent is gathering his men to secure a village and to retreat in an orderly fashion. Unable to find Sergeant Cording who is supposed to accompany him, Kent asks Goodwin to identify the sergeant's location: "Down there I think, Goodwin answered." (79) Upon hearing this, Kent falls into an exaggerated demonstration of his power:

'Down there you think,' Kent mimicked quietly, and then raised his voice angrily: 'Think what?'
'Sir.' Goodwin spoke sullenly to the ground.
'Get up when you talk to an officer, damn you.' Kent spoke viciously, a rage that he did not understand seethed in his mind and as Goodwin scrambled awkwardly to his feet it was as much as he could do not to kick him savagely in the side. (79)

Kent's aggression towards Goodwin, indicated by the insistence on being called "Sir" and be spoken to in a manner befitting his rank, shows that masculinity is not automatically attributed to officers, but requires constant demonstration of power and the subordination of lower ranks. Kent emphasises his superiority by "rais[ing] his voice" and ordering Goodwin to stand up. Alan Bairner stresses that it is important to "remember that some of those men who […] engage in [...] violence […] do so not because they are powerful, other than in a purely physical sense, but precisely because they feel that they lack power"[93]. Outwardly, Kent's exaggerated display of masculinity functions as a demonstration of power, but it is his anxiety regarding the adequacy of his general performance and qualities as an officer, which underlies his actions.

Moments before this scene, Kent and his company sergeant-major Tarrant had discovered three dead men, who had gone ahead of the platoon to secure the path. Juxtaposing Kent's and Tarrant's reaction to the horrible sight demonstrates why the company commander is not recognised for a tough and masculine performance:

[Kent] smelt the sickeningly appetising smell of cooked flesh and drew back sharply, white with nausea, the tips of his fingers shaking as he pictured how these men had died. He looked up and saw Tarrant watching him closely and he tried to smile.

92 Nickie Charles, *Gender in Modern Britain* (Oxford: Oxford University Press, 2002), p. 10.

93 Alan Bairner, "Masculinity, Violence and the Irish Peace Process" in *Capital and Class* Vol. 69 (1999), p.143.

'I suppose the rest of them are keeping warm inside,' Tarrant said lightly, successfully hiding his own qualms, thinking that the men were dead and that there was no point going as white as a sheet about it. (78)

The paradoxical "sickeningly appetising smell" that fills Kent with "nausea" illustrates his conflicting position: on the one hand, he has to fulfil his position as an officer by giving orders and setting a good example for his men. On the other hand, he is a weak individual who cannot hide his insecurities and who is morally compromised when the smell of human flesh stirs his appetite. Despite evoking feelings of hunger, Kent is clearly more moved by the sight than Tarrant, who can "successfully" hide his "qualms", whereas Kent has turned pale and his fingers are visibly "shaking". Tarrant immediately judges his officer as spineless for showing an emotional response: "there was no point going as white as a sheet about" dead men. Whereas Kent is incapable of talking, Tarrant's black humour that "the rest of them is keeping warm inside" demonstrates masculine toughness. In contrast, Kent's masculinity is threatened by his inability to appear in control of his body, which signals a stereotypically feminine reaction. Lynne Segel asserts that the definition of what 'men ought to be' does

not derive from any intrinsic characteristic of individuals, but from the social meanings which accrue to these ideals from their supposed superiority to that which they are not. To be 'masculine' is *not* to be 'feminine', *not* to be 'gay', *not* to be tainted with any marks of 'inferiority' – ethnic or otherwise.[94]

Butler similarly argues that men are always dependant on women to know of their superior status: this "radical dependency of the masculine subject on the female 'Other' suddenly exposes his autonomy as illusionary"[95]. By remaining silent and letting his body take control, Kent has unwittingly displayed traditional feminine traits of emotionality and weakness, which signals emasculation. Consequently, Kent's increasing self-doubts result from moments such as this one when he fails to live up to his commanding position and the ideal of hegemonic masculinity. His exaggerated rage against Goodwin in the scene quoted previously is a belated reaction to and compensation for his inability to hide his discomforts at the sight of death. Subconsciously, Kent recognises that his treatment of Goodwin is unfounded ("a rage that he did not understand"), but the

94 Lynne Segal, *Slow Motion: Changing Masculinities, Changing Men*, [1990], (London: Virago Book, 1997), p. xxxiv.

95 Judith Butler, *Gender Trouble: Feminism and the Subversion of Identity*, [1990], (London and New York: Routledge Classics, 2006) p. XXX.

need to counter his earlier trespass towards femininity is greater than any sense of justice.

Kent is constantly confronted with his inability to perform an authentic military masculinity, which is once more evident after witnessing the threat of aerial bombing. Again, Kent's reaction is contrasted to Tarrant's who says: "I counted eighteen planes, did you make it that or were there more?", to which Kent replies: "About eighteen, I think, [...] although it had not occurred to him to count them" (52). Whereas Tarrant substantiates his previously examined masculine performance, Kent had fallen "on the ground" feeling "the explosions kick through the ground against his body" (52), unable to make any attempt at counting planes. Immediately afterwards, Kent takes his anger over his inability to think rationally like Tarrant out on Anson: "Did you think I'd need a nice strong cup of tea after the nasty bombing? You really are an old woman." (53) The bombing had evidently unnerved Kent, who projects his own shame onto Anson's kind gesture. Kent's anger that Anson may have approached him as a subject tainted with fear instead of presuming that he is superior to such emotions, resonates in Kent's sarcasm: "nice strong cup of tea"; "nasty bombs". His style of speaking is designed to mock Anson by highlighting the duties of a batman as stereotypically female tasks thus not only downgrading women's social position but also Anson's within the military.

Mimi Schippers argues that when men like Anson transgress into performances of typically feminine quality through "homosexual desire [or] being weak and ineffectual", their performance is "*not* symbolically constructed as problematic *masculine* characteristics; they are constructed as decidedly feminine"[96]. Kent's comparison of Anson to an "old woman" functions to emasculate his batman. However, this is only momentary and derives from Kent's need to establish himself as superior to Anson. If non-conforming men became immediately associated with femininity – which permanently removes them from recognition and power – hegemonic masculinity could no longer rely on subordinated and marginalised masculinities to assist in the process of regulation and perpetuating patriarchy. While I agree that subordinated men are often (but not always) stigmatised as feminine, their masculinity remains superior to femininity if only by possessing a male body. If Anson was immediately and permanently perceived as feminine because he assumes 'the domestic female role', Kent would not need to constantly prove his masculine superiority. It is doubtful that a society strictly and lastingly denying masculinity to effeminate or otherwise marginalised men could retain hegemonic masculinity as a compelling concept for men to

96 Mimi Schippers, "Recovering the Feminine Other: Masculinity, Femininity, and Gender Hegemony" in *Theory and Society* Vol. 36, No. 1 (2007), p. 96.

strive for. Instead, by allowing for momentary emasculation as punishment and the promise of hegemonic masculinity as an achievable goal, Connells' theorisation of "[r]ecognizing multiple masculinit*ies*", which form difference and proximity to hegemonic masculinity and femininities, is far more compelling than Schipper's concept of immediate and permanent emasculation.[97] Connell distinguishes between hegemonic, subordinate, complicit and marginalised masculinities in order to more fully grasp the coordination of masculine power that perpetuates patriarchy. Complicit men are those who unconsciously contribute to the patriarchal system by benefitting from male superiority. Marginalised masculinities, on the other hand, are performed by individuals who differ from a social standard and are often discriminated against through institutionalised racism and/or classism. Lastly, homosexual men perform subordinated masculinities and are constantly in danger of becoming emasculated because "[t]he institutional dimension of hegemonic masculinity gives it a social authority that shapes perceptions of gayness"[98]. Homosexuality is consequently left doubly subordinated and "at the bottom of a gender hierarchy among men"[99]. However, marginalised and subordinated masculinities do not automatically and permanently transform into femininity as Schippers argues, but function to 'cluster around' hegemonic masculinity. Despite Anson's position and occasional emasculation, fellow soldiers such as Goodwin respect him, which highlights military masculinity as a complex system of negotiation and compromise.

This respect for Anson is evident when he and Kent approach Goodwin in their attempt to find Sergeant Cording. Whereas Goodwin is unimpressed by Kent's position as an officer, he averts his gaze at the sight of Anson: "He saw Anson and dropped his eyes" (79). Goodwin's behaviour indicates that Anson is more respected by the men than Kent. Goodwin and Anson used to be close friends, but when Goodwin punches Anson during one of his drunken escapades, their break up is initiated, which leads Anson to become Kent's batman. In his new position, Anson benefits from Kent's status as an officer and locates his own masculinity in relation to Kent's. Goodwin, in contrast, verbally as well as physically subordinates Anson, and in doing so acts in opposition to hegemonic masculinity that needs to conceal its dominance whenever possible in order to retain it: "[i]t is the successful claim to authority, more than direct violence, that is the mark of hegemony", according to Connell.[100] Goodwin's mistake of un-

97 Connell, (2016), p. 76, [my emphasis].

98 Connell, "A very Straight Gay: Masculinity, Homosexual Experience, and the Dynamics of Gender" in *American Sociological Review* Vol. 57, No. 6 (1992), p. 746.

99 Connell, (2016), p. 78.

100 Ibid., p. 77.

necessarily using violence against Anson has not only provoked the latter to terminate their friendship and to obtain a higher position, it has also subordinated Goodwin to a fellow soldier who is homosexual *and* performs traditionally female tasks when caring for Kent. Goodwin's respect for Anson demonstrates that gender performance is a highly paradoxical matter and disallows for categorical explanation. It follows that although Connell's differentiation between four masculinities (hegemonic, complicit, subordinated and marginalised) is a helpful guide to understand different forms of masculinity, it is ultimately too restrictive to capture the multiplicity and inherent contradictions that accompany masculine gender performance.

Moreover, contrasting Woods' examination quoted earlier, Kent cannot be recognised as a "positive representative of homosexuality: masculine, patriotic, mature and capable (in all these respects matching the less visible but steadier Anson)"[101]. Kent fails to identify with the People's War, yells at soldiers for no discernible reason and cannot control his body and emotions when encountering death. Kent is certainly neither "masculine, patriotic, mature and capable" nor "a positive representative of homosexuality" but marked as fighting his emerging feelings for his batman. Anson, however, is depicted as more capable and less fearful than Kent but remains marginalised and bracketed in Wood's analysis. Due to personal and professional shortcomings, Kent needs to exaggerate Goodwin's manner as inappropriate and Anson's domestic duties as feminine in order to contrast himself from the common soldier to become recognised as an officer of higher rank. Unquestioningly attributing masculinity to all soldiers because according to Smith "[t]here is no need to extrapolate masculinity from man – in the soldier they become one"[102] thus overlooks this complicated structure of the military where various forms of masculinities are constantly in flux and emasculation a threat to guarantee hierarchy among soldiers and their enclosed obedience towards officers.

This structure of various masculinities organising the military and facilitating a corporeal appearance of toughness and dominance is further diversified in the British army's opposition with the Japanese enemy. A stereotypical view that racialised bodies are subordinated to the white colonisers is illustrated and perpetuated in the inscribed 'moral hierarchy' of the British compared to the savage Japanese military, particularly in a scene where Goodwin and another soldier named Venner part with their platoon to have a swim in a nearby stream. Thinking themselves relatively safe, despite the noise of the water impairing their

101 Woods, (2014), ix.

102 Smith, (2004), p. 4.

senses, the two men enjoy their swim, but when Venner sunbathes on top of a rock, Goodwin observes a man with a sword emerging behind Venner's back:

> Venner's head hit his left knee, bounced on the rock and fell into the pool. A fountain of blood shot into the air and drenched his naked body as it toppled slowly over. The big man seemed to laugh as he picked up Venner's shirt and wiped his sword. (48)

The detailed description of displaced body parts in this scene is disturbing and the sequence of the head first falling on Venner's knee, then bouncing on the rock and finally landing in the water makes it appear utterly unreal. Goodwin's fascination with the materiality of the body – the head – and lack of horror when witnessing the murder, mirrors a twisted psyche and denotes utter lack of compassion. The hyperbolic "fountain of blood" not only works to demonstrate the brutality of the Japanese, but also reflects on Goodwin's personality, who lives in constant need for drama and delights in causing abuse. Not only does he fail to show any kind of emotional response to the murder, he also praises himself for his "marvellous escape" (48).

When telling Corporal Bonar about the incident, Goodwin "suddenly remembered the extraordinary way Venner's head had bounced on the rock and he wanted to roar with laughter" (48). The term "extraordinary" signals the grotesque movement of Venner's head and its displacement from his body. Goodwin's hidden pleasure is revealed in his wish to laugh, which connects him to the murderer, who also laughs whilst cleaning his sword with Venner's shirt, showing no signs of respect for the dead. Whereas Kent is criticised as effeminate for being too emotional when encountering death, Goodwin has to hide his excitement ("he *wanted* to roar with laughter"), because delighting in death would mark him as inhumane as the Japanese. Once more the impossible position of military personnel is demonstrated: they can neither show an emotional response nor delight in violence.

Goodwin's lack of horror concerning the murder, in contrast to Corporal Bonar's unease when hearing about it indicates Goodwin's hidden fascination for and eroticisation of violence. This gains more traction when considering that Goodwin commits a murder himself at the very beginning of the novel. Drunk and in need of money, he decides to break into a temple. Upon encountering a sleeping figure outside, he infers that this must be the watchman and that "he'll have the keys of the gate" (25). Without any warning and absolutely unfounded, Goodwin begins to choke the person to death.

> He reached the body and straddled it gracefully, at the same time his fingers dug viciously into the throat and his fingers pushed the blanket tight around the neck and then locked together. He smiled gently at the terrible paroxysms of the body as it writhed in the blanket and twisted in terror and agony, trying to break away from this unseen, unimaginable horror. [...] [H]e felt a slowly swelling pressure of desire that took its tempo from the twisting body against which he now pressed his own, exquisite pleasure that made him whimper; in that split second between the unbearable pleasure breaking and the flood of relief he dug inwards and upwards with his thumbs and felt the neck snap. (26)

This murder scene reveals a perverse pleasure of possessing masculine power and illustrates Kathy J. Phillips' argument that "people trained in a sex-hating society may feel excitement at suffering, even without any sex"[103]. Goodwin does not simply feel excitement – he feels sexual pleasure. The detail of how his fingers enclose the person's head, who is blinded by a blanket, accentuates that the perverse violence of the murder increases Goodwin's "sense of power" (26), which makes the whole incident pleasurable to him. These desires are strongly connected to his wish for dominance and superiority. Subordinated to both his officer Kent and his former friend Anson, Goodwin reclaims his masculine power by exerting it over an innocent victim. The more the defenceless body struggles, the more aroused Goodwin becomes, which is indicated by the use of semicolons and compound sentences to convey the impression of excitement and speeding simultaneously towards orgasm and death. Combining the sibilance "slowly swelling pressure" with the harsh t-sounds in the alliteration "took its tempo from the twisting body" conflates sexual and murderous desire. The 'soft' sexual pleasure seems to almost legitimize the harsh homicide when the scene focuses on Goodwin's rising desire culminating in an orgasm to the motion of murder. The snap of the neck is the final tone of both the victim's life and Goodwin's humanity.

Goodwin's savage brutality against a civilian suggests that the perverted violence aligns him with the Japanese. However, in contrast to Venner's death, his murder is kept a secret only shared by the reader. Through this disguise the novel demonstrates a need to conceal exaggerated British military masculinity from becoming public knowledge because "those who behaved in too aggressive or too strident a manner or advocated 'toughness' over 'goodness' risked being thought of as fascistic"[104]. A fascistic masculinity as associated with the enemy does not belong into the scripts of British nationalism. The display of violence

103 Kathy J. Phillips, *Manipulating Masculinity: War and Gender in Modern British and American Literature* (New York: Palgrave Macmillan, 2006), p. 106.

104 Rose, (2003), p. 287.

brought against Venner and witnessed by Goodwin, who finds his own perversion mirrored in its sight and expressed in his murder, explains why Kent, when rebuking Goodwin in the scene quoted previously, needs to satisfy his desire to subordinate by yelling instead of kicking: because Kent is the representative of the British nation, he needs to openly refrain from unnecessary demonstration of violence. Otherwise, he would become undistinguishable from the Japanese enemy – brutal, merciless and primitive.

Metaphorically, Goodwin's victim wields a belated revenge and subverts Goodwin's fantasies of demonstrating masculine "power" (26), when it is revealed that his victim was actually a woman. Whereas hegemonic masculinity subordinates femininity, narratives of chivalry state that women and children need to be protected from harm. Goodwin's execution of masculine power against an innocent and *female* victim further endangers the respectable code of conduct British soldiers had to follow during the war. Goodwin's repeated violation of that code is punished when it becomes known that the woman was infected with leprosy. Throughout the novel, Goodwin is repeatedly paranoid over being infected with the disease, which completely changes his manner from disrespectful and brutal to deeply troubled:

> One of the straps supporting his pack was chafing his shoulder. Or was it the start of a sore? [...] He knew nothing about the disease [leprosy] and was too frightened to ask in case it might connect him with the murder [...]. [...] In any case they never hanged white people out here. Or did they? That was something else he dared not ask. (45-46)

No longer confident that his murder will remain a secret if he begins to show infectious spots, Goodwin ponders the symptoms of the disease but is too scared to ask for medical advice. His malicious and narcissistic attitude that has manoeuvred him into this situation is momentarily gone, and he is left a frightened man scared for his life. Yet, Goodwin finds comfort in the belief that "they never hanged white people out here", because white soldiers are privileged over colonial subjects. Since the victim is a poor, female Indian, her case is not a priority to be solved and Goodwin's assumption that he would not be hanged is not put to the test.

Kent buttresses Goodwin's racism when he complains about the police's half-hearted investigations if any British soldiers were near the temple during that night:

> 'Wasn't that absolutely typical of the civilian attitude toward the troops – anything they can't solve, blame it on the Army. I suppose they weren't getting anywhere and probably

> paid some wretched Indian to say that he saw a soldier in the temple. Can you imagine any of our men going there in the middle of the night [, Tarrant]?' (31)

Kent's racism against the Indians and his naive protection of his men prevents him from considering the possibility that a soldier might be responsible for the murder. Instead, he blames the local police for not doing their job properly – that questioning the army is exactly the police's job is conveniently passed over by Kent. The officer's evaluation of events subverts the role of victim and culprit: "The whole thing was a nonsense, we were only dragged in as a face-save for the police." (32) Vehemently defending his men, Kent's attitude illustrates how decisive it is for the British army to keep clear of scandal and to represent a 'moral war' in contrast to the enemy who is associated with savage brutality.

The mercilessness of the enemy is substantiated when Kent and Anson get captured by a group of Japanese who torture Kent for information. After enduring severe beating, Kent finally concedes: "There are three regiments, don't hit me again, please, please ... I'll tell you everything, three regiments, two of them Indian and mine and some gunners, and I'll tell you about the tanks." (164) Interestingly, Kent's high treason has no consequences for the immediate storyline or for his career, because gun fire breaks out and the Japanese party scatters into the woods leaving Anson and Kent to take care of themselves. It is distinctly left open whether or not Kent's information has given the enemy any advantage because from this point onwards, the story concentrates on his and Anson's flight from Burma without giving a broader context. However, when Kent recovers from his wounds and re-encounters Tarrant, there occurs a moment of tension when Tarrant talks about "the river fiasco" (189) after which the platoon is "only about quarter strength" (190). Although using a telling reference, Tarrant does in no way suggest that Kent has caused the "fiasco", and Kent reflects that the inconsistencies, gaps and contradictions of other reports will make it hard to discover what really happened, which saves him from being court-marshalled:

> He had already listened to five or six accounts from different men who had visited him in hospital, and now he knew that all the versions he might hear would differ fundamentally from the others, that they were, and could only be, accounts of what had happened to individual people. (190)

Due to the many and personal versions of the event, it is credible that Kent focuses on his fate when recalling his flight from the Japanese: "I'm rather vague about the whole thing, I had only half come to from the crack on my head and being beaten up didn't help me to think any more clearly." (190) Emphasising his wounds and pointing towards the despicable acts of the Japanese who beat him up, Kent positions himself as a victim who should not be questioned any further. In doing so, he acts in exactly the manner Anson assumes of him, when he imagines two versions of how the incident could have played out that would both save Kent's reputation and honour as an officer. In an internal monologue Anson ponders:

> [Kent] could pretend that he didn't remember anything that happened in the clearing because of the wound in his head, or that he had only been trying to save Anson. He might even pretend that he didn't believe there were any tanks at all, and only said it to confuse the Japanese. (167-168)

Because people "would say Kent had behaved like a coward and a traitor in the clearing (167) if they knew the truth, Anson needs to narrate the incident in a certain way that establishes Kent as either badly injured, or as brave, controlled and calculating. Anson's tactic emphasis on Kent's alleged bravery despite the "wound in his head" shows how History is written by the victors – a History that is impersonal (Anson is referring to himself as a third person) and fundamentally created to convey the image of national success.

At the same time as fashioning a heroic tale, Anson believes that most people would have acted in the same way Kent did as soon as "the stick was raised a second time and with the thought present in their minds that this was only the beginning of repeated pain. There were heroes of course, he thought, [...] that woman Joan of Arc for instance, she must have been one" (167). Of all the heroic figures that history has produced, Anson distinguishes one of the very few women, and he challenges the assumption that heroism is reserved for the male body when, by the use of female pronouns, forcing the reader to recognise Jeanne D'arc *as* a woman.

Ultimately however, even a heroine is a myth, for "there always seemed to be something odd about heroes, either they got religion or believed in something else or just wanted to show off" (167). A hero(ine) is largely dislikeable, according to Anson, and in need of some form of divine guidance in order to fulfil greater-than-human deeds. "It wouldn't be easy for most people to be heroes, most people didn't believe in anything very much, at least nothing important, nothing except themselves." (167) Moving from the concrete example of Joan of Arc as a heroine to "most people", Anson legitimises why Kent can never be a hero: he is like "most people" preoccupied with himself and not interested in the well-being of another person or cause. Consequently, Kent can never live up to the heroic ideal nationalism demands of its officers – not as long as heroism is synonymous with bravery and altruism. Anson thus reveals a paradox in narratives of national heroism: if soldiers are masculine and heroic, but Anson believes that heroes are either not real or female, the soldier discourse cannot be real or attainable for men either.

Joseph Campbell's study *The Hero with a Thousand Faces* examines another significant difference that hampers heroic action today compared to "the comparatively stable periods of those great co-ordinating mythologies which now are known as lies"[105]: whereas the hero of ancient times was formed and forged by a group, "today no meaning is in the group [...] all is in the individual"[106]. It follows that heroism needs to rise and produce from within a person: "It is not society that is to guide and save the creative hero, but precisely the reverse."[107] Warfare is thus built on a structure that annihilates itself when military personnel are required to perform heroically although heroism is an insubstantial myth as displayed by Anson. The military thus fails to create a convincing corporate image of masculinity and heroism when men like Kent privilege their personal well-being over the collective cause of winning the war.

Kent substantiates Anson's critique on heroic action when he rescues Goodwin from certain death but does so for reasons contradicting stereotypical narratives of masculine heroism. Goodwin is lying on plain ground injured and exposed to possible enemy fire, which endangers the rest of the platoon. About to order two men to catch Goodwin and save him from death, Kent realises:

> If they were ordered to go they would, but there was no inner compulsion to make them do it for its own sake, all they understood was that it was infinitely desirable to be alive, that the mere act of living was a sufficient justification, the only true reality. (81)

This distinction between a "true reality" for the soldiers, which means being alive, and a 'false' or 'insignificant' reality, which is Goodwin's survival, is the reason for Kent's conflict. Instead of disregarding the feelings of his men, he foregrounds them to the effect of reversing his role as an officer required to give orders. Kent's predicament is then not only an inability to command but connected to his feelings for his men and their survival. Kent's behaviour resembles stereotypically female preoccupation with the realm of the emotional and stands in contradiction to the dominant narrative of male rationality. Since any trace of femininity needs to be excluded from male thinking, Kent translates his sympa-

105 Joseph Campbell, *The Hero with a Thousand Faces*, [1949], (Princeton: Princeton University Press, 1973), p. 388.

106 Ibid., p. 388.

107 Ibid., p. 391.

thy into a challenge for himself to counteract his self-doubts. After pondering his choices, he comes to the conclusion that

> he himself would have to go and fetch Goodwin in, because if he did not people would say he had been afraid, that he had failed as a company commander. He might not succeed in the attempt, that was not important, the attempt had to be made. (81)

If staying alive constitutes "true reality" for the soldiers, then it is the rescue of Goodwin which determines Kent's fate. An act of masculine heroism that saves another person's life whilst demonstrating fearlessness, courage and leadership qualities in front of fellow soldiers would confirm Kent's position within the army and could silence his self-doubts concerning the adequacy of his gender performance. Masculine heroism is drummed into military personnel, especially officers, during their training, and "works by linking the sense of personal worth to the needs of an organization that specializes in violence"[108]. This pattern is, according to Campbell a stereotypical element of heroism because "[t]he hero is the man of self-achieved submission"[109]. That Kent is prepared to perform masculine heroism shows a shift in focus away from his subjectivity towards the military, reinforced in his sudden self-identification as the "company commander" to emphasise and submit to his rank. In consequence, Kent's individuality is marginalised and his position within the military as an anonymous and nationalistic force becomes highlighted. The possibility of dying to save Goodwin is irrelevant, what counts is "the attempt" and therefore the substantiation of Kent's role as an officer in perpetuating the myth of the Unknown Soldier.

Anson indirectly proposes to 'accidently kill' Goodwin when "mov[ing] the muzzle of his tommy-gun" (82). However, killing Goodwin would undermine Kent's rank and might take away privileges. Anson's subsequent offer to rescue Goodwin himself and thus spare Kent the danger is met with equal despair as it would reverse their social and military positions. By standards of class and rank, Kent's situation is a more privileged one making his masculinity superior to Anson's. In offering to rescue Goodwin without showing signs of fear as observed in Kent, the batman unconsciously challenges the positions of power between them. It is Anson's masculinity that comes closer to the hegemonic ideal in this situation, consequently subordinating Kent. Agreeing to Anson's proposal to rescue Goodwin would substantiate Kent's failing masculine performance – a trespass that is momentarily broached when his "head dropped forward as relief

108 Connell and Rebecca Pearse, *Gender In World Perspective*, [2002], (Cambridge: Polity Press, 2009), p. 140.

109 Campbell, (1973), p. 16.

swept through him. He tried to control a long sigh but it was impossible." (82) The dropped head signalling gratitude that someone else might put their life in danger demonstrates Tomkins' analysis of shame:

> Shyness, shame, and guilt are not distinguished from each other at the level of affect [...]. [...] This is not to say that shyness in the presence of a stranger, shame at a failure to cope successfully with a challenge, and guilt for an immorality are the same experience. Clearly they are not. [...] Yet the affect that we term shame-humiliation, which is a component of each of these total experiences, is one and the same affect.[110]

The shame-humiliation complex deriving from "failure to cope successfully with a challenge" is evident in Kent's gesture to drop his head and audible as "a long sigh". Kent experiences shame over personal weakness, which functions to induce conformity despite hesitations. He seems to follow a conservative path where "cultural norms force men to endure trauma and master fear, in order to claim the status of 'manhood'"[111]. Such a reading is challenged when Kent "turned his head and looked at Anson, his eyes soft with gratitude" (82).

> They looked at each other for what seemed a long time; the dust still glittered on Anson's cheek, the sweaty streak of dirt, a dried spot of blood on his chin, the pulse in his throat, all were beautiful and suddenly, without knowing why, Kent was calm and happy. He smiled and put up his hand and rubbed the smeared dirt on Anson's face with his finger. He could feel the roughness of the beard on his finger-tips.
> 'No,' he whispered, shaking his head, 'not you.' The words were spoken without thinking, and immediately he was embarrassed. He went on quickly: 'I want a batman, not a corpse, besides I know you loathe the man.' (82)

The scene describes how Kent gives in to his feelings and realises that he could not bear to lose Anson. Instead of being forced into action by the military, Kent's love for another man has an empowering effect on him. This change undermines the military, and by extension the British nation, for its relentless manipulation of subjects when pressuring male bodies into acts of masculine heroism to perpetuate a collective national identity. When the two men look into each other's eyes unabashedly, conventional meaning and conduct is disturbed. Their mutual gaze increases the impression of making time stop and troubles traditional ac-

110 Tomkins, (1995), p. 133.

111 Joshua S. Goldstein, *War and Gender: How Gender Shapes the War System and Vice Versa*, [2001], (Cambridge and New York: Cambridge University Press, 2003), p. 264.

counts on time as "typically coded masculine and space, being absence or lack, as feminine"[112]. According to Adele Jones, time reigns over space since "constructions of space are naturalized by the temporal practices to which they are subordinated"[113]. In accordance with the gender binary, time is figured as masculine, tightly linked to the public and politics, whereas space is coded feminine. In this depiction, the connotation of time as masculine "aligned with history, progress, civilization, politics and transcendence" [114] fades by not only bringing time to a halt, but also by connecting it to the feminine sphere of being looked at.

When considering that the scene takes place just before Kent is rescuing Goodwin, who is still lying on the road exposed to enemy fire, space is accentuated because it is Goodwin's geographic location, which most severely endangers Kent's life in the rescue. Space being contrasted to time as "stasis, passivity and depoliticization" therefore seems to detract its immediate impact in a life or death situation.[115] As the scene features two males with romantic feelings for each other, the very concepts of time and space are challenged and the event turns into a parody of traditional conduct. This parody of gender norms is enhanced when the sight of Anson's sweaty face where dirt has dried, plunges Kent into a calm happiness. Kent's reaction shows that blood can become beautiful and a male beard can be tenderly touched with male finger-tips – a gesture abnormal in conventional terms. It is thus the *conflation* of typically masculine and feminine qualities which challenges the duality of gender because masculinity is no longer associated with strength (and time) and femininity with emotional weakness (and space). This inversion of concepts enables a performance of masculine heroism that is informed by love for another man and not induced by an institution using femininity as a threat to soldiers.

Kent's experience of 'feminine emotions' enables him to fulfil his hegemonic role, whereas pressure and shame as regulating mechanism had left him doubtful and clinging to his own life. As long as hegemonic masculinity rests on the assumption of a 'pure masculinity', its performance is doomed to border on the grotesquely extreme, evident in Kent's outburst towards Goodwin or the latter's murder outside the temple. Constantly haunted by the fear of exposing femininity, hegemonic masculinity kills off human sensitivities and compels men to become the Unknown Soldier devoid of emotions. Kent's hesitations and reluctance to give his life for the benefit of the nation shows that the reward of recognition does not equal the sorrows men have to endure to earn it. In light of this

112 Doreen B. Massay, *Space, Place, and Gender* (Cambridge: Polity Press, 1994), p. 6.

113 Jones, "Disrupting the Continuum" (2014), p. 33.

114 Ibid., p. 6.

115 Ibid., p. 6.

context Kathy J. Phillips' evaluation of why men fight is too simplistic: "Whenever a culture locates masculinity pre-eminently in fighting, a constantly fanned uncertainty about masculine status helps push men of all sexual orientations to war."[116] The analysis of Kent's behaviour has shown that while aware of the attribution of hegemonic masculinity when rescuing Goodwin, and prone to social shaming, Kent is only persuaded to commit the act after experiencing emotions commonly dismissed as feminine. Consequently, in contrast to Phillips' argument it is not a desire for masculinity that pushes Kent into action, but his love for Anson which makes his heroism a parody of traditional narratives.

Nevertheless, Kent's performance, although originating from feminine feelings, effectively substantiates the stereotypical image of hegemonic masculinity ascribed to a person of his rank. This (re)attribution can be observed in the moment after the successful rescue of Goodwin where the image of a proud, roaring lion is used to reflect Kent's brave act in the language of patriarchy: "He scrambled to his feet and wanted to roar with laughter for pride and relief." (84) When before Kent was shown to diverge from masculinity, he is now behaving like a stereotypical man who performed masculine heroism successfully. Consequently, it would be too superficial to understand hegemonic masculinity as the *only* engine working sovereign power – instead an examination of the complex and often paradoxical structure of gender performances in connection to the nation-state is always essential for understanding its diverse functions.

FILLING THE GRAVE WITH MORTAL REMAINS: DISINTEGRATION OF THE *UNKNOWN* SOLDIER MYTH

The analyses of the four novels uncover the Western system of nationalism, patriotism and propaganda as highly unstable and in need of perpetually constructing heroic myths as unifying troops to guarantee national immortality. By disregarding the subject in the relentless inscription of meaning onto their bodies, the British national leadership tries to counter this body's emancipation and challenge to the system. The fabrication of a forced national identity is especially obvious in characters who refuse to willingly die for their country. At this point the tomb of the Unknown Soldier is figuratively opened and filled with mortal remains of soldiers who never stop questioning the cause of their death. In the last section of this chapter I will disclose that the bodies of soldiers challenge the myth of the *Unknown* Soldier when directing attention to male physicality that

116 Phillips, (2006), p. 98.

traditional order likes to trivialise through emphasising male reason. In his work on *British Writing of the Second World War*, Rawlinson asserts that "[f]ar from being visible, the wounded body is always liable to disappear"[117]. I wish to challenge this assumption by arguing that the very opposite process is at work in the novels under discussion. Instead of creating a "linguistic route for the disappearance of the hurt body"[118], Baxter enhances the body's significance in *Look Down in Mercy*, when Kent and Anson get captured by the Japanese. Kent's somatic control fades entirely and embarrassingly as a result of the Japanese's officer's beating: "He lay there helplessly, shaking in every limb and suddenly there was a rush of gas and excreta as he voided his fæces into his shorts." (165) The symbolic significance of this and other scenes in which the male body is illustrated as weak, wounded and lacking control becomes clear with regard to Simone de Beauvoir's ground-breaking study *The Second Sex*, in which she states:

> Woman has ovaries and a uterus; such are the particular conditions that lock her in her subjectivity; some even say she thinks with her hormones. Man vainly forgets that his anatomy also includes hormones and testicles. He grasps his body as a direct and normal link with the world that he believes he apprehends in all objectivity, whereas he considers woman's body an obstacle, a prison, burdened by everything that particularises it.[119]

De Beauvoir asserts not only that men are conventionally considered to perform an active role in the world, making women their passive counterpart, but also that the two sexes are trapped by their bodies in different ways. She argues that because women are stereotypically identified by and through their bodies due to their reproductive capacities, they are strongly linked and limited to them. Their disempowered social position is a direct consequence of this abjected corporeality and its negative association with pain and restraint. Men, however, are empowered through disembodiment, making them different to, or positioned outside of, their physical shell: "[h]e thinks of his body as a direct and normal connection with the world, which he believes he apprehends objectively, whereas he regards the body of woman as a hindrance, a prison, weighed down by everything peculiar to it."[120] De Beauvoir, therefore, distinguishes between female *em*bodiment and male *dis*embodiment, which is further elaborated on by Butler, who links this concept to the constitution of 'the rational man' whose body is

117 Rawlinson, (2000), p. 25.

118 Ibid., p. 27.

119 Simone de Beauvoir, *The Second Sex*, [1949], (London: Vintage Books, 2011), p. 15.

120 Ibid., p. 5.

"reason dematerializ[ing] [women's] bodies that may not properly stand for reason"[121]. Butler rightly criticises the familiar binary of sex and gender and the different rendering of bodies in order to maintain a set of standards.

The Night Watch exaggerates this paradigm by making female embodiment appear almost grotesque to the point where the dichotomous construction of bodies is revealed as imaginary: Winnie, a co-worker of Duncan at a candle factory after the war, is "a girl with a deformity of the face, a squashed-in nose and a pinched-up mouth, and a pinched-up nasal voice to match" (37). The focus on the face and its deformed mouth reflects the stereotype of female unreason addressed by Butler and emphasizes Winnie's female embodiment. Len, another co-worker, builds a wax figure with "oversized breasts and hips, and waving hair" to resemble Winnie. Len's action not only reveals the misogynistic image of culturally fashioned femininity, but also women's arbitrary position as both grotesquely deformed and beautifully manufactured to fulfil men's sexual fantasies. The latter becomes abundantly clear when Len "passionately kissed [the wax figure] [...] [and] put[s] his fingernail to the fork of its legs and pretended to tickle it" (37). The implication of sexual intercourse demonstrates the paradox of female embodiment: women's bodies are not only "a hindrance, a prison, weighed down by everything peculiar to it", they also need to be the source of desire for men in order to return to their function as reproductive vessels. Winnie and the wax figure render visible that women simultaneously represent the abjected sphere of reproduction and bodiliness, whilst the female physique (breasts, hips) is perceived as attractive to men. Consequently, that which is being rejected by the rational male as grotesquely embodied at the same time attracts him and guarantees the survival of the human species.

The debate on bodily transcendence versus immanence brought ub by Sedgwick was revived during Second Wave Feminism by Iris Marion Young, who argues that "[t]he lived body as transcendence is pure fluid action, the continuous calling-forth of capacities that are applied to the world"[122]. Contrary to de Beauvoir, Young understands transcendence not as disembodiment, but as a lived experience that originates from the body and transforms into uninhibited action. Bodily movement and action is lived differently by women and men, and "[r]ather than simply beginning in immanence, feminine bodily existence remains in immanence or, better, is *overlaid* with immanence, even as it moves out

121 Judith Butler, *Bodies that Matter: On the Discursive Limits of "Sex"*, [1993], (London and New York: Routledge Classics, 2011), pp. 21-22.

122 Iris Marion Young, *On Female Body Experience: "Throwing Like A Girl" and Other Essays* (Oxford: Oxford University Press, 2005), p. 36.

toward the world in motions of grasping, manipulating, and so on"[123]. What Beauvoir has named the particularities of the female body, Young understands as her inability of moving beyond immanence to achieve transcendence. The grand trope of male 'disembodiment' *versus* female 'embodiment' thus continues to be of issue in feminist studies.

When Kent in *Look Down in Mercy* is beaten by the Japanese, his body is abjected, which challenges male transcendence and illustrates Butler's argument that despite his ideological disembodiment, man is "one which is nevertheless a figure of a body"[124]. Aware that the Japanese will torture Kent to get vital military information, Anson tries to deceive the enemy by pretending to be in command. The Japanese officer, however, suspects the diversion and begins to violently abuse Kent, calculating that any officer would object to be treated in such a disrespectful manner. When Kent exclaims in commanding tone: "Don't treat me like this [...] I'm an officer, I've done nothing wrong" (162), the Japanese is proven right and "smile[s] affably" (162). It is the clear structure of distributing hegemonic masculinity to white, middle class, male bodies which makes it possible for the Japanese to recognise Kent as a potential officer. Having been treated with respect throughout his life, Kent cannot accept abuse from a man whose racially marked masculinity is subordinated to the white male. When demanding respect, Kent manoeuvres himself into an ever more desperate situation. The profound wish for recognition and respect determines his resistance to being beaten and shows that masculinity is not only abusive towards femininities and other masculinities but also works as a blindfold for critical self-reflection.

Even though Kent, being a Caucasian fighting in Burma, is located outside the realm of his home and race, which makes him a "body out of place"[125], his performance illustrates Ahmed's argument that the "reduction of the stranger to a being" becomes a "fetishisation"[126]. Ahmed pledges to "examine the affect of the transnational movement of peoples" without "assuming an ontology of the stranger"[127]. This is relevant for the analysis of Kent's position *vis-à-vis* the Japanese enemy, because a reading of him as an inferior stranger, who has left "the home of [his] nation", would exaggerate his body as a site of dislocation, whilst marginalising his privileged social position bestowed upon him by the British nation.[128] In fact, Kent continues to benefit from historically constructed white

123 Young, (2005), p. 36.

124 Butler, (2011), p. 21.

125 Ahmed, (2000), p. 78.

126 Ibid., p. 79.

127 Ibid., p. 79.

128 Ibid., p. 78.

supremacy regardless of his dislocated body. This is most obvious when the Japanese officer strikes "Kent across the face with his stick" (162). Although physically abused, Kent manages to maintain control over his body when only flinching in fear. Rather than the beating, it is the officer's poor hygiene which causes the highest level of discomfort in Kent and leads him to "involuntarily turn[...] his head away, sickened by the smell of fishy dental decay, and the wet splutter that showered into his face" (162). The Japanese officer's nauseating outward appearance distracts from his position of power when causing pain. Due to the contrast between Kent's Western standards of aesthetics and the officer's rotten teeth and bad breath permanently marking his face, the roles of capturer and captive are momentarily disturbed. This reversal of power redirects Kent towards a hegemonic and masculine position in control of his body to identify him as superior to Japanese violence.

In the next moment, Kent fails to maintain this self-control, and "a mouthful of hot frothy vomit [...] shot on to the sleeve of the officer's uniform" (162). Whilst this is a classic example of Julia Kristeva's theory on abjection where "I expel *myself*, I spit *myself* out, I abject *myself*"[129], the cause of Kent's repulsion – "a gob of stinking slime and phlegm [spat out by the Japanese] coat[ing] Kent's nostrils" – emphasises the Japanese's insufficient physical hygiene as well as manners and redirects abjection back to the colonial subject. It is thus ultimately the Japanese, and not Kent, who becomes the victim of degradation/abjection (being vomited on), initiated by the colonising white race. At this and other points in the story, *Look Down in Mercy* displays the internalised colonial narratives of oppression that no inversion of power can re-write: the Japanese officer can inflict the white man's body with pain, but he cannot cleanse Kent of disgust.

Ultimately, Kent's white superiority over the Japanese dwindles and unable to accept any more pain, Kent's control over his body fades. Gail Kern Paster's analysis in *The Body Embarrassed* shows why neither the female nor the male body is dead matter that can be transcended. "Humoral physiology ascribes to the workings of the internal organs an aspect of agency, purposiveness, and plenitude to which the subject's own will is often decidedly irrelevant."[130] When regaining consciousness after being captured by the Japanese, Kent realises that "his hands were throbbing with pain and that one side of his head seemed to be full of blood trying to burst through his skull" (160). This exemplifies Paster's

129 Julia Kristeva, *Powers of Horror: An Essay on Abjection* (New York: Columbia University Press, 1982), p. 3.

130 Gail Kern Paster, *The Body Embarrassed: Drama and the Disciplines of Shame in Early Modern England* (Ithaca and London: Cornell University Press, 1993), p. 10.

claim that agency may be assigned to the body's interior. Kent is incapable of monitoring and subordinating his "opinionated body"[131]. Furthermore, Paster asserts a link between the stereotypic assumption of women as the physically 'weak vessel' to their bodily peculiarity as the 'leaky vessel' deriving from female menstruation.

> The male body, opened and bleeding, can assume the shameful attributes of the incontinent female body as both cause of and justification for its evident vulnerability and defeat. *At such moments, the bleeding male's blood comes to differ, shamefully, from itself.*[132]

The *bleeding* body alters the semantic meaning of contained blood and gives agency to the body beyond subjective control. Kent's involuntary defecation worsens his case and asserts complete loss of control. Both moments – bleeding and defecation – are judged as depriving the male subject of rationality because "man [is] one who is without a childhood; is not a primate and so is relieved of the necessity of eating, defecating, living and dying"[133]. Kent is thus not only forfeiting his privileged position as a rational, disembodied and empowered male, but comes to be emasculated by bleeding, which aligns him with the female sex. With this new emphasis given to his body, Kent is becoming progressively more abjected. Butler, like Kristeva, returns to the physical roots of abjection as imprinted on the body arguing that "[t]he 'abject' designates that which has been expelled from the body, discharged as excrement, literally rendered 'Other'"[134]. This means that when the body becomes abjected, comes to disdain the controlling mind, the subject forfeits recognition on the social level. The myth of male disembodiment is thus challenged when Kent's injuries subordinate the officer's ability of semantic control. Men are thus not above the physical reality of their bodies which is similarly shown in Waters' novel.

Whereas the initial description of the workers in *The Night Watch* has singled out Winnie as physically deformed whilst disregarding Duncan's and Len's male bodies, the narrative amends this impression by showings Len "lurching a little from side to side, like a stout old lady; for his left leg was short, and fused at the knee" (81). The reference to a woman – the "stout old lady" – illustrates

131 Isabelle Stengers, "Wondering about Materialism" in Levi Bryant and Nick Srnicek and Graham Harman (eds.), *The Speculative Turn: Continental Materialism and Realism* (Melbourne: National Library of Australia Cataloguing-in-Publication Data, 2011), p. 373.

132 Paster, (1993), p. 92, [my emphasis].

133 Butler, (2011), p. 21.

134 Butler, (2008), p. 181.

how embodiment is still conflated with women and relegated from the realm of male thinking. Duncan, in contrast, is "one of our ablest workers" (42) according to the factory boss Mrs. Alexander – simultaneously denoting his skills and his physical health.

However, during a conversation with Fraser, who wonders how Duncan can stand working in the factory, Duncan explicitly compares himself to the other workers when saying: "Everybody else there stands it. Why shouldn't I?" (87) The question Fraser is really asking is why a physically healthy person works at a place for disabled people. Duncan does not see a paradox in his occupation because he believes that his deviating sexuality is marked on his body just like Winnie's female embodiment is marked on her face. This levelling of physical disability and homosexuality is similarly noted by Claude J. Summers, who judges the war injury of Mary Renault's protagonist Laurie to be "symbolic not only of his oedipal dependence [...] but also of his homosexuality itself"[135]. According to Summers, the characters' homosexuality is manifesting in their physical injuries – in Ralph's "clawlike" (144) hand, and in Laurie's lameness. While I generally agree with this observation, Summers' conclusion that Laurie's "sexual difference [is] more crippling than his physical disability"[136] seems to be reductive.

When Laurie is being given a boot with which to walk without having to use crutches, he refers to it as a "cripple's boot", "ugly" and with a thick sole (90). The terms 'cripple' in Laurie's version and 'crippling' in Summers' analysis refer to opposite things. The former denotes his stiff leg, while the latter ascribes it to Laurie's homosexuality. To say that Laurie's "sexual difference [is] more crippling than his physical disability" reverses the character's own assessment of his condition. This becomes even more obvious when considering Laurie's identity formation informed by the cripple's boot: "One might as well learn to laugh it off, because this was not transitional like the crutch or the stick. This, henceforward, was Laurie Odell." (90-91) Even if Laurie had regarded his homosexuality as a hindrance before, in this moment of adopting to the boot, which will be a part of him for the rest of the life, his identity has changed from homosexual to cripple making his "physical disability" a greater burden than his "sexual difference".

A similar observation can be made for Ralph, who keeps his deformed hand hidden by a glove because there is "[n]o point in upsetting people" (190) by which he means particularly women. His insecurity over showing his injury is

135 Claude J. Summers, *Gay Fictions: Wilde to Stonewall: Studies in a Male Homosexual Literary Tradition* (New York: Continuum, 1990), p. 162.

136 Ibid., p. 162.

more tightly linked to his deviating sexuality than Laurie's struggles, for Ralph has experienced women as cruelly judgemental and "expect[s] that they would punish him with his deformity" (185). Since only "get[ting] along with real bitches", which might be read as a form of self-punishment for having 'abnormal' desires, Ralph's experiences with women have been wholly negative, and a woman's startled reaction upon seeing his uncovered hand confirms his premature judgement. In contrast to Laurie, whose injury replaces his homosexual identity, Ralph's hand substantiates his abjected status and infiltrates into his attitude of hiding his true self from women (and heteronormative society in general). Waters' *The Night Watch* illustrates female cruelty in similar ways when Viv makes an effort of being nice to a man with a stiff leg "because she didn't want him to suppose she wouldn't [think about going out with him], because of his leg" (251). Both *The Night Watch* and *The Charioteer* suggest that it is not only men who consider themselves as disembodied, but that women, too, find the sight of injured male flesh difficult to endure. Despite or maybe because of this aversion, the novels emphasise that men's bodies are prone to injury and male disembodiment reveals itself as a myth at wartime when the very bodies of men turn into protagonists and are, contrary to Rawlison's argument, *not* "liable to disappear"[137]. In giving the body an identity that struggles to the fore in representations of deformations, blood, and even faeces, the myth of the *Unknown* Soldier disintegrates and collapses.

The novels depict diverse ways of resisting the war either by disclosing the lingering social differences that render the People's War inauthentic, or by portraying characters who actively oppose their roles as soldiers. In their shared antagonism towards the Second World War, the novels reveal that it was not only *not* heteronormative as shown in the previous chapter, but also that it was not received with the kind of enthusiasm broadcasted by propaganda. Moreover, the People's War and Unknown Soldier myth fashioned to create a national community are in danger of revealing their insubstantiality when the wounded bodies of men strive for attention. The body is therefore a significant space of and for resistance, as it enables to break with various norms regarding gender, sexuality and the ideology of male disembodiment. In the following chapter I wish to elaborate on the significance of spaces by examining the inscriptions of gender norms onto the body and into the home, in order to disclose a narrative resistance to follow heteronormative scripts regarding the gendered politics of space.

---

137 Rawlison, (2000), p. 25.

“The Collapse of a Wall [...] Starts with a Few Loose Bricks” –

Queering Space, Body and Time

QUEER FICTION – QUEER CONCEPTS

Sarah Waters’ *The Night Watch* (2006) self-reflectively questions its own investment in the past and challenges a straightforward reading of time. In “Disrupting the Continuum: Collapsing Space and Time in Sarah Waters’s [sic] *The Night Watch*”, Adele Jones nicely pinpoints the outlook of Waters’ novel by stating:

> In collapsing the certainty of linearity, reinforced by the subversive narrative, Waters undermines the primacy of time and, faced with the possibility of no future at all, each character escapes the relentless forward movement into the future and thus the heteronormative ‘paradigmatic markers’ which define that future – birth, marriage, reproduction, and death [...].[1]

Kay Mitchell similarly observes that Waters

> thwarts the identification of lesbianism as backwardness through the adoption of a backwards structure that is, thus, rendered truly queer – as it deploys moments of romantic optimism, suggests new possibilities of relationality and initiates affective ‘touches across

1 Adele Jones, “Disrupting the Continuum: Collapsing Space and Time in Sarah Waters’s *The Night Watch*” in *Journal of Gender Studies* Vol. 23, No. 1 (2014), p. 34.

time', while exploring the *longue durée* of melancholy and refusing the consolation of too facile a futurity.[2]

Both critics emphasise that Waters' narrative structure deconstructs heteronormative time, as *The Night Watch* refuses "the consolation of too facile a futurity" and destabilises the "relentless forward movement into the future". The characters repeatedly express relief over the needlessness of thinking about what comes after the war, since the presence allows for variations of heteronormative life that cannot be conceptualised in peacetime. Adam Fitzroy's *Make Do and Mend* (2012) takes a similar approach to the atrocities of wartime when the farm labourer Jim Brynawel realises that "[y]ou're a long time dead" – now is the time to "*carpe diem*" (188) [emphasis original]. The constant threat of war and death prompts Jim to find the courage to admit to his feelings for the protagonist Harry Lyon. In *The Night Watch* Helen's lesbian relationship with Kay is also only imaginable because "so many impossible things were becoming ordinary, just then" (274). Yet, because these "impossible things" are fixed to the war, their endurance is equally linked to it, which makes it not only "pointless" (275) to think of a time after the war, but, paradoxically, also uncanny. It seems almost consequential that *The Night Watch* has to move back in time and swiftly abandons the bleakness of 1947 to nostalgically recall the past.

Whereas Jones and Mitchell focus on queer time as the most significant marker in *The Night Watch*, I shall add(ress) the interlinking matters of "Queering Space, Body and Time". This chapter will critically analyse the body (particularly Kay's lesbian body) as a space for gender non-conformity in performances of (female) masculinity that call into question sex-gender coherence. At the same time as troubling heteronormative assumptions regarding the body, Kay's excessive performance of masculinist behaviour towards her girlfriend Helen aligns and equates her with the role of a traditional dominant male. My reading of Kay is therefore twofold: demonstrating that *The Night Watch* destabilises gender norms written on the body, whilst examining Kay's subsequent investment in unwittingly perpetuating patriarchal standards when she subordinates Helen and relegates her into the confined space of their home. Following Jones' and Mitchell's reading of *The Night Watch* as embodying queer time, I will push this 'queering' of traditionally normative concepts further and analyse the home as queer space; not only because the stereotypically heteronormative space of

2 Kate Mitchell, "'What Does it Feel like to be an Anachronism?': Time in *The Night Watch*" in Kaye Mitchell (ed.), *Sarah Waters: Contemporary Critical Perspectives* (London: Bloomsbury, 2013), p. 98.

'home' at times actively enables queer desire, but because it queerly defies any and all clear-cut definitions.

My approach to the conception of home will illustrate that it is a highly paradoxical, flexible and fluid space of controlling and manipulating desires to conform to a standard. The home is controversial because it denies movement and desires beyond heteronormative patterns whilst purposefully allowing for deviating pleasures in order to control them. To clarify this ambivalent and inconsistent structure, I wish to briefly turn to Wendy Brown's theory of tolerance, which pointedly explains the various and subconscious mechanisms that manage social life. The *Oxford English Dictionary* states that the common definition of "the action or practice of tolerating" comprises "freedom from bigotry or undue severity in judging the conduct of others"[3]. In *Regulating Aversions*, Brown convincingly questions this positive outlook and observes that

> [t]olerance regulates the presence of the Other both inside and outside the liberal democratic nation-state, and often it forms a circuit between them that legitimates the most illiberal actions of the State by means of a term consummately associated with liberalism.[4]

Tolerance is, according to Brown, not a liberalist notion to integrate deviating subjects, but a tactical manoeuvre to perpetuate a tacit hierarchy between those who tolerate and those who are being tolerated. Rather than striving to decrease differences, tolerance "is necessitated by something one would prefer did not exist"[5] and derives from a need to manage 'foreignness' in a way that suits the dominant order. "In this activity of management, tolerance does not offer resolution or transcendence, but only a strategy for coping."[6]

> The very invocation of tolerance [...] indicates that something contaminating or dangerous is at hand, or something foreign is at issue, and the limits of tolerance are determined by how much of this toxicity can be accommodated without destroying the object, value, claim or body. Tolerance appears, then, as a mode of incorporation and regulating the presence of the threatening Other within.[7]

3 "tolerance, n." *OED Online*. Oxford University Press, June 2017. Web. 28 August 2017.

4 Wendy Brown, *Regulating Aversions: Tolerance in the Age of Identity and Empire* (Princeton: Princeton University Press, 2006), p. 8.

5 Ibid., p. 25.

6 Ibid., p. 25.

7 Ibid., p. 27.

Brown argues that tolerance is deceptive when it disguises itself as a desirable and open-minded quality. Far from advocating equality, tolerance functions to *assimilate* the threatening element into dominant discourse in order to control it.

The home functions in remarkably similar ways: whereas the stereotypical home features the nuclear family that is connected to domestic labour, female oppression, reproduction and a sense of stasis, it may also contain deviating desires in order to keep the public street faultlessly heteronormative. Whereas tolerance works through assimilation to control deviating subjects, the home can perpetuate both hetero- and homosexual desires in a manageable parameter. The following analysis will demonstrate that even lesbian characters like Kay can come to project heteronormative ideals onto their home, which means that Kay's potential for queering space is similarly limited as the queering of her body.

Renault's *The Charioteer* also displays a curious attitude towards the home by repeatedly emphasising its relevance for the characters' psychic condition: without a home, Laurie feels lost and unsure where he belongs. When he observes that his disrespectful behaviour towards Andrew during an argument "came home to him" (240), Laurie alludes to the conceptual proximity of 'home' and 'self'. This chapter will examine the far-reaching connotation of his poetic language in order to illustrate that the 'self' is constrained by an 'inner home' that induces conformity onto characters similar to the physical home in order to enforce certain scripts of conduct. Only when "the wall" of stereotypical conventions collapses "start[ing] with a few loose bricks" (240), can the characters begin to negotiate their sexual identity without the restraining quality of the heteronormative home. The novels' emphasis on destruction of houses caused by the war further questions buildings as symbols of inevitable futurity grounded in their alleged physical endurance. In this way, wartime novels in general and those with a homosexual subject matter in particular enable a reading of queer time, body and space that reverses traditionally forward orientated culture based on homely belonging.

The home is stereotypically tightly linked to the family and perceived as a heteronormative space of reproduction – a notion that will be elaborated on in the course of this chapter.[8] In "The House as Symbol of the Self" Clare Cooper argues:

> The house both encloses space (the house interior) and excludes space (everything outside it). Thus, it has two very important and different comportments; its interior and its façade. The house therefore nicely reflects how man [and woman] sees himself[/herself], with

8 Doren B. Massey, *Space, Place, and Gender* (Cambridge: Polity Press, 1994).

both an intimate interior, or self as viewed from within and revealed only to those intimates who are invited inside, and a public exterior [...] or the self that we choose to display to others.[9]

The "enclose[d] space" is most often inhabited by the nuclear family, whereas the "exclude[d] space" is comprised of those subjects without permission to cross the boundary. Cooper moves from the physical conditions of walls dividing between interior and exterior, to the incorporation of these boundaries within the self. The doubling of the self between what is made public and what remains private relates to the public/private dichotomy made possible through house and home. Consequently, the rules of conduct that govern the interaction of subjects within the home find rehearsal in the 'inner home' of the self.

Of equal importance are the physical house and its connection to the body. Anthony Vidler traces three moments in the history of architectural embodiment: "(1) the notion that building *is* a body of some kind; (2) the idea that the building embodies states of the body, or, more importantly, states of mind based on bodily sensation; and (3) the sense that the environment as a whole is endowed with bodily or at least organic characteristics."[10] His analysis shows the continuity of drawing links between physical buildings and embodiment to highlight their conceptual proximity. I am diverting from Vidler's critical evaluation of architectural embodiment and houses as diverse "corporeal metaphors" [11], when looking at the characters' psychological incorporation of homely standards. Instead of arguing for the body as a model for houses, I propose to look at the home as a mirror image for fabricating an 'inner home' that controls the self. In order to understand the complex meaning of 'the self', it is helpful to turn to Judith Butler's theory on gender performativity as it discloses the interlocking relationship between social norms, gender identity and the body.

Butler defines gender performativity as the repetitive and unconscious enactment of norms. She challenges the assumption that gender derives from a stable inner self that refers back to a biological body and its dual sex on two

9 Clare Cooper, "The House as Symbol of the Self" (Barkley: University of California, 1974), p. 131. For further information see also Clare Cooper, *House As a Mirror of Self: Exploring the Deeper Meaning of Home*, [1995], (Berwick and Maine: Nicolas-Hays, 2006).

10 Anthony Vidler, *The Architectural Uncanny: Essays in the Modern Unhomely* (Cambridge, London: MIT Press, 1992), p. 70.

11 Vidler, (1992), p. 69. Vidler elaborates on the connection of bodies and buildings by stating that "The body, its balance, standards of proportion, symmetry, and functioning, mingling elegance and strength, was the foundation myth of building." p. 71.

grounds: firstly, sex is as much a constructed fiction as gender based on the idea of opposing and dichotomous categories, given that hormonal and chromosomal abnormalities resulting in genital variability occurs frequently. Secondly, gender is the social expression of a fantasy that disguises itself as identity. "There is no gender identity behind the expression of gender; that identity is performatively constituted by the very 'expressions' that are said to be its result."[12] Consequently, "gender cannot be said to follow from a sex in any one way", which signals the multiplicity of gender performances across sexed bodies.[13] There is no 'proper' gender because, according to Butler, "[w]here that notion of the 'proper' operates, it is always and only *improperly* installed as the effect of a compulsory system."[14] "[A]cts, gestures, and desire produce the effect of an internal core or substance, but produce this *on the surface* of the body, through the play of signifying absences that suggest, but never reveal, the organizing principle of identity as a cause"[15]. Embodied action fabricates the impression of an inner core (a self) that is allegedly gendered in accordance with the body's sex. Butler claims that such an "interior essence" does not exist – that the gendered body "has no ontological status apart from the various acts which constitute its reality"[16]. This does not deny the reality of lived experience expressed through the body but calls into question the assumption that corporality signifies gender identity. Cooper similarly asserts that "[t]he first and most consciously selected form to represent self is the body, for it appears to be both the outward manifestation, and the encloser, of self"[17]. Accordingly, the body becomes the primary object for monitoring social conformity, because it is assumed to represent and make visible an interior core abstractly called 'the self'.

Consequently, when Vidler is right that architecture has a tradition of modelling buildings after the human body, and when the body is assumed (however wrongly) to express the interior self that is gendered in accordance with the body's sex, it follows that specific gender norms become infiltrated into the home and pass as 'natural' due to their connection with the "locale of gender identity"[18] – the sexed body. In order to fully challenge the gender order, it is

12 Judith Butler, *Gender Trouble: Feminism and the Subversion of Identity*, [1990], (London and New York: Routledge Classics, 2006), p. 34.

13 Ibid., p. 9.

14 Judith Butler, "Imitation and Gender Insubordination" in Diana Fuss (ed.), *Inside/Out: Lesbian Theories, Gay Theories* (New York: Psychology Press, 1991), p. 21.

15 Butler, (2006), p. 185.

16 Ibid., p. 185.

17 Cooper, (1974), p. 131.

18 Butler, (2006), p. 183.

necessary to disclose in what way house and home function as an echo chamber of that body. Iris Marion Young observes that ending exploitation based on gender, class, race and other modern signifiers of social inequality "requires rejecting entirely the project of supporting identity and subjectivity embodied in the patriarchal ideology of home"[19]. Young's argument reinforces the connection between body and home and the significance of deconstructing any assumption regarding the fixity of gender and its projection onto the heteronormative home.

I will argue for the interlinking of various spatial parameters (body, home, street etc.) in order to disclose their interdependency that reifies the structural perpetuation of heteronormative standards. Because the sexed body is thought to display a gendered self coherent with biological markers, the body becomes a sign for gender conformity. As a model for architectural buildings, the heteronormative body is not only situated within the home but also the ground on which society quite literally builds. Consequently, by challenging sex-gender coherence displayed on the body, the implicated norms of the home become equally disturbed. It follows that the formerly heteronormative home restricting desires and movement beyond known boundaries turns into a non-conforming space that facilitates homosexual pleasures. At the same time as liberating itself from dominant parameters, the homosexual home becomes a space of confinement as it keeps desires in the private in order to not disturb the public. The following analysis will demonstrate the complex interconnections between various spaces that correlate in controlling gender performances. In order to more fully conceptualise the potential of body spaces to challenge gender conformity, I wish to turn to Halberstam's theory of female masculinity.

Halberstam's influential study *Female Masculinity* elaborates on Butler's gender performativity by observing that "masculinity must not and cannot and should not reduce down to the male body and its effects"[20]. In this way, forms of hegemonic masculinity and masculine heroism examined in the previous chapter are not strictly fixed to the male body, but can also be performed by women like Waters' mannish lesbian character Kay. In consequence, "*man* and *masculine* might just as easily signify a female body as a male one, and *woman* and *feminine* a male body as easily as a female one"[21]. This separation of masculinity from male bodies shows the constructedness and ambiguity of gender and its arbitrary relation to biological bodies. The division of sex and gender – of

19 Iris Marion Young, *On Female Body Experience: "Throwing Like A Girl" and Other Essays* (Oxford: Oxford University Press, 2005), p. 130.

20 Halberstam, *Female Masculinity* (Durham and London: Duke University Press, 1998), p. 1.

21 Butler, (2006), p. 9, [emphasis original].

male/female bodies and masculinity/femininity – is absolutely vital for understanding why Kay can obtain a form of masculine gender performance during the war. This does not imply that Kay perceives herself as a man, but that masculinities and masculine power prevail independently of male bodies. Halberstam calls this performance female masculinity – "*a specific gender with its own cultural history rather than simply a derivative of male masculinity*"[22]. Although conceding that "[s]ometimes female masculinity coincides with the excess of male supremacy", Halberstam's primary aim is to turn "a blind eye to conventional masculinities and refusing to engage"[23]. The spirit of *Female Masculinity* is therefore to distance itself from male masculinity and to embrace forms of masculinities performed by female bodies that have been unrecognised or abjected in traditional socio-historic contexts.

Kay's performance during the war discloses that Halberstam's ambitious aim to disregard masculine power in female masculinity is difficult – a flaw Halberstam is aware of when repeatedly justifying when and why a masculine woman exceeds a masculine power sought to be dismissed.[24] The claim for female masculinity to seek a different form of empowerment is problematic, because Kay repeatedly subordinates her girlfriend Helen, and is perceived as "more of a gentleman than any real man" (425) by others. This suggests that while female masculinity *might* be a way of staying ambivalent towards masculine power (which seems inherently paradoxical given the retention of the term 'masculine'), Kay fails in this attempt. Halberstam's theory is additionally problematic because the focus on a masculine singular indicates that there is only one version of masculinity and this seems to suggest that women need to embrace hegemonic masculinity in order to escape their traditional powerlessness. Carrie Paechter rightfully criticises Halberstam for this move when stating: "The dualistic relationship between masculinity and femininity, whether claimed by males or females, positions both extreme and normative femininity as without power, and, indeed, as pathological."[25] Paechter's critique is built on the premise that women such as Kay perform female masculinity in order to contrast themselves from more feminine women. This refurbishment of gender norms by female bodies is as oppressive as traditional gender performances based on a dichotomy of sexed bodies.

22 Halberstam, (1998), p. 77, [my emphasis].

23 Ibid., p. 9.

24 Ibid., p. 109.

25 Carrie Paechter, "Masculine Femininities/Feminine Masculinities: Power, Identities and Gender" in *Gender and Education* Vol. 18, No. 3 (2006), p. 257.

In order to indicate that Kay's gender performance is neither that of male nor female masculinity, I will be using brackets: (female) masculinity. By choosing to bracket the 'female', and not the 'masculinity' part of the term, I insinuate that Kay's performance is more informed by the traditional discourse of patriarchy, than by Halberstam's thesis, making Waters' character an image of female complicity in patriarchal power structures.

Wendy Brown explains why female complicity is a fundamental and material concept:

> The state can be masculinist without intentionally or overtly pursuing the 'interests' of men precisely because the multiple dimensions of socially constructed masculinity have historically shaped the multiple modes of power circulating through the domain called the state – this is what it means to talk about masculinist power rather than the power of men.[26]

This statement recalls that male bodies do not necessarily denote masculinity, but those bodies that participate in and distribute the power structure encompassing the construct of masculinity. The problem with gender performativity is then that "[m]asculinity maintains its position of superiority in relation to femininity and men maintain legitimate possession of those superior characteristics *regardless* of who is embodying femininity or masculinity."[27] An analysis following Butler, in which gender is deconstructed as performativity, therefore offers little room for conceiving the dynamics of masculinity and femininity in new terms, since the privileging of the masculine and subordination of the feminine continues to prevail. This structure is pointedly evident when Kay "got talking to a tipsy girl [in the cinema], and had finished by leading the girl into an empty lavatory and kissing her and feeling her up. The thing had been rather savagely done; she felt ashamed, thinking of it now." (106) In these instances when women like Kay either adopt masculine power, or when women like this girl leave their own subordination unchallenged, they unwittingly support the logics of patriarchy in their complicity.

This chapter will set out by examining Kay's performance of (female) masculinity and its effect on simultaneously the perception of her female body and her attitude towards her wartime girlfriend Helen. By destabilising the body as a space on which to project gender norms correlating with one's sex, Waters' de-

26 Wendy Brown, *States of Injury: Power and Freedom in late Modernity* (Princeton University Press, 1995), p. 177.

27 Mimi Schippers, "Recovering the Feminine Other: Masculinity, Femininity, and Gender Hegemony" in *Theory and Society*, Vol. 36, No. 1 (2007), p. 96, [my emphasis].

piction of Kay emphasises variances and gender fluidity. This queering of the body challenges not only the assumption of a heteronormative home, but also the battlefield as a masculine space where men negotiate their masculinity. Kay's (female) masculinity devastates the dominant gendered politics of space in diverse ways, but due to her female complicity, described by Brown, the effect is neither desirable nor lasting.

BODY SPACE – DESTABILISING GENDER

In her study "'Grisley [sic] 'L' business': Re-valuing Female Masculinity and Butch Subjectivity in *Tipping the Velvet* and *The Night Watch*" [28] Claire O'Callaghan argues that Kay "challenges prejudiced heterosexist and lesbian-feminist stereotypes of the butch lesbian that have contributed to her denigration"[29]. My reading of Kay in this section is vastly different and discloses the many ways in which Kay, rather than shattering, contributes to the stigmas that accompany butch subjectivity. Whilst the following analysis does not deny the appropriateness and importance of developing a concept for thinking gender which allows for fluidity, and indeed welcomes performances that break up the rigidity of the gender binary, Kay shows that the claim for female masculinity to *not* adopt and transfer traditional masculine power is too idealistic, and in Kay's case largely amiss. She adheres to stereotypical representations of 'being butch', in which the "mythic mannish lesbian", to borrow Esther Newton's term,[30] is often characterised as level-headed thus mimicking masculine rationality. Although I partially agree with O'Callaghan that "[b]y granting [Kay] heartache, Waters highlights the emotional vulnerability of the butch lesbian and invests her with dignity and feeling"[31], Kay's gender performance is pervaded with moments clearly distinguishable as masculinist, and she does therefore not perform a positive and counter-discursive form of female masculinity.

---

28 Claire O'Callaghan, "'Grisley [sic] 'L' business': Re-valuing Female Masculinity and Butch Subjectivity in *Tipping the Velvet* and *The Night Watch*" in Adele Jones and Claire O'Callaghan (eds.), *Sarah Waters and Contemporary Feminism* (London: Palgrave Macmillan Nottingham, 2016).

29 Ibid., p. 196.

30 For an analysis of the 'mythic mannish lesbian' see Esther Newton, "The Mythic Mannish Lesbian: Radclyffe Hall and the New Woman" in *Signs* Vol. 9, No. 4, The Lesbian Issue (1984), pp. 557-575.

31 O'Callaghan, (2016), p. 207.

By attempting to read Kay as a liberated butch subject, O'Callaghan additionally fails to differentiate between wartime and peace when she claims that "Kay's dress and masculine demeanour underline her identification with masculine sensibilities. The opening pages [of *The Night Watch*] include a lengthy description of Kay's wardrobe and dressing routine, [and] reinforce the importance of such aesthetics to her."[32] O'Callaghan rightly identifies that the emphasis on Kay's clothes occurs at the very beginning of the novel set in 1947. However, it seems misleading to read Kay's careful dress code at this point as a form of liberation when it stands in direct contradiction to her lack of emphasis on outward appearance during the war. O'Callaghan continues arguing that Kay's "employment in the London Auxiliary Ambulance Service exemplifies the changing dress code that broke with conventions of femininity (uniforms and trousers)"[33]. Shifting back to the war years, O'Callaghan's examination conflates two very distinct periods in women's and lesbians' lives that cannot serve as a continuous example for butch subjectivity in the 1940s. In order to clarify this further, I will initially examine Kay's failing performance of (female) masculinity with the establishment of peace grounded in the overarching re-inscription of gender norms, to then elaborate on her female complicity based on her patronising behaviour towards Helen during the war.

In the part set in 1947 Kay becomes obsessed with her own appearance as a way of compensation for her feelings of worthlessness when Helen has left her. Through her tailored style, her "men's shoes" (5), cuff links and greased short hair, Kay tries to re-claim a former power and autonomy that the establishment of peace took away from her. Halberstam's *In a Queer Time and Place: Transgender Bodies, Subcultural Lives* argues that such display of "the masculine woman in the past has rarely been pictured as an interesting phenomenon – usually, she has been portrayed as the outcome of failed femininity, or as the result of pathetic and unsuccessful male mimicry"[34]. Halberstam asserts that attempts of dressing in a masculine style, as shown in Kay, are often disregarded or ignored in order to not raise attention to such failed gender identity. The narrative illustrates Halberstam's criticism when Kay's appearance, unnoticed during war, is now recognised but misread, because people call her "'young man', and even 'son'" (5). This misreading of Kay's body does not have the same empowering effect on her as the occupation as an ambulance driver during the war, because it indicates youth, immaturity and even pre-sexuality. Since Duncan is

32 O'Callaghan, (2016), p. 204.

33 Ibid., p. 204.

34 Halberstam, *In a Queer Time and Place: Transgender Bodies, Subcultural Lives* (New York and London: New York University Press, 2005), p. 17.

also perceived as a boy who cannot manage his own life, the depiction of Kay as a son equally indicates helplessness and resignation. Instead of dissolving this mis-recognition by placing emphasis on her female body, the narrator clarifies her age – "she would be thirty-seven on her next birthday" (5) – in order to unhinge Kay from implications of immaturity. The emphasis on her age rather than her female body reinforces the significance of being noticed as a war participant and survivor. Despite emphasising that she will be "thirty-seven" soon, making her a conscious witness of the war, Kay's heroism of the past years is marginalised and her former confidence is destroyed. It therefore takes persuasion on her part not to stay at home – "she wouldn't turn back" (6) – but to face the world outside where she no longer feels welcome.

To further compensate for her lack of recognition, Kay "walk[s] with a swagger, make[s] a 'character' of [herself]", but immediately concedes that this gender performance is "tiring" "when you hadn't the energy for it" (100). Hearing the same jokes over her appearance "a thousand times" (100) makes Kay nostalgically glorify the past in comparison to the "creature" (208) she has become now. Her self-identification as a "creature" delineates that without the war to distribute masculine power to female bodies, Kay has lost her subjectivity and any ambition in life. I therefore agree with Stewart's argument that "[d]espite the horror [Kay] witnesses as an ambulance driver, during the war [she] feels a sense of purpose then that is lacking to her in the peacetime"[35]. Her situation after 1945 also partially demonstrates Plain's argument that women were "asked to assume *temporarily* the *semblance* of masculinity"[36]. Whereas I agree that women only "*temporarily*" found recognition and lost their autonomy with the emergence of peace, Kay illustrates that she obtains more than a "*semblance* of masculinity", because she deeply identifies with her masculine role. In order to more fully understand the dynamics that lead to Kay's desperate situation after the war, her failing relationship with Helen in 1944 needs to be taken into account. Although Kay is admittedly the betrayed lover which evokes sympathy for her, she actively contributes to her fate, which significantly changes the sub-text that leads to her peacetime suffering.

Ignoring Kay's female complicity in a patriarchal power structure, O'Callaghan criticises that "Helen and Julia's affair functions (troublingly) as a form of punishment to Kay for her apparent investment in heterosexual idealism"[37]. Arguing *against* Kay's re-enactment of heteronormative patterns,

35 Victoria Stewart, *The Second World War in Contemporary British Fiction: Secret Histories* (Edinburgh: Edinburgh University Press, 2011), p.155.

36 Plain, (1996), p, 28, [first emphasis added, second emphasis original].

37 O'Callaghan, (2016), p. 208.

O'Callaghan asserts that "Waters's [sic] representation of their [Helen and Julia's] developing romance serves only to align the reader's sympathies with Kay [...] because the novel's reverse chronological structure creates an affective discourse surrounding Kay"[38]. Whilst Helen and Julia's affair takes place, Kay is portrayed as heroically saving the city in her job as an ambulance driver. These contradictory storylines function, according to O'Callaghan, as the "affective discourse" that negates Helen's sense of confinement in her relationship in favour of creating a nimbus of sympathy for Kay's situation as the betrayed lover. O'Callaghan grounds her argument in a conversation between Helen and Julia, who perceive Kay's gentlemanly behaviour towards her girlfriend as a burden:

> 'Come and sit down, Helen.' [said Julia] [...]
> She'd drawn up chairs, but looked dubiously from the dusty seats to Helen's smartish coat. [...]
> 'It's all right,' said Helen. 'Really.'
> 'Sure?' I'll take you at your word, you know. I won't be like Kay about it.' [...]
> For Kay *would* have made a fuss about the dust, [Helen] thought; and she knew instinctively how tiresome that sort of thing would seem to Julia. (271) [emphasis original]

Moments later Helen continues pondering:

> She wanted to ask how it had been for Julia, with Kay. She wanted to know if Julia had felt what she herself sometimes, guiltily, felt: that Kay's constant fussing, which had once been so appealing, so exciting, could also be rather like a burden; that Kay made an absurd kind of heroine of you; that Kay's passion was so great there was something unreal about it, it could never be matched ... (275)

Helen represents Kay as someone who displays an almost neurotic need to help, and in doing so infantilises her partner. She nevertheless reflects that Kay's gallant demeanour was part of the reason why she fell in love with her in the first place: "It did seem romantic. Kay's rather glamorous, isn't she? [...] She made such a – such a fuss of me. [...] It was hard to resist, anyway." (274) At the beginning of their romance, Kay's fussing over Helen constitutes the ground of her feelings, now it restrains Helen's autonomy. Julia, who pretends that she was never drawn to Kay's gallantry, wonders about Helen's ability to endure it, which, according to Julia, characterises Helen as balanced and level-headed: "You *are* well adjusted" (275) [emphasis original]. The truth is that Julia does not so much mind Kay's behaviour but cannot forgive Kay for rejecting her.

38 O'Callaghan, (2016), p. 208.

Julia's unrequited love has filled her with bitterness and leads her to seek emotional revenge by pursuing Kay's girlfriend for herself. In a confessional conversation with Helen, Julia delineates why she and Kay could never become lovers:

> Julia hesitated. Then, 'She was never in love with me,' she said. [...] 'I was the one. I was in love with Kay for years. She tried to love me back, but – it never took. I'm just not her type, I suppose. We're too similar; that's all it is.' [...] She wants a wife – someone good, I mean; someone kind, untarnished. Someone to keep things in order for her, hold things in place. I could never do that. I used to tell her she wouldn't be happy until she'd found herself some nice blue-eyed girl – some girl who'd need rescuing, or fussing over, or something like that...' (424-425)

Still hurt, Julia perceives Kay's rejection as an evaluation of her gender performance as insufficiently feminine for someone who "wants a wife". Several weeks before this conversation, Julia had used the exact same words: "Kay wants a wife. [...] That sounds like a children's game, doesn't it? Kay wants a wife. She always has. One must be the wife with Kay, or nothing." (353) This statement substantiates the impression that Julia and Kay's relationship did not work out because Julia was not prepared to take up the role of wife whilst Kay performs the role of husband. Like Kay, Julia's appearance and manner is mostly masculine, albeit combined with feminine markers such as red lips and make-up. One night, Julia asks Helen if she looks "like a male impersonator on stage" (355), which highlights her masculine style. Due to this similarity, neither character is willing to be "the wife". Julia's aversion towards traditional gender roles is obvious in her pejorative use of the phrase "Kay wants a wife", which she then modifies to "[o]ne must be the wife with Kay, or nothing." The impersonal pronoun "one" directs the focus away from Julia to include Helen and every future woman who might become Kay's partner. It implies that being with Kay entails living in a heteronormatively gendered relationship since "one" will always perform the feminine part – and this "one" is never Kay. Julia's additional observation that Kay's masculine performance and desire for a wife "sounds like a children's game" betrays not only Julia's hurt ego, but also dramatises how "female masculinity is generally received by hetero- and homo-normative cultures as a pathological sign of misidentification and maladjustment"[39]. Halberstam's emphasis on "hetero- and *homo*-normative cultures" critically observes that gay and lesbian communities live as much in a normative discourse as heterosexual subjects. Kay's performance of (female) masculinity is thus not only abjected by heteronormative society, but also considered a "misidentification and malad-

39 Halberstam, (1998), p. 9.

justment" by people like Julia, which makes Kay doubly marginalised. Read in this way, Kay's performance of power towards Helen becomes easily obscured, which is evident in O'Callaghan's claims that the conversation between Julia and Helen "replay[s] criticisms of the butch lesbian"[40]. Accordingly, Julia and Helen "perceive [Kay's] affections as stifling because it limits their agency and, above all, they believe that Kay's 'gentlemanly' behaviours indicate that she wants to be a man"[41]. O'Callaghan's reading of Kay as the victim of 'butch bashing' overlooks scenes in which Kay actively contributes to the fabrication of such negative voices. Maite Escudero-Alías also asserts that "Kay's drained existence in the aftermath of the war trauma is drastically marked by the betrayal of her former lover"[42]. Even more sympathetic with Kay than O'Callaghan, Escudero-Alías claims that Kay "becomes the recipient of social injustice, shameful secrets and nameless suffering, in spite of her status as an upper-class lesbian"[43]. Recognising Kay for her privileged class status, Escudero-Alías leaves unmentioned her masculine gender performance, which pushes Helen into the arms of Julia where she can "confide in [her], almost as one wife to another" (275). The repeated and negative reference to being a "wife" indicates how deeply the characters feel and fear their entrapment into a feminine gender role, which makes it necessary to read Kay's (female) masculinity as an oppressive force that subordinates her girlfriend.

In order to enhance her masculine status during the war, a distinct lack of focus on Kay's outward appearance is evident, which contrasts her masculine dress code after the war. There are no mirror scenes in which she examines her naked body wishing it to be any different such as depicted in *The Well of Loneliness* by Radclyffe Hall (1928), where the gender deviant protagonist Stephen Gordon perceives her body as a "monstrous fetter" (*TW*, 187)[44]. Neither does Kay engage in any other kind of self-loathing, but instead relishes her lesbian lifestyle with her equally homosexual group of friends. I would therefore agree with Natasha Alden's observation that "although [Kay] dresses in men's clothes, can pass as a man, wishes to have the kind of active job traditionally restricted to men and sleeps with women, [she] does not view herself as inverted, and never alludes to

40 O'Callaghan, (2016), p. 205.

41 Ibid., p. 206.

42 Maite Escudero-Alías, "'There's that curtain come down' The Burden of Shame in Sarah Waters' *The Night Watch*" in Marita Nadal and Mónica Calvo (eds.), *Trauma in Contemporary Literature: Narrative and Representation* (New York: Routledge, 2014), p. 229.

43 Escudero-Alías, (2014), p. 228.

44 Radclyffe Hall, *The Well of Loneliness*, [1928], (New York: Anchor Books, 1990).

such a model"[45]. Besides the knowledge of her wearing a uniform to work and trousers in her spare time, the reader is only once allowed to catch a short glimpse of how Kay cuts her hair in 1944: "I'd just started to cut my hair. I've dropped hair everywhere, now." (285) It remains unclear whether this cutting of hair was to keep it short for practical reasons, or a decision to abandon the symbolic long hair of femininity. Yet the briefness of this passage and the ease with which Kay talks about it, suggests that feminine symbols, such as long hair, lost their significance in wartime. This relaxation allowed women to experience a degree of liberation from the monitoring of their bodies.

Make Do and Mend (2012) similarly addresses this change in female appearance when the housemaids Kitty and Blanche make "small attempts to set one another's hair once a week" (77). This is often dismissed in favour of "sewing or knitting in an endeavour to produce new garments from old or to circumvent the coupon system for clothing in other ingenious ways" (77). The female characters in this novel are not deviating in their sexuality like Kay, but the fact that their sense of hairstyle has altered and given way to the production of clothes shows how 'ordinary' women, too, moved the norms of female appearance. Accordingly, Kay attracts little attention with her style during the war which makes it needless to foreground it as especially masculine. Moreover, by calling her 'Kay', the character's gender ambiguity is heightened because the name is unisex, and when her friends refrain from classifying her as Mr or Miss by just calling her 'Langrish', they deflect attention from her female body. However, female pronouns are continuously deployed throughout the novel, which paradoxically reinforces Kay's indifference towards sex and gender norms. She seems to appropriate a number of arbitrary standards and fashions a unique gender performance to suit her personality.

Kay's masculine demeanour controversially perpetuates gender roles within her relationship when she aspires to provide a heteronormative life for her partner Helen. In two scenes set in 1944 and 1941 respectively, Kay expresses her idealistic vision:

> Well, I'm sick of gazing into Helen's face and seeing it look more and more tired and worn. If I were her husband I'd be off fighting; there wouldn't be a thing I could do about it. But the fact is, I'm here – (255)

45 Natasha Alden, "'Possibility, Pleasure and Peril': *The Night Watch* as a Very Literary History" in Kaye Mitchell (ed.), *Sarah Waters: Contemporary Critical Perspectives* (London: Bloomsbury, 2013), p. 195.

It was one of the tragedies of her life, that she couldn't be *like* a man to Helen – make her a wife, give her children ... (326) [my emphasis]

Kay clearly voices grief and anger over her position that prevents her from caring for Helen in the way she believes a man could by making her "a [legal] wife" and giving her "children". Kay's mournful musings regarding her inability to adopt an authentic male role might suggest that she is heading into transgender, possibly even transsexual terrain, where the subject feels "real and desperate desires for reembodiment"[46]. Indeed, both quotes end in silence; the dash ("–") and the ellipses ("...") at the end of the sentences indicate that Kay does not want to speak the inevitable: that however much she might wish to be a husband to Helen, her biological body is female and in the early 1940s this was a condition not modifiable by medicine.

However, Kay only ever wants to be "*like*" a man for Helen's sake, who is deeply dissatisfied with her relationship when saying: "If we could only be married, something like that." (326) Helen's emphasis on marriage as a fantasy that Kay cannot fulfil, feeds into Kay's pre-existing insecurity regarding *Helen's* happiness in their relationship, which increases Kay's fear of losing Helen to a man. That she does not believe Helen to be with another woman is revealed shortly afterwards when she suggests that Helen should "go to a pub and get canned, and pick up some boy, some soldier –'" (327). Kay's style of speaking ("get canned", "pick up") indicates that she effectively mimics male working-class parlance. This active disguising of her upper-class status by using bawdy slang complements Kay's understanding of what constitutes tough and autonomous subjecthood: a rational working-class masculinity that represses emotions and insecurities. Kay does consequentially not question her identity as a masculine woman, nor does she wish to be a man. Her lingering insecurities over Helen's sexual orientation instead cause her to believe that Helen secretly wishes for a male partner and for them to be in a conventional heterosexual relationship. Initially, Kay's fashioning of heterosexual roles is therefore a reaction to Helen's inability to cope with the disguising of their love from the public. However, Kay imitates masculinist conduct to the point where she actively subordinates Helen and restraints her to the role of "wife".

The use of stigmatising language as well as the objectification of the female body emphasise the unequal dynamics between Helen and Kay. Instead of focusing on her own appearance, it is Helen's body that is carefully dressed, undressed and lengthily described under Kay's voyeuristic masculine gaze: "she caught a glimpse, beyond the turned-up collar of Helen's coat, of the cream lapel

46 Halberstam, (1998), p. 143.

beneath it, and beneath that, the smooth, blemishless skin" (321). By staring at Helen, Kay tries to conquer these layers of clothing and in doing so, she almost undresses Helen with her eyes. Like a lustful man, Kay remembers Helen in her new silk pyjamas, and how she had buttoned up the dress Helen is wearing underneath her coat. The silk pyjamas, "the colour of pearls" (256), have a symbolic meaning in the narrative. As a luxurious birthday present to Helen, Kay not only draws attention to her higher class and financial background, thus challenging the authenticity of her working-class parlance. She also substantiates her lesbian desire for Helen and fixates her in the role of girlfriend/wife. Adele Jones rightly concludes that "although challenging gendered norms, [Kay] attempts to recreate a lesbian version of those norms in her relationship with Helen"[47] and the pearl coloured pyjamas substantiate these efforts. *The Night Watch* situates the symbol of pearls simultaneously in lesbian feminism and in queer theory, because pearls are, according to O'Callaghan, "avowedly 'feminine' via their historic association with women", but they also "denote a multifarious, suggestive range of meanings" reminiscent of queer theory's diversity and reluctance to essentialise.[48] O'Callaghan concludes that "Waters's [sic] novels convey a queer conception of identity while privileging the specificity of women and female same-sex desire."[49] Kay's gift therefore obtains several meanings: indicating class and higher status because pearls are associated with wealth, highlighting her own identity as queer, and distinguishing her relationship in lesbian terms assigning the role of woman and wife to Helen.

Kay's affectionate enthusiasm upon showing the pyjamas to her friends is sexualised by Binkie who jokes: "She won't be putting up any resistance once she's in this." (256) The term "resistance" was brought up in the context of the war: because the pyjamas are French, Helen will "be doing her bit for the Re-

47 Jones, "Disrupting the Continuum", (2014), p. 41.

48 Claire O'Callaghan, "The Equivocal Symbolism of Pearls in the Novels of Sarah Waters" in *Contemporary Women's Writing* Vol. 6, No. 1 (2012), p. 21. Waters' usage of the pearl metaphor in *The Night Watch* and in her other novels situates the author in a lesbian tradition where pearls have often symbolised love between women. O'Callaghan shows that writers such as Radclyffe Hall, Janette Winterson or Sarah Schulman repeatedly rely on the implied meaning of pearls/oysters to encode lesbian desires. She argues that "pearls provide a 'language' in which to encode same-sex orientation in a period (albeit a fictional one) in which such terminology was unavailable to women." O'Callaghan, (2012), p. 27. For Waters pearls/oysters do not only highlight a lesbian tradition, they also provide a language to pronounce lesbian desire in tandem with earlier narratives.

49 O'Callaghan, (2012), p. 21.

sistance" (256) by wearing them. Translating Resistance into resistance, Binkie fixes the symbolic meaning of pearls exclusively to the "categories *woman* and *lesbian*"[50] due to the implication of sexual intercourse and Helen's role as woman dressing up, or rather undressing, for her husband Kay. The essentialism resonating in Binkie's words is substantiated when Kay holds the pyjamas against herself saying: "They look absurd on me, of course, but you get the idea." (256) Clearly not identifying with the feminine part of the pearl trope, Kay denies association with it. However, her reluctance highlights O'Callaghan's theory that "pearls are [also] a queer symbol"[51] beyond the category of women and its implied femininity: because Kay identifies as queer, the twofold meaning of the pyjamas is established. Moreover, when giving the pyjamas to Helen at her birthday, Kay recalls the moment they have first met and says: "I held your face in my hand. You were smooth, like a pearl." (313) Kay's memory emphasises that pearls represent the "shifting, provisional nature of identity"[52] since Helen travels from heterosexuality to homosexuality upon meeting Kay. Waters' usage of pearls is thus not unilateral but contains hidden meanings for the reader to ponder.

The pearl metaphor is finally abandoned when Helen receives her birthday present. Recognising that the gift must have been expensive, Helen feels uncomfortable: "I don't deserve it" she says, and when putting on the pyjamas, their glamour and pearl-like colour vanishes and it transforms into an ill-fitting item:

> The sleeves were long: she buttoned the cuffs and folded them back, but they slid out of the folds at once and fell almost to her fingertips. She stood, as if shyly, for Kay to look her over. [...] She didn't look glamorous really, however; she looked young, and small, and rather solemn. (312)

The text highlights every negative aspect of the oversized pyjamas and repeats Helen's fretful attempt of rolling up the sleeves. When catching her reflection in the mirror, Helen "quickly [turns] away" (312) as if refusing to encounter the image of her body wearing a token of Kay's love and desire whilst remembering her own disloyalty when seeing Julia behind Kay's back. O'Callaghan argues that the wearing of pearl-coloured pyjamas "inscribes lesbian desire on the body"[53]. In this way, Helen's body becomes significant as a lesbian and feminine body belonging to Kay. Unable to identify with this projection, Helen avoids

50 O'Callaghan, (2012), p. 21.

51 Ibid., p. 21.

52 Ibid., p. 24.

53 Ibid., p. 29.

both her own gaze reflected in the mirror and Kay's, who continues marvelling at Helen. The characters' contradictory perspectives clash and create a twofold meaning for the reader who knows of Helen's emerging feelings for another woman and Kay's undying love for her 'wife'. The sympathy for Kay disguises her patriarchal attitude towards Helen, who becomes sexually objectified by her 'husband': Kay "remembered standing in the bedroom, fastening up the handsome dress; she remembered the sliding of the silk pyjamas, the feel of the weight of Helen's hot, suspended breasts." (321) That Kay is female does not lessen the objectifying character of her fantasy evoked when staring at Helen but suggests that female bodies are prone to objectification by both men *and* women. The meaning behind gazes becomes clearer when comparing and contrasting Kay's voyeurism with Kent and Anson's hidden gazes in *Look Down in Mercy*.

Kent displays an almost compulsive need to switch off the lights before having a sexual encounter with Anson as well as with his mistress Helen. That he does not adjust this behaviour according to his partner's sex demonstrates that a person's desire for recognition is bound to social conventions which, in this case, is the avoidance of *any* objectifying gaze for a man, who understands himself as straight and white, thus obtaining the social position of the active and privileged. In *Masculinity, Psychoanalysis, straight Queer Theory*, Calvin Thomas draws a connection between gender stereotypes and gazing. He argues that the stereotypically assigned positions of active masculinity and passive femininity are tightly interwoven with the power-powerless dichotomy intrinsic to the concept of the objectifying gaze. The one actively looking (conventionally male) and the other passively being looked at (conventionally female) claim very different social positions: "it is [...] the *straight* male figure, perhaps the straight *white* male figure, who cannot bear the burden of sexual objectification, the straight white man who is reluctant to gaze at his exhibitionist like"[54]. This reluctance to meet a person's gaze is similarly noted by Silvan Tomkins in *Shame and Its Sisters*, where he reflects that "[t]o the extent to which mutual looking maximizes shared intimacy, whatever taboos there may be on intimacy as such are immediately enforced on interocular exchange, just as they are enforced on sexuality."[55] Tomkins' argument unfolds along the narrative of learned shame as a mechanism to control and adjust a subject's way of conduct before negative, integrity threatening, sanctions such as abjection take place. For him, learned shame is a

54 Calvin Thomas, Masculinity, Psychoanalysis, Straight Queer Theory: Essays on Abjection in Literature, Mass Culture, and Film (New York: Palgrave Macmillan, 2008), p. 7.

55 Silvan Tomkins, *Shame and Its Sisters: A Silvan Tomkins Reader* Eve Kosofsky Sedgwick and Adam Frank (eds.), (Durham: Duke University Press, 1995), p. 144.

> vehicle for the transmission and preservation of social norms from generation to generation. It also provides a mechanism for the preservation of social norms among adult members of the community, inasmuch as the evocation of the shame of the other and its evocation of the shame of the self provide powerful negative sanctions against the transgression of shared social norms.[56]

Kent's behaviour is not only an unconscious adjustment of heteronormative ways of conduct, but also intrinsic to a learned shame complex monitoring society that transforms intimacy between two subjects into various levels of shame, depending on the stigma assigned to the sexual act preceding the gaze.

After Kent's first intimate moment with Anson, he is more troubled about facing Anson the next morning than regretting what has just happened: "all that he was certain of before he fell asleep was that he dreaded the morning, when sooner or later he would have to look at Anson and be looked at in return" (153). The objectifying gaze of which Kent will be the initiator as well as the receiver, both in non-heteronormative ways, functions as a kind of manifestation of what can be tolerated and even overlooked only when, quite literally, kept in the dark. With the light of the day, however, "[h]e and Anson opened their eyes at the same moment and drew apart as swiftly as though they had been awake" (154). Through their movement they attempt to re-establish the heteronormatively required distance between their male bodies. Thus, the sight of the homosexually caressed white, male body violates its and its observer's masculinity and privileged position as a recognisable subject. This paradigm is challenged when Kent and Anson become increasingly more comfortable in each other's company:

> [Kent] stopped to allow the platoon to close up, and while he waited glanced quickly at Anson, who had taken off his hat and stood where a patch of moonlight fell on his face. He was watching Kent and when their eyes met he smiled and Kent's blood stirred and he smiled back, surprised to find that it was so easy. (155)

Kent's reaction to Anson's unexpected gaze illustrates what Tomkins argues is the twofold character of shame: Kent is "caught between the shame of looking and the shame of being ashamed to do so"[57]. He has to endure Anson's gaze, even when it makes his "blood stir[...]" in order to not encounter double shame,

56 Tomkins, (1995), p. 156.

57 Ibid., p. 146.

which Gail Kern Paster calls the "redundancy of shame [:] social shame of *feeling ashamed*"[58].

In twisting the implied norms of the objectifying gaze, this scene demonstrates that the shamefulness of looking and being looked at is dependent on two conditions: the *clarity* of the vision and the *reception* of the gaze. Only when both moments irrevocably occur together, does the gaze challenge the social position of the stereotypically active male. Hence why it can be argued that when Kent seeks out an unnoticed moment to look at Anson he shows no visible sign of remorse or discomfort, because he is in the position of performing the active, masculine role which, although in a non-heteronormative context, can still be tolerated. When in the next instance Anson returns his gaze, Kent manages to endure it "and he [even] smiled back", because the emerging night impairs his own vision as well as the image he is looking at. Altered by the moonlight, the clarity of the morning's daylight, when both had found it impossible to look at each other with the still fresh memory of the night in their minds, is no longer observable in their gazes and faces. It follows that the objectifying gaze is bound to other moments in order to operate normatively: clarity of vision, lighting conditions and reciprocity. When one element is impaired or rendered insignificant, the regulatory force of the gaze fades.

Moreover, gazes are only threatening when a subject's desire for recognition is still at work, binding it to heteronormative conduct. Throughout the novel, Kent steadily departs from social conventions, and he experiences his own and Anson's gaze as increasingly less distressing: "As they talked they looked each other straight in the face; it became difficult to disengage their eyes even when a silence fell, and the silences began to fall more frequently and last longer." (206) This clearly shows Kent's changing attitude towards his relationship with Anson and exemplifies that desiring gazes can change in quality. No longer objectifying, their mutual looking is pleasurable for *both* characters.

In *The Night Watch*, Kay obtains a much more traditional role when she distracts from her own body by objectifying Helen's. While Kent and Anson learn the pleasure of mutual looking, Kay remains fixed in her position as the objectifier, whereas Helen, not looking and unaware of being looked at, becomes objectified. Kay thus illustrates Halberstam's critique that "[a]s long as masculinity is annexed in our society to power and violence and oppression, we will find some masculine women whose gender expression becomes partially wedded to the worst aspects of a culturally mandated masculinity"[59]. O'Callaghan strongly dis-

58 Gail Kern Paster, *The Body Embarrassed: Drama and the Disciplines of Shame in Early Modern England* (Ithaca and New York: Cornell University Press, 1993), p. 36.

59 Halberstam, (1998), p. 109.

agrees with a reading that criticises Kay because she claims that *The Night Watch* "challenge[s] such damaging views of butch subjectivity" [60], since Kay is depicted as emotional and passionate. To strengthen her argument, O'Callaghan compares Kay's use of the term "glamour girl" to Reggie's and asserts that "because Reggie and Viv's heterosexual relationship [...] is empty and contains none of the love that Kay displays, Waters re-values and reinforces Kay's ardent love for Helen, and in doing so, exalts the figure of the butch lesbian"[61]. While I generally agree that Viv and Reggie's illicit relationship is damaging rather than elevating, Viv is extremely excited to meet her lover in 1944: "It was so wonderful to stand in his arms, she felt suddenly almost light-hearted. She even thought, for an awful moment, that she might cry." (182) This display of passion, and the cards Reggie sends Viv "after one of their Saturdays" to tell her that "he was all right" (244), might not reveal the same kind of "ardent love" Kay feels for Helen, but to argue that Viv and Reggie's relationship is from the outset thoroughly "empty" seems reductive.

Furthermore, the comparison between Reggie and Viv's relationship to Kay and Helen's does not alter Kay's masculinist implications when using the phrase 'glamour girl'. O'Callaghan seems to refute her own argument when she concedes that "[t]he term 'glamour girl' equates femininity with heteronormative stereotypes of women from the period in which the ideology of 'beauty as duty' reinforced heteronormative ideals of gender"[62]. Her supplement that "the repetition between Kay and Reggie's use of the phrase undermines the notion that Kay is attempting to feminise Helen in line with heterosexual ideals" is not only unconvincing because it solely rests on Kay's display of passionate love for Helen. It is also essentializing, as O'Callaghan's argument is built on Kay's female body and lesbianism that apparently 'naturally' contrast her from Reggie and his heterosexist language. It seems unfounded to presume that because Kay and Reggie differ in terms of gender and sexuality, their use of the term 'glamour girl' connotes vastly different implications.

The shortcomings of O'Callaghan's analysis become more obvious with regard to Reggie's and Kay's use of the phrase "Good girl" – another correlation between the characters that is conveniently overlooked by O'Callaghan, because it more compulsively reveals Kay's proclivity of resorting to masculinist phrases. Reggie utters the words "Good girl" whenever Viv behaves in a way that pleases him. This is evident at the beginning of the novel, when they make a trip to the countryside. No longer enchanted by his 'charm', Viv begins to eman-

60 O'Callaghan, (2016), p. 206.

61 Ibid., p. 207.

62 Ibid., p. 207.

cipate herself from Reggie when she does not want to have sex with him in public. Yet, she assists him in masturbating. When Reggie is done, he commands Viv to be careful not to let the semen stain his trousers. Content with her efforts, he rewards Viv by calling her a "Good girl" (71). The same pattern is evident at the beginning of their relationship. During one of their clandestine meetings in a remote hotel room, Reggie kisses Viv. His beard pricks her skin:

'You need a shave.'
'I know,' he answered, rubbing his chin against her forehead. 'Does it hurt?'
'Yes.'
'Do you mind?'
'No.'
'Good girl. [...]' (182)

This scene is patronising in several ways. Not only does Reggie call Viv a "Good girl" to reward her behaviour as seen before, he also tests Viv's level of discomfort when he deliberately repeats what feels uncomfortable by "rubbing his chin against her forehead." Viv does not simply have to agree that Reggie does not need to shave, she has to endure *and not mind* the uncomfortable feeling of his beard in order to earn a "Good girl". Reggie's masculinity is substantiated by displaying his beard as a sign for high testosterone and in relation to a woman, who places her desires after his. In doing so, Viv fixes herself in a traditional and passive feminine role against which Reggie's masculinity becomes active and dominant. Placed in such highly stereotypical positions, Viv replies only when directly spoken to and only in one-word sentences, which underlines her total dependency on Reggie. Throughout the novel, Reggie's "Good girl" repeatedly functions to maintain these gender stereotypes, which signals Kay's use of it towards Helen during a telephone call as similarly patronising:

'I'll see you later. You're coming straight home? Come quickly, won't you?'
'Yes, of course.'
'Good girl... Goodbye, Miss Giniver.'
'Goodbye, Kay.' (284)

The dynamics in this conversation are reminiscent of those between Viv and Reggie. Kay calls Helen a "Good girl" to reward her agreement that she will be "coming straight home". The way Kay pressures Helen to "come quickly" does not mark longing and love for Helen as much as Kay's desire to dominate and control her girlfriend. Helen's short responses reflect Viv's one-word answers, signalling the women's shared obedience and submissiveness. In calling her *Miss* Giniver Kay highlights Helen's female role in their relationship. However, since Miss denotes an unmarried woman it also emphasises their extramarital status. Kay's attempt of claiming possession over her girlfriend fails further when Helen uses Kay's first name. This difference in address emasculates Kay and subordinates her to Helen who questions Kay's superiority in their relationship by using her first name. Kay's (female) masculinity is therefore built on shaky legs and in constant danger of being revealed as a performance lacking bodily substance. Nevertheless, the use of masculinist phrases substantiates Kay as a character which partakes in the patriarchal power system and reveals O'Callaghan's reading as an activist approach into refurbishing a butch subjectivity, which, although generally desirable, misinterprets significant details of how Kay is represented in the novel.

QUEERING THE BATTLEFIELD

Whilst establishing heteronormative roles in her relationship with Helen, Kay's active job as an ambulance driver at the home front challenges the stereotypical definition of the 'battlefield', which according to Angela K. Smith, is "the ultimate location for 'being a man'" – for displaying masculinity.[63] *The Night Watch* shows that the spatiality and definition of 'battlefield' as a signifier for masculinity is more complex than Smith perceives. With the exception of Walter Baxter's *Look Down in Mercy*, none of the novels actually depict the traditional battlefield of the Second World War as locus to negotiate masculinity. Life at the home front is much more determining, and *The Night Watch*, in particular, shows that the battlefield of London is comparable to Burma, Dunkirk and elsewhere in brutality, danger and bleakness, only made bearable by the courage of those who protect their city. Kay's efforts demonstrate that "the contribution of the Home Front was as significant as that of the military"[64], and Kay's commitment allows her to claim part of the masculinity Smith so narrowly ascribes to the battlefield

---

63 Angela K. Smith, "Introduction" in Angela K. Smith (ed.), *Gender and Warfare in the Twentieth Century: Textual Representations* (Manchester: Manchester University Press, 2004), p. 2.

64 Corinna M. Peniston-Bird, "The People's War in Personal Testimony and Bronze: Sorority and the Memorial to the Women of World War II" in Lucy Noakes and Juliette Pattinson (eds.), *British Cultural Memory and the Second World War* (London: Bloomsbury, 2014), p. 67.

for herself. I wish to examine how *The Night Watch* pointedly dramatises this role of the 'fighting woman' at home, and thus reverses Gill Plain's argument that women working at the home front remained decidedly feminine, as they only obtained "the *semblance* of masculinity"[65]. Instead, Waters' Kay performs a much more 'phallic version' of masculinity than Plain's "semblance" suggests. Kay therefore challenges both the streets of London and the battlefield as heteronormative spaces. However, she can cope with the horrors she sees during her shifts in the comfort of her own home, whereas soldiers at the front are deprived of such privacy. I will argue that the comforts Kay claims for herself at home enable her to buttress her masculine performance in the public, whereas the lack of homes influences military operations in negative ways because soldiers become careless in their pursuit of homeliness. Kent's growing insecurity and the soldiers' recklessness during missions in *Look down in Mercy* further questions the traditionally masculine connotation of the battlefield.

The theorisation of masculine heroism discussed previously, argues that men need to perform heroic acts in order to strengthen and underline the adequacy of their masculine gender performance. It was shown that this enactment is littered with moments of fear, force and failure when subjects are compelled to risk their lives for their country. Kay, in contrast, is represented as much more courageous than Kent when she feels "awake, alert, alive in all her limbs" (192), despite the fact that she will be sent off on another night's ambulance run. Instead of feeling the threat of war, it fills her with life and purpose. These dynamics are represented in a card game with her colleague Hughes. In clothes, age, posture and complexion Hughes is described as resembling the image of the Reaper – the metaphoric embodiment of death. Kay consciously observes that it feels "like gaming with Death" (189) – a sensation that is increased by Hughes' gesturing: he "pointed a finger, then turned and crooked it. '*Tonight*,' he whispered in horror-film tones." (189-190) Despite feeling spooked, Kay wards off his threat by throwing a coin at him – a reference to the Charon in Greek mythology – indicating Kay's reluctance to consider her own death and her symbolic refusal to pay for passage to the world of the dead. Later, Hughes performs the same act in front of the mirror. "[L]ooking quite unnerved", he admits uneasily that he "had a whiff of [his] own grave" (190). Juxtaposing the reaction of Kay and Hughes it can be argued that in wartime Kay faces danger without fear because the proximity of death heightens her alertness and initiative. Paradoxically, the possibility of her own death fills Kay with life, which is substantiated when she volunteers to do a "mortuary run" (211) in order to protect a seventeen-year-old girl from

65 Gill Plain, *Women's Fiction of the Second World War: Gender, Power and Resistance* (Edinburgh: Edinburgh University Press, 1996), p. 28, [emphasis original].

witnessing such a horrible sight. Kay's altruism has a troubling effect: at once highlighting her as a noble character who takes care of others, whilst substantiating her masculinist subject position when she assumes her young female colleague to be unprepared for the job.

Together with another colleague named Cole, Kay arrives at the scene where a bomb had detonated in a backyard.

> A man led Kay and Cole around it, to show them what had been recovered: a woman's body, clothed and slippered but minus its head; and the naked, sexless torso of an oldish child, still tied round with its dressing-gown cord. These lay under a blanket. Wrapped in an oilcloth sheet beside them were various body-parts: little legs; a jaw; and a chubby jointed limb that might have been a knee or an elbow. [...]
> Kay nodded. She turned, and went back to the van. It was better to be moving, doing something, after sights like that. [...] The worst thing to handle was the jaw, with its little milk-teeth. Cole picked it up, then almost threw it into the box – overcome, in the end, not with sadness, but simply with the horror of the thing.
> 'All right?' asked Kay, touching her shoulder.
> 'Yes. I'm all right.'
> 'Walk about over there. I'll see to this.'
> 'I said I'm all right, didn't I?' (212-213)

The war neither spares women from witnessing death, nor children from dying, and the bluntness with which the scene is narrated signals that despite the horrible sight, Kay and Cole have almost grown used to carrying not only the dead but also the dispersed. Being an ambulance driver at the home front during the Second World War was obviously challenging, and Kay and Cole need to be tough in order to deal with what they witness. The rapid transition from describing how Kay and Cole move towards the blanket, to detailing what they find on it, plunges the reader into a state of horror as if themselves witnessing what the characters see. Although prepared that the woman is dead, the sober display of her body lying there "minus its head" is deeply unsettling and captures the atrocity of war.

The depiction of how Cole has to take care of the child's jaw is especially moving and indicates the character's struggle to handle the situation. In contrast to Cole's "horror of the thing", Kay remains calm and busies herself in order to cope with the task of transporting the body parts to the place where they are stored. When she tells Cole to leave the rest to her, she unconsciously puts herself above her colleague who feels patronised and reacts accordingly: "I said I'm all right, didn't I?" Kay's offer is perceived as a challenge to Cole's abilities and greeted with hostility – a reaction to Kay's 'gentlemanly behaviour'. Kay's instinct to save the young colleague from encountering such atrocities in addition to her patronising behaviour towards Cole evidence that her performance is more heroic and masculine than Kent's in *Look Down in Mercy*, who already begins shaking at the sight of burnt men without having to deal with their transportation. Consequently, Kay's behaviour as a fighting woman at the front is more convincing according to traditional masculine standards than Kent's commanding skills on the battlefield. This difference challenges any assumption regarding the automatic attribution of masculinity to soldiers, whilst women obtain nothing more than what Plain calls a "*semblance* of masculinity".[66] In fact, Kay's (female) masculinity makes her "*more* of a gentleman than any real man" (425) [my emphasis], according to Helen and Julia.

Moreover, Kay's subconscious trauma caused by the sight of dispersed body parts is only displayed when she is in the privacy of her apartment, which adds to the narrative of tough masculinity that hides its qualms from the outside world:

> She was fine, for a moment or two. But then the whisky began to shiver in the glass as she raised it to her mouth, and the cigarette to shed ash over her knuckles. She'd started to shake. Sometimes it happened. Soon she was shaking so hard she could barely keep her cigarette in her mouth or sip from her drink. It was like the passing through her of a ghost express-train; there was nothing to be done, she knew, but let the train rattle on. Through all its boxes and cars ... (216)

O'Callaghan argues that this and other scenes highlights the "the emotional vulnerability of the butch lesbian"[67], despite the fact that Kay drinks "whisky" – a stereotypically male drink that confirms her glorification of masculine conduct. However, it is significant that this scene happens inside her flat, whilst Helen is fast asleep: Kay is not being watched and only the reader glimpses this emotional reaction towards the "ghost[s]" that haunt Kay after her shift. She meticulously follows the scripts of masculinity that allow for emotions only in the private in order to retain an outside performance of sturdiness. Kay's behaviour illustrates Genevieve Lloyd's polemic argument that

> Woman's task is to preserve the sphere of the intermingling of mind and body, to which the Man of Reason will repair for solace, warmth and relaxation. If he is to exercise the

66 Plain, (1996), p. 28, [emphasis original].

67 O'Callaghan, (2016), p. 207.

most exalted form of Reason, he must leave soft emotions and sensuousness behind; woman will keep them intact for him. [68]

Lloyd's "sphere of the intermingling of mind and body" denotes the home where women stereotypically take care of the "Man of Reason", who "must leave soft emotions and sensuousness behind". Kay's behaviour after her shift partakes of these characteristics when she displays outward toughness. However, as soon as she leaves the public and stops "exercise[ing] the most exalted form of Reason" (in this case driving an ambulance), she returns to the home for "warmth and relaxation". In Lloyd's thesis, men are dependent on women to mirror the homely and emotional sphere: "women will keep [soft emotions and sensuousness] intact for him". Kay shows an interesting variation of this paradigm when she, independent of her partner Helen, allows the comforting atmosphere of the home to gradually relax her because she combines the distinct spheres of masculinity and femininity in her body and gender performance.

In the all-male environment of the military, men like Kent in *Look Down in Mercy* cannot find similar comforts because their male bodies exclude them from savouring "soft emotions and sensuousness" without women to "keep them intact for them". The characters' growing sense of homelessness challenges Young's argument that "he has a home at the expense of her homelessness, as she serves as the ground on which he builds"[69]. While it might be coherent to argue that women nurture men at home whilst themselves becoming disengaged with their workplace, Baxter's novel consistently shows that efforts of providing homeliness are failing for men, too. Brown disputes Young's claim for similar reason when arguing that "*If* he is 'at home' anywhere, it is in the sphere of civil society insofar as his nature is expressed there and he performs all of his significant activities there."[70] Striking is her implied questioning *if* men *ever* feel at home, which further challenges male homeliness "at the expense of her homelessness". In accordance with earlier evaluations of Kent's failing masculinity, the officer's homelessness calls to attention the social pressure on men to perform gender stereotypes of toughness and indifference to homely comfort, which not only disengages them from their emotions, but also keeps them from embracing the home. Interestingly, the only male character to find a home is Thomas in Adam Fitzroy's *Make Do and Mend*, since he is staying "at home" (144) not as a

68 Genevieve Lloyd, The Man of Reason: "Male" and "Female" in Western Philosophy (London: Routledge, 1984), p. 51.

69 Iris Marion Young, *On Female Body Experience: "Throwing Like A Girl" and Other Essays* (Oxford: Oxford University Press, 2005), p. 128.

70 Brown, (1995), p. 149, [my emphasis].

consciousness objector, but because his occupation as a lawyer is considered too valuable for him to do war work. By establishing a home with a family, Thomas is ironically cast out of the dominant paradigm of male homelessness during war, which reinforces his position as a stranger within the nation as has been elaborated on in the previous chapter. Other characters like Kent who are far from home, begin to long for the comfortable space that scripts of masculine conduct deny them to embrace.

In order to "put aside the slowly accumulating burden of [Kent's] responsibilities" (53), Anson brings him tea and other small pleasantries. Unlike Kay, whose occupation as an ambulance driver takes her into the public space of London's street, Anson's domestic tasks are those traditionally connected to the home. Massey argues that the "place called home is frequently personified by, and partakes of the same characteristics as those assigned to Woman/Mother/lover"[71]. *Look Down in Mercy* destabilises this categorical assumption of encountering female bodies at home when Kent is teased by a fellow officer about wanting to leave the club early: "I suppose your girl friend's [sic] sitting at home doing a bit of sewing and waiting for you, eh?" (213). This statement deploys every stereotype of women and home in order to underscore the masculine atmosphere of the military by evoking the image of the passive woman staying at home doing domestic work, whilst awaiting her active and public man to return. Yet, Kent's blushing upon these words deconstructs the scene's implied meaning: he and the reader know that it is not a woman awaiting him at home, but Anson who had asked to stay at Kent's bungalow because "[s]ome of the new shirts want pips sewing on, and those new socks could do with another wash through" (212). By using the exact same word and grammar – "sewing" – the officer's imagined woman is connected to Kent's batman, which challenges the stereotype of female domesticity. However, since Anson violates traditional masculinity by being homosexual and performing feminine tasks, he does not alter the female home but opens its definition to include male bodies that become emasculated through domestication. The alignment of the home as feminine emphasises how "traditionally [it has] been subject to the patriarchal authority of the husband and father"[72]. Kent's social and military superiority over Anson substantiates this claim albeit indicating that "patriarchal authority" is not only practised over biologically female bodies, but over everyone who fulfils the female gender role, for example by sewing. Consequently, while the narrative decon-

71 Massey, (1994), p. 10.

72 Nancy Duncan, "Renegotiating Gender and Sexuality in Public and Private Spaces" in Nancy Duncan (ed.), *BodySpace: Destabilizing geographies of gender and sexuality* (London and New York: Routledge, 1996), p. 131.

structs the home as inhabiting solely female bodies through representing a male body awaiting Kent, it does not deny that homeliness is connected to domesticity, femininity and patriarchy.

Despite Anson's efforts to ease Kent's discomforts at the front, he never achieves for Kent to feel homely, because both characters suffer from "the void caused by the barren years of being a private soldier, of having no home" (4). The term "void" merges experiences of physical homelessness with a disturbed feeling of belonging. The primary meaning of "void" is "emptiness, vacancy, vacuity, vacuum" denominating spaces that are cleared off objects or inhabitants. Living in provisional barracks, the soldiers' lives are void of both personality and luxurious objects.[73] This physical emptiness of the military camp enters and reflects the soldiers' psyche and transforms the "void" into a psychological meaning: an "unsatisfied feeling or desire"[74]. The soldiers experience a growing sense of dissatisfaction when suffering homelessness, which manifests in "an impalpable atmosphere of chaos" (4) despite constant cleaning and tidying. In the course of the novel, this chaos increasingly impairs military action, and Kent reflects that "[b]y now everything was in utter confusion, no one seemed to know whether there was still any organised resistance to the Japanese nor how far away they were" (233). The chaos of the barracks has penetrated the body of the military noticeable in a lack of information and order.[75] A conversation between Kent and the Sergeant Major illustrates Kent's exhaustion caused by the constant movement: "I'm so anxious to get settled in a position we intend holding on to for a bit […] that I'm frightened to ask too many questions in case I give myself away." (140) Not only is the repeating theme of Kent's professional insufficiency obvious in this scene, his homelessness has additionally aggravated a feeling of anxiety. He is scared to display his desire "to get settled in a position we intend holding on to for a bit", because such a confession would substantiate his inability to endure discomfort. Additionally, his hesitance seems to be a sign of embarrassment to seek homely belonging, because the home is traditionally connected to female bodies whereas to be a man means "*not* to be 'feminine', *not* to be 'gay', *not* to be tainted with any marks of 'inferiority' – ethnic or oth-

73 "Void, adj. and n.1." *OED Online*. Oxford University Press, June 2016. Web. 8 June 2016.

74 "Void, adj. and n.1." *OED Online*. Oxford University Press, June 2016. Web. 8 June 2016.

75 In *The Charioteer* Laurie similarly comments on the disorganisation of the hospital: "the whole place was in a chronic muddle" (36). Mary Renault, *The Charioteer*, [1953], (New York: Vintage Books, 2003),

erwise"[76]. Man must display indifference to the home, which explains why Kent cannot admit to his need for homely comfort.

Moreover, the home is not only unreachable but also treacherous in *Look Down in Mercy*, when a group of British soldiers stops at a bungalow to bury a dead comrade and to make tea for the rest of their battalion following on foot in flight of the Japanese:

> The driver had managed to unscrew the padlock on the front door and wandered about the gloomy rooms lit by chinks of mote-flecked sun that slipped through the shutters. The place was bare except for a few rickety pieces of furniture, but he found a tattered copy of *Blackwood's* dated July 1926; he dragged an arm-chair to the veranda and sat drinking his tea and reading odd paragraphs that caught his eye, his lips forming the words. (73)

The padlock assures the driver that the house is empty even though there is no solid proof for this assumption. Without concern, he moves into the "gloomy rooms". Whilst the driver's behaviour is highly unusual for a military personal trained to fully secure a building before entering it, and staying alert throughout the mission, it is characteristic of a private person, who has not felt the comfort of home for several years. The image of a solid house, contrasting the provisional barracks which the soldiers are used to, has swept away any concerns regarding the enemy and leads the driver to be careless and unalert. When entering the bungalow regardless of his impaired vision, the concept of house and home is revealed as connoting a sense of safety. The driver's surprising ease is evident in his movements: he is "wander[ing]" inside this unoccupied house, unconcerned and leisurely, without considering the possibility of danger. Through his movement he claims the deserted house for himself and compensates for his debilitating homelessness. This possessive attitude is additionally demonstrated in his approach towards the furniture. Instead of cautiously leaving it where he found it, the driver arranges the arm-chair, takes up the July 1926 issue of the *Blackwood's Magazine* and makes himself comfortable to enjoy his tea. In doing this, he re-enacts a form of domesticity usually absent from military discourse. Even when he hears noises, he remains calm, only "casually look[ing] across to his lorry" (73) to then continue with his reading. His behaviour shows how great the need for feeling homely figures – greater than the instinct of staying attentive in case danger emerges. Unsurprisingly, the driver's sense of safety is punished when the Japanese appear and burn the whole group alive. In his pursuit of a home, the driver did not act rationally as it is required of him. It follows that de-

76 Lynne Segal, *Slow Motion: Changing Masculinities, Changing Men*, [1990], (London: Virago Book, 1997), p. xxxiv.

spite demonstrating a masculine appearance, the battlefield is occupied by humans whose need for comfort superimposes rational thinking. The novel insinuates that the home is simultaneously safe and dangerous because it provides an ideological space that is assumed safe to live in, whilst restraining critical though.

Harry similarly addresses the seductive safety of homes in *Make Do and Mend* when during a dance sirens sound alarm and the entire village hurries under cover. The jollity of the dance is interrupted to remind the reader of the always present threat of war.[77] Harry reflects that

> The church [where the people take cover] may well have stood for a thousand years before tonight, but it would be no proof against a direct hit; if that happened, there would be a thousand years of solid masonry and carved oak down around the ears of the shelterers in an instant. (97)

While the rest of the village feels relatively secure in the shelter, Harry is aware that their sense of safety is illusionary and the age of the building nothing but a false promise of protection. Harry's repeated use of the phrase "a thousand years" is striking because it indicates the old age of the church, but more importantly the ability of the war to destroy it with one "direct hit". In Harry's worst case scenario, the building which should save the people, will bury and kill them.

Equally ironic is Harry's recollection of a case in Cardiff where a whole family was killed because "a bomb fell through their house and exploded in the cellar where they were sheltering; only the horse, in the stable next door, had survived" (147). Harry's comparison between the stable and the supposedly safe shelter reinforces the impression that houses are conveying a kind of security that is nothing but a fabrication built on human fantasies. It is therefore not surprising that in all novels shelters are regarded with suspicion. Neither Helen and Julia in *The Night Watch*, nor Harry in *Make Do and Mend*, agree to be kept locked up, and choose movement over apparent safety. Laurie in *The Charioteer* even violates his aversion towards homosexual company like Sandy's when accepting his invitation to a party in order to avoid the communal shelter after his treatment in the city hospital. Kent is the wariest of the deceptive safety of build-

77 All novels use the sound of sirens to cut through any narration of tranquillity and happiness, which disrupts a progressive narration and is a constant reminder of the threatening events in continental Europe in the 1940s. The deployment of a sound as a signal for imminent danger disrupts language and alludes to the uncontrollability of wartime and its threat to humanity.

ings. When he and Anson pass through a village on their flight out of Burma, he expects the houses to "burst into flames and betray him" (174). Despite his physical discomforts in the wilderness, Kent avoids the threatening cities "full of sickness" (250). To him, city life is the epitome of abjection, pervaded with "cases of cholera" (226), Indians hastily leaving their homes at the falling of "a few bombs" (100) and anti-aircraft fire never to return. Consequently, Kent avoids anything that represents domesticity and prefers battling nature – a forceful but less manipulative power in his view.

CHALLENGING THE PARENTAL HOME

Kent perceives the home as a construction that limits its inhabitants through monitoring desire and perpetuating heteronormativity: he saw "charred furniture [standing] in front of the heaps of ash that represented homes" (217) in a village deeply effect by the war. By distinguishing the "heaps of ash" as "represent[ing] homes", Kent not only observes that the physical houses are gone and have been reduced to piles of ash, but, more importantly, that whatever constitutes a home is only a representation of what *should* be a home.[78] Implicitly, Kent questions if there is anything such as a home detached from what has socio-historically forged understandings of homeliness. This section will demonstrate that the far-reaching connotations of home are mostly marked by paradoxes: simultaneously protecting a 'norm' whilst keeping 'difference' from infiltrating the public. Nancy Duncan argues that "[t]he public/private dichotomy (both the political and spatial dimensions) is frequently employed to construct, control, discipline, confine, exclude and suppress gender and sexual difference preserving traditional patriarchal and heterosexist power structures."[79] The private home does all of these things, but Duncan conflates two lines of argument: the home "construct[s], control[s] [and] discipline[s]" heterosexuality and gender conformity to guarantee heteronormative standards in the public, but it also "confine[s], exclude[s] and suppress[es]" deviating desires in order to eliminate them from society. This shows the twofold function of home as *monitoring* or *controlling* heterosexual desires and *confining* homosexual preferences. In this way, the concept of home illustrates Brown's argument that when the hegemonic order fails

78 Kent's emphasis does not lie on the physical building but on the psychological implication of it since he uses the word "home" instead of "house".

79 Duncan, (1996), p. 128.

to successfully abject something (such as homosexual desire), it then assimilates and submerges it under the dominant order.[80]

At the same time as controlling and confining various forms of desires, the home has a powerful impact on the self because the 'norms' learned at home become internalised and create an understanding of 'proper' conduct. Judith Butler observes a similar phenomenon with view to gender:

> Although being a certain gender does not imply that one will desire a certain way, there is nevertheless a desire that is constitutive of gender itself and, as a result, no quick or easy way to separate the life of gender from the life of desire. [...] To speak in this way may seem strange, but it becomes less so when we realize that the social norms that constitute our existence carry desires that do not originate with our individual personhood.[81]

Butler convincingly argues that desires do not originate from one's personhood but are influenced by social norms. Subjects adhere to heteronormativity and its strict regulations despite its potentially destructive effects. Since social norms develop within patriarchal and heteronormative settings, masculinity or femininity are artificial *constructs* one desires to achieve, which consequently makes one's *desire* concerning gender identity constituted and constructed by heterosexual norms as well. Because of the force with which heteronormativiy is assigned to sexed bodies, individuals usually do not question their desires, but instead believe them to purely and autonomously originate from themselves. Masculinity for men and femininity for women is therefore a powerful act of performance that the performer does not want to break. This reluctance to violate standards partly results from the threat of being abjected, but also because alternative performances necessitate an investigation of why gender norms are insufficient for one's personality, and how to improve this insufficiency. It is the combination of these two factors – knowledge of gender being performative followed by a willingness to risk abjection for a potentially 'incorrect' gender performance – that is needed for accidental slippages in order to transform discourses. Gender performances outside heterosexual norms are 'abjected' because their presence threatens heteronormativity and therefore patriarchy. Julia Kristeva's example of death in *Powers of Horror* helps to understand the paradoxical position of the abject: "as in true theatre, without makeup or masks, refuse and corpses show me what I permanently thrust aside in order to live"[82]. Kristeva asserts here that acknowledging what is abjected can give normative life new value

80 Brown, (2006), p. 27.

81 Judith Butler, *Undoing Gender* (London and New York: Routledge, 2004), pp.1-2.

82 Kristeva, (1982), p. 3.

and room for change. However, since society sees regulating discourses of power relations seldom as a threat but mostly as a guide – not consciously noticeable but always existing – a disturbance of these discourses is not desirable, for they imply transformation and forced adjustment. Consequently, instead of acknowledging trauma and abjection, or even desires beyond the control of heteronormative discourse, we learn to largely deny the existence of difference.

The home works in very similar ways because the self becomes conditioned to follow a certain set of rules that stands in close proximity to the heteronormative home. Before a person perceives deviating desires that need to be confined in the private space, that very space regulates, controls and manipulates desires according to heteronormative parameters. The self is therefore conditioned in heteronormative terms because "the social norms that constitute our existence carry desires that do not originate with our individual personhood"[83]. A formulation in Mary Renault's *The Charioteer* calls to attention the meaning of self and its implication for the conceptualisation of 'home' and feeling 'homely', when the protagonist Laurie becomes conscious of his impulsive reaction towards his friend Andrew during an argument. Their dispute occurs on account of a fellow hospital patient named Charlot, who has a fatal relapse after witnessing explosions that recall his traumatic experiences at Dunkirk. Laurie suggests that Andrew should pretend to be a priest and fulfil Charlot's last wish to confess his sins. Their argument over whether or not it is morally acceptable to deceive a dying man ends with Laurie's pointed accusation that Andrew would not understand a war victim's sorrows anyway, because he is a conscientious objector and has not witnessed the horrors of combat. Immediately after saying "Charlot and I understand each other" (240), Laurie ruefully reflects: "What he had said came home to him only gradually, like the collapse of a wall which starts with a few loose bricks." (240) Laurie's remorse originates from his realisation that Andrew's Quaker beliefs are incompatible with Laurie's romantic feelings towards him. He also understands that, sub-consciously, his friend's pacifism unsettles Laurie more than he is prepared to admit. These paradigm shifting comprehensions regarding their relationship are illustrated in the image of a "home" and "a wall" eroded by a "few loose bricks". The phrase "[w]hat he had said came home to him" is particularly interesting, as it deploys the "home" as a metaphorical synonym for Laurie's self. According to the *Oxford English Dictionary* 'to come home to oneself' means to come "to one's senses", "to a state of self-

83 Butler, (2004), pp.1-2.

control" or "self-awareness"[84]. This definition denotes a direct focus on the interior self in control of a subject's behaviour and desire. Laurie's idiomatic expression additionally connects home and self to akin theoretical concepts and calls to attention their similar semantic function. In this section I will flesh out how 'the self' is metaphorically restrained by an 'inner home' that monitors desire and inhibits movement. Ahmed argues that the traditional home "becomes associated with stasis, boundaries, identity and fixity"[85]. "To be at home is the absence of desire, and the absence of an engagement with others through which desire engenders movement across boundaries."[86] What Ahmed calls the "absence of desire" is more clearly characterised as a lack of exploring and exploiting abjected desires theorised by Butler and Kristeva. My analysis will show that beyond denying desires, the home can be overly filled with a range of forbidden pleasures.

In Renault's *The Charioteer* and Fitzroy's *Make Do and Mend*, the characters Laurie and Harry are conditioned to accept certain social standards, fashioned by parental authority *at home*. In this way, the parental home becomes identified as a space of control rather than of comfort, which restrains the characters' excess to non-normative desires. However, Laurie's and Harry's increasing reluctance to follow such norms liberates "the closed 'bound' self"[87] to experience new kinds of passions that are subsequently suppressed and confined in the home. The connotation of home and feeling homely is therefore complex: the heteronormative home monitors desires to stay within known borders, whereas the homosexual home is overly filled with abjected desires that are relegated into the private in order to not disturb the heterosexual public. The home therefore functions as a counterpart to the street that needs to remain untarnished by nonconforming subject.

When Laurie receives a letter from his mother regarding her upcoming marriage to Mr. Straike, the allegory between home and self is recalled with a slight twist: "Now for the first time it started coming home to him: the Best Man, the reception, the archaic vestiges of sacrifice, of capture, and of sale." (257) Whereas Laurie's outburst towards Andrew for refusing to pretend being a priest

84 "home, adv.". OED Online. March 2016. Oxford University Press. http://www.OED.com/view/Entry/87872?redirectedFrom=come+home+to+oneself [last accessed: 02/06/2016].

85 Sara Ahmed, *Strange Encounters: Embodied Others in Post-Coloniality* (London and New York: Routledge, 2000), p. 87.

86 Ibid., p. 87.

87 Jenny Hartley, *Millions like Us: British Women's Fiction of the Second World War* (London: Virago, 1997), p. 60.

was resolved by Laurie's self reclaiming control over his emotions, his self is now invaded by negative feelings, which have been seething in his subconscious for some time. At this point, "self-control" becomes "self-awareness" – the letter disables Laurie's protective 'inner home' and begins to penetrate his psyche with emotions and desires beyond his control.

A comparison between Laurie's approach to the home and Philip's in *Make Do and Mend* illustrates the different resolution for stabilising a shaken self. Harry and the vicar, Philip, talk about Jim Brynawel, who withdraws from village life and keeps his past private. Philip concludes that "[i]t would be a shame to disturb Jim just when he's beginning to be comfortable within himself." (65) Philip's evasive formulation is incomprehensible for both Harry and the reader, especially because neither knows that the reason for Jim's "wounds" (65) is the suicide of a man who was madly in love with him, and whom Jim rejected. Assuming that Jim 'has come home to himself' – that his self has re-taken control over his emotions after a moment of uncertainty over his sexuality – he is now beginning to feel homely. However, homeliness is rightly criticised by Ahmed "as too familiar, safe and comfortable to allow for critical thought"[88]. "Beginning to be comfortable within himself" does then not denote critical reflection and self-evaluation but the very opposite: Jim's temporarily shaken self returns to stability and conformity by denying himself deviating desires and autonomous movement. This demonstrates that traditional homely comfort is not a sign for satisfaction but for conformity.

In contrast to Jim, who denies himself discerning self-evaluation and returns to a place of stasis, Laurie begins to question his failing sense of homeliness upon receiving the message that his mother is going to re-marry: "I've often had a feeling that there's nowhere I really belong." (291)[89] In consequence of Laurie's diminishing sense of homeliness, he begins to liberate himself from his relationship of dependence with his mother, which has been shakily built on the secret of Laurie's homosexuality and Mrs. Odell's wish to stay oblivious to it. Until this revelation of non-belonging, the reader had the impression that by keeping his bedroom in his mother's house throughout the war, Laurie is holding onto his

88 Ahmed, (2000), p. 87.

89 This passage may also be read with regard to Freud's evaluation of 'un-heimlich', which is reproduced by Vidler when he states: "For Freud, 'unhomeliness' was more than a simple sense of not belonging; it was the fundamental propensity of the familiar to turn on its owners, suddenly to become defamiliarized, derealized, as if in a dream." Anthony Vidler, *The Architectural Uncanny: Essays in the Modern Unhomely* (Cambridge and London: MIT Press, 1992), p. 7. Laurie's formerly familiar home turns into unhomeliness because his relationship with his mother falters.

childhood-feelings of comfort. However, it is not the material house that satisfies Laurie; he cannot even conceptualise what to do with it after his mother's marriage to Mr. Straike: "Mrs. Trevor had written again about the house, and –" (257). Laurie's sentence is interrupted by the emergence of a nurse and the reader never finds out what will happen to this "seventeenth-century cottage" (84), which is the only description ever given of the building. Laurie's past is a subconscious memory that cannot be re-materialised by making a home of the inherited house "even if war regulations had allowed him to keep it as a weekend place" (272). Consequently, homeliness is not related to the house in Laurie's understanding, but to his mother. He admits that "[w]omen still stood to him for background and stability, as they do to children, because they had never stood for anything more" (248). Laurie perceives women as nothing more than caretakers of homes and homes become embodied through female bodies because Laurie has never related to them in any other form or context. When his mother has re-married, Laurie's past sense of homeliness collapses and he realises that he has never really belonged anywhere. In consequence, he begins to liberate himself from his relationship of dependence with his mother.

Baxter's representation of Harry at the Hendra farm in *Make Do and Mend* is strikingly similar to Renault's dramatisation of Laurie's failing sense of homeliness in the matriarchal home. Harry at the same time loves and hates the Hendra house because it represents both the building he grew up in, and the conservative father he despises. Harry explains that "[l]ack of interest in the day-to-day operation of the estate had been one of the reasons he had opted for the Navy in the first place" (9). Even as a child, Harry used to seek ways of hiding, but "[u]ntil Harry had left to join the Navy, running away from Hendra had never involved running very far" (16). Instead of trying to understand his son's reluctance to stay at the farm, Harry's father Sir Charles "had always chosen to see [Harry's running away] as evasion on his responsibilities, but Harry had simply wanted some excitement in his life" (9). Harry's reflection demonstrates a distance to his father and a lingering disidentification with the daily routine on the farm. Even when returning to Hendra to recover from his lung injury caused by his submarine running aground, his feelings continue to be ambivalent despite establishing "his private quarters in his [father's old room]" (71) – an attempt of shaking off the authoritative memory of Sir Charles.[90] Home is here not connected to the

90 That Harry's brother Jack equally felt neglected by his father is evident in Jack's sarcastic statement that their father's perpetual shortage of money could have been prevented by "selling us [the children] and keeping the books" (17). Jack's critical evaluation of their childhood shows that Harry's and Jack's childhood home was lacking

mother monitoring her child's sexuality as in *The Charioteer*, but to the father rendering visible the home as a space of patriarchal control.

Harry begins to approach his childhood house, which he has inherited after his father's death, by describing it as "home-*like*" (7) [my emphasis], instantly revealing his damaged identification with it. The vicarage, in contrast, is represented as his *chosen* "second home" (16), indicating a more positive testimony. While Hendra symbolises conservative standards through the figure of the late father whose ideologies have been 'inherited' by his son Thomas, Harry perceives the vicarage, inhabited by a homosexual pastor, as a place for difference and liberation. Philip's "quiet room" (64), where Harry feels most satisfied, reveals that the concept of home is not fixed to one's family or ancestry. Nevertheless, Harry's need to qualify home in terms of "like" or "second" illustrates that he has nowhere to easily identify as home. In this way, the novel demonstrates Ahmed's approach to the home as a "lived experience" detached from "fantasies of belonging"[91], by which she denotes the phantasmic assumption that ancestry determines homeliness. Instead of perpetuating family structures through staying where one 'belongs by birth', Ahmed approaches the home in terms of satisfaction and dis-satisfaction: the question to ask is not only "*how one feels*" about that which is meant to be a home but "*how one might fail to feel*"[92]. Through failing to feel at home at Hendra, Harry rebels against subconscious standards of heteronormativity at the Hendra estate. Both *The Charioteer* and *Make Do and Mend* demonstrate the continuous and constructed interconnection between home and family, and how the choice to leave family bonds behind influences the characters' feeling of homeliness.

At the beginning of *Make Do and Mend*, Harry is about to enter his father's chambers for the first time since he has left his family several years before the outbreak of the war: "It was like the ceremonial opening of a tomb." (18) Calling the rooms a "tomb" has several implications: it foremost indicates that family members rarely entered Sir Charles' chambers. Harry therefore describes his entrance as "ceremonial", which enhances the scene's significance. Juxtaposing Harry's reference to the "tomb" with Laurie's reaction in *The Charioteer* upon entering Alec and Sandy's (friends of Ralph's) home, the term "tomb" obtains another quality. As Laurie is invited to join a homosexual party, he describes Alec and Sandy's house as a "mausoleum" (114). The party turns out to feature those homosexual individuals Laurie has come to disdain for their promiscuity,

warmth and love, and that this was not only felt by Harry but by at least one of his brothers, too.

91 Ahmed, (2000), p. 89.

92 Ibid., p. 89, [emphasis original].

flamboyancy and cattiness. Consequently, Laurie "could recall few doors which he had felt such reluctance to enter" (114). This uneasy feeling becomes substantiated when Laurie realises that homosexuals like himself cannot escape socialising, however reluctantly, with these "advanced psychopaths", since they are *all* "driven underground together" (199). The description of the hosts' house as a "mausoleum" symbolises society's many layers and the force with which homosexuals are made to share the abjected space at its bottom. Consequently, the tomb in *Make do and Mend* becomes more than the chambers of Sir Charles and a symbol of his death or the decay of the house, because it may also indicate a space of/for homosexuality.

This becomes more traction considering that *Make do and Mend* develops a latent feeling of secrecy regarding Sir Charles' sexuality when his best friend Philip talks about their friendship and his own sexual deviance. These suspicions regarding Sir Charles' sexuality are manifesting, when Philip straightforwardly claims in front of Harry and his brother Jack: "Oh, he'd realised [my sexual preferences] all right [...] How could he not?" (241) The narrator clarifies the significance of Philip's words:

> The tone of voice was such as to divert the attention of both brothers [Harry and Jack], for a moment, from their immediate concerns; there was a wealth of sadness concealed behind the ordinary words. Philip, however, seemed disinclined to elaborate [...]. (241)

The text leaves the possibility as to whether or not Sir Charles was homosexual distinctly open, but Philip implies that he and Sir Charles have shared some kind of secret. Philip's interrogation "How could he not", combined with the "wealth of sadness" resonating in his words, strongly suggests that they were on intimate terms and potentially shared more than confidentialities. Harry and Jack realise that Philip knows more than he is prepared to admit, but they do not pressure him to elaborate. Considering Philip's career as a vicar which demands a lifetime of celibacy, and his explanation that in his time "it was safest to deny one's urges altogether" (63), it seems plausible that Harry's father, too, felt less sure about his heterosexuality than he let people to believe. The metaphoric bridge between *Make Do and Mend's* "tomb" and the "mausoleum" in *The Charioteer* has thus been built: both narratives use the symbolism of death to demonstrate how homosexuals are abjected from society that does not accepts outlawed desires. The repeated emphasis on death metaphors highlights the medical discourse surrounding homosexuality where subjects were regarded as sexually deviat – an 'illnesses' that threatened heteronormative and reproductive society.

In order to not be persecuted, homosexuals had to keep their desires private and in the home, which shows the paradoxical function of the home: at once navigating desires into heteronormativity, and when this process fails, containing non-conforming pleasure in order to keep them away from the heteronormative public. Whereas Sir Charles had to conceal his homosexual desires in order to fashion an appearance of heteronormativity, Harry flees his childhood-home because of its representation of conservative ideologies. The novel, therefore, displays not only the conflicting functions of home – policing and containing desires – but also a generational distance between father and son. Ultimately, Harry is able to live a less suppressed life because he manages to liberate himself from the negative connotation of heteronormative homeliness, whereas his father remains trapped inside a restraining home fashioned after conservative social scripts regarding gender and sexuality.

Upon his return to the Hendra house after years of serving in the Navy, Harry begins to re-claim his childhood home by entering his father's chambers:

> Cautiously he opened the door to the bedroom as if half-expecting to find his father lurking behind it, an emaciated and malevolent prisoner. What he found instead was an old iron bedstead with its thick horsehair mattress still in place, a washstand complete with basin, ewer and slop bucket, a chest of drawers with a mirror on top and a few of his father's ebony-backed hairbrushes lined up neatly as if awaiting his return. There was also a tall and forbidden mahogany wardrobe smothered in elaborate carving. In the grate lay a cone of fallen soot the counterpart of the one in the adjoining room. (22)

Harry is uncertain what might be waiting behind the door: Harry's father? His ghost? Or possibly a third, as yet unknown, "prisoner"? The use of the term "prisoner" to characterise Harry's father, reinforces my reading of Sir Charles being imprisoned in a heteronormative home due to his potential homosexuality. The "old iron bedstead" "still in place" contributes to the uncanny scene and betrays the impression of the father "awaiting his [son's] return". Harry, as the new owner of the house, is reminded of his present mediocrity by his very own furniture, especially by the "forbidden mahogany wardrobe", which seems to recollect a time where Harry was a child and not allowed to look inside it. The word "forbidden" recalls a memory that infantilizes the adult Harry and demonstrates the father's authority over his children when he was still alive. It also suggests a semantic representation of 'being in the closet' to add to previous arguments regarding Sir Charles' disguised homosexuality.

Harry has to constantly remind himself that he "divorced himself from his family" (148) by serving in the Navy, and that consequently his father has long lost any power over his son. His choice of words – "divorced himself from his family" – substantiates Harry's self-understanding as a homosexual, whose "divorce" not only expresses a split with his family but also with the heteronormative lifestyle symbolised by the Hendra house. Reassuring himself of his independence, Harry wards off the threat of the ghostly "prisoner" that is the memory of his father. The fallen soot from the chimney convinces Harry that the room is absolutely empty and that it has not been in use for a long time. Subsequently, Harry begins repairs on the house in order to claim authority over his father's ghostly soul by moving into his chambers and using his furniture.

However, Harry's latent feeling of unhomeliness at Hendra carries through the whole narrative despite his increasing control over the estate. This becomes particularly obvious after a relapse of pleurisy during which Harry stays at Jim's remote farm hut, where their mutual affection becomes apparent for the first time. After his recovery, Harry reluctantly states that he must "return to Hendra, to his home and family" (134). Despite indicating slightly more identification with Hendra when no longer qualifying it as "home-like" but as "home and family", the resentment of going back to a place where his desires still need to be closeted is clear. The narrator clarifies that the imminent separation of Jim and Harry did not "fill either man with enthusiasm, and a shadow fell across them at the mentioning of it" (134).

Even when 'coming out' to his brother Jack, who accepts Harry's relationship with Jim, homosexual desire is still cast out of the Hendra house because Jim and Harry's love works as a storyline subordinated to Jack's heterosexual marriage and becomes relegated to the remote farm hut in order to not disturb the heterosexual public. Moreover, since the father's convictions live on in Harry's second brother Thomas, heteronormative standards continue to dominate within the family. Consequently, Harry's endeavour to engender a new home is only partially successful when he finds a lover but fails to completely claim Hendra as a non-normative home.

In *The Charioteer*, Laurie's parental bond is similarly difficult to sever. Despite realising and accepting his homosexuality early on as a teenager, Laurie continues to be conditioned within the bounds of his mother's home and finds relief only after having been intimate with Ralph. Laurie's realisation that he "[got] what he must long have been desiring" (291) evidences that before the sexual shattering of his heteronormatively conditioned self, 'abnormal' physical desires were prevented from penetrating his psyche in order to maintain an "orthodox" (58) lifestyle – meaning his staying away from homosexual conduct and conforming to gender norms of masculinity. His statement can be read as a confession that his mother's home has never fully satisfied Laurie, who failed to be open and comfortable as a result of his closetedness. Laurie's sudden realisation that something was missing from his life demonstrates that the conventional concept of home not only keeps the self from desiring outside of heterosexual norms, but also that it regulates experiences of social belonging. Through becoming conscious of his situation, Laurie begins to liberate himself from his dependence on his mother, and his sense of homely belonging grounded in the denial of his homosexual desires is shattered when he sleeps with Ralph.

Responding to his and Laurie's sexual encounter, Ralph announces: "You belong with me [, Laurie]. As long as we're both alive, this will always be your place before anyone else's." (291) Since Ralph believes that Laurie's non-belonging was a result of his dishonest bond with his mother, he concludes that a relationship with him, in which Laurie does not need to hide his sexuality, would fulfil his deepest desires. Momentarily, Laurie is tempted by this proposal and he admits that "[t]here had not been time to discover, till now, the sensation of coming home again which is one of the more stable by-products of physical love" (310). The recurring formulation of "coming home" as an emotional experience, restates the interconnection between home and self. Henri Lefebvre argues that "[t]he relationship between Home and Ego, meanwhile, borders on identity"[93]. Identity thus stands in a reciprocal connection with home and self, which is substantiated by Ahmed's understanding of feeling homely: "subject and space leak into each other, *inhabit each other*"[94]. However, whereas the phrase "to come home to him" illustrates the self's re-taking control in monitoring desires, the kind of identity envisioned in Ralph's "coming home" does not perpetuate fixity and monogamy, and thus defies heteronormative markers of home and self. Whilst Laurie's self and his inherited house have controlled his desires and prevented him from negotiating a homosexual identity, the "coming home" to a male body opens a new horizon of possibilities. Instead of narrowly envisioning home as a heteronormative identity, Laurie and Ralph broaden it to implicate belonging without stasis or gender conformity. Ralph even proposes an open relationship in which Laurie is free to see Andrew whenever he wants to, without implying that this endangers their shared feeling of belonging together. Ralph's negotiation of the meaning of "coming home" reveals that feeling homely can be detached from conventional understandings of identity whilst retaining its quality of evoking safety. He subverts Ahmed's understanding of home "associated with stasis, boundaries, identity and fixity" because "[t]o be at home is the absence of desire"[95], when insinuating that home is a space of *forbidden* desires.

93 Henri Lefebvre, *The Production of Space*, [1974], (Malden: Blackwell, 2003), p. 121.

94 Ahmed, (2000), p. 89, [emphasis original].

95 Ibid., p. 87.

Once more the contradictory discourse of home becomes clear: whereas Ahmed characterises the heteronormative home as a space without desire to "engender[...] movement across boundaries"[96], Ralph's metaphoric image of two male bodies 'coming home' argues for the concealment of unsavoury desires inside the home. In his perception, the home is no longer a space for heteronormativity and the family but designed to disguise homosexual desires.

Kay's home in *The Night Watch* is also meant to be a space for difference when she describes its rooms as "L-shaped" (314) to denote their resident as Lesbian. The apartment has quite literally grounded Kay throughout her chaotic life before the war when "[s]he'd had too much money; she'd drunk too much; she'd careered from one unhappy love-affair to another" (314). It was the only constant in her life for "seven years" (314) since it had been given to her by a prostitute "she'd once been lovers with" (314). Because it does not resemble family ties but various outlawed desires, Kay's home is initially introduced as a non-heteronormative place. It thus queers both time and space – time when surviving the war for seven years, and space by being non-reproductive, non-familial but filled with lesbian desire. Kay describes how much she likes living in the flat with its "funny little mews or yard that the flat overlooked" (314), repeatedly using the word 'like' for emphasis. However, Kay confines Helen to this home when she says that "[s]he felt about the flat rather as she felt about Helen: that it was secret, special, hers" (314). Kay's comment highlights her male role in their relationship, and by comparing her feelings for Helen to her sense of homeliness, Kay unconsciously reduces Helen to a thing that can be possessed. The explanation that both were "secret, special, hers" confines Helen further and removes her autonomy and the possibility for Helen to move because Kay claims possession over her.

Whereas Kay's attitude towards her flat demonstrates Ahmed's theorisation that "subject and space leak into each other", Helen, who feels uncomfortable in Kay's home, cannot identify with it in the same way her partner does.[97] Consequently, Helen does not 'like' the flat but uses the term 'silent' to describe her feelings: "The flat seemed very silent after [switching off the radio]: it was always especially silent in the evenings and at weekends […]. The silence and the stillness sometimes got on Helen's nerves." (343) Silence is here not an expression of peace of mind and inner quietness – feelings which might rather compare to Kay's sense of homely identity – but the very opposite: an uncertainty and unhomeliness signalling Helen's growing defamiliarisation with Kay. Moments later, this silence transforms into restlessness and a devastation over "wasting

96 Ahmed, (2000), p. 87.

97 Ibid., p. 89.

time" (344): "Now she became aware of the minutes as they passed: she felt them, suddenly, for what they were, as fragments of her life, her youth, that were rushing away like so many drops of water, never to return." (344) Despite wartime's uncertainty over the future, Helen realises that she is aging nonetheless. Kay's flat has turned into the figure of stasis and lack of movement for Helen just like the stereotypical heterosexual home. Because Kay represents the ideologies of heteronormative structures, and restricts Helen's initiative by patronising her, her home loses the unique lesbian qualities of anti-establishment and subsumes into the broad discourse of heteronormative homes.

The Charioteer develops a similar resolution between Laurie and Ralph when the former realises that the latter's proposition of an open relationship is not sincere but derives from Ralph's distance from the homosexual subculture: "scenes of jealousy were relegated in Ralph's mind to a special category, along with bracelets and eye-shadow" (319). Ralph is desperate to prove that he does not belong to the group of effeminate homosexuals, who wear "bracelets and eye-shadow" and throw jealous tantrums. In order to demonstrates his transcendence of such jealousy, Ralph "never discussed the future; he never mentioned Andrew; he never tried to make Laurie admit any change of heart" (319). The repeated pattern of saying "he never" is indicative of Laurie and Ralph's repetitive and monotonous relationship. It also signals undiscussed issues that prevent the characters from being truly honest with each other.

Only at home, where privacy and blackout conceal their homosexuality, can Laurie and Ralph be a couple, and their intimacy, which needs concealment in the open street, can reign. It seems hardly surprising that Laurie and Ralph's relationship becomes dreary rather quickly. Laurie comes to feel as restless in Ralph's home as Helen does in Kay's, and to him "[t]he next few evenings all merged [...] into a common memory and he thought of them almost as one" (318). Laurie's comment demonstrates his boredom with the couple's routine that alternates between bars and Ralph's home: "Sometimes Laurie would feel himself almost forgotten; but in the middle of it Ralph would look at his watch; the blackout would reseal itself behind them; in the dim street he would smile and say, Let's go home." (318) Ralph's differentiation between "the dim street" and the "home" relegates the focus towards a public space that stands in oppositional relationship to the home. It follows that the home does not rigorously deny desires as Ahmed argues[98], but purposefully permits them in order to keep deviance away from the public street.

The 'coming home of two male bodies' is thus accompanied by a new kind of encagement – privacy. Laurie's sense of belonging, initially recognised as a

98 Ahmed, (2000), p. 87.

liberation from the matriarchal home, has turned him into a still closeted and additionally abjected subject, who needs to conceal his desires from the public gaze. After a fight with Ralph, Laurie comes to the conclusion that "[a]s little as three weeks ago, his life had been full of strings: a home, three people he had been tied to. Now he was as free as air, he could go anywhere, it made no difference to anyone." (336) Laurie's construction of a homely bond with Ralph has failed and Laurie has become dissatisfied with the strings in his life once more. He remains incapable of forging a relationship with either Ralph or Andrew, and thus questions the possibility of finding love when his aspired form of love continues to be abjected from the public and confined within the private home.

THE PUBLIC HOME – THE PRIVATE STREET: INVERSION OF CONCEPTS

Laurie's and Helen's experiences illustrate that even non-heteronormative homes can come to be constraining because the realm of movement is restricted to a limited space. It follows that the queering of homely spaces through non-conforming bodies does not have the desired effect of shattering a constrained self. I wish to move from the re-negotiation of homely spaces to the deconstruction of physical buildings in order to examine the effect of wartime demolition on the characters, and to investigate whether the disintegration of public and private is a more fruitful attempt for queering space. Although wartime necessitates different scripts of conduct as seen in Kay's occupation as an ambulance driver, certain norms like the perpetuation of privacy seem to linger. The acceptance and protection of standards even when mirror images such as houses are destroyed, signifies the enduring power of heteronormative discourse. However, this section will also show that the street may offer more space for privacy than the home in wartime, and that this inversion of concepts demonstrates the arbitrariness of spatial connotations.

Whilst working as an ambulance driver, Kay frequently witnesses the disintegration of public and private spaces when countless houses collapse. At one point she thoughtfully reflects:

> What amazed her, too, was the smallness of the piles of dirt and rubble to which even large buildings could be reduced. This house had had three intact floors to it, an hour before; the heap of debris its front had become was no more than six or seven feet high. She supposed that houses, after all – like the lives that were lived in them – were mostly made of space. It was the spaces, in fact, which counted, rather than the bricks. (195)

The "piles of dirt and rubble" reflect the morbidity of the 1940s where normative concepts of house and home collapse. Kay's observation that "houses, after all – like the lives that were lived in them – were mostly made of space" is ironic given that she tries to confine Helen in a little apartment. Her understanding of lives as space instead of time (birth to death), challenges futurity, which refers not only to Kay's deviating sexuality that will never result in pregnancy, but also to peoples' reluctance to make plans for a future that they might not live to see. Since time (future) is no longer within the realm of the imaginable, as has been argued by Jones and Mitchell[99], spatiality has become the determining factor in peoples' lives – indicated in the narrative's preoccupation with ruins. Kay's amazement over the small size of collapsed houses illustrates that the materiality of buildings is much more secondary than the physical impression suggests, and that this condition is concealed as long as normative discourse (linearity of peacetime) prevails. Only when threatened by the war, do people realise and perceive houses with regard to their materiality and fragility.

Julia nuances this observation when she says that houses, that have been bombed but are not fully collapsed, appear to be "more miserable, somehow, than if a house has been blasted to bits: it's like a life with a cancer in it" (225). Julia, too, lays emphasis on lives that are determined by space. When a house is only partially broken, the life that comes to strive in it has neither passed away completely. It is this partial death of the self, gradually spreading like a cancer growing inside, which makes the image of a half-broken house worse to bear than one which is undeniably destroyed. Not only does Julia's statement exemplify the connection between self and home, she suggests that the destruction of houses has an effect on the self. Warfare and its disintegration of heteronormative spaces bear consequences for subjective and coherent life since the self is constantly threatened from the outside.

Throughout the war Julia helps her father to survey the extent of damage to London's housing. At one point, she is struggling to open a door and is mistaken for an intruder. On account of her apparently 'foreign looks', a woman calls the police believing Julia to be "a Nazi or a vagrant refugee", who is "trying to force her way into a house" (267-268). Afterwards, Julia muses that her appearance is too dark to make her look doubtlessly British, whereas Helen possesses "English flower looks" (268) that will always identify her as an "Ally" (268). The woman's suspicion when calling the police is grounded in Julia's appearance and shows that the distinction between friend and stranger, as was exemplified in the analysis of Fitzroy's Jim Brynawel, is decisive and determines how a subject is perceived during war. Moreover, the sacredness of property and private space,

99 Jones, (2014), p. 34, Mitchell, (2013), p. 98.

even when numerous houses are fully or partially destroyed through bombs, continues to prevail. The woman calling the police therefore fears that Julia might be conquering someone else's private space.

In contrast to Julia, who enjoys her peculiar role and proudly reflects that "Marylebone has no more secrets from me" (267), Helen's instinct of respecting other people's property remains strong, despite the raging of the war. Her reluctance is highlighted when she and Julia enter a critically damaged, yet not collapsed, house. In this scene the former home has lost its homeliness in the shadow of the war, but Helen remains aware of her status as an intruder – a feeling that is reinforced when encountering the uncanny display of furniture:

> The bedrooms still had their beds and wardrobes in them, and the wardrobes were damp, because of the broken windows the ancient clothes inside them eaten through by moths or growing mouldy. (276)

Unlike Baxter's driver in *Look Down in Mercy*, Helen feels uncomfortable in the presence of the furniture, the clothes and the moths, and she cannot shake off the uneasy feeling that the flat may still be inhabited despite its destruction. To Helen, the house has not ceased to resemble what is left of a home, which is reinforced by a broken mirror "hung on the wall with a weird, blank face: its glass had shattered and fallen, and filled the basin beneath it in a hundred silvery shards" (276). The mirror's bleak blackness no longer reflects people, but the overall condition of the damaged house, thus contributing to the destructive theme of war. While the soul of the home (the people) is destroyed, the mirror's unbroken frame uncannily reminds of the house's past as an inhabited and functional space. When Helen and Julia have finished their cigarettes, Helen's concerns become more obvious:

> She took the cigarette to the fireplace, to crush it out there; and she did the same with Julia's, when Julia had finished. But then she didn't want to leave the two stubs behind in the empty grate: she waved them about to cool them down, and put them back, with the fresh ones, in her packet. […] 'You don't think [the owners would] be a shade more troubled by the rainwater, the broken windows, the bomb in the bed?' [, said Julia.]
> 'Rain and bombs and windows are just things,' said Helen. 'They're impersonal, not like people …' (278)

Julia's reaction to Helen's peculiar behaviour shows a technique of coping with the war and its extraordinary circumstances that all characters share at various points: sarcasm. The dry humour in Julia's words contrasting Helen's seriousness curiously enforces both positions. Only by reminding the reader that the two women are in a house in which nothing is still functional, in which a bomb is in the bed, and rain has ruined everything, does Helen's approach to the smoked cigarettes seem completely alien. Yet, when explaining that "[r]ain and bombs and windows are just things", Helen's intentions appear noble and less exaggerated. In her concern for the people who used to live in the house and who, according to Julia, will not come back to collect their belongings, Helen feels awkward and does not want to leave a trace of herself or of Julia behind. Helen ranks the interference of humans with abandoned houses a greater threat than the house's possible collapse, just like the woman had done when calling the police about Julia. While Julia and her father's work is necessary in order to keep people from moving back into unsafe houses, Helen finds this interference and her own part in it tolerable only as long as she takes any evidence of her presence back outside with her, in order to protect an imaginary privacy.

Another scene in *The Night Watch* illustrates that whilst the war might take away privacy, personal matters still need to be discussed in private. Viv lives with other typists in the John Allen House where she and her colleagues develop ingenious ways of communicating in order to circumvent the lack of privacy that accompanies shared living. Victoria Stewart remarks that the John Allen House "becomes 'claustrophobic' rather than nurturing", which reveals the house as an "anti-home"[100]. The telephone even warns its users not to mistake it for a private communication device with a label saying "*Think before You Speak*" (378) [emphasis original].

When Viv calls Reggie to tell him about their unwanted pregnancy, she explicitly distinguishes the apartment from her childhood house where her family lives: "I'm in a cupboard, she whispered, at home. I mean, at John Allen House." (381) Nothing inside this house engenders homeliness and the relatively private place from where Viv calls is contrasted with the "horribly public" (378) alcove where the telephone was originally positioned before the "girls had unpicked the staples which attached the wire to the wall" (378) to be able to drag it in the "darkness" (378) of the cupboard. The dualism of public/private is emphasised by another binary, that of light/darkness. Although wartime regulations kept all rooms dark, the staircase is "lit very badly with one blue bulb" (376-377), which contrasts it to the complete darkness of the cupboard and adds to the impression that the house has lost its primary quality of keeping privacy.

Rachel Wood asserts that "[w]artime opened up new spaces and offered new opportunities for sexual encounter; the blackout in particular offered a sense of

100 Stewart, (2011), p. 131 and p. 144.

privacy in public spaces."[101] Not only sexuality was elevated in the blackout, secrets, too, found confidential acknowledgements. Consequently, when Viv decides to tell her friend about her pregnancy, she does so on a public bench and not at 'home'. Again, darkness conceals Viv's secret, which she directly contrasts to the "lights blazing" at "John Allen House at this time of night" (292). The novel thus shows that in wartime the physical demolition of buildings is not necessary for deconstructing the public/private divide. The need of sharing spaces functions in similar ways, as people seek other and often public places for communicating private matters.

Stewart similarly claims that the war "acts to disturb the separation between public and private"[102], which is aptly demonstrated in *The Charioteer*: "the streets were almost empty, till [Laurie and Ralph] came to one where a house lay half across the road with a rescue squad working, and they had to go another way" (204). The street Ralph and Laurie encounter is "almost empty", which rehearses the wartime paradigm of keeping people in shelters at night to protect them from air raids. Moreover, the image of the house laying "half across the road" symbolises the physical inseparability of public/private.[103] Conflating that which has been divided analytically reveals public/private as a constructed dichotomy. Reading the "rescue squad" through the lens of *The Night Watch* shows that this scene not only deconstructs conceptions of private domesticity but challenges the stereotypical role of women at home more sweepingly: since Waters constructs wartime work as predominantly performed by women, it stands to reason that Renault's rescue squad equally features females rather than males. In this way, women are taken out of the private space of the British hearth and home and transcended into the public sphere as active participants of war. The stereotypic construction of home as female is challenged when women participate in the war effort and when house and home turn into piles of ash. When the private becomes public and the public becomes private, a total inversion of ideological concepts takes place. The war thus destroys not only the heteronor-

101 Rachel Wood, "'Walking and Watching' in Queer London: Sarah Waters' *Tipping the Velvet* and *The Night Watch*" in *Journal of Lesbian Studies* Vol. 17, No. 3-4 (2013), p. 308.

102 Stewart, (2011), p. 10.

103 For an overview over the debate on unpaid housework and the intersections between Second Wave Feminism and Marxism see among others: Mary O'Brien, *The Politics of Reproduction*, [1983], (New York and London: Routledge, 1983). Adrienne Rich, *Blood, Bread, and Poetry: Selected Prose*, [1986], (New York: Norton and Company, 1994). Michèle Barrett, *Women's Oppression Today: The Marxist/feminist Encounter* (London: New Left Books, 1980).

mative home by challenging the durability of buildings, but also reveals female domesticity as shattered when men like Anson take care of officers and women like Kay become heroes.

In consequence of the increasing devastation of heteronormative discourse through the power of war, Helen, who previously kept the public/private divide faultless by taking the cigarettes out of the bombed-out house, eventually leaves Kay's home to confide in Julia, who is becoming Helen's secret lover in the following scene:

> Then, 'In here!' said Julia, tugging Helen's hand. She had seen, lit up by the second flash, a sort of baffle-wall that had been built across the entrance to an office or a bank. The space it made was deep, jute-scented, impossibly dark: she moved into it, as if passing through a curtain of ink, and drew Helen in after her.
>
> They stood without speaking, catching their breaths; their breath sounded louder, in that muffled space, than all the sounds of the chaos in the street. Only when they heard footsteps did they look out: they saw the warden they had spoken to, still running, but running back in the opposite direction. He went straight past and didn't see them. (374)

Helen and Julia's erotically filled space is distinguished from the street in which the "chaos" (374) of the raid is raging. Stewart concludes that Helen and Julia's first sexual encounter "occurs in these inauspicious circumstances [where] sexuality is thus constructed as a response to the danger that they are experiencing, with the blackout facilitating their intimate contact by providing a cloak of secrecy"[104]. Stewart's 'make love not war' analysis does not do much to liberate Helen and Julia from the stigma of sexual deviance when she states that it is the "blackout [which] facilitat[es] their intimate contact by providing a cloak of secrecy". Her reading remains within the realm of the public/private divide addressed by Gill Valentine in "(Re)Negotiating the 'Heterosexual Street'":

> Whilst the space of the centre – the street – is produced as heterosexual, the production of 'authentic' lesbian and gay space is relegated to the margins of the 'ghetto' and the back street bar and preferably, the closeted or private space of the 'home' [...].[105]

Following this argument, sexually deviating subjects are forever hidden from the public. Stewart allows for variation of this concept only due to the mercy of

104 Stewart, (2011), p.157.

105 Gill Valentine, "(Re)Negotiating the 'Heterosexual Street': Lesbian Productions of Space" in Nancy Duncan (ed.), *BodySpace: Destabilizing geographies of gender and sexuality* (London and New York: Routledge, 1996), pp. 146-147.

darkness which conceals Helen and Julia and protects the heteronormative gaze from encountering difference. Although the "muffled space" (374) "impossibly dark" (374) in which Julia and Helen become "invisible" (375) substantiates Valentine's and Stewart's analysis that homosexual couples are cast out of the street and into its margins, Julia and Helen's shared sexual experience simultaneously shatters the concepts of home as containing homosexuality and of the public as denying it. Rachel Wood similarly argues that "[t]he destruction of the city lifts many of the restrictions upon who has access to space. Waters represents same-sex desire as a direct product of the disrupted landscape of wartime London."[106] Indeed, because the street is empty except for Helen and Julia as well as a disorientated warden, it enables the lesbian couple to inscribe it with deviating desires.

Helen and Julia's refusal to go into a shelter significantly changes the perception of the street: while usually occupied by heterosexual couples, it is now emptied of any scrutinising gazes policing their desires. The focus of the warden, as the only other person mentioned, does not lie on Helen and Julia's sexuality, but on his duty to take all remaining people down into the shelters: but "[h]e went straight past and didn't see them". Helen and Julia's hiding place is therefore not a disguise of their lesbianism, but reflects their rebellious unwillingness to relinquish their mobility by going into a shelter. As the only subjects left in the street, they reclaim it by their mere presence. Rightly Adele Jones argues that "the queering of public space undermines the dominant narrative of that space"[107]. Julia and Helen actively challenge the heterosexual street and deconstruct its implied normativity through their non-conforming sexuality.

They additionally disturb conceptions of home as a private space where sexuality is concealed, because they *chose* to be in the street instead of the home where the "intimate light" (354) had unsettled Helen. This "intimate light" which in other romantic encounters such as between Kent and Helen in *Look Down in Mercy* is meant to create a relaxed atmosphere, sheds too much light on Helen's feelings for Julia. She is more comfortable in the dark street where her body is in focus to distract from her deceiving of Kay. Instead of reading the "impossibly dark" space as a metaphor for the couple's sexual deviance, it can denote muting of the 'moral self'. Julia and Helen's choice to leave the home and to enter the street culminating in intercourse questions Valentine's pessimistic observation that public spaces can only be challenged subliminally and occasionally through disguised gazes between non-conforming subjects.[108] Unlike Laurie and Ralph

106 Wood, (2013), p. 314.

107 Jones, "Disrupting the Continuum", (2014), p. 36.

108 Valentine, (1996), pp. 146-147.

who leave the heterosexual implication of the street unchallenged when going home, Waters' characters deconstruct it with their sexually active lesbian bodies.

When Helen and Julia engage in lesbian love, Kay's home is destroyed in two ways: not only has her girlfriend betrayed her, "a side and part of the roof of Palmer's had fallen and flattened" (451) her apartment as well. The word "flattened" indicates the nothingness that is left of Kay's former home. Since the flat represents Kay's identity as a lesbian, the image of it being gone shatters Kay to the core: "The knowledge undid her." (451) When Helen and Julia emerge, Kay's worst fear that Helen is buried underneath the rubble is relieved. However, tragedy strikes even harder because Kay is slow to realise why Helen and Julia are together and unhurt. The last words of the part set in 1944 read: "Julia. Oh, Julia! Thank God! I thought I'd lost her" (454). The reader, of course, knows that Helen has long been lost, but Kay is as yet unaware of her own fate. The destroyed building underlines the finality of her broken relationship. In losing her home and her lover, Kay has lost part of herself making her a restless body that cannot settle after the war. Helen, in turn, finds liberation from Kay's home when the physical building is turned to dust.

"PLUCKED FROM TIME": KILLING THE CHILD AS A TOKEN OF FUTURITY

The frequent association of home and female bodies has been revealed as an unstable system designed to perpetuate patriarchy. The child is another indication for female restriction to the home as implied in Massey's assertion that the "place called home is frequently personified by, and partakes of the same characteristics as those assigned to Woman/*Mother*/lover"[109]. This definition reveals the child as a significant token of the heteronormative and reproductive home. In *The Night Watch*, Waters depicts a gruesome abortion of Viv's unwanted child with Reggie and illustrates that the killing of the foetus has a vengeful reversal on the mother, who defies her traditional role of mother. The abortion demonstrates Lee Edelman's critique on "reproductive futurism" – a concept which

109 Massey, (1994), p. 10, [my emphasis].

> impose[s] an ideological limit on political discourse as such, preserving in the process the absolute privilege of heteronormativity by rendering unthinkable [...] the possibility of a queer resistance to this organizing principle of communal relations[110].

Edelman criticises the dominance of the nuclear family and the perpetuation of heterosexual reproduction to ensure the family's superior position within society. In consequence of this, other forms of being, what he terms "queer resistance", come to be neglected if not abjected in the organisation of society. His concept of "reproductive futurism" denotes this social convention of looking ahead with a specifically heterosexual gaze that guarantees the future to be no different from its present and past. In this version of heterosexual endurance "the Child [becomes] the obligatory token of futurity"[111] and consequently of the home. By initiating the abortion, Viv releases herself from the burden of the family that often dominates women's life choices. The following analysis will investigate Viv's abortion as a form of resistance to imposed codes of conduct. Despite Viv's objectification during the process, the exposure of her body, the bloody aftermath in which she almost dies, she troubles heteronormative assumptions of progressivity and the dominance of the family by claiming a right over her reproductive body. This is substantiated when during the "procedure" (390) – one of several euphemisms to not speak the word 'abortion' – Viv feels like she has been "plucked from time" (393) which is not simply a description for her lost sense of time due to the narcotics but insinuates her abortion as a moment of defeating reproductive futurism – possibly, although the narrative leaves this open, leaving her reproductively challenged in the future as well.

Stewart comments that "[i]n line with present-day attitudes, authors such as Waters attempt to construct abortion as a choice, and to shear away its association with guilt, irresponsibility and promiscuity"[112]. While this assessment is doubtlessly desirable and ascribes great educational value to *The Night Watch*, I believe the narrative deploys a more complicated approach to abortion: although Viv is punished for killing her unborn child indicated by the great blood loss in its aftermath, her initiative in seeking the abortion strongly votes for a contemporary thinking in which women have the right to choose the fate over their own body. Yet again it is Viv's dependency on Reggie to find a doctor willing to perform the operation, which questions the autonomy of her decision. Her initiative is thus constantly challenged to illustrate a woman's complicated situation dur-

110 Lee Edelman, *No Future: Queer Theory and the Death Drive* (Durham and London: Duke University Press, 2004), p. 2.

111 Edelman, (2004), p. 12.

112 Stewart, (2011), p. 139.

ing an unwanted pregnancy in the 1940s. Notwithstanding these conflicts, Viv takes control when she rings the doorbell to Mr Imrie's house, who will conduct the abortion, whereas Reggie is left motionless out of fear of doctors.

Before entering the doctor's home, the surroundings are described as queerly unreal: "Everything looked depthless, the fronts of houses flat as scenery on stage, the trees like trees of papier mâché touched up with glitter and silver paint." (386) Illuminated by the full moon, the street with its houses and trees looks artificial. This resembles Viv and Reggie's insubstantial relationship in which Reggie fails to support Viv in any meaningful way and leaves her alone when she is not recovering from the operation. Covered in "glitter" and "silver paint" to soften the blow of truth, Viv does not see Reggie for who he really is – a narcissistic, misogynist and cold-hearted man interested in nothing but his own well-being. Even her knowledge that "he wished she had come with Betty, her sister – anyone but him" (386), does not 'unglitter' her perception of him. This highly symbolic prelude to the abortion locates Viv as a constrained woman at the mercy of two men – Reggie and the doctor, Mr Imrie – who try to fix her 'unruly female body'.

Inside his questionable practice, Mr Imrie (suspiciously never referred to as 'Dr. Imrie') treats Viv "in a mild and matter-of-fact kind of way" (391), resembling the attitude of medicals towards the female body as a hindrance. Young aptly explains how "[p]regnancy does not belong to the woman herself", since it always also involves the 'expertise' of doctors, midwives, husband and father.[113] The same is true for abortions, which are even more stringently controlled by everyone but the woman herself. The symbolic significance of Viv's abortion is enhanced by setting it in Mr Imrie's private home to substantiate a traditional dominance over female bodies executed within private spaces. This reading is strengthened when Viv has to take off her clothes and feels exposed to Mr Imrie's gaze with "her bottom half bare" (390). When beginning with "the, er, treatment" (388) – linguistically highlighting that everybody feels uncomfortable with the situation – Viv is experiencing it as a dream evoked by the narcotics in which she replaces Mr Imrie's terrifying "instruments" and "queer machines" (390) with "*The German Bull*": "a new and very terrifying kind of weapon" (392). In her dream, this bull spears Viv in her stomach leaving her with the horrible feeling of knowing where the "horn had run right through her…" (392). By doing so, the narrative creates an allegory in which the German Bull replaces the white man's hand that fixes the female body. When Viv awakens, she recalls her dream to Reggie and realises that "all the time I suppose it was Mr Imrie" (400),

113 Young, (2005), p. 46.

thus adding to the atmosphere of objectification.[114] Although claiming her right over whether or not to have a child, Viv is severely punished for her decision – first by being exposed to Mr Imrie and later when suffering from severe blood loss that almost kills her.

Viv recovers from the operation in a show-flat designed "to show you what your place would be like, if you bought one" (398-399). Everything in there is false – the putative brandy is coloured water, the telephone is not attached to a line and the cigarettes are merely made of pasteboard. The objects of domesticity are artificial and in the case of the telephone even life threatening when Viv desperately needs an ambulance, which is denied to her by the non-functional phone. Viv observes that "[i]t was like someone's idea of a film-star's bedroom; or as though prostitutes or playboys lived here" (398). Not only does this comment sustain the impression of falsity, the comparison to a film-star's flat is equally telling: during the conversation preceding the operation, Mr Imrie had constantly repeated Viv's made-up name, Mrs Margaret Harrison, which made her feel like the name "sounded so false and made-up, it might have been an actress's name, or the name of a character in a film" (387). By becoming Mrs Margaret Harrison, Viv is becoming the actress who might live in this soulless flat. Moreover, her impression of the flat possibly belonging to a prostitute or playboy reveals Viv's feelings regarding her relationship with Reggie who, as a married man, can never be more than an illicit affair to her. Viv seems to feel that by being Reggie's mistress, she is no better than a prostitute and deserves to suffer in this "anti-home"[115].

Like Viv's unborn child, the flat is a token of reproductive futurism to signal that after the war there will be 'normal times' again. Viv realises that "flats, like this, [are scattered] on every side" (401) of the street to ensure the endurance of heteronormative standards. Startled, Viv asks if really "Nobody lives here?", which implies the waste of space whilst the whole city is desperately trying to find replacement for destroyed homes. Viv's remark highlights the hypocrisy of Helen's job as a re-housing agent that is made impossible through the disorganisation of wartime and the redundancy of bureaucratic processes that devastate clients as well as Helen herself: "people we rehoused three years ago are coming back; they've been bombed out all over again." (229) Helen's job seems to be a constant effort of maintaining peace-time standards of homeliness doomed to fail due to the concrete erasure of homes in wartime. During a conversation with

114 For more information on the role of medicine in feminism see: Anne Fausto-Sterling, *Sexing the Body: Gender Politics and the Construction of Sexuality* (New York: Basic Books New York, 2000).

115 Stewart, (2011), p. 144.

Julia who pretends to have lost her house "and everything in it" (228), Helen sarcastically states:

> 'Everything?' Helen thought it over. 'That's about six separate departments, I'm afraid. I could only help you with a grant for light repairs. You'd have to see someone over at the War Damage Commission about rebuilding work; they're just as likely, however, to send you back to us. [...] What's that? You've lost the chit [we gave you]? Oh, dear. You must get another, and start all over again ... It's like snakes and ladders, you see. And this is always assuming, of course, that we've found time to see you in the first place. (228-229)

Helen's sarcastic outburst hides her deeply felt distress over her inability to offer actual help. The institutionalised disorganisation described by Helen broadens the discourse of military chaos and substantiates the impression that with regard to house and home, the Government remains unable to cope. Jenny Hartley argues that "[t]he open house is the emblem of the nation's adaptation to war: the values it exemplifies are those of hospitality, tolerance and community"[116]. In light of Helen's evaluation, Hartley's statement becomes unconvincing: although Helen tries to be hospitable, tolerant and communal and even used to give her own money away, the institution keeps her from being truly helpful. Helen reflects that "the war made you careless. [...] You ended up thinking only of yourself" (282), which emphasises the exact opposite of Hartley's claim. Instead of showing the nation's ability to cope with the damage caused by the war, Helen's sarcasm illustrates helplessness and despair.

Viv, on the other hand, realises that the Government is knowingly and willingly sacrificing its people in order to hold onto a concept of home from the past in an effort of protecting it for the future. Extravagantly outlandish, the flat in which Viv recovers from the abortion is a means of guaranteeing the return of heteronormativity. "[E]verything was chill to the touch and dusty; and here and there were piles of powder: paint and plaster, that must have been shaken down in raids. The rooms smelt damp, unlived-in." (398) Interestingly, this soulless flat has sustained the threat of air raids, which guarantees the reproduction of homely concepts when people are willing and able to contemplate renting flats like that again. However, when Viv stains the flat with her blood, its image of perfection is devastated: "the blood came faster than ever" (404). "Then she saw a little blood on the carpet" (405). Viv's blood is closely related to the abortion of her child and staining the "anti-home"[117], where everything is meant to be clean and in order ultimately challenges the untarnished reproductive space of

116 Hartley, (1997), p. 54.

117 Stewart, (2011), p. 144.

the home. Although Viv's female body is supposed to represent stereotypical codes of gender including maternal feelings, Viv defies reproductive futurism and infiltrates deviance into the show flat. No longer flawless and impeccable, the stains of blood render the symbolic meaning of the flat futile and Viv's body a site of resistance. Paradoxically, Viv's heterosexual body can more powerfully oppose regulations than Kay's queer body. This seemingly contradictory resolution of destabilising gender norms derives from Kay's complicity in the patriarchal structure and renders visible the complex mechanisms that influence (non-) heteronormative bodies.

Examining the dynamics between various spaces in connection to the body helps to more fully understand the determining mechanisms that perpetuate social conformity. The roles of 'man' and 'woman' seem to be of little importance compared to the overarching power of 'masculinity' and 'femininity'. It is therefore not simply a conservative and patriarchal power structure that relegates female bodies into the domestic private and male bodies into the political public, but a much more entrenched and interconnected ideology where gender norms become simultaneously projected onto the body and induced into the home to mutually influencing effect. By gender norms I do not mean sex-gender coherence but the qualities that are assigned to masculinity and femininity: as long as 'masculinity' is associated with 'public', 'active', 'rational', 'disembodied', however subliminally or reluctantly, 'femininity' becomes 'private', 'passive', 'emotional' and 'embodied'. This dichotomy seems to prevail irrespective of the performer's sex, which makes gender performativity a desirable but ultimately compromised form of resistance when subjects like Kay consciously perform masculinity in order to escape a passive femininity accompanied by the burden of private domesticity.

This chapter set out to broaden discussion on *The Night Watch* beyond current research regarding its narrative structure that defies progressivity. Not only the deconstruction of time is at the centre of Waters' novel, space is every bit as much represented and devastated in the fictionalisation of demolition and chaos. In addressing and evaluating various spaces from body to home, my analysis demonstrates that the gendered politics of space are grounded in a complex system of gender norms that are not only marked on the body, but also stringently projected into the home in order to protect a heteronormative public. Whilst some bodies like Kay's may escape this rigid monitoring during the war, the privileging of masculinity over femininity and the inscription of such ideologies onto spaces seems to endure. Only when the house as a symbolic echo chamber of the body is destroyed or tarnished by blood, can we perceive the extent of gender monitoring beyond corporal reference points.

“No Sense of a Tidy Ending”:

Resisting Closure

Narratives of same-sex desires at a time defined through heteronormativity, call into question the dominance of wartime scripts regarding gender segregation that follow Government propaganda. In challenging the authority of such stereotypical ideologies, Walter Baxter's *Look Down in Mercy* (1951), Mary Renault's *The Charioteer* (1953), Sarah Waters' *The Night Watch* (2006) and Adam Fitzroy' *Make Do and Mend* (2012)[1] disclose the fragility of patriarchal structures. *History's Queer Stories* mediates between homosexuality and war and brings these presumably contradictory parameters into conversation. It also seeks to challenge hegemonic knowledge of the Second World War and its literary representation, in order to devastate assumptions of a coherent history grounded in heterosexuality and gender conformity. Through deconstructing an allegedly heteronormative past, claims for a conservative future lose their footing and credibility. The novels discussed in this thesis provide a starting point for future research into a non-heteronormative past to diversify our present.

Les Brookes describes his “Coda” to *Gay Male Fiction Since Stonewall* “as a tailpiece rather than a conclusion” because conclusion “is a problematic word: it suggests closure, when what most investigations uncover is a lack of closure”[2]. He states further that there is “no sense of a tidy ending”[3] regarding research into gender and sexuality because such studies try to channel rather than withhold the

1 Walter Baxter, *Look Down in Mercy*, [1951], (Virginia: Valancourt Books, 2014), Mary Renault, *The Charioteer*, [1953], (New York: Vintage Books, 2003), Sarah Waters, *The Night Watch* (London: Virago, 2006) and Adam Fitzroy, *Make Do and Mend* (UK: Manifold Press, 2012).

2 Les Brookes, *Gay Male Fiction Since Stonewall: Ideology, Conflict, and Aesthetics* (New York and London: Routledge, 2009), p. 186.

3 Brookes, (2009), p. 186.

fluidity, vicissitude and potential of their subject matter. Defying closure substantiates the possibility of creating a "place of ongoing, indeed permanent, contestation and disruption"[4]. This study, in particular, cannot end in a conclusion because it set out to retrieve and navigate a range of queer fictions with a conscious awareness that there may be many more novels of and about the Second World War that challenge dominant narratives but remain largely disregarded in current research. It was my aim to broaden the existing literary canon on world war fiction, and not to subsequently restrain my own research by compiling a set of handy findings that satisfy the desire for completion.

Instead I wish to draw attention to Han Suyin's narrative negotiations of her experiences during the Second World War in her novel *Winter Love* (1962)[5]. In doing so, I not only add a female voice to the auto-biographical narrative *The Naked Civil Servant* (1968) by Quentin Crisp with which this study began, I also buttress the necessity of correcting a homogenous narrative of the war that was created by a dominant readership with a specific idea of how the war should be represented in literature. Through repeatedly engaging with *Winter Love* in this chapter, I call to attention thematic rehearsals or discrepancies compared to other texts, in order to assemble and recap important features in the portrayal of wartime homosexuality in the four novels that have been in focus. The intersecting discourses of war and homosexuality, homophobia and subculture, freedom and setbacks are enthralling, but forever complicate a homogenous reading of these novels. I therefore follow Brookes in giving a "tailpiece" rather than a conclusion as an impulse to encourage further studies into a war that troubles assumptions regarding heterosexuality, masculinity, nationalism and patriotism.

Similar to the novels discussed at length, Han Suyin's *Winter Love* devastates dominant wartime writings, because the narrative contradicts expectations of the soldier poet describing the war at the front. Suyin, born in 1917 as Rosalie Matilda Kuanghu Chou to a Chinese father and a Belgian mother, moved from China to London in 1942 where her husband was stationed as a soldier. She completed her education at the Hunter Street School of Medicine for Women in London, which provided "her first awareness of the possibilities of sexual love between women"[6], according to Alison Hennegan. "[A]spects of the institution itself [...] provide the setting for her 1962 novel *Winter Love*"[7]. Thus, drawing on personal experiences, Suyin creates a first-person narrator, Red, who recalls the

4 Brookes, (2009), p. 186.

5 Han Suyin, *Winter Love*, [1962], (London: Virago Press, 1994).

6 Alison Hennegan, "Introduction" in Han Suyin *Winter Love*, [1962], (London: Virago Press, 1994), p. Viii.

7 Ibid., p. Viii.

late war years when she first met Mara – a well-off woman who is bored with married life and starts studying at Red's college. The central storyline focuses on how these two women become first close friends and later lovers, and Red's struggle to accept that Mara continues to be married to her husband, Karl. War action or Blitz experiences figure as side-effects framing the more important plot on lesbian love. I am incorporating aspects of *Winter Love* in this last chapter in order to not only grasp a broader picture of homosexuality during the Second World War composed by an author with first-hand experience, but mainly because Suyin's text is a fascinating composition that reflects on many issues discussed in this study. The fate of Red after the war when she becomes a married woman also allows me to rehearse the extraordinary circumstances of wartime and the return to 'normality' in central Europe on May 8, 1945.

At the outset of this study I introduced Quentin Crisp's *The Naked Civil Servant* as a narrative that illustrates, like *Winter Love*, personal experiences rather than the grand narrative of destruction. Instead of trying to capture the atrocities that threatened London from the sky in earnest language following the tradition of realist wartime writings by soldiers representing battlefield experiences, Crisp's text is filled with humorous passages to distract from the dangers of his time.

> Perhaps it was because the First World War had left me so unmoved that I did not take the second one very seriously. When news reached me in 1940 that London was burning I was sitting in a cottage outside Basingstoke with a pregnant actress. I had nothing to lose but my aerograph and my typewriter but, explaining that I ought to spread my brooding pinions over these, I rushed home. The truth was that I couldn't bear to miss the great drama of my time. (152)

Typical of his style of writing, Crisp characterises the war as hardly worth mentioning. In fact, he gives more attention to negligibilities like the pregnant actress, the small cottage and the aerograph and typewriter that need covering, than to the fact that the Blitz is destroying England's capital. Moreover, whereas other people leave the city to save their lives, Crisp returns to watch "the great drama of [his] time". And a great drama it was indeed: "The Blitz transformed the relationship between home front and front line by forcing civilians to fight like soldiers and soldiers to watch and wait like civilians"[8]. The great scale of events made everyone a prime witness, but because Crisp had experienced so much hostility brought against him on account of his effeminate looks and deviating

8 Kristine A. Miller, *British Literature of the Blitz: Fighting the People's War* (London: Palgrave Macmillan, 2009), p. 5.

desire, he describes the war as merely one more threat to his life. This exaggerated indifference – which, of course, is another way of coping with the events – paints the war in a new light. Not focusing on the soldier's struggle to survive or the civilian who defends their city, Crisp's disinterest marginalises the war and its effects, thus challenging the dominant narrative of total devastation. He represents the war as "a 'preposterous' experience, by implication absurd and topsy-turvey [sic], rather than a fundamental threat to life"[9]. In this way his autobiography and Suyin's *Winter Love* are extraordinarily similar, for Suyin, too, emphasises Mara and Red's relationship in 1944 rather than the dominant images of wartime destruction. The two texts share an ability to concentrate on how life at the home front bore as many new possibilities as old setbacks.

Crisp gleefully states that "[n]ever in the history of sex was so much offered to so many by so few" (160), and Red reflects that whereas other winters were chiefly unpleasant, "about this winter, Mara's winter, I continue to feel its substance, the wrench of its happiness like a pain" (26). Combining markers of cheerfulness and misery, Red highlights the paradoxical time of war that simultaneously facilitated her brief romance with Mara but took it away from her when Mara's husband begins to question his wife's faithfulness. Red struggles to grasp her muddled emotions of "vampire memories of the past which suck meaning out of every hour of my existence; memory of love sharp and sweet and nothing like it ever to be" (27). A deep devastation rings in her poetic language, but her love for Mara is not only "sharp" but also "sweet". In this way, *Winter Love* aligns itself with the other novels discussed in this study in its earnest attempt of infiltrating diversity into the discourse of wartime that was assumed to be clearly organised to represent a homogenous picture following patriotism, nationalism and propaganda. It also shows that recollecting the Second World War is governed by incongruities: Red's past is simultaneously filled with nostalgia and painful memories, which challenges a categorical assessment of the time as well as of its literature.

Neither *The Naked Civil Servant* nor *Winter Love* fit the category of traditional war literature because they defy the readers' and critics' desire to be shown the "war as it really was, or rather, as they expected it to be"[10]. No-one expected the war to be about an unemployed and effeminate homosexual who struggled for money or about a lesbian couple and their endeavours to stay together despite all odds. Instead of such personal accounts infused with homosex-

9 Gill Plain, *Literature of the 1940s: War, Postwar and 'Peace'* (Edinburgh: Edinburgh University Press, 2013), p. 8.

10 Ann-Marie Einhaus, "Modernism, Truth, and the Canon of First World War Literature" in *Modernist Cultures* Vol. 6, No. 2 (2011), p. 299.

uality, wartime fiction was meant to represent the violence and "the dislocating impact of war on self and society"[11]. Despite, or rather because of this clear conception of what war literature ought to be, contrasting what literature of and about the time really engages with, critics like Gill Plain assumed that "there was a great deal of [literary] activity in the decade, but no lasting legacy"[12]. She and other scholars reiterate that "the events of the 1940s were simply too diffuse and too varied for a homogenous literary response to the war or to its shocking and complicated aftermath"[13]. It follows that until the 1990s, the Second World War was considered to be a largely non-literary period, because texts of and about the war were assumed to be non-existent.

Recent studies have done away with this immediate post-war claim that the Second World War was fought on too great a scale to find a literary voice. Kristine A. Miller found that rather than being a non-literary period, the Second World War was predominantly non-novelistic: diary entries, letters, articles, short stories and propaganda flourished, but longer works of drama and fiction as well as frontline narratives were produced less often. In order to remediate the traditional image of the soldier giving his life for the benefit of the nation, researchers set out to reclaim a female position fighting at the home front. Studies such as Karen Schneider's *Loving Arms* or Plain's *Women's Fiction of the Second World War* reveal the extraordinary circumstances for women during a contradictory time full of liberties and setback, where they were needed at the home front in often traditionally male occupations and contributed to the war effort in their battle against the air raids. However, "while women in 'men's jobs' were for the most part ultimately accepted as necessary, they were subject to derision and ridicule and were paid less than men for the same work"[14]. Schneider and Plain agree that "[t]he patriarchal system [...] stands firm despite the chaos of war"[15], because women were "asked to assume temporarily the *semblance* of masculinity – to act like men, but to remain constantly aware of their femininity"[16].

Crisp's *The Naked Civil Servant* mentions the forceful inscription of female gender conformity when describing an incident where a policeman challenges Crisp's blunt observation that women have taken to masculine clothing. The po-

11 Plain, (2013), p. 25.

12 Ibid., p. 2.

13 Ibid., p. 4.

14 Karen Schneider, *Loving Arms: British Women Writing the Second World War*, [1997], (Lexington, Kentucky: The University Press of Kenntucky, 2015), p. 22.

15 Plain, (1996), p. 26.

16 Ibid., p. 28.

liceman's reaction reveals that a woman who embraced a masculine appearance, was considered a disgrace. Suyin's *Winter Love* demonstrates this attitude towards women more forcefully. At one point Mara and Red are in a café when a bomb explodes nearby and destroys the building. Subsequently a number of people emerge and pressure the two women if they need help: "someone came up to me and asked if I wanted a shock injection, I said crossly: 'For God's sake, I'm all right I tell you.' (37) Moments later another "man coming up again to say: 'Sure you don't need a shock injection?" (38) He then turns to Mara to sooth the visibly upset woman whilst saying to Red:

> 'You'd better take her home, she's had quite a shock.'
> And Mara whispered: 'Let's go home, let's go home,' not a bit brave or anything.
> I felt conspicuous because of Mara not being brave and not offering to help, so I said, 'O.K., pull yourself together, we're going.
> But the A.R.P. man said sharply: 'Now, don't fuss her, miss. Your friend's upset, can't you see?' (38)

Whereas in *The Night Watch* the ambulance team is mostly female to substantiate women's role in protecting Britain's cities during the war, Suyin's Air Raid Precautions worker is male and obtains a superior role over Red in telling her how to treat Mara. Unlike Kay who gains autonomy during the war, Mara, in particular, is treated like a child who needs guidance because she can apparently not decide for herself what to do. Red shows her discontent and immediately gets criticised when the A.R.P. man openly disapproves of her manner. It is striking that Mara is "not a bit brave" in this scene considering that she is courageous enough to leave her husband to move in with Red. These contradictions, albeit puzzling at first, fit perfectly well with Plain's examination of femininity during war: whereas temporary trespasses in form of clothing and occupation where accepted, women had to continue following the scripts of femininity. For an upper-middle class woman such as Mara, helping after a bombing would defile not only her social status but also her femininity. In *The Night Watch* Kay similarly states: "This filthy war's knocked all the glamour out of life for women like [Helen]. It's all right for us, we can just kick about the muck and pretty well like it –" (254-255). Obviously, only a certain kind of woman was permitted to "kick about the muck and pretty well like it", and neither Helen nor Mara belong to that category. Yet both share a flat with their lesbian lovers without causing undesirable consequences to their feminine appearance. In fact, Mara is regularly perceived as a heterosexual and highly attractive woman because she looks neat and fashionable, "so utterly different from all the drab, untidy females the war had made of us, it took one's breath away" (58). Similar to Kay, Red distinguishes her own "drab" and "untidy" appearance from Mara's "wonderful coat" (57) "deep brown, soft, and a red pixie cap, and of course lipstick" (58). Among themselves the women differentiate between those who accept and even indulge the slackened norms of beauty (Kay and Red), and those who continue to perform a pre-war version of femininity despite experiencing a non-heteronormative love (Helen and Mara). Consequently, Mara compensates for her trespass towards lesbianism by showing exaggerated signs of the weak female who needs protection, and who is not brave at times of crisis. Red, in contrast, resembles Waters' depiction of the mannish lesbian Kay. The dynamics within lesbian relationships suggest a lingering gender binary where femininity is dominated by masculinity regardless of the non-heteronormative nature of the performance. Troublingly, homosexual narratives seem to struggle to abandon this conservative dynamic between genders, which illustrates how entrenched that kind of binary thinking remains to be in our society.

In order to broaden feminist research focusing on the contradictory role of women during the war, scholars increasingly investigated its memory, and the merit of historical fiction to retroactively and retrospectively reclaim the war. Ackerman's recent study on fictional and medial commemoration, investigates this lingering fascination with the Second World War.[17] He concludes that novels serve as a mediation between subject and collective, public and private, art and commerce, tradition and transformation, communicative and cultural memory, script and symbol, literature and modern (mass)media.[18] As a poetic cultural memory, texts can communicate and connect distant parameters across time. They may also inscribe a modern consciousness into the past that often conflates history with the present to create a hybrid version of events that simultaneously reflects on contemporary as well as past issues. Waters' *The Night Watch* (2006) and Fitzroy's *Make Do and Mend* (2012) fall into this genre of historical fiction that retrospectively narrates the war whilst adding a particular modern consciousness to the past. In depicting the rivalry between England and Wales, Fitzroy's *Make Do and Mend*, for instance, rehearses a long-standing conflict among the countries of Great Britain that continues to influence current

17 Zeno Ackermann, Gedächtnis-Fiktionen: Mediale Erinnerungsfiguren und literarischer Eigensinn in britischen Romanen zum Zweiten Weltkrieg (Heidelberg: Universitätsverlag Winter, 2015), p. 25.

18 Original: "Der Roman steht demnach in der Mitte und vermittelt: Zwischen Subjekt und Kollektiv, Eigensinn und Gemeinsinn, Kunst und Kommerz, Tradition und Transformation, kommunikativem und kulturellem Gedächtnis, Schrift und Bild, Literatur und modernen (Massen-)Medien." Ackermann, (2015), p. 383.

political and economic decisions. Whereas People's War propaganda during the Second World War promulgated unity between England, Wales, North Ireland and Scotland, narrative accounts like *Make Do and Mend* repeatedly show that social and localised differences continued to prevail. Fitzroy's novel emphasises that the ideology of the People's War becomes undone when the protagonist Harry Lyon and his partner Jim Brynawel resurrect the myth of a Welsh national legend. Rather than reifying a collective national unity to fight the enemy, the text challenges the authority of Government propaganda.

However, whilst some Welsh nationalists did find the People's War oppressive towards their country, the great majority of people did not, and on Victory Day "[t]hey flew the Welsh dragon alongside the Union Jack"[19]. This discrepancy between the novel and historical accounts, in addition to Fitzroy's use of frank language in describing sexual acts, identifies the novel as a retrospective fiction that seeks ways of amending a past by infiltrating it with contemporary political themes. Less obvious than *Make Do and Mend*, *The Night Watch*, too, speaks from a distinctly modern position where sexuality is liberated and women find their possibilities to be larger than during the 1940s. Drawing on these new opportunities, Waters' women live surprisingly independent lives during the war, able to have an abortion, engage in lesbian sex in the open street or perform the active life usually reserved for male bodies. Detecting markers of a contemporary consciousness is not meant to marginalise these novels: they are vital re-writings of the past, because they infiltrate a non-heteronormative subject matter into historical accounts that broadens our knowledge of the war. They also encourage a feeling of continuity and genealogy for homosexual subjects, who often feel unhinged from history because their desires have seldom been taken into account in historical research.

In order to mediate the function of novelistic representation of the past, Stewart's *The Second World War in Contemporary British Fiction: Secret History* points to the lingering gaps and blindfolds detectable in mainstream narratives recovering the war. She incorporates Waters' *The Night Watch* into her research to show that "certain narratives [...] may have been actively concealed by individuals for fear of familial or social disapproval, and alternative versions have, for ideological reasons, taken prominence"[20]. This assumption of a lingering heteronormative war culture formed the foundation of my research and was com-

19 Dr Martin Johnes, "Welsh Identity in Wartime" (2014) *BBC Online* [last accessed: 01/08/2017] <www.bbc.co.uk/wales/history/sites/themes/periods/ww2_welsh_identity.shtml>.

20 Victoria Stewart, *The Second World War in Contemporary British Fiction* (Edinburgh: Edinburgh University Press, 2011), p. 2.

plemented by an investigation into gay and lesbian literature and its navigation of homosexuality during the Second World War. I asked how homosexuality is represented in retrospective narratives that are interested in a different kind of war story in order to disclose at what point the dominant discourse of war disintegrates. These questions led to a whole new set of issues regarding the historiography of homosexual desire concerning both its literary as well as academic negotiation.

The gay liberation movement since 1969 prompted a temporary amnesia of its troubled past that lastingly influenced the perception of pre-Stonewall literature as "not good for the gays"[21]. Instead of investigating a period in history where large numbers of men and women shared confined spaces with their own sex, which, according to Allan Bérubé facilitated same-sex desires[22], gay and lesbian scholarship had little interest in retrieving a past they saw as oppressive and hampering claims of emancipation. Looking into the future, literature was not recognised as a mediator between homophobic society and individual experiences navigating desires. The first chapter of this study set out to re-negotiate this perception and to challenge recurring readings of pre-Stonewall writings as "homosexual problem novels"[23] in order to demonstrate that an often positive consciousness resides in earlier novels that can help to promote and complement current genealogical efforts within the gay and lesbian community.

Despite latest queer theoretical endeavours to establish a literary tradition of queer fiction, there seems to reside an "ethos of celebration"[24] that praises some texts as important narratives of same-sex desire whilst neglecting others. It follows that novels such as Renault's *The Charioteer* and Fitzroy's *Make Do and Mend* have either not received broad scholarly attention or became criticised for their inscription of homophobia and self-loathing. However, it needs to be remembered that these early novels about the Second World War featuring homosexual protagonists cannot be reduced to their sexual discourse, since the war constitutes the characters' framework of action. Through merging the issues of war and homosexuality in my analysis, I demonstrate that deviating desires are part of society, even when heteronormative discourses such as the military deny

21 Michael Bronski, *Pulp Friction: Uncovering the Golden Age of Gay Male Pulps* (New York: St. Martin's Griffin, 2013), p. 10.

22 Allan Bérubé, *My Desire for History: Essays in Gay, Community, and Labor History* (Chapel Hill: University of North Carolina Press, 2011), p. 112.

23 Claude J. Summer, *Gay Fictions: Wilde to Stonewall: Studies in a Male Homosexual Literary Tradition* (New York: Continuum, 1990), p. 26.

24 Lisa Lynne Moore, "Lesbian Migrations: Mary Renault's South Africa" in *GLQ: A Journal of Lesbian and Gay Studies* Vol. 10, No. 1 (2003), p. 23.

their existence. Instead of treating homosexuality and war as distinct matters, my analysis brings them into conversation in order to reveal at what points the characters' struggles are grounded in a broader homophobic discourse that hampers their initiative, or when they have indeed internalised their burden as self-hatred.

Although it seems coherent to judge Laurie's anxious monitoring of his desires as a sign for *The Charioteer*'s emphasis on stigmatisations, it is the confined space of the military hospital, which simultaneously threatens Laurie's secret and facilitates his romantic feelings for Andrew. His constant negotiation between representing the nation at war as a soldier, albeit an injured one, and almost recklessly embracing his new love when spending prolonged time with Andrew in the hospital kitchen, challenges a categorical reading of *The Charioteer*. In fact, the repeated display of double discourses between Laurie and Andrew questions our comfort of heteronormative knowledge: by using distinctly homosexual parlance when referring to Tchaikovsky as "queer" (56), Laurie unsettles the heterosexual discourse of the military hospital and infiltrates it with "queer" knowledge. It follows that Claude J. Summers' analysis focusing on "homosexuality as a personal failing"[25] and Natasha Alden's claim that "[t]here is no free and easy acceptance of sexual orientation"[26] in *The Charioteer*, reduce the text to the rare moments in which Laurie becomes conscious of his inability to make his sexuality public because of a homophobic society. Contrasting Summers and Alden, I have argued that Laurie accepts his homosexuality, even as a teenager, but he struggles to find an elevating love that remains respectable according to his personal standards of morality fashioned after Plato's *Phaedrus*. Laurie is thus not burdened by a deviating sexuality, but by an ideology that determines his desire for decency and positions non-conformity in tension with this desire. Consequently, *The Charioteer* represents the struggle of finding a place within society for a homosexual subject at a time where homogeneity and conformity were assumed to be 'normal' and 'natural'. Laurie has to make a choice that never questions his homosexuality – after all, his choice is between Ralph and Andrew and not between a man and a woman. This is the footing on which *The Charioteer* rests and passages of self-doubt and despondency work to disguise a daring narrative in conventional language to guarantee publication.

The necessity of cloaking the homosexual context becomes most apparent in the analysis of Baxter's two versions of *Look Down in Mercy*. Whereas the American audience was confronted with tender kisses and actual intercourse between the protagonist Toni Kent and his batman Anson, the more conservative

25 Summers, (1990), p. 26.

26 Natasha Alden, *Reading Behind the Lines: Postmemory in Contemporary British War Fiction* (Manchester und New York: Manchester University Press, 2014), p. 193.

British readership were not exposed to such trespasses. Following homophobic scripts of the 1950s that made homosexuals "scapegoats"[27] that were harassed and degraded, Baxter's British ending where Kent commits suicide, fits Summers' wary evaluation of pre-Stonewall texts much better than Renault's novel. The Kent of the British version conceptualises and negotiates between the seemingly distant worlds of soldering and homosexual pleasure in a more troubled and less bold way than Renault's Laurie. Any form of intimacy between the characters is censored according to the Obscene Publications Act of 1857. Similar to Renault's use of allusive language to circumvent censorship of "obscene writing" that "deprave[ed] and corrupt[ed] the minds and morals of those who are open to such immoral influences"[28], Baxter's British version only hints at the physicality in Kent and Anson's relationship. However, both editions show that Kent tries to fashion and maintain a relationship with Anson, who is not only a man but his batman and therefore neither of Kent's class, nor of his rank.

Even the British version cannot escape the lingering "homosocial desire"[29] that becomes apparent through the depiction of Kent, despite intense attempts of presenting the military as an institution untainted by homosexuality and effeminacy. Because Kent enjoys the company of his men during dances and of Anson in particular, and repeatedly trespasses into feminine displays of joyful gossip, he unwittingly challenges what Connell identifies as a "*corporate* display of masculinity"[30] within the military. Connell argues that although hegemonic masculinity is a concept most men will not achieve to perform; the military constitutes a convincing and broad ground for masculine performances. Kent's behaviour contradicts Connell's evaluation and *The Naked Civil Servant* demonstrates the military's struggles to keep the institution free from gender trespasses. Quentin Crisp is discharged from service on account of his effeminate looks, which reveals that more often than sexuality, it was gender that became policed by conservative forces guided by the Government. The patriarchal system of monitoring gender conformity was therefore a lingering factor during the Second World War. Paradoxically, because the military fashions such a masculine self-image, Kent in *Look Down in Mercy* is allowed to enjoy male company without

27 Summers, (1990), p. 26.

28 Definition of 'obscenity' by Benjamin Hickling in 1868, known as the 'Hicklin ruling'. Cited in Rachel Potter, "Introduction" in David Bradshaw and Rachel Potter (eds.), *Prudes on the Prowl: Fiction and Obscenity in England, 1850 to the present* (Oxford: Oxford University Press, 2013), p. 2.

29 Eve Kosofsky Sedgwick, *Between Men: English Literature and Male Homosocial Desire* (New York: Columbia University Press, 1985).

30 Connell, *Masculinities*, [1995], (Cambridge: Polity Press, 2016), p. 77.

raising suspicions, until he comes to realise that his feelings for Anson are more than friendship.

Kent's confidence is increasingly shattered because his performance lacks masculine markers of toughness. He becomes emasculated and suffers the loss of respectability when showing an emotional response at the sight of death. Whilst this depiction initially seems to reiterate stereotypes of the weak homosexual incapable of command, the narrative reverses the situation by depicting a vicious enemy to create a counter-narrative to the alleged moral integrity of the British military. Not only is the enemy to be fought on the battlefield, its methods of beheading, burning and torturing need to be contrasted to the respectable British officer who is increasingly failing to withstand such atrocities. Representing a brutal enemy and contrasting them to a British officer illustrates the nation's self-understanding as "a benevolent imperial power"[31] that is, even during combat, humane and distinct from an aggressor such as Japan. The trauma of masculinity is then the perpetual fanning of insecurities over the adequacy of men's performance, because they are neither allowed to delight in violence as the dominant order rests on a system of *silent* monitoring, nor permitted to be affected by signs of brutality which would thwart their appearance of toughness. Kent's emasculation is thus partially vindicated when resisting the desire to act in similarly savage ways.

In *Winter Love*, Red gives a new perspective on masculinity when she reflects on her unhappy marriage with Andy after the war and captures not only her emotional brutality towards her unwanted husband, but also how easily men's masculinity can be threatened: "In the ways of wives, I keep him in doubt of himself as a man by making him feel small, by nagging him about his being late for meals, and by rationing him where bed is concerned." (79) This display becomes even crueller:

> And I can think up ways of nagging him so that his manhood will be shorn from him, little by little, so that all that's left of him is a preening body, still pretending to maleness, but getting it over quickly now, getting flabby and coming quickly, and the quicker the better for me. He's really getting impotent; I know, and he knows but we never talk about it, and I keep an eye on him he won't stray, and he's scared of me I know. (83)

Through her nagging, Red enhances Andy's pre-existing doubts over his masculinity which can be recognised in his earlier attempts of seducing Red during the war. The seeking of sex as a validation of men's manhood by subordinating the female body makes women an instrument to satisfy men's physical and emotion-

31 Rose, (2003), p. 286.

al needs for power and dominance. Red turns this stereotypical narrative on its head when she humiliates Andy by pronouncing his increasing impotence. Kent, too, fears this fate and dreams about being "in bed with Celia, and impotent. He caressed her body with his lips, but it was no use, she was twining her soft legs round his, fumbling at him with her fingers. For God's sake! She was saying, for God's sake!" (57). Similar to Mara as the nagging wife, Kent fears Celia's reaction when dreaming that he is sexually insufficient. Prone to social shaming, Kent is constantly in doubt over his masculinity and seeks ways to prove himself worthy. In consequence of this desire to countervail doubts and to stabilise his shaken ego, Kent seduces the Eurasian nurse Helen who thinks herself in love with the white officer. The hypocrisy of censorship is most blaringly evident when comparing the toned-down passages of homosexual love with Kent's explicit raping of Helen. In an act of alleged passion, Kent reduces Helen to her body, kisses her forcefully and finally assaults her. In contrast to previous scenes depicting Kent and Anson, this moment of rape is explicitly described in both the American and British version, which shows the double-standard of censorship: female objectification that elevates a man's masculinity seems to be too common place to raise objections, whereas consensual homosexual acts needed to be deleted from the British version.

Kent's action resembles Red's experience with her husband: both men feel insufficiently masculine and subordinate a female in order to elevate their self-worth. Kent additionally challenges himself to rescue a soldier named Goodwin when he is injured and unable to seek cover. In an act of bravado, Kent risks his life to save his manhood but does so only after recognising his deep emotional bond with Anson whose offer to complete the task himself stirs Kent's passion for him. His act of masculine heroism is thus a parody of 'the real thing' when love for another man and not the nation compels Kent into action. In this way *Look Down in Mercy* challenges the relentless monitoring of men based on shame and abjection and illustrates that homosexual feelings can produce heroic action. Contrary to stereotypical assumptions, Kent's homosexuality does not hamper his initiative, but releases an unknown power, which the military's mechanisms of enforcing conformity fail to do. Although momentarily moving into the sphere of feminine emotions, Kent's deed is translated into patriarchal language of the roaring lion, which derogates the possibility of creating a lasting masculinity that is informed by feminine emotions rather than tough violence. Novels narrating homosexual desires at times of war thus find various ways of interrupting scripts of gender and sexuality, but may also resolve their own challenge back into dominant order.

The display of failure when trying to live up to the idealistic inscription accompanying his position, shows Kent as a character who is burdened by more than his emerging homosexuality. Similar to Laurie's situation in hospital, Kent's plight is aggravated through the war when the nation seduces men to perform heroically and to metaphorically serve their country as Unknown Soldiers to further national collectivity. The struggles endured by Kent and Laurie can therefore not be located in their sexuality – at least not exclusively. The extraordinary situation of war bears challenges for them that peacetime did not, because the sharing of confined spaces endangers their closetedness whilst also fostering attraction to their own sex.

The main body of this study focuses on this paradoxical role of the war simultaneously policing and enabling outlawed desires. I discussed the interlinking issues of gender, nation, patriotism, public and private spaces to show that all of these seemingly neutral parameters are deeply embedded in a dichotomous gender structure. Wartime literature illustrates a highly complex and intersecting matrix where each of these markers (and more) determines how characters perceive themselves and others during this period. Presenting itself as stable and enduring, the nation actually lacks these desirable qualities. It is, according to Anderson, an "imagined community"[32] that needs a "repertoire of images"[33] to disguise its fundamental insubstantiality. Narration is thus as much the basis of nation-states as the distinction between 'friend' and 'stranger', both in relation to other nations and within its own borders. At times of war a constant control is required over who belongs to the nation – who represents the propagated norms of patriotism and nationalism – and who fails to rehearse such ideologies: conscientious objectors, deserters and other non-conforming subjects. The 'us' versus 'them' dynamic is one strategy to induce conformity and national belonging. In order to fight so-called Nazi Germany, British nationalism nurtured the desire for belonging to one community by repeating the united strength of Britain and its people. However, "it is that very emotional power of the idea of being one with others that makes the definition of the national community so fraught" [34], Sonya O. Rose explains. Wartime nationalism designed on the back of national unity is marked by incongruities when some people fail to adopt the war as their war. Waters' character Julia expresses the inherent paradox of a fabricated

32 Benedict Anderson, Imagined Communities: Reflections on the Origin and Spread of Nationalism, [1983], (London and New York: Verso, 1991), p. 6.

33 Sara Ahmed, *Strange Encounters: Embodied Others in Post-Coloniality* (London and New York: Routledge, 2000), p. 98.

34 Sonya O. Rose, Which People's War?: National Identity and Citizenship in Britain 1939-1945 (Oxford: Oxford University Press, 2003), p. 286.

communality during the war: "I hate this passion for uniforms, too. Uniforms, armbands, badges. I thought the military impulse, as it's grown up in Germany, was what we were against!" (273) Demonstrating the double-standards of the People's War when simultaneously claiming to level classes, whilst differentiating people's social status through uniforms, Julia discloses the arbitrariness of an ideology according to which what one fights against and what one represents becomes indistinguishable. This instability is retroactively captured in Adam Fitzroy's *Make Do and Mend* (2012) where the protagonist Harry demonstrates how manipulative and ultimately failing the propagation of a People's War is.

When Harry is injured after a submarine accident, he begins to disidentify with his role as Navy officer to instead re-collect a Welsh identity represented in the legend of Owain Glyn Dŵr – a Welsh independent fighter who announced sovereignty of Wales against English rule in the Middle Ages. As a heroic figure of Welsh independence, whose life and deeds are recollected in many stories, Glyn Dŵr illustrates Geoffrey Bennington's argument that "we undoubtedly find narration at the centre of nation: stories of national origins, myths of founding fathers, genealogies of heroes"[35]. The legend of Glyn Dŵr is compelling because it can be neither proven right nor wrong as his grave has never been found, making the tomb of the metaphoric Unknown Soldier forever empty. At the same time as being a localised legend, Glyn Dŵr envisions and embodies Welsh independence from English rule.

Harry's path towards indulging his Welsh origin is accompanied by his increasing renunciation of the war and his role as officer to the point where he considers actively protesting against the war by "wearing a white poppy" (247-248) next Armistice Day. The legend of Glyn Dŵr subordinates the People's War and positions England and Wales not as a united nation battling conquest, but as independent countries each fighting on their own. Harry comes to the conclusion that "if ever England is invaded, we'll know that without a doubt Wales will still hold on" (297). Clearly, the narrative of a *United* Kingdom is challenged in *Make Do and Mend* when the characters prefer a local over a collective identity. Even Harry's trespass into actively writing propaganda for the BBC, limiting his experience to "accommodation, food, routine, the occasional funny story" (151), is marginalized as an interlude and superimposed by the novel's ending where Harry and Jim fantasise over an enduring Wales.

Another telling reference to the faultiness of People's War propaganda is the conflict between Harry's brother Thomas Griffith-Lyon and Harry's partner Jim

35 Geoffrey Bennington, "Postal Politics and the Institution of the Nation" in Homi K. Bhabha (ed.), *Nation and Narration* (London and New York: Routledge, 1990), p. 121.

Brynawel. My analysis has shown that the novel's use of Welsh surnames is decisive for determining which character is portrayed as belonging to 'us' (Thomas) and which is belonging to 'them' (the conscientious objector Jim). Whereas Thomas claims to be a representative of the nation when adopting his wife's surname Griffith meaning 'lord' to hyphenate it with his last name Lyon ('lion')[36], Jim Brynawel translates to 'windy hill'[37] and denotes his non-conforming position within the nation at war. Thomas implicitly declares himself the keeper of patriotism and he accuses Jim of murder. The novel cleverly subverts Thomas' efforts to degrade Jim when revealing that the latter is a historian whose real name is Montgomery, which loosely translates to 'top of man power'.[38] Jim's now upper class and high intellect puts him on similar footing with Thomas, who does not accept his defeat and continues to row against Jim even though everybody else has accepted the former stranger. *Make Do and Mend* shows that the People's War is not only unconvincing in terms of uniting Britain, but also with regard to the dichotomy of friend and stranger. Consequently, propaganda created to sustain the elusive and illusive nation faces the danger to unravel when subjects begin to emancipate themselves from the common and communal path.

The narrative of resistance to the Government's promulgating a People's War is equally evident in *The Night Watch*, when Duncan's friend Alec asserts that it is not the soldiers' war "but a load of government men's. It's not our war, either; we have to suffer in it though. We have to do the things they tell us." (481) Disillusioned and unconvinced by the promises of glory and reputation made by their country's leadership, Duncan and Alec want to commit suicide, but whereas Alec succeeds Duncan survives and becomes a prisoner. The prison silences and confines critical voices concerning the war in order to protect the national war effort. Duncan and the other inmates logically feel like outcasts since they are incapable of changing the events happening outside. As a tactical manoeuvre to increase this sense of debarment, the prisoners are symbolically emasculated when they cannot represent their nation at war. Although Alec's negative attitude towards the war has lastingly influenced Duncan, he finds no way to convincingly express his resistance. Despite his seemingly powerful hold on inmates, Duncan queers the prison space by transforming his bunk neighbour Fraser's heterosexual fantasy of a "plain, stout, stupid, grateful girl" (305) into

36 Basil Cottle, *The Penguin Dictionary of Surnames* (Harmondsworth: Penguin Publishers, 1967), p. 123 and p. 174.

37 Evans H. Meurig and William Owen Thomas and Christopher Daviers, *Y Geiriadur Mawr: The Complete Welsh-English English-Welsh dictionary* (Llandysul: Gwasg Gomer, 1980), p. 59 and p. 36.

38 Cottle, (1967), p. 196.

homosexual desire, when pleasuring himself to the sound and motion of Fraser's own masturbation. Although the prison functions as an extension of the nation to keep non-conforming subjects safely contained behind bars, it is powerless against Duncan's body devastating the semblance of order from within.

In *The Charioteer*, the protagonist Laurie also infiltrates homosexual desire into the heterosexual space of the hospital and performs a masculinity that is informed by his emotional attachment to the young Quaker, Andrew, rather than by exaggerated displays of toughness. In fact, Laurie's injured leg makes his movements appear stiff and laborious. Any form of heroism, no matter how minimal, is hampered, which is depicted in his failing attempt to save Nurse Adrian's handkerchief from flying away: "Instinctively he started to run after it, felt the stiff drag of his leg, and stopped." (249) Laurie's injury will leave him unable to perform the kind of masculinity the nation demands of its soldiers ever again, and hc progressively learns to handle his situation until he identifies with his "cripple's boot" (90): "This, henceforward, was Laurie Odell." (90-91) Unlike Kent in *Look Down in Mercy*, whose injuries are never permanent enough to expel him from the discourse of war, Laurie's body bears its marks as a reminder of his service as well as the war's ruthlessness. Instead of the nation manoeuvring Laurie into war and manipulating him into further acts of masculine heroism, it is Mr. Straike, the devious new husband of Laurie's mother, who pesters his stepson and demands a masculine performance. Laurie manages to withstand Mr. Straike's desire to rechristen him as Laurence, the 'non-sissy version' of his nickname, and instead reveals the vicar's own unchristian attitude towards men whose Quaker religion condemns fighting. Betraying his Christian values when denouncing Quakers working as male orderlies, Mr. Straike discloses that in wartime, religion can become subsumed under nationalism. Instead of respecting Christian values, built on peace and altruism, he represents the nation's efforts of manipulating men into battle. Mr. Straike's hypocrisy is underlined by the fact that he is a non-fighter himself, which makes him unfit to judge others' who refuse to fight. In contrast to his stepfather, Laurie adopts a much more lenient approach to conscientious objectors when saying sarcastically: "Perhaps we ought to have tried burning them [Quakers] alive. Perhaps we just needed to be civilians and not soldiers. I wouldn't know." (269) Laurie criticises that those who are not forced to physically encounter the war on the battlefield have a more radical attitude towards conscientious objectors than soldiers. He therefore criticises the relentless monitoring of men by the nation or other institutions such as the church to push men into combat.

Negotiating his place in a world full of extremes, Laurie finds a friend in Andrew, which strengthens the protagonist's rebellious campaign against Mr.

Straike. However, their innocent relationship is built on a fortress of silences and gaps because communicating his feelings would risk revealing to Andrew that their close relationship exposes Andrew's homosexual tendencies. Laurie stays clear from articulating his desires and instead introduces Andrew to Plato's *Phaedrus*. Seeking to find a love that is both of the mind and of the body, Laurie cannot identify with the available scripts of wartime that constantly demand him to deny part of his identity, and he eventually and tragically confides in Ralph who seems to resolve and combine these conflicting desires. However, Laurie cannot quite cope with having lost Andrew and the novel hints at the brevity of their love when stating that "they are reconciled for a night in sleep" (347). One is bound to ask what the morning might hold?[39] – a question that the novel never resolves.

The relationships between Kay, her girlfriend Helen and Julia, Helen's secret lover in *The Night Watch*, disintegrates in similar ways as Laurie and Ralph's, because Kay's female complicity in a patriarchal structure restraints Helen and drives her into the arms of Julia. In Kay's world men have no role to play because she is the man – the husband – who "wants a wife" (353). Not only does Kay heroically rescue Helen in 1942, she also awakens Helen's lesbianism represented in a metaphorical rebirth when she is freed from the rubble under which she is stuck. Kay gazes "at her in a sort of wonder; unable to believe that something so fresh and so unmarked could have emerged from so much chaos" (503). Ending the novel on this note, Waters lays emphasis on Kay's love for Helen. However, the section set in 1944 paints Kay in a less positive light when she shows her affection for Helen in a way that oppresses her girlfriend who consequentially flees into the arms of Julia where she can "confide in [her], almost as one wife to another" (275). Whereas Kay's performance of (female) masculinity during the war enhances her initiative, it is domineering towards Helen – evident in Kay's use of the phrase "Good girl" (284). Designed to express what Red in *Winter Love* calls "lower-middle-class talk [that] made one feel somehow more 'in' with everybody else, less class-feeling about, more chummy and sturdy" (6), Kay's "Good girl" has the opposite effect on Helen as it fixates her into the role of a dependant woman yearning for the approval of a man – in this case, a woman performing the role of man. Whereas Kay's habit of speaking in working-class style coincides with Red's observation that this "reflected the 'I-can-look-after-myself' feeling" (6), Helen, who is the receiving end of such talk, is denied the same autonomy. It follows that whilst a reading of Kay as an independent

39 Nikolai Endres, "Horses and Heroes: Plato's Phaedrus and Mary Renault's *The Charioteer*" in *International Journal of the Classical Tradition* Vol. 19, No. 3 (2012), p. 161.

and strong woman contributing to the war effort is highly desirable from a queer theoretical point of view, it oversimplifies her damaging attitude towards Helen, which turns Kay into a female complicit within the patriarchal power structure. Consequently, not all women assumed merely a "*semblance* of masculinity"[40] whilst retaining their femininity, they could also deeply identify with masculinity to the effect of privileging it over femininity.

Although unconscious of her masculinist performance, Kay becomes increasingly aware of Helen's growing emotional distance and she begins to fear that Helen desires a 'real' man and she angrily tells Helen to go and "pick up some boy, some soldier –'" (327). Red, too, struggles with her increasingly unstable relationship to Mara and wonders "why, [Mara is] weak, she's influenceable, she doesn't harden herself against things as I do. And for a fleeting panicky moment I thought how easy it would be to lose her. To someone else. A man, for instance." (114) In remarkably similar terms, underlining Waters' incorporation of earlier lesbian texts, Kay and Red question their lovers' lesbianism before suspecting their faithfulness. This implies the constant fanning of insecurities regarding a masculine gender performance and its exhaustion for the performer. Both Kay and Mara lose their lovers towards the end of the war. Whereas Kay's excessive performance of (female) masculinity has led to Helen's betrayal, Red's fate rehearses a more traditional resolution of lesbian love when she marries Andy and has children with him.

Winter Love's ending demonstrates Castle's criticism that lesbian women are always "in the shadows, in the margins, hidden from history" because their desire is often not even recognised by heteronormative society: in the moment of marriage, Red's lesbianism becomes forever invisible. [41] This gains more traction with view to another scene when Mara's husband Karl realises that his wife is no longer faithful and calls on her at Red's place. Instead of realising their friendship for what it really is, he ignores Red and when she inquires about how Mara and Karl's conversation went, her partner contributes to her sorrows: "It never crossed his mind. Another man yes, but not you. I think he was reassured, seeing it was only you." (92) Red reflects that "Karl hadn't even looked at me as a person. Suddenly I hated them both, Karl and Mara, together." (92) Invisible to Karl, Red and Mara's relationship loses substance and becomes more forcefully trapped inside their flat where it remains hidden from heteronormative discourse.

The narrative of home as monitoring heterosexual and concealing homosexual desires is part of the experiences of all characters. The home becomes the

40 Plain, (1996), p, 28, [emphasis original].

41 Terry Castle, *The Apparitional Lesbian: Female Homosexuality and Modern Culture* (New York, Columbia University Press, 1993), p. 2.

limiting space that entraps subjects to guarantee a set of norms to prevail within public society. As the "the house [is] a metaphor for the closed 'bound' self, which the war opens and airs"[42], its limiting functions find undoing on the physical as well as the psychological level. Starting "with a few loose bricks" "the collapse of a wall" (*TC*, 240), as represented in the destruction of buildings, enables a re-negotiation of homely belonging. Whereas Helen flees into the street to escape the confinement of Kay's flat, Viv, another one of Waters' characters, aborts a child and turns the impeccable "show-flat" where she suffers from the operation into an "anti-home" stained with blood. In killing her child and by manipulating her domestic and reproductive role, Viv finds a kind of liberation denied to many other women of the time. In *Winter Love* Red and Mara meet such a woman whose husband "used to make her pregnant all the time, did it to tie her down, to destroy her" (106). Upon this revelation of the woman's fate, Red reflects that "women aren't happy just being married and having kinds and doing the housework, they want something else too" (111). What these women want is to be independent and not trapped inside the domestic home where they become caretaker of men and children. Through aborting the child, Viv liberates herself from the confining narrative of the home and by tarnishing the show flat, she defies "reproductive futurism"[43] further. As a truly queer character, Helen's body becomes the site of resistance, more so than the mannish lesbian Kay. Consequently, gender non-conformity cannot guarantee counter-discursiveness when conservative ideologies continue to reign on the body as well as in the home.

In retrieving and navigating war stories with a queer subject matter, this study has simultaneously challenged the perception of wartime as a heteronormative endeavour and the assumption of pre-Stonewall novels as bleak and burdensome. Negotiating the seemingly distant parameters of unlawful sexual desire and violent combat fought on the back of men and women alike, these novels disclose the war as a time of crisis for heteronormative society on more scales than one. Whereas enforced civil separation between men and women fostered military affectation of masculinity, it also enabled intense camaraderie and more deeply felt emotions. Women, too, found their circle of mates first diminished and then increased to compile experiences that peacetime society prohibited. Homosexual wartime fiction thus manoeuvres between protesting against the

42 Jenny Hartley, Millions like Us: British Women's Fiction of the Second World War (Virago, 1997) and Phyllis Lassner, British Women Writers of World War II: Battlegrounds of their Own (Palgrave Macmillan, 1998), p. 60.

43 Lee Edelman, *No Future: Queer Theory and the Death Drive* (Durham and London: Duke University Press, 2004), p. 2.

ruthlessness of the war that threatens to dismember society and celebrating the coming together of people sharing the same desires.

However, throughout this study I have repeatedly emphasised that retrospective war novels like *The Night Watch* and *Make Do and Mend* display anachronisms when projecting a distinctly modern consciousness into the past. This is overtly obvious in scenes of sexual contact, but also implicitly stated when characters display an exaggerated sense of pride in their sexuality and non-conforming gender performance. These implied slippages need to be exposed in order to reveal the novel's at times compromising attitude. In contrast to these modern re-writings that deliberately over-emphasise a liberal consciousness, *The Charioteer* and *Look Down in Mercy* show more restraint. However, I assert that pre-Stonewall novels offer discernible critique on heteronormative society in more allusive ways which, paradoxically, elevates their potential of undermining dominant knowledge. Because neither Kent nor Laurie are recognisable for their homosexuality, they present a constant threat to the social order and challenge the military's masculine self-image, whereas Kay and Harry perpetuate hegemonic standards by replicating heterosexual relationships and gender stereotypes, or by becoming assimilated as the controllable abject. Pre-Stonewall novels therefore seem to offer greater potential for disclosing the diverse layers of society, which makes it necessary to abandon the "is it good for the gays"[44] question that hampers wide-raging research.

Sexual variance is not a contemporary invention but a constantly present variance of dominant life. Gazes into the past are thus not necessarily restrictive but potentially elevating and educational, because they contribute to feminist efforts of negotiating a disguised and overlooked *Her*story. Future studies should build and expand on the potential queer stories in order to diversify not only current culture, but also its history. Whilst this study has focused on homosexuality during the war, other aspects such as race, class, ethnicity, age and generation could not find sufficient negotiation due to limited space and because of the explicit emphasis on representations regarding sexuality and gender. It therefore seems important to flag these missing themes in order to delineate ground for subsequent investigations.

We live in a world full of new challenges, some of which are built on patriarchal ideologies fashioned in earlier periods. By exposing the continuity of social diversity, we can deconstruct the roots of sexism, racism, classism, homophobia and the fear of anything that is 'different', in order to devastate arguments for a conservative future that is no different from its past. *History's Queer Stories* contributes to this form of research by revealing that not even a conserva-

44 Bronski, (2013), p. 10.

tive period such as the Second World War is undisputedly controlled by dominant forces that induce a collective conformity. Narrative negotiations of a non-heteronormative war offer a point of departure for subsequent research into a queer history in order to create a more colourful present and future.

Bibliography

PRIMARY MATERIAL

An Englishman in New York (2009), Dir. Richard Laxton, DVD, Momentum Pictures.

Baxter, Walter. *Look Down in Mercy*, [1951], (Virginia: Valancourt Books, 2014).

———. *The Image and the Search* (London: Hutchinson, 1953).

Bell, Barbara. *Just Take Your Frock Off* (Brighton: Ourstory Books, 1999).

Bowen, Elizabeth. *The Heat of the Day*, [1948], (New York: Anchor Books, 2002).

Churchill, Winston. "The Women of Britain" in Charles Eade (ed.), *Onwards to Victory: War speeches by the Right HON. Winston S. Churchill* (London: Cassell and Company Ltd., 1944).

———. "'Westward, Look, the Land is Bright,' Address Broadcast April 27, 1941" in Charles Eade (ed), *The Unrelenting Struggle* (Boston: Little, Brown and Co., 1942).

Crisp, Quentin. *The Naked Civil Servant*, [1968], (London: Harper Perennial, 2007).

Fitzroy, Adam. *Make Do and Mend* (UK: Manifold Press, 2012).

Forster, E. M. *Maurice*, [1971], (London: Penguin Classics, 2005).

Hall, Radclyffe. *Miss Ogilvy Finds Herself* (New York: Harcourt, Brace, 1934).

———. *The Well of Loneliness*, [1928], (New York: Anchor Books, 1990).

Isherwood, Christopher. *The Sixties: Diaries Volume Two 1960-1969* (London: Chatto and Windus, 2010).

Kipling, Rudyard. "The White Man's Burden: The United States & The Philippine Islands" in Rudyard Kipling (ed.), *Rudyard Kipling's Verse: Definitive Edition* (Garden City, New York: Doubleday, 1940).

Orwell, George. *The Lion and the Unicorn: Socialism and the English Genius*, [1941], (The University of Adelaide: eBooks@Adelaide, 2014)

<https://ebooks.adelaide.edu.au/o/orwell/george/lion_and_the_unicorn/> [last accessed: 18/07/2017].

Platon. *Phaidros* (München: Ernst Heimeran Verlag, 1964).

Renault, Mary. *The Charioteer*, [1953], (New York: Vintage Books, 2003).

———. *The Friendly Young Ladies*, [1944], (London: Virago Press, 2014).

Shute, Nevil. *Requiem For a Wren*, [1955], (London: Vintage Books, 2009).

Suyin, Han. *Winter Love*, [1962], (London: Virago Press, 1994).

Vidal, Gore. *The City and the Pillar*, [1948], (New York: Vintage Books, 2003).

Waters, Sarah. *The Night Watch* (London: Virago, 2006).

SECONDARY MATERIAL

Abraham, Julie. *Are Girls Necessary?: Lesbian Writing and Modern Histories*, [1996], (Minneapolis and London: University of Minnesota Press, 2008).

Ackermann, Zeno. *Gedächtnis-Fiktionen: Mediale Erinnerungsfiguren und literarischer Eigensinn in britischen Romanen zum Zweiten Weltkrieg* (Heidelberg: Universitätsverlag Winter, 2015).

Ahmed, Sara. "Orientations Matter" in Diana Coole and Samantha Frost (eds.), *New Materialisms: Ontology, Agency, and Politics* (Durham and London: Duke University Press, 2010).

———. "Racialized Bodies" in Mary Evans and Ellie Lee (eds.), *Real Bodies: A Sociological Introduction* (New York: Palgrave, 2002).

———. *Strange Encounters: Embodied Others in Post-Coloniality* (London and New York: Routledge, 2000).

———. *The Cultural Politics of Emotion* (London and New York: Routledge, 2004).

Alcoff, Linda Martín. "Feminist Theory and Social Science: New Knowledges, New Epistemologies" in Nancy Duncan (ed.), *BodySpace: Destabilizing Geographies of Gender and Sexuality* (London and New York: Routledge, 1996).

Alden, Natasha. "'Accompanied by Ghosts': The Changing Uses of the Past in Sarah Waters's Lesbian Fiction" in Adele Jones and Claire O'Callaghan (eds.), *Sarah Waters and Contemporary Feminism* (London: Palgrave Macmillan, 2016).

———. "'Possibility, Pleasure and Peril': *The Night Watch* as a Very Literary History" in Kaye Mitchell (ed.), *Sarah Waters: Contemporary Critical Perspectives* (London: Bloomsbury, 2013).

———. *Reading Behind the Lines: Postmemory in Contemporary British War Fiction* (Manchester and New York: Manchester University Press, 2014).

Anderson, Benedict. *Imagined Communities: Reflections on the Origin and Spread of Nationalism*, [1983], (London and New York: Verso, 1991).

Armitt, Lucie. "Interview with Sarah Waters" in *Feminist Review* No. 85, Political Hystories (2007), pp. 116-127.

———. "Teasing (Out) a New Generation: The Writing of Sarah Waters" in Adele Jones and Claire O'Callaghan (eds.), *Sarah Waters and Contemporary Feminism* (London: Palgrave Macmillan, 2016).

Armstrong, Elizabeth A. and Crage, Suzanna M. "Movements and Memory: The Making of the Stonewall Myth" in *American Sociological Review* Vol. 71, No. 5 (2006), pp. 724-751.

Bairner, Alan. "Masculinity, Violence and the Irish Peace Process" in *Capital and Class* Vol. 69 (1999).

Barker, Paul. *Polari – The Lost Language of Gay Men*, [2002], (London and New York: Routledge, 2003).

Barrett, Michèle. *Women's Oppression Today: The Marxist/feminist Encounter* (London: New Left Books, 1980).

Barthes, Roland. *Image Music Text*, Essays Selected and Translated by Stephen Heath (Fulham: Fontana Press, 1977).

———. *Mythologies: The Complete Edition, in a New Translation*, [1972], (New York, Hill and Wang, 1973).

Bauer, Heike and Cook, Matt. (eds.), *Queer 1950s: Rethinking Sexuality in the Postwar Years* (Palgrave McMillan, 2012).

Bennington, Geoffrey. "Postal Politics and the Institution of the Nation" in Homi K. Bhabha (ed.), *Nation and Narration* (London and New York: Routledge, 1990), pp. 121-137.

Berlant, Lauren and Edelman, Lee. *Sex, or the Unbearable* (Durham and London: Duke University Press, 2014).

Berlant, Lauren and Warner, Michael. "Sex in Public" in *Critical Inquiry* Vol. 24, No. 2 (1998), pp. 547-566.

Bersani, Leo. "Is the Rectum a Grave?" in *The MIT Press* Vol. 43 (1987), pp. 197-222.

———. *Homos* (Cambridge and London: Harvard University Press,1995).

Bérubé, Allan. "World War II" in B. R. Burg (ed.), *Gay Warriors: A Documentary History from the Ancient World to the Present* (New York and London: New York University Press, 2002).

———. *My Desire for History: Essays in Gay, Community, and Labor History* (Chapel Hill: The University of North Carolina Press, 2011).

Bhabha, Homi K. "DissemiNation: Time, Narrative, and the Margins of the Modern Nation" in Homi K. Bhabha (ed.), *Nation and Narration* (London and New York: Routledge, 1990).

———. "Introduction" in Homi K. Bhabha (ed.), *Nation and Narration* (London and New York: Routledge, 1990).

Bird, Sharon R. "Welcome to the Men's Club: Homosociality and the Maintenance of Hegemonic Masculinity" in *Gender and Society* Vol. 10, No. 2 (1996), pp. 120-132.

Boehm, Katharina. "Historiography and the Material Imagination in the Novels of Sarah Waters" in *Studies in the Novel* Vol. 43, No. 2 (2011), pp. 237-257.

Bordo, Susan. "Reading the Male Body" in: Laurence Goldstein (ed.), *The Male Body: Features, Destinies, Exposures* (Ann Arbor, Michigan: The University of Michigan Press, 1994).

Bourke, Joanna. *Dismembering the Male: Men's Bodies, Britain and the Great War* (London: Reaktion Books, 1996).

Bradshaw, David. "American Beastliness, the Great Purge and its Aftermath (1946-1959)" in David Bradshaw and Rachel Potter (eds.), *Prudes on the Prowl: Fiction and Obscenity in England, 1850 to the present* (Oxford: Oxford University Press, 2013), pp. 138-158.

Brah, Avtar. *Cartographies of Diaspora: Contesting Identities* (London and New York: Routledge, 1996).

Braidotti, Rosi. *Metamorphoses: Towards a Materialist Theory of Becoming* (Cambridge: Polity Press, 2002).

Breen, Margaret Sönser. *Narratives of Queer Desire: Deserts of the Heart* (London: Palgrave Macmillan, 2009).

Bristow, Joseph. "Homosexual Writing on Trial: from *Fanny Hill* to *Gay News*" in Hugh Stevens (ed.), *The Cambridge Companion to Gay and Lesbian Writing* (Cambridge: Cambridge University Press, 2011).

Bronski, Michael. "The Shock of the Old: Christopher Bram Chats with the Author of *Pulp Friction*" in *The Gay & Lesbian Review Worldwide* Vol.10, No. 2 (2003), pp. 32-33.

———. *Pulp Friction: Uncovering the Golden Age of Gay Male Pulps*, [2003], (New York: St. Martin's Griffin, 2013).

Brookes, Les. *Gay Male Fiction Since Stonewall: Ideology, Conflict, and Aesthetics* (New York and London: Routledge, 2009).

Brown, Bill. "Thing Theory" in *Critical Inquiry* Vol. 28, No. 1 (2001).

Brown, Wendy. *Regulating Aversions: Tolerance in the Age of Identity and Empire* (Princeton: Princeton University Press, 2006).

———. *States of Injury: Power and Freedom in late Modernity* (New York, Princeton University Press, 1995).

Burden, Robert. "Introduction: Englishness and Spatial Practices" in Robert Burden and Stephan Kohl (eds.), *Landscapes and Englishness* (New York: Radopi, 2006), pp. 13-26.

Butler, Judith. "Contagious Word: Paranoia and 'Homosexuality' in the Military" in Iain Morland and Annabelle Willox (eds.), *Queer Theory* (Hampshire: Palgrave Macmillan, 2005).

———. "Imitation and Gender Insubordination" in Diana Fuss (ed.), *Inside/Out: Lesbian Theories, Gay Theories* (New York: Psychology Press, 1991), pp.13-21.

———. "Sexual Politics, Torture, and Secular Time" in *The British Journal of Sociology* Vol. 59, No. 1 (2008), pp. 1-23.

———. *Bodies that Matter: On the Discursive Limits of "Sex"*, [1993], (London and New York: Routledge Classics, 2011).

———. *Excitable Speech: A Politics of the Performative* (London and New York: Routledge, 1997).

———. *Gender Trouble: Feminism and the Subversion of Identity*, [1990], (London and New York: Routledge Classics, 2006).

———. *Undoing Gender* (London and New York: Routledge, 2004).

Calder, Angus. *The People's War: Britain 1939-1945* (London: Pimlico, 1969).

———. *The Myth of the Blitz*, [1991], (London: Pimlico, 1992).

Cambell, Joseph. *The Hero with a Thousand Faces*, [1949], (Princeton: Princeton University Press, 1973).

Castle, Terry. *The Apparitional Lesbian: Female Homosexuality and Modern Culture* (New York: Columbia University Press, 1993).

Charles, Nickie. *Gender in Modern Britain* (Oxford: Oxford University Press, 2002).

Clune, Maggie and Day, Gary and Maguire, Chris. "Decline and Fall? The Course of the Novel" in Gary Day (ed.), *Literature and Culture in Modern Britain: Volume Two: 1930-1955* (London and New York: Longman, 1997).

Cohn, Carol. "Gays in the Military: Texts and Subtexts" in Marysia Zalewski and Jane Parpart (eds.), *The "Man Question" in International Relations, [1997],* (Boulder, Colorado: Westview Press, 1998), pp. 129-149.

Conekin, Becky E. "'Magazines are Essentially about the Here and Now. And this was Wartime': British Vogue's Responses to the Second World War" in Philippa Levine and Susan R. Grayzel (eds.), *Gender, Labour, War and Empire: Essays on Modern Britain* (Hampshire: Palgrave Macmillan, 2009).

Connell, R. W. and Messerschmidt, James W. "Hegemonic Masculinity: Rethinking the Concept" in *Gender and Society* Vol. 19, No. 6 (2005), pp. 829-859.

Connell, R. W. and Pearse, Rebecca. *Gender in World Perspective*, [2002], (Cambridge: Polity Press, 2009).

Connell, R. W. "A very Straight Gay: Masculinity, Homosexual Experience, and the Dynamics of Gender" in *American Sociological Review* Vol. 57, No. 6 (1992), pp. 735-751.

———. "Masculinities and Men's Health" in Bettina Baron and Helga Kotthoff (eds.), *Gender in Interaction: Perspectives on femininity and masculinity in ethnography and discourse* (Amsterdam: John Benjamins Publishing Company, 2001), pp. 139-152.

———. *Masculinities*, [1995], (Cambridge: Polity Press, 2016).

Conrath, Alan Brady. "Mary Renault as the First Gay Novelist" in *The Gay and Lesbian Review Worldwide* Vol. 21, No. 6 (2014), pp. 28-30.

Cooper, Clare. "The House as Symbol of the Self" (Barkley: University of California, 1974).

———. *House As a Mirror of Self: Exploring the Deeper Meaning of Home*, [1995], (Berwick and Maine: Nicolas-Hays, 2006).

Cottle, Basil. *The Penguin Dictionary of Surnames* (Harmondsworth: Penguin Publishers, 1967).

Dasenbrock, Reed Way. "The Novel and the End of Empire" in Brian W. Shaffer (ed.), *A Companion to the British and Irish Novel 1945-2000* (Malden and Oxford: Blackwell Publishing, 2005).

Davies, Robert Rees. *The Revolt of Owain Glyn Dŵr* (Oxford: Oxford University Press, 1995).

De Beauvoir, Simone. *The Second Sex*, [1949], (London: Vintage Books, 2011).

De Lauretis, Teresa. "Queer Theory: Lesbian and Gay Sexualities An Introduction" in *Differences: a Journal of Feminist Cultural Studies* Vol. 3, No. 2 (1991), pp. iiix–viii.

Dean, Tim. *Beyond Sexuality* (Chicago and London: University of Chicago Press, 2000).

DeCoste, Damon Marcel. "The Literary Response to the Second World War" in Brian W. Shaffer (ed.), *A Companion to the British and Irish Novel 1945-2000* (Malden and Oxford, Blackwell Publishing, 2005).

Dennis, Abigail. "'Ladies in Peril': Sarah Waters on Neo-Victorian Narrative Celebrations and why She Stopped Writing about the Victorian Era" in *Neo-Victorian Studies* Vol. 1, No. 1 (2008), pp. 41-52.

Dick, Bernard F. *The Hellenism of Mary Renault* (Carbondale, Illinois: Southern Illinois University Press, 1972).

Dinshaw, Carolyn and Edelman, Lee and Ferguson, Roderick A. and Freccerp, Carla. "Theorizing Queer Temporalities: A Roundtable Discussion" in *GLQ: A Journal of Lesbian and Gay Studies* Vol. 13, No. 2-3 (2007), pp. 177-195.

Dinshaw, Carolyn. *Getting Medieval: Sexualities and Communities, Pre- and Postmodern* (Durham and London: Duke University Press, 1999).

Doan, Laura and Waters, Sarah. "Making Up Lost Time: Contemporary Lesbian Writing and the Invention of History" in David Alderson and Linda R. Anderson (eds.), *Territories of Desire in Queer Culture: Refiguring Contemporary Boundaries* (Manchester: Manchester University Press, 2000).

Doan, Laura. *Disturbing Practices: History, Sexuality, and Women's Experience of Modern War* (Chicago and London: University of Chicago Press, 2013).

———. *Fashioning Sapphism: The Origins of a Modern English Lesbian Culture* (New York: Columbia University Press, 2001).

Duncan, Nancy. "Renegotiating Gender and Sexuality in Public and Private Spaces" in Nancy Duncan (ed.), *BodySpace: Destabilizing geographies of gender and sexuality* (London and New York: Routledge, 1996).

Easthope, Anthony. *Englishness and National Culture* (London and New York: Routledge, 1999).

Edelman, Lee. *No Future: Queer Theory and the Death Drive* (Durham and London: Duke University Press, 2004).

Einhaus, Ann-Marie. "Modernism, Truth, and the Canon of First World War Literature" in *Modernist Cultures* Vol. 6, No. 2 (2011), pp. 296-314.

Endres, Nikolai. "Horses and Heroes: Plato's Phaedrus and Mary Renault's *The Charioteer*" in *International Journal of the Classical Tradition* Vol. 19, No. 3 (2012), pp. 152-164.

Escudero-Alías, Maite. "'There's that Curtain Come Down' The Burden of Shame in Sarah Waters' *The Night Watch*" in Marita Nadal and Mónica Calvo (eds.), *Trauma in Contemporary Literature: Narrative and Representation* (New York: Routledge, 2014).

Fausto-Sterling, Anne. *Sexing the Body: Gender Politics and the Construction of Sexuality* (New York: Basic Books New York, 2000).

Foucault, Michel. "What is an Author?" in James D. Faubien (ed.), *Aesthetics, Method, and Epistemology: Volume two, Essential Works of Foucault 1954-1984* (New York: New Press, 1998), pp. 205-222.

———. *Discipline and Punish: The Birth of the Prison*, [1975], (London: Vintage Books, 1995).

———. *The Will to Knowledge: The History of Sexuality: 1*, [1976], (London: Penguin Books, 1998).

Freeman, Elizabeth. *Time Binds: Queer Temporalities, Queer Histories* (Durham and London: Duke University Press, 2010).

Freud, Sigmund. *Three Essays on the Theory of Sexuality. Complete Psychological Works, Standard Edition* [1905] (Vol. VII, 1955).

Fussell, Paul. *Wartime: Understanding and Behavior in the Second World War* (New York and Oxford: Oxford University Press, 1989).

George, Rosemary Marangoly. "Homes in the Empire, Empires in the Home" in Rosemary Marangoly George (ed.), *Burning Down the House: Recycling Domesticity* (Boulder, Colorado: Westview Press, 1998).

Gilroy, Paul. *There Ain't No Black in the Union Jack*, [1987], (New York: Routledge Classics, 2002).

Goldstein, Joshua S. *War and Gender: How Gender Shapes the War System and Vice Versa*, [2001], (Cambridge and New York: Cambridge University Press, 2003).

Gopinath, Gayatri. "Homo-Economies: Queer Sexualities in a Transnational Frame" in Rosemary Marangoly George (ed.), *Burning Down the House: Recycling Domesticity* (Boulder, Colorado: Westview Press, 1998).

Grayzel, Susan R. *Women's Identities at War: Gender, Motherhood, and Politics in Britain and France during the First World War* (Chapel Hill and London: University of North Carolina Press, 1999).

Gunn, Drewey Wayne and Harker, Jaime (eds.). *1960s Gay Pulp Fiction: The Misplaced Heritage* (Amherst and Boston, Massachusetts: University of Massachusetts Press, 2013).

Gunn, Drewey Wayne. *Gay Novels of Britain, Ireland and the Commonwealth, 1881–1981: A Reader's Guide* (Jefferson, North Carolina: McFarland & Company, 2014).

Halberstam. *Female Masculinity* (Durham and London: Duke University Press, 1998).

———. *In a Queer Time and Place: Transgender Bodies, Subcultural Lives* (New York and London: New York University Press, 2005).

Halperin, David M. *How to do the History of Homosexuality* (Chicago and London: University of Chicago Press, 2002).

Hammond, Paul. *Love Between Men in English Literature* (New York: St Martin's Press, 1996).

Hartley, Jenny. *Millions like Us: British Women's Fiction of the Second World War* (London: Virago, 1997).

Hennegan, Alison. "Introduction" in Han Suyin *Winter Love*, [1962] (London: Virago Press, 1994).

Herman, David and Phelan, James and Rabinowitz, Peter J. and Richardson, Brian and Warhol, Robyn. *Narrative Theory: Core Concepts and Critical Debates* (Columbus, Ohio: The Ohio State University Press, 2012).

Hoberman, Ruth. "Masquing the Phallus: Genital Ambiguity in Mary Renault's Historical Novels" in *Twentieth Century Literature* Vol. 42, No. 2 (Summer, 1996), pp. 277-293.

Hocquenghem, Guy. *Homosexual Desire*, [1972], (Durham: Duke University Press, 1993).

Howson, Richard. *Challenging Hegemonic Masculinity* (New York: Routledge, 2006).

Hutcheon, Linda. *A Poetics of Postmodernism: History, Theory, Fiction* (New York and London: Routledge, 1988).

Jackson, Paul. *One of the Boys: Homosexuality in the Military during World War II*, [2004], (Montreal & Kingston: McGill-Queen's University Press, 2010).

Jagose, Annamarie. *Queer Theory: An Introduction* (New York: New York University Press, 1996).

Jentsch, Ernst. "On the Psychology of the Uncanny" in *Angelaki* Vol. 2, No. 1 (1995), pp. 7-16.

Jones, Adele and O'Callaghan, Claire. "Sarah Waters's Feminism" in Adele Jones and Claire O'Callaghan (eds.), *Sarah Waters and Contemporary Feminism* (London: Palgrave Macmillan, 2016), pp. 1-21.

Jones, Adele. "Disrupting the Continuum: Collapsing Space and Time in Sarah Waters's *The Night Watch*" in *Journal of Gender Studies* Vol. 23, No. 1 (2014), pp. 32-44.

Jones, Norman W. *Gay and Lesbian Historical Fiction: Sexual Mystery and post-Secular Narrative* (New York: Palgrave Macmillan, 2007).

Jones, Sonya L. *Gay and Lesbian Literature Since World War II: History and Memory*, [1998], (New York: Routledge, 2014).

Kaplan, Gisela T. and Rogers, Lesley J. "The Definition of Male and Female: Biological Reductionism and the Sanctions of Normality" in Sneja Gunew (ed.), *Feminist Knowledge: Critique and Construct* (London and New York: Routledge, 1990).

Kinsey, Alfred C. *Sexual Behavior in the Human Male*, [1948], (Bloomington and Indianapolis: Indiana University Press, 1975).

Kristeva, Julia. *Powers of Horror: An Essay on Abjection* (New York: Columbia University Press, 1982).

Kumar, Krishan. *The Making of English National Identity* (Cambridge: Cambridge University Press, 2003).

Kynaston, David. *Family Britain, 1951-57*, [2009], (London: Bloomsbury, 2010).

Lance, Mark Norris and Tanesini, Alessandra. "Identity Judgements, Queer Politics" in Iain Morland and Annabelle Willox (eds.), *Queer Theory* (Hampshire: Palgrave Macmillan, 2005), pp. 171-186.

Lanser, Susan Sniader. *Fictions of Authority: Women Writers and Narrative Voice* (Ithaca and London: Cornell University Press, 1992).

Lassner, Phyllis. *British Women Writers of World War II: Battlegrounds of their Own* (London: Palgrave Macmillan, 1998).

Lefebvre, Henri. *The Production of Space*, [1974], (Malden: Blackwell, 2003).

Lloyd, Genevieve. *The Man of Reason: "Male" and "Female" in Western Philosophy* (London: Routledge, 1984).

Love, Heather. *Feeling Backward: Loss and the Politics of Queer History* (Cambridge and Massachusettes: Harvad University Press, 2007).

Lovell, Terry. "Resisting with Authority: Historical Specificity, Agency and the Performative Self" in *Theory Culture Society* Vol. 20, No. 1 (2003), pp. 1-17.

Margaronis, Maria. "The Anxiety of Authenticity: Writing Historical Fiction at the End of the Twentieth Century" in *Historical Workshop Journal* Vol. 65, No. 1 (2008), pp. 138-160.

Massay, Doreen B. *Space, Place, and Gender* (Cambridge: Polity Press, 1994).

———. "Masculinity, Dualism and High Technology" in Nancy Duncan (ed.), *BodySpace: Destabilizing geographies of gender and sexuality* (London and New York: Routledge, 1996).

McClintock, Anne. *Imperial Leather: Race, Gender and Sexuality in the Colonial Contest* (New York: Routledge, 1995).

McEwan, Neil. *Perspective in British Historical Fiction Today* (Houndsmill: MacMillan, 1987).

Meurig, Evans H. and Thomas, William Owen and Daviers, Christopher. *Y Geiriadur Mawr: The Complete Welsh-English English-Welsh dictionary* (Llandysul: Gwasg Gomer, 1980).

Miller, Kristine A. *British Literature of the Blitz: Fighting the People's War* (London: Palgrave Macmillan, 2009).

Millett, Kate. "Instances of Sexual Politics" *Sexual Politics*, [1970], (Urbana and Chicago: University of Illinois Press, 2000), pp. 3-22.

Mitchell, Kaye. "'I'd Love to Write an Anti-Downtown!': An Interview with Sarah Waters" in Kaye Mitchell (ed.), *Sarah Waters: Contemporary Critical Perspectives* (London: Bloomsbury, 2013).

———. "'What Does it Feel like to be an Anachronism?': Time in *The Night Watch*" in Kaye Mitchell (ed.), *Sarah Waters: Contemporary Critical Perspectives* (London: Bloomsbury, 2013).

———. "The Popular and Critical Reception of Sarah Waters" in Kaye Mitchell (ed.), *Sarah Waters: Contemporary Critical Perspectives* (London: Bloomsbury, 2013).

Moore, Lisa Lynne. "Lesbian Migrations: Mary Renault's South Africa" in *GLQ: A Journal of Lesbian and Gay Studies* Vol. 10, No. 1 (2003), pp. 23-46.

Morgan, Robin. *Sisterhood is Powerful: An Anthology of Writings from the Women's Liberation Movement* (London: Vintage Books, 1970).

Morley, David and Robins, Kevin. "No Place like Heimat: Images of Home(land) in European Culture" in *New Formations* Vol. 12 (1990), pp. 1-23.

Newton, Esther. "The Mythic Mannish Lesbian: Radclyffe Hall and the New Woman" in *Signs* Vol. 9, No. 4, The Lesbian Issue (1984), pp. 557-575.

Noakes, Lucy and Pattinson, Juliette. "Introduction: 'Keep Calm and Carry on': The Cultural Memory of the Second World War in Britain" in Lucy Noakes and Juliette Pattinson (eds.), *British Cultural Memory and the Second World War* (London: Bloomsbury, 2014).

Norton, Rictor. "The Homosexual Literary Tradition: Course Outline and Objectives" in *College English* Vol. 35, No. 6 (1974).

O'Brien, Mary. *The Politics of Reproduction*, [1981], (New York and London: Routledge, 1983).

O'Callaghan, Claire. "'Grisley [sic] 'L' business': Re-valuing Female Masculinity and Butch Subjectivity in *Tipping the Velvet* and *The Night Watch*" in Adele Jones and Claire O'Callaghan (eds.), *Sarah Waters and Contemporary Feminism* (London: Palgrave Macmillan Nottingham, 2016).

———. "The Equivocal Symbolism of Pearls in the Novels of Sarah Waters" in *Contemporary Women's Writing* Vol. 6, No. 1 (2012), pp. 20-37.

———. *Sarah Waters: Gender and Sexual Politics* (London: Bloomsbury, 2017).

Paechter, Carrie. "Masculine Femininities/Feminine Masculinities: Power, Identities and Gender" in *Gender and Education* Vol. 18, No. 3 (2006), pp. 253-263.

Palmer, Pauline. "'She began to show me the words she had written, one by one': Lesbian Reading and Writing Practices in the Fiction of Sarah Waters" in *Women: A Cultural Review* Vol. 19, No. 1 (2008), pp. 69-86.

Parry, Amie. "Modernism and Domesticity: From Conrad's Eastern Road to Stein's Empty Spaces in the Home" in Rosemary Marangoly George (ed.), *Burning Down the House: Recycling Domesticity* (Boulder, Colorado: Westview Press, 1998).

Paster, Gail Kern. *The Body Embarrassed: Drama and the Disciplines of Shame in Early Modern England* (Ithaca and New York: Cornell University Press, 1993).

Pattinson, Juliette. "'The best disguise': performing femininities for clandestine purposes during the Second World War" in Angela K. Smith (ed.), *Gender and Warfare in the Twentieth Century: Textual Representations* (Manchester: Manchester University Press, 2004), pp. 132-153.

Pattinson, Juliette and Noakes, Lucy. *British Cultural Memory and the Second World War* (London: Bloomsbury, 2014).

Pearl, Monica. *AIDS Literature and Gay Identity: The Literature of Loss* (New York and London: Routledge, 2013).

Peniston-Bird, Corinna M. "The People's War in Personal Testimony and Bronze: Sorority and the Memorial to the Women of World War II" in Lucy Noakes and Juliette Pattinson (eds.), *British Cultural Memory and the Second World War* (London: Bloomsbury, 2014).

Pérez Rodríguez, Eva M. *How the Second World War Is Depicted by British Novelists since 1990: The Passage of Time Changes Our Portrayal of Traumatic Events* (New York: Edwin Mellen Press, 2012).

Peyre, Henri. "The Most Neglected Books of the Past Twenty-Five Years Selected by Writers, Scholars and Critics" in *The American Scholar* Vol. 25, No. 4 (1956), p. 492.

Phillips, Kathy J. *Manipulating Masculinity: War and Gender in Modern British and American Literature* (New York: Palgrave Macmillan, 2006).

Phelan, Shane. "The Shape of Queer: Assimilation and Articulation" in *Women & Politics* Vol. 18, No. 2 (1997), p. 55-73.

Plain, Gill. *Literature of the 1940s: War, Post-war and 'Peace'* (Edinburgh: Edinburgh University Press, 2013).

———. *Women's Fiction of the Second World War: Gender, Power and Resistance* (Edinburgh: Edinburgh University Press, 1996).

Potter, Rachel. "Introduction" in David Bradshaw and Rachel Potter (eds.), *Prudes on the Prowl: Fiction and Obscenity in England, 1850 to the present* (Oxford: Oxford University Press, 2013), pp. 1-10.

Pronger, Brian. *The Arena of Masculinity: Sports, Homosexuality, and the Meaning of Sex* (New York: St. Martin's Press, 1990).

Pusch, Luise F. *Das Deutsche als Männersprache* (Frankfurt am Main: Suhrkamp, 1984).

Puwar, Nirmal. *Space Invaders: Race, Gender and Bodies out of Place* (Oxford and New York: Berg Publishers, 2004).

Rau, Petra (ed.). *Long Shadows: The Second World War in British Fiction and Film* (Evanston, Illinois: Northwestern University Press, 2016), pp. 3-32.

Rawlinson, Mark. "Memory and Nation in British Narratives of the Second World War After 1945" in Manuel Bragança and Peter Tame (eds.), *The Long Aftermath: Cultural Legacies of Europe at War, 1936-2014* (New York and Oxford: Berghan, 2016).

———. "The Second World War: British Writing" in Kate McLoughlin (ed.), *The Cambridge Companion to War Writing* (Cambridge: Cambridge University Press, 2009).

———. "Does Tolstoy's War and Peace Make Modern War Literature Redundant?" in Laura Ashe and Ian Petterson (eds.), *Essays and Studies 2014: War and Literature* (Cambridge: The English Association, 2014).

———. *British Writing of the Second World War* (Oxford: Clarendon Press, 2000).

Renault, Mary. "Afterword" *The Friendly Young Ladies*, [1944], (London: Virago Press, 2014).

Rich, Adrienne. *Blood, Bread, and Poetry: Selected Prose*, [1986], (New York: Norton and Company, 1994).

Roland, Barthes. *Mythologies*, [1957], (New York: The Noonday Press, 1972).

Rose, Gillian. "As if the Mirrors had Bled: Masculine Dwelling, Masculinist Theory and Feminist Masquarade" in Nancy Duncan (ed.), *BodySpace: Destabilizing geographies of gender and sexuality* (London and New York: Routledge, 1996).

Rose, Sonya O. *Which People's War?: National Identity and Citizenship in Britain 1939-1945* (Oxford: Oxford University Press, 2003).

Royle, Nicholas. *The Uncanny* (Manchester: Manchester University Press, 2003).

Rubenstein, Roberta. "The Feminist Novel in the Wake of Virginia Woolf" in Brian W. Shaffer (ed.), *A Companion to the British and Irish Novel 1945-2000* (Malden: Blackwell Publishing, 2005).

Schippers, Mimi. "Recovering the Feminine Other: Masculinity, Femininity, and Gender Hegemony" in *Theory and Society* Vol. 36, No.1 (2007), pp. 85-102.

Schneider, Karen. *Loving Arms: British Women Writing the Second World War*, [1997], (Lexington, Kentucky: The University Press of Kenntucky, 2015).

Sedgwick, Eve Kosofsky. "Axiomatic" in Iain Morland and Annabelle Willox (eds.), *Queer Theory* (Hampshire: Palgrave Macmillan, 2005).

———. *Between Men: English Literature and Male Homosocial Desire* (New York: Columbia University Press, 1985).

———. *Epistemology of the Closet*, [1990], (Berkeley and London: University of California Press, 2008).

Segal, Lynne. *Slow Motion: Changing Masculinities, Changing Men*, [1990], (London: Virago Book, 1997).

Shaffer, Brian W. *Reading the Novel in English 1950-2000* (Malden, Oxford and Victoria: Blackwell Publishing, 2006).

Sharp, Joanne P. "Gendering Nationhood: A feminist engagement with national identity" in Nancy Duncan (ed.), *BodySpace: Destabilizing geographies of gender and sexuality* (London and New York: Routledge, 1996), pp. 97-108.

Sinfield, Alan. *Gay and After* (London: Serpent's Tail, 1998).

———. *Literature, Politics and Culture in Post-war Britain* (Oxford: Blackwell, 1989).

Slide, Anthony. *Lost Gay Novels: A Reference Guide to fifty Works from the First Half of the Twentieth Century*, [2003], (New York: Routledge, 2011).

Smith, Angela K. "Introduction" in Angela K. Smith (ed.), *Gender and Warfare in the Twentieth Century: Textual Representations* (Manchester: Manchester University Press, 2004).

Smith, Harold L. "British Feminism in the Second World War" in Philippa Levine and Susan R. Grayzel (eds.), *Gender, Labour, War and Empire: Essays on Modern Britain* (Hampshire: Palgrave Macmillan, 2009).

Stengers, Isabelle. "Wondering about Materialism" in Levi Bryant and Nick Srnicek and Graham Harman (eds.), *The Speculative Turn: Continental Materialism and Realism* (Melbourne: National Library of Australia Cataloguing-in-Publication Data, 2011).

Stevens, Hugh (ed.). *The Cambridge Companion to Gay and Lesbian Writing* (Cambridge: University Press, 2011).

Stewart, Victoria. *The Second World War in Contemporary British Fiction: Secret Histories* (Edinburgh: Edinburgh University Press, 2011).

Sullivan, Nikki. *A Critical Introduction to Queer Theory* (New York: New York University Press, 2003).

Summerfield, Penny. "The Generation of Memory: Gender and the Popular Memory of the Second World War in Britain" in Lucy Noakes and Juliette

Pattinson (eds.), *British Cultural Memory and the Second World War* (London: Bloomsbury, 2014).

Summers, Claude J. *Gay Fictions: Wilde to Stonewall: Studies in a Male Homosexual Literary Tradition* (New York: Continuum, 1990).

Sweetman, David. *Mary Renault: A Biography* (London: Chatto & Windus, 1993).

Thomas, Calvin. *Masculinity, Psychoanalysis, Straight Queer Theory: Essays on Abjection in Literature, Mass Culture, and Film* (New York: Palgrave Macmillan, 2008).

Titunik, Regina F. "The Myth of the Macho Military" in *Polity* Vol. 40, No. 2 (2008), pp. 137-163.

Tomkins, Silvan. *Shame and Its Sisters: A Silvan Tomkins Reader* Eve Kosofsky Sedgwick and Adam Frank (eds.), (Durham: Duke University Press, 1995).

Travis, Alan. *Bound and Gagged: A Secret History of Obscenity in Britain* (London: Profile Books, 2000).

Valentine, Gill. "(Re)Negotiating the 'Heterosexual Street': Lesbian Productions of Space" in Nancy Duncan (ed.), *BodySpace: Destabilizing geographies of gender and sexuality* (London and New York: Routledge, 1996), pp. 145-154.

Vidler, Anthony. *The Architectural Uncanny: Essays in the Modern Unhomely* (Cambridge and London: MIT Press, 1992).

Volcano, Del LaGrace and Windth, Indra. "GenderFusion" in Iain Morland and Annabelle Willox (eds.), *Queer Theory* (Hampshire: Palgrave Macmillan, 2005).

Warhol, Robyn and Richardson, Brian and Rabinowitz, Peter J. and Phelan, James and Herman, David. *Narrative Theory: Core Concepts and Critical Debates* (Columbus, Ohio: The Ohio State University Press, 2012).

Warner, Michael. *The Trouble with Normal: Sex, Politics, and the Ethics of Queer Life* (Cambridge and Massachusetts: Harvard University Press, 1999).

Waters, Chris. "The Homosexual as Social Being in Britain, 1945-1968" in Brian Lewis (ed.), *British Queer History: New Approaches and Perspectives* (Manchester: Manchester University Press, 2013).

Waters, Sarah. *Wolfskins and Togas: Lesbian and Gay Historical Fictions, 1870 to the Present* (London: University of London, 1995).

Watkins, Susan. "Issues of Gender and Sexuality" in Kathrine Cockin and Jago Morrison (eds.), *The Post-War British Literature Handbook* (New York, Continuum, 2010).

Watson, Janet. "Total War and Total Anniversary: The Material Culture of Second World War Commemoration in Britain" in Lucy Noakes and Juliette

Pattinson (eds.), *British Cultural Memory and the Second World War* (London: Bloomsbury, 2014).

Weinberg, Thomas S.. *Gay Men, Gay Selves: The Social Construction of Homosexual Identity* (Virginia: Irvington Publishers, 1983).

Whittle, Stephen. "Gender Fucking or Fucking Gender? in Iain Morland and Annabelle Willox (eds.), *Queer Theory* (Hampshire: Palgrave Macmillan, 2005).

Wickberg, Daniel. "Homophobia: On the Cultural History of an Idea" in *Critical Inquiry* Vol. 27, No. 1 (2000), pp. 42-57.

Wolfe, Peter. *Mary Renault* (New York: Twayne Publishers, 1969).

Wood, Rachel. "'Walking and Watching' in Queer London: Sarah Waters' *Tipping the Velvet* and *The Night Watch*" in *Journal of Lesbian Studies* Vol. 17, No. 3-4 (2013).

Woods, Gregory. "Introduction" *Look Down in Mercy*, [1951], (Richmond: Valancourt Books, 2014).

———. *A History of Gay Literature: The Male Tradition* (New Haven and London: Yale University Press, 1998).

Young, Iris Marion. *On Female Body Experience: "Throwing Like A Girl" and Other Essays* (Oxford: Oxford University Press, 2005).

Zeikowitz, Richard E. *Letters Between Forster and Isherwood on Homosexuality and Literature* (New York: Palgrave Macmillan, 2008).

Zilboorg, Caroline. *The Masks of Mary Renault: A Literary Biography* (Columbia, Missouri: University of Missouri Press, 2001).

ONLINE SOURCES

British Broadcasting Corporation (*BBC*). "WW2 People's War: An Archive of World War Two Memories – written by the public gathered by the BBC" <http://www.bbc.co.uk/history/ww2peopleswar/stories/36/a2688636.shtml> [last accessed: 06/10/2016].

Duden online. <www.duden.de/node/674398/revisions/1315157/view> [last accessed: 30/08/2017].

Independent. "Obituary: Fergus Provan" <http://www.independent.co.uk/news/people/obituary-fergus-provan-1247639.html> [last accessed: 24/08/2016].

Johnes, Dr. Martin. "Welsh Identity in Wartime" (2014) BBC Online <www.bbc.co.uk/wales/history/sites/themes/periods/ww2_welsh_identity.shtml> [last accessed: 01/08/2017].

Jones, Adrien and Evans, Eirwyn. “Owain Glyn Dŵr Society” <www.owain-glyndwr.wales/index.html> [last accessed: 20/07/2017].

Oxford English Dictionary (*OED*) online. Oxford University Press <www.public.oed.com/about/> [last accessed: 09/09/2017].

Sexsmith, Sinclair. “Jack Halberstam: Queers Create Better Models of Success” (2012) <http://www.lambdaliterary.org/interviews/02/01/jack-halberstam-queers-create-better-models-of-success/> [last accessed: 11/08/2017].

Time. “Books: Man Under Pressure“ <http://content.time.com/time/magazine/article/0,9171,816164,00.html> [last accessed: 24/08/2016].

The Phrase Finder. “The meaning and origin of the expression: The chickens come home to roost” < http://www.phrases.org.uk/meanings/chickens-come-home-to-roost.html > [last accessed: 02/09/2017].

Index